Texas and Texans in World War II

Ralph A. Wooster

EAKIN PRESS Fort Worth, Texas
www.EakinPress.com

Copyright © 2005
By Ralph A. Wooster
Published By Eakin Press
An Imprint of Wild Horse Media Group
P.O. Box 331779
Fort Worth, Texas 76163
1-817-344-7036
www.EakinPress.com
ALL RIGHTS RESERVED
1 2 3 4 5 6 7 8 9
ISBN-10: 1-68179-003-3
ISBN-13: 978-1-68179-003-9

Contents

Preface	....	v
CHAPTER ONE	On the Eve of War	1
CHAPTER TWO	Texas Mobilizes for War...........................	23
CHAPTER THREE	The Pacific War, December 1941–July 1942...........	43
CHAPTER FOUR	Expansion of the War, July 1942–December 1943.......	60
CHAPTER FIVE	The Home Front: A People at War	82
CHAPTER SIX	Politics, Race, and Prisoners of War	104
CHAPTER SEVEN	Allied Success, 1944	127
CHAPTER EIGHT	Victory	155
APPENDIX ONE	After the War	174
APPENDIX TWO	Texas Medal of Honor Recipients	185
Endnotes	....	189
Bibliography	....	236
Index	....	255

MAPS

Pearl Harbor, December 7, 1941	17
Major Army Training Camps in Texas	27
Major Army Air Fields in Texas	32
Luzon, 1941	53
The Italian Campaign, September 1943–June 1944	75
Largest Prisoner of War Camps in Texas	122
The Pacific Theater	130
Normandy	136
The War in Western Europe, November 1944–January 1945	141

MAPS PREPARED BY GEORGE FARRAR

Preface

Several years ago, while writing the entry for Texas in World War II for the *New Handbook of Texas*, I was struck by the fact that no overall study of Texas and Texans in the second world war had been written. While a number of articles and monographs have been published concerning individual Texans and groups of Texans (such as the 36th Division and the "Lost Battalion"), I could find no published work that covered the activities of all Texans both at home and abroad during the war. It is my hope that this book will help fill that gap.

My interest in the events of World War II has a long background. I was 13 years old when I heard over the family radio on Sunday afternoon in December that the Japanese had attacked Pearl Harbor. Like many teenagers, I had a great interest in sports and movies, but I was also quite interested in military and political affairs, even at that young age. I listened to world news on the radio every evening and heard commentator H. V. Kaltenborn warn us that war was near. Even so, like most Americans I was shocked to hear that the Japanese had actually attacked our bases in the Pacific.

Pearl Harbor changed our lives. As older friends and relatives went off to war, I took an after school and Saturday job at my father's service station (we called them "filling stations" in those days) to replace one of his employees who was drafted. Like many others, I did what I could to support the war effort by buying savings stamps and bonds, collecting newspapers, scrap iron, aluminum foil, and anything else the government needed, taking part in civil defense drills (I was a messenger for my father, a local air raid warden), and writing letters and cards to uncles and other relatives in the Army and Navy.

For me, World War II was in many ways "the Good War" described by Studs Turkel. None of my relatives or close friends were killed in the conflict, and although we faced the inconveniences of rationing and shortages, we had more spending money than ever before. More important, we were supporting our nation in the fight against the evils of German fascism and Japanese imperialism.

I was in my junior year in high school when the war ended. Somehow it never occurred to me that if the war had lasted two more years I might have been in the fighting. A few years later I was called into military service and sent to Germany as an infantry squad leader. I had completed my graduate education and was reassigned to the Historical Division, United States Army, Europe, where I worked on classified documents relating to military operations in World War II. I also had the opportunity to meet and work with soldiers, both American and German, who had been in the war. I profited a great deal from this experience and developed a deeper appreciation for the sacrifices that Americans made in that war.

Since my military service 50 years ago, I have continued to be interested in the second world war. While my primary historical specialization is the American Civil War, I have taught a course on World War II for nearly 40 years. Writing the essay for Texas in World War II for the *New Handbook of Texas* convinced me that someday I would do a book on the subject.

As is always true, many people contributed to the completion of this work. Several are veterans who have shared their memories of the war with me. I particularly wish to thank Dan Dennis, a longtime friend and former B-17 navigator with the 486th Bomb Group, who has encouraged me in many ways. His interest in the U.S. Eighth Air Force helped me to understand the hardships and sacrifices made by those airmen. My brother-in-law, Bert Norris of Highlands, Texas, armorer and gunner on a B-24 in the same Air Force, described the war from the viewpoint of an enlisted airman. Thanks are also expressed to Joe Stewart, a bombardier with the 445th Bomb Group who participated in one of the most costly bombing raids of the war; Gene Priest, a P-47 pilot who was seriously injured in a mission over Germany; Lonnie Hood, who flew 114 missions in the South Pacific; Tom Floyd, rifleman in the 30th Infantry Division that fought its way across France and Germany; and W. T Block, the premier historian of Jefferson County and a member of the 78th Infantry Division, who has provided much information on Southeast Texans in the war.

Phil Latimer, former head of the mathematics department of Lamar University and my colleague for over 30 years, shared much information on the 761st Tank Battalion. Latimer was one of the white officers in this African American battalion that distinguished itself in the fighting in Europe. As one of the few living officers in the battalion Latimer, a retired lieutenant colonel in the Army reserves, has played a major role in getting some recognition for the accomplishments of the "Black Panthers."

Numerous friends and associates provided information and support for the book. George Farrar, artist and Viet Nam Navy veteran, once again made the maps contained in the book. Valerie Majors Domingue, former student and friend, made available material concerning her grandfather, B. B. Majors, who served in the campaign in Burma. Theresa Storey, documents librarian at Lamar University, used her considerable skills in obtaining government reports on enlistments and casualties of Texans in the military. E. James Hindman, president of Angelo State University and a former colleague at Lamar, and

Suzanne Campbell, archivist at Angelo State, provided information on the San Angelo Army Air Field. Kevin Ladd, a former student and now director of the Wallisville Heritage Park, furnished much material on the role of Chambers and Liberty County citizens in the conflict. David Montgomery, formerly director of the Tyrrell Historical Library in Beaumont, pointed out a number of local sources and furnished several photographs. Robert Schaadt, director, and Darlene Mott, librarian and reading room supervisor, at the Sam Houston Regional Library and Research Center in Liberty were most helpful in providing materials. My good friend Howard Peacock, a Navy veteran of World War II and an accomplished writer, provided information on the Jingu and Maverick families of San Antonio. To all of these individuals I am much in debt.

Adrian Anderson, my longtime colleague at Lamar and one of the state's leading Texas historians, encouraged me to undertake this study and has provided valuable support and wisdom throughout the project. Several other colleagues at Lamar helped in various ways.

Robert Robertson provided information on civil rights matters, organized labor, and Southeast Texas in general. Tom Reid, a former graduate student and veteran of many years of Army service, offered insights and assistance in obtaining information from military and governmental sources. Shawn Molina, former Marine and graduate student, provided material on military special service operations.

My son, Robert Wooster, military historian at Texas A&M University, Corpus Christi, and his wife Catherine Cox, professor of English at the same institution, were helpful in a variety of ways.

As always, my wife, Edna, whose uncle, Forest Mathews, met his death early in the war serving his country on the U.S.S. *Peary*, provided encouragement needed to complete the project. She and I met in the closing months of World War II and have shared 60 happy years together. The war brought her to Texas from her native Oklahoma; for me this was the most important event of the war years.

The book is dedicated to the American men and women who fought in the war. They are truly the great generation to whom those of us a few years younger owe a debt that can never be repaid.

RALPH A. WOOSTER
Beaumont, Texas

CHAPTER ONE

On the Eve of War

The Japanese attack upon the United States naval base at Pearl Harbor on December 7, 1941, caught most Texans by surprise. The state, like the nation, was slowly recovering from the Great Depression. Although the programs of Franklin D. Roosevelt's New Deal had not solved all the nation's economic ills, there was some optimism that the worst was over. The growing concern over the possibility of American involvement in European and Asian wars had led to a preparedness campaign that involved industrial and commercial expansion. New military bases, airfields, and training camps were being built all over the state. Older facilities such as Kelly Field at San Antonio and Biggs Field at El Paso were being up-dated and expanded. New employment opportunities were opening up everywhere.[1]

On the eve of war the population of the state was growing but not as rapidly as in previous years. The 1940 census reported 6,414,824 people living in Texas, an increase of 10.1 percent over the previous decade. This was the smallest decade increase for the state in the 20th century. The 1930 census had shown a 24.9 percent increase during the previous decade, the 1920 census a 19.7 percent increase, and the 1910 census a 27.8 percent increase.[2]

Even with the overall growth during the 1930s, Texas fell from fifth to sixth among the states in total population, slipping behind more rapidly growing California.[3]

Although a majority of Texans still lived in rural areas, more Texans than ever resided in towns and cities. Nearly 3 million Texans, or 45.4 percent of the state's population, lived in urban areas, an increase of 21.8 percent over 1930. Again, however, the rate of urban growth was less than in the previous three decades, each of which had an increase of over 50 percent in urban residents.[4]

Houston, with 384,515 people, was the state's largest city, as it had been since 1930 when it passed Dallas and San Antonio in total population. Fort Worth and El Paso were the state's fourth and fifth largest cities (behind Dallas and San Antonio). Austin, which had a 65.6 percent population increase during the 1930s, was now the sixth largest city. Galveston, Beaumont, Corpus Christi, and Waco rounded out the state's ten largest cities.[5]

University Park, a Dallas suburb, was the fastest growing of the state's 50 largest incorporated cities, increasing from 4,200 residents in 1930 to 14,458 in 1940, or 244.2 percent. Longview, 29th largest city in Texas, grew from 5,036 to 13,759 people, or 173.2 percent. Corpus Christi, whose population increased from 27,421 residents in 1930 to 57,301 in 1940, had the greatest percentage gain of the state's ten largest cities, 106.6 percent. El Paso, with nearly 6,000 fewer inhabitants in 1940 than 1930, was the only one of the state's ten largest cities to lose population in the decade. Port Arthur, Big Spring, Cleburne, and Sweetwater were other Texas cities losing population in the 1930s.[6]

Nearly one-fourth (23.2 percent) of all Texans lived in the state's four most heavily populated counties: Harris, Dallas, Bexar, and Tarrant. The density of population in 1940 Texas was 24.4 people per square mile, a little more than half as much as the national average.[7]

On the eve of Pearl Harbor, Texas men outnumbered women by slightly more than 30,000. The percentage of women in the total population was increasing, however; from 49.1 percent in 1930 to 49.8 percent in 1940.[8]

Nearly 86 percent of Texans were enumerated as "white" in the 1940 Federal census, a percentage that had grown steadily since the Civil War. The African American population, while increasing in total numbers, was declining in percentage of total population, from 30.3 percent in 1860 to 20.4 percent in 1900, 15.4 percent in 1920, to 14.4 percent in 1940. The foreign born population in the state dropped from 361,068 in 1930 to 234,388 in 1940, in large measure because of poor economic conditions. The number of individuals born in Mexico, the foreign country with the largest number of natives in Texas, fell from 261,046 in 1930 to 159,266 in 1940.[9]

Slightly more than 60,000 deaths were reported in Texas during 1941. Heart disease (12,420 deaths) continued to be the major killer, followed by pneumonia, cancer, tuberculosis, and nephritis (kidney disease). Nearly 2,000 Texans were killed in automobiles in 1941; 3,000 Texans died in other accidents. More than 600 Texans committed suicide that year; nearly 600 Texans were victims of homicide.[10]

Slightly over 1.5 million Texas children were enrolled in public schools in 1940. Two-thirds of these attended schools in independent school districts, the other third in common school districts. Texas public schools, like other public institutions and facilities, were segregated by race in 1940. In most of Texas this meant separate schools for black and white children; in some areas of south and west Texas it also meant separate schools for Mexican children. The 11-year curriculum was still maintained in nearly half of the state's school districts. The other half of the public schools had adopted the 12-year curriculum, first established in the Port Arthur Independent School District.[11]

While most Texans took pride in their public schools, teacher salaries were inadequate (averaging only $1,120 annually), facilities were poor, and the percentage of students in daily attendance was low. The *Texas Almanac* for 1941-42 noted that "Texas is usually ranked from thirtieth to fortieth among the states" in its educational system.[12]

On the eve of Pearl Harbor Texas had 41 senior and 58 junior colleges. Fourteen of the senior institutions, including one (Prairie View) for African Americans, were state supported. Twenty-five senior institutions (including five for African Americans) were church endowed, and two, both in Houston (one of which was for African Americans), were municipal senior colleges. The University of Texas, with 11,677 students, was the largest senior college in the state, followed by Texas A&M (6,541 students) and Texas Tech (4,246 students). The Texas State College for Women, the University of Houston, Baylor University, North Texas State Teachers College, and Southern Methodist University were the only other institutions with 2,000 or more students enrolled in 1940.[13]

More than 2 million Texans were members of a religious denomination in 1941. More than half of these belonged to one of the state's three largest religious bodies, Baptist, Roman Catholic, and Methodist. Baptists, with 388,044 members of African American congregations and 360,421 members of white Southern Baptist Convention congregations, were the most numerous. Slightly more than 600,000 Texans were Roman Catholics and 316,664 were Methodists. Churches of Christ, Presbyterians, Disciples of Christ, Lutherans, Episcopalians, and Assemblies of God were the other Christian religious groups with the most members in Texas. More than 43,000 Texans were of the Jewish faith.[14]

As noted above, the majority of Texans still lived in rural areas in 1940. The number of these rural Texans engaged in farming, however, declined from 2,342,553 in 1930 to 2,154,758 in 1940. Rural non-farm population increased from 1,092,819 in 1930 to 1,348,672 in 1940. Many rural Texans who had previously grown cotton were turning to livestock as their source of livelihood. Cotton cultivation dropped from nearly 17 million acres to slightly more than 8 million in 1940; the number of cattle increased from 5,583,471 in 1930 to 6,281,537 in 1940. Similar increases occurred in the number of hogs and sheep. In 1940 Texas ranked first among the states in the number of cattle, sheep, Angora goats, mules, and turkeys. The state was second (to Iowa) in the number of horses, chickens, and eggs and in total income from livestock.[15]

The oil and gas industry was increasingly important in the Texas economy on the eve of the second world war. Texas was the largest petroleum producing state in the nation, producing nearly half a billion barrels of crude oil in 1940, or 36.5 per cent of all domestic production. Because of the discovery of new sources of oil and gas in the Texas Panhandle, Permian Basin, and East Texas in the 1920s and 1930s, the total value of Texas mineral products nearly doubled in the 1930s, increasing from $400 million in 1930 to approximately $700 million in 1940. As the nation increased its preparation for war the total value of Texas mineral products, largely oil and natural gas, rose to over $950 million dollars in 1941.[16]

Texans depended heavily upon the radio for much of their entertainment and information. By 1940 there were 56 radio stations operating in the state, 28 of them owned wholly or in part by newspapers such as the *Dallas Morning News*, *Houston Post*, and *Houston Chronicle*. The most powerful of these were the 50,000 watt stations: KRLD (Dallas), WBAP (Fort Worth), WFAA (Dallas), and WOAI (San Antonio). Many of the Texas radio stations were members of regional networks: the Texas Quality Network, with four stations in Dallas, Fort Worth, Houston, and San Antonio; the Lone Star chain, six stations; and the Texas State Network, 16 stations.[17]

Nearly two-thirds of all Texas homes had radios by 1940. During the daytime hours many Texans listened to national network serials or "soap operas" such as "Guiding Light," "Ma Perkins," "Stella Dallas," "David Harum," "Just Plain Bill," and "Our Gal Sunday." Unlike modern television, which is divided into 30-minute or one-hour segments, these pre-war programs usually ran for 15 minutes.[18]

The most popular radio program originating in Texas was the "Light Crust Doughboys," originally featuring Bob Wills, Herman Arnspiger, and Milton Brown. Sponsored by Burrus Mills of Fort Worth, which made Light Crust flour, the Doughboys played popular western and country music as well as sacred and sentimental songs. W. Lee O'Daniel, manager of Burrus Mills, was originally critical of "hillbilly" music, but became the announcer for the group and organized a radio network that broadcast the Doughboys' music throughout the state. Although O'Daniel left Burrus Mills in 1935, formed his own flour company and his own band (the Hillbilly Boys), and later ran for and was elected governor, the Light Crust Doughboys continued to be highly popular. By 1940 the Light Crust Dougboys broadcast over 170 radio stations in the South and Southwest.[19]

"The Early Birds," an early morning show on WFAA (Dallas), was another popular Texas radio program in the 1930s. Using the theme "Happy Days Are Here Again," the show featured a live orchestra playing up-beat, popular melodies. Another local favorite was the Stamps Quartet, a gospel music group originating in Dallas on KRLD.[20]

In the early evening Texans enjoyed local news and weather programs as well as national commentators such as H. V. Kaltenborn, Elmer Davis, and Raymond Graham Swing. For young listeners, the evening news was preceded by "Jack Armstrong, the All-American Boy," "Little Orphan Annie," "The Green Hornet," "The Lone Ranger," and "Don Winslow of the Navy."[21]

After the newscasts Texans had various national network programs from which to choose. The "Kate Smith Show" and "Kraft Music Hall" presented a variety of music and comedy. Pure comedy was featured on the "Edgar Bergen and Charlie McCarthy Show," "the Aldrich Family," the "Jack Benny Show," the "Fred Allen Show," "Fibber McGee and Molly," "Lum and Abner," and "Amos and Andy." For those listeners seeking drama "Lux Radio Theater," with movie director Cecil B. DeMille as host, and the "Mercury Theater of the Air," (which became the Campbell Playhouse in the late 1930s) with Orson Welles, presented a variety of productions. "Gangbusters," "Big Town," and "Mr. District Attorney," were 1930 versions of today's "Law and Order." "One Man's Family," the story of the Barbour family of San Francisco, was a popular early evening serial.[22]

Sports fans in pre-World War II Texas enjoyed a variety of broadcasts. Heavyweight boxing matches, particularly the two Max Schmeling-Joe Louis fights broadcast by the national networks, attracted thousands of listeners in the Lone Star state. Professional wrestling matches in Texas' largest cities were often described on Saturday night local radio stations and drew sizable listening audiences. Saturday afternoons were reserved for the Humble Sports Network, featuring announcers Kern Tips and Ves Box describing Southwest Conference college football games.[23]

Texans were avid moviegoers in the 1930s. Almost every city or town had a motion picture theater. In the early thirties movie houses were generally located in the center of town, such as Dallas' Elm Street or Houston's Main Street, but as the effects of the Depression lessened, neighborhood or suburb theaters began to appear in the larger cities. This was also the era of the grand movie palaces built in the style of European opera houses. By 1941 all the larger Texas cities could boast of theaters with lavish, often ornate, interiors. Among these were the Majestic, Metropolitan, and Loew's State in Houston, the Paramount in Austin, the Jefferson in Beaumont, the Plaza in El Paso, the Texas, Aztec, Empire, and Majestic in San Antonio, the Majestic and Palace in Dallas, and the Worth and Hollywood in Fort Worth.[24]

These grand palaces were reserved for first run movies featuring the most popular stars or highly rated pictures such as Margaret Mitchell's *Gone With the Wind* starring Vivian Leigh and Clark Gable. Texans in smaller towns had to wait until the major features had their run in the big city or, if they were impatient, drive into the city to see the picture.

Texans, like other Americans, were drawn to motion pictures by popular actors and actresses. James Stewart (*The Philadelphia Story*) and Texan Ginger Rogers (*Kitty Foyle*) were Academy Award winners for 1940. Gary Cooper (*Sergeant York*) and Joan Fontaine (*Suspicion*) were award winners for 1941. *Rebecca* was chosen best picture of 1940 and *How Green Was My Valley* in 1941. Orson Welles' movie *Citizen Kane* was nominated for nine honors in 1941, but received only one award (for best screenplay).[25]

Texas boasted an array of motion picture stars including Ginger Rogers (Fort Worth), Linda Darnell (Dallas), Ann Sheridan and Joan Blondell (Denton), Ann Sothern (Ranger), Mary Martin (Weatherford), Zachary Scott (Fort Worth), Ann Miller (Houston), Dana Andrews (Huntsville), and Ken Maynard (Mission).[26]

The outdoor or "drive-in" movie made its appearance in Texas just before the outbreak of World War II. The first such theater in Texas, and one of the first in the nation, was on Galveston beach in 1933 but closed after three weeks when a storm blew down the screen. The first "permanent" drive-in theater in the state was the Texas, which opened in Corpus Christi in 1939. Another drive-in, also named the Texas, opened on Houston's South Main on June 7, 1940. The drive-in was slow to take hold in Texas, in part because of mosquitoes and in part because the indoor theater offered air-conditioning; it was often the only place in pre-war Texas to do so.[27]

Sporting events provided the main competition to the movies in pre-war Texas. Baseball and football were the major sports, although a large number of Texans attended professional boxing and wrestling events in the 1930s. Even though there were no major baseball teams in Texas (or in any other city west of the Mississippi River except St. Louis), the Class A Texas League had clubs in Beaumont, Dallas, Fort Worth, Houston, and San Antonio (as well as Tulsa, Oklahoma City, and Shreveport). Although League attendance lagged in 1941, partly because of an unusually rainy season that saw 85 postponements (1941 was the wettest year in Texas history), nearly half a million fans watched Texas League games that year. The Houston Buffaloes, a farm club of the St. Louis Cardinals, won 103 games and the regular season championship behind three 20-game pitchers, Howie Pollett, Freddy Martin, and Ted Wilks. The Buffs lost to the Dallas Rebels in the first round of the playoffs. The Rebels went on to defeat the Tulsa Oilers in the League championship playoff, but were themselves beaten by Nashville in four straight games in the Dixie Series.[28]

On the national scene the New York Yankees once again were the World Champions, defeating the Brooklyn Dodgers in five games. Highlights of the season were Joe DiMaggio's 56 game hitting streak, a record that still stands, and Ted Williams' batting average of .406 (the last time a major leaguer hit above .400 in a season).[29]

While baseball remained the national pastime on the eve of World War II, Texans were equally interested in football. The National Football League, still in its infancy, was like baseball confined to the East Coast and the Mid-West. While Texans followed the play of Texas athletes such as Sammy Baugh of the Washington Redskins and Davey O'Brien of the Philadelphia Eagles in newspapers and on radio, there were no professional teams in the state.

College football on Saturdays and high school football on Friday nights provided entertainment for thousands of Texans. Texas A&M, which went undefeated in 1939 and claimed the mythical national championship, was defeated by the Texas Longhorns in a shocking upset on Thanksgiving Day 1940, but the Aggies partially redeemed themselves with a 13-12 victory over Fordham in Dallas' Cotton Bowl on January 1, 1941.[30]

The University of Texas Longhorns were the prohibitive favorite to win the Southwest Conference and a possible trip to the Rose Bowl in 1941. Led by backs Jack Crain and Pete Layden and linemen Mal Kutner and Chal Daniel, the Longhorns overwhelmed their first six opponents (including Oklahoma and LSU). *Life* magazine featured the Horns in its November 17, 1941, edition with front page photographs and a seven-page spread entitled "Texas Football–A Great University Has Nation's Top Team."[31]

Even before the *Life* story hit the newsstand, the luster of the Texas team had begun to fade. In early November the Baylor Bears held the mighty

Longhorns to a 7-7 tie, and on the following Saturday (two days before the *Life* story was published), the TCU Horned Frogs upset the Longhorns, 14-7. The national championship and a trip to the Rose Bowl denied them, the Longhorns took out their revenge on the Texas Aggies 23-0 on Thanksgiving Day, and on the day before Pearl Harbor buried the Oregon Ducks by a score of 71-7.[32]

In communities across the state, it was high school football that drew citizens together on Friday nights during the regular season and Saturday afternoons during the championship playoffs. The Amarillo Golden Sandies, state champions in 1934-1936 and 1940, appeared to be headed for another title in 1941, winning their first eight games. The Sandies' 22 game winning streak was ended in November, however, with a defeat by district rival Pampa. The Masonic Home Mighty Mites of Fort Worth, coached by Rusty Russell, were another perennial powerhouse in the late 1930s even though they were usually heavily outweighed by their opponents. Like Amarillo, Masonic Home seemed unbeatable throughout much of 1941 but had to forfeit most of its games when it was discovered the team had used an ineligible player. The ineligible rule also caught two other high school powers, Lufkin and Odessa, in 1941.[33]

The first round of the 1941 playoffs, the bi-district games, were played on December 6, the day before Pearl Harbor. On that date Wichita Falls, Ysleta, Highland Park, Dallas Sunset, Temple, Tyler, Houston Lamar, and Austin advanced to the state quarterfinals. The attack on Pearl Harbor on December 7 shocked the state and the nation, but playoff games continued throughout the month. Two days after Christmas, the Wichita Falls Coyotes were crowned state champions, defeating Temple 13-0.[34]

Many of the young men who participated in the 1941 high school football playoffs would soon be in the service of their nation fighting on distant, and more deadly, fields. Even before the Japanese attack on Pearl Harbor most Texans realized war was near. The fall of France in the summer of 1940, the battle for Britain that summer, and the Japanese occupation of French Indo China in 1941, brought the prospects for American involvement closer and closer. While Texans were still going about their daily tasks, abundant evidence of an increased military preparedness convinced many that it was only a matter of time before the United States was at war.[35]

Texans generally supported the efforts of President Roosevelt to strengthen the nation's defenses. The state's two United States senators, Morris Sheppard and Tom Connally, were key proponents of the president's efforts. Sheppard, the dean of Congress in length of service, was first elected to the U.S. House of Representatives in 1902. A quiet, unassuming man, Sheppard moved to the U.S. Senate in 1913. Here he became a supporter of Woodrow Wilson and a champion of prohibition. In the 1930s he consistently backed Roosevelt in his domestic programs, even the court reorganization plan. As chairman of the Senate Military Affairs Committee, Sheppard guided the administration bill for increased military spending through the Senate in 1939. He later supported passage of a Selective Service Act and the Lend Lease Act. His death from a brain hemorrhage on April 9, 1941, removed one of Roosevelt's most loyal supporters from the Senate.[36]

Sheppard's Texas colleague in the Senate, Tom Connally of Marlin, opposed the president's court reform measure but backed him on foreign policy matters. Something of a showman with his black bow tie and flowing locks of white hair, Connally was an effective and colorful public speaker. As a senior member (and later chairman) of the Senate Foreign Relations Committee, he took a lead in successful efforts to modify the neutrality law to allow cash and carry arms sales to nations resisting aggression.[37]

Most House members from Texas (all Democrats) supported President Roosevelt's policies in military and foreign affairs. Sam Rayburn of Bonham was leader of the state's House delegation. First elected to Congress in 1912, Rayburn was majority leader in the House, 1937-1940, and became speaker in 1940. As majority leader and speaker, Rayburn guided administration proposals through Congress. He was assisted by other Texas congressmen, especially Luther Johnson of Corsicana, Lyndon B. Johnson of Stonewall, Lindley Beckworth of Gilmer, and Albert Thomas of Houston.[38]

Not all Texans supported the President's preparedness measures. Hatton Sumners of Dallas, chair of the House Judiciary Committee, broke with the

L-R: Tom Connally, unidentified, Morris Sheppard, unidentified.
—Center for American History, UT-Austin

8 ★ Texas and Texans in World War II

President over the court-packing bill and was only a lukewarm supporter of Roosevelt's foreign and military measures. Wright Patman of Texarkana was an ardent advocate of New Deal domestic programs but flirted with isolationism in the 1930s. Martin Dies of Orange, chairman of the House Un-American Activities Committee, was more interested in ferreting out Communists in the government than in Roosevelt's measures to improve national defense. Prior to his defeat for re-election in 1938 Maury Maverick of San Antonio supported New Deal domestic programs and became the darling of the Eastern liberal press. However, Maverick generally favored neutrality measures and opposed FDR's naval expansion program. He did support expansion of the air service and improvements at San Antonio's Kelly Field in his own district.[39]

Martin Dies and Hatton Sumners were the only Texas congressmen who did not vote in favor of the Burke-Wadsworth bill creating the nation's first peacetime draft in late summer 1940. Morris Sheppard, chairman of the Military Affairs Committee, played a major role in moving the bill through the Senate over the opposition of Hiram Johnson of California and Burton K. Wheeler of Montana. Aging, in poor health, and not a skilled public speaker, Sheppard worked tirelessly to secure passage of the measure. In July he guided the bill through his committee and on August 9 opened floor discussion of the proposal. "The doctrines and aggressions of certain dictator-controlled nations," made limited conscription necessary, he argued. The nation had to be able to defend itself and its neighbors; since the number of voluntary enlistments was inadequate, the only solution was a selective draft in which the burdens would be "borne equally by all classes, regardless of economic means."[40]

Supported by fellow Texan Tom Connally and Allen Ellender from neighboring Louisiana, Sheppard helped beat back a series of delaying measures. In late August, the bill cleared the Senate. In the House, majority leader Sam Rayburn worked to defeat amendments. With the support of the entire Texas delegation except Dies and Sumners (who did not vote) the Selective Service bill was adopted by the House. The final measure, creating a system whereby 900,000 American males between ages 21 and 35 would be inducted into the Army for one year, was signed by President Roosevelt on September 16, 1940.[41]

In October 1940, more than 16 million young Americans, including 800,000 Texans, registered for selective service. Late that month a national lottery determined which of these men would be inducted into military service. In November, the first of the new recruits began reporting to camps for training.[42]

At the same time the first draftees were being inducted, 12,000 members of the Texas National Guard were reporting to newly opened Camp Bowie near Brownwood. Under legislation approved by Congress the previous August, the president called a number of National Guard units into federal service. The Texas National Guard, one of those called, became the 36th Infantry Division of the United States Army.[43]

Passage of the Selective Service bill came during the presidential election campaign. Breaking with the precedent of George Washington, Franklin D. Roosevelt sought a third term. Although many Texas political leaders had earlier endorsed Vice President John Nance Garner from Uvalde for the post, once the Democratic Party renominated FDR, Texas, part of the traditionally Democratic Solid South, supported the president's re-election. Receiving over 800,000 votes in the state compared to nearly 200,000 for Republican nominee Wendell L. Willke, Roosevelt carried all but seven Texas counties. At the same time Governor W. Lee O'Daniel and other Democratic nominees were victorious in state races. When Senator Morris Sheppard died on April 9, 1941, O'Daniel was elected to succeed him, winning a close election over Congressman Lyndon B. Johnson.[44]

Shortly after his re-election as president, Roosevelt called for continued expansion of the nation's industrial and military capabilities and increased aid for Great Britain in its struggle against Nazi aggression. In January 1941 administration supporters introduced into Congress legislation that would authorize the president to sell, transfer, lend, or lease materials to any country whose defense he deemed vital to American security. Assigned the number H.R. 1776 by Sam Rayburn (who was now Speaker of the House) and known generally as the "Lend Lease bill," the measure moved first through the House. Historian Warren F. Kimball, who traced passage of the bill through the Congress in his book *The Most Unsordid Act: Lend-Lease, 1939-1941*, noted that Sam Rayburn and fellow Texan Luther Johnson of Corsicana played major roles in House passage. Rayburn persuaded the White House to accept amendments placing time restrictions and reporting requirements on the measure. Without such amendments the Speaker was convinced the bill would not pass. Luther Johnson, a senior Democrat on the House Foreign Affairs Committee, provided important leadership in moving the measure through a skeptical House. With the efforts of Rayburn and Johnson the Lend Lease bill passed the House, 260-165. With the exception of Joseph Mansfield, the entire Texas House delegation voted for passage.[45]

In the Senate another Texan, Tom Connally, played a major role in passage of the Lend Lease bill. As second ranking Democratic member of the Foreign Affairs Committee, Connally worked to modify some of the restrictions of the House bill both in committee and on the Senate floor. With Connally's assistance, the Senate passed the Lend Lease measure by a 60-31 vote on March 11, 1941.[46]

With continued aid for the financially pressed British now assured, President Roosevelt could give more attention to the growing Japanese threat in the Far East. The Japanese had moved into Manchuria in 1931 and after months of fighting set up a puppet regime headed by the last emperor of the Manchu dynasty. In 1937 the Japanese launched an all-out campaign to occupy the whole of China. The United States, which opposed Japanese expansion in the Far East, extended limited aid to the Chinese Nationalist government headed by Chiang Kai-shek. When Japan moved to occupy northern Indo China in summer 1940 Roosevelt placed an embargo on the shipment to Japan of premium grades of scrap iron and steel and high octane aviation gasoline. As a further deterrent to Japanese moves toward the Philippines and the Dutch East

Sam Rayburn
—UT Institute of Texan Cultures at San Antonio

Indies, the Roosevelt administration determined to keep the United States fleet, which had been conducting training exercises in the mid-Pacific, in Hawaii rather than return to its permanent base at San Pedro, California. When the fleet commander, East Texan Admiral James O. Richardson, protested too vigorously that such a move might endanger the fleet, the president removed him from command and appointed Rear Admiral Husband E. Kimmel, to the post. The fleet remained at Pearl Harbor in Oahu, Hawaii.[47]

To assist the Chinese in their war with Japan, Roosevelt extended Lend Lease aid to Chiang Kai-shek. In April 1941 the president authorized the resignation of American military personnel who wished to become members of the American Volunteer Group flying fighter aircraft for China. Headed by a retired Army Air Corps pilot, Texas-born Claire L. Chennault, these American airmen were soon under contract with the Chinese government to engage Japanese fighters over the skies of China. Flying Curtiss P-40 fighter planes with the teeth of the tiger shark painted on the front of the plane, these daring pilots were regarded as courageous heroes by the Chinese and the American public and outlaw mercenaries by the Japanese.[48]

These early efforts of the Roosevelt administration did not deter the Japanese. In July 1941 they extended their movement into south Indo China, occupying eight air and two naval bases. Believing this action required a strong response, President Roosevelt issued an order freezing all Japanese assets in the United States. This was soon extended to a full embargo of trade with Japan, including petroleum.[49]

Meanwhile, Texans in Congress were called upon to support an additional measure to prepare the nation for war. The 12-month enlistment of the men first called into service under the Burke-Wadsworth bill would soon be up. Upon the recommendation of his military advisors, President Roosevelt asked Congress to extend the draftees' term of enlistment for the duration of the national emergency.[50]

Despite the press of world events (the German army invaded the Soviet Union in June 1941) members of Congress, including Speaker Sam Rayburn, were skeptical. Many believed that such an extension of the draftees' term of enlistment was breaking a commitment. Public opinion was divided on the issue. Nearly two-thirds of newspaper editorials supported the extension, but the Gallup Poll showed only 51 percent of individuals surveyed favored extension. Forty-five percent opposed extension, and four percent had no opinion. The draftees themselves wanted early release, many adopting as their symbol the word "OHIO," meaning "Over the Hill in October."[51]

The debate over extending the term on enlistment went on throughout late July and early August. Some early skeptics such as Speaker Rayburn came to accept the need for keeping the 1940 draftees in uniform. Senate leaders, including Tom Connally, worked out a compromise whereby service was extended to 18 months rather than for the duration of the emergency as the administration wanted. The extension bill passed the Senate 45 to 30, with 21 members not voting. Senator Connally voted for the passage. W. Lee O'Daniel, who had just taken his seat filling the vacancy created by the death of Senator Morris Sheppard, voted against the extension. The vote was much closer in the House, 203 for extension and 202 opposed. All Texas House members (with the exception of Rayburn, who as presiding officer did not vote) voted in favor of the extension. Extension opponents in the House called for a vote recount but Speaker Rayburn refused to allow a recount. On August 18, President Roosevelt signed the bill. At the same time he issued an executive order deferring those who were 28 or older on July 1, 1941.[52]

The tempo of military preparations was stepped up in autumn 1941. In September the nation's largest peacetime maneuvers began in Louisiana with General Ben Lear's Second Army, made up primarily of troops from the Southeast, attacking General Walter Krueger's Third Army consisting of troops trained in the Southwest. The Texas National Guard, federalized as the 36th Infantry Division in November 1940 and now commanded by Regular Army Major General Fred L. Walker, was part of Krueger's Third (or Blue) Army in the maneuvers. Dwight D. Eisenhower, born in Denison, Texas, and future commander of Allied armies in Europe, served as Krueger's chief of staff. In the course of the maneuvers, the overflow into East Texas brought many soldiers and machines into the Lone Star State.[53]

While Americans at home were preparing for war, American seamen were coming into direct contact with German submarines in the Atlantic. In September the American destroyer *Greer* had an exchange of fire with a German U-boat in the south Atlantic. In mid-October another German submarine put a torpedo into the U.S. destroyer *Kearny*, killing 11 American seamen. Later that month the destroyer *Reuben James* was sunk when a German torpedo hit the ammunition magazine, ripping the ship in two. One hundred fifteen American seamen were killed, including the ship's captain, Heywood "Tex" Edwards from San Saba. A member of the Annapolis class of 1926, Edwards had been captain of the wrestling team and star of both boxing and football squads at the naval academy.[54]

Even though clouds loomed on the horizon that autumn, Texans were surprised when on December 7, 1941, Japanese carrier-based planes attacked the American naval base at Pearl Harbor in the Hawaiian Islands. Many can remember exactly where and when they learned of the attack. Dave Naugle of KFJZ in Fort Worth was on duty in the "teletype room when the bells starting ringing—about eight or ten of them. 'Flash!—Japs attack Oahu.'" Dan Dennis, then a student at Lamar Junior College in Beaumont, recalls that he was reading the Sunday comics when he heard of the Japanese attack. Vito Dimiceli of Nederland, who was in the Army Reserves, was driving back to Port Arthur from Franklin, Louisiana, when he heard on the car radio that Pearl Harbor had been bombed. All reserve personnel were ordered to report to the local armory. Valeta Crow of Hamlin, who was attending beauty school in Fort Worth, was sitting on the balcony of her boarding house when the music on her radio was interrupted with news of the attack.[55]

Since the news of the attack was received in Texas early Sunday afternoon many Texans were at a motion picture theater at the time. Martha Sue Stroud of Clarksville recalls that she was at the Avalon Theater when an announcement was made that the Japanese had attacked Pearl Harbor. Hazel Shelton, a 14-year-old sophomore at Nacogdoches High School, had gone to a double feature with friends. When she came out of the theater at 4:30, newsboys were selling "extra" editions of the Nacogdoches *Sentinel* announcing the Japanese attack. Fred O. Garza of Cuero had a similar experience. When he came out of the movie newspaper "extras" were describing the attack.[56]

Ann Tweedy of San Angelo had married young bomber pilot Philip Ardery the day before Pearl Harbor. On December 7 she and her new husband were driving to Kentucky to visit his parents when they stopped at a gasoline station in Little Rock. There they learned of the attack. Lieutenant Ardery telephoned his base in San Angelo, but was told to continue his trip to Kentucky.[57]

Most military personnel were ordered to report to their bases once the attack on Pearl Harbor was known. Paul Austin, a native of Fort Worth, had joined the Texas National Guard in 1937 when he was only 16. He and his brother were in a movie theater in Brownwood watching Gary Cooper in "Sergeant York." The movie suddenly stopped and a voice over the loudspeaker announced that all members of the 36th Division should report to Camp Bowie immediately.[58]

Bill Dallas of Austin was another member of the 36th Division who was watching *Sergeant York* at a movie that afternoon. Dallas was in a theater in Fort Worth when announcement of the attack was made. When the announcer went on to say that the United States would soon be in war, the audience started applauding. Young Dallas, who was in uniform, wondered why they were clapping. "I thought, 'What the hell are they applauding for? We're going to war.'"[59]

Ubaldo Arizmendi of Brownsville was in training with the 30th Field Artillery at Camp Roberts, California, when he learned of the attack. He and several companions were in a bus going into town. When the bus stopped, military police prevented them from going on. One of the soldiers asked, "What's going on? We've all got passes." The MP replied that Japan had just bombed Pearl Harbor. The men returned to camp where, according to Arizmendi, they "got guns and real bullets."[60]

Philip Latimer, a young math teacher from Detroit, Texas, who had been drafted in June 1941, was hitchhiking his way from Beaumont back to Camp Polk, Louisiana, when a motorist informed him of the Japanese attack. Like many Texans, Latimer wondered where Pearl Harbor was.[61]

George Gay of Houston, later the sole survivor of a naval torpedo plane squadron at the battle of Midway, was stationed at Norfolk, Virginia, on December 7. He and a fellow officer were in a park having a picnic with their dates that afternoon. In late afternoon they went to a movie not knowing of the attack. They did not learn of the attack until that evening. When they returned to base a Marine sentry informed them that they were to report to their squadron immediately.[62]

While most Texans learned of the bombing of Pearl Harbor from their radios and newspapers, some Texans witnessed the attack first hand. Best known of these Texans today is Doris Miller, an African American from Waco, who was credited with shooting down one or more Japanese aircraft. Miller, who enlisted in the Navy in September 1939, was serving as a mess attendant on the battleship *West Virginia* when Japanese bombs hit the ship that morning. Miller went to the main deck and, after assisting in moving the ship's fatally wounded captain, manned an unattended machine gun. This was his first experience firing the weapon, as African-American seamen were not given gunnery training in the segregated U.S. Navy. Newspaper accounts credited Miller with shooting down several enemy planes, but these were never officially verified. Miller himself was confident he shot down at least one Japanese airplane. For his actions Miller was later awarded the Navy Cross in a ceremony conducted by fellow Texan Admiral Chester W. Nimitz.[63]

Doris Miller

The battleship U.S.S. *Oklahoma*, moored directly in front of *West Virginia*, was hit by Japanese bombs at the same time. Seaman First Class William W. Fomby from Hamlin, a small town 35 miles north of Abilene, was assigned to one of Oklahoma's 5-inch broadside guns. That morning Fomby was pulling mess duty. He had just helped serve breakfast when a sailor rushed into the mess hall to report that aerial maneuvers were being held that morning with planes diving all over the place. Anxious to view the action, Seaman Fomby rushed to the open deck. He observed the planes but could not understand why they were diving with their wheels down as he knew American planes always dived with their wheels up. When a bomb hit Ford Island he thought someone would "catch hell for that!" Just then, he heard orders to man antiaircraft and broadside guns. By the time he reached his battle station, the ship was under heavy attack. He jumped overboard just before *Oklahoma* heeled over, and he swam through burning oil and flames to the U.S.S. *Maryland*, which was moored on the inside of the *Oklahoma*.[64]

Just as the *Oklahoma* rolled over, a torpedo rocked the U.S.S. *Arizona*, moored to the rear of the *Tennessee* and *West Virginia*. Private First Class James Cory, a young Marine from Dallas assigned to the *Arizona*, had eaten

U.S.S. Arizona, *Pearl Harbor, December 7, 1941*

—National Archives

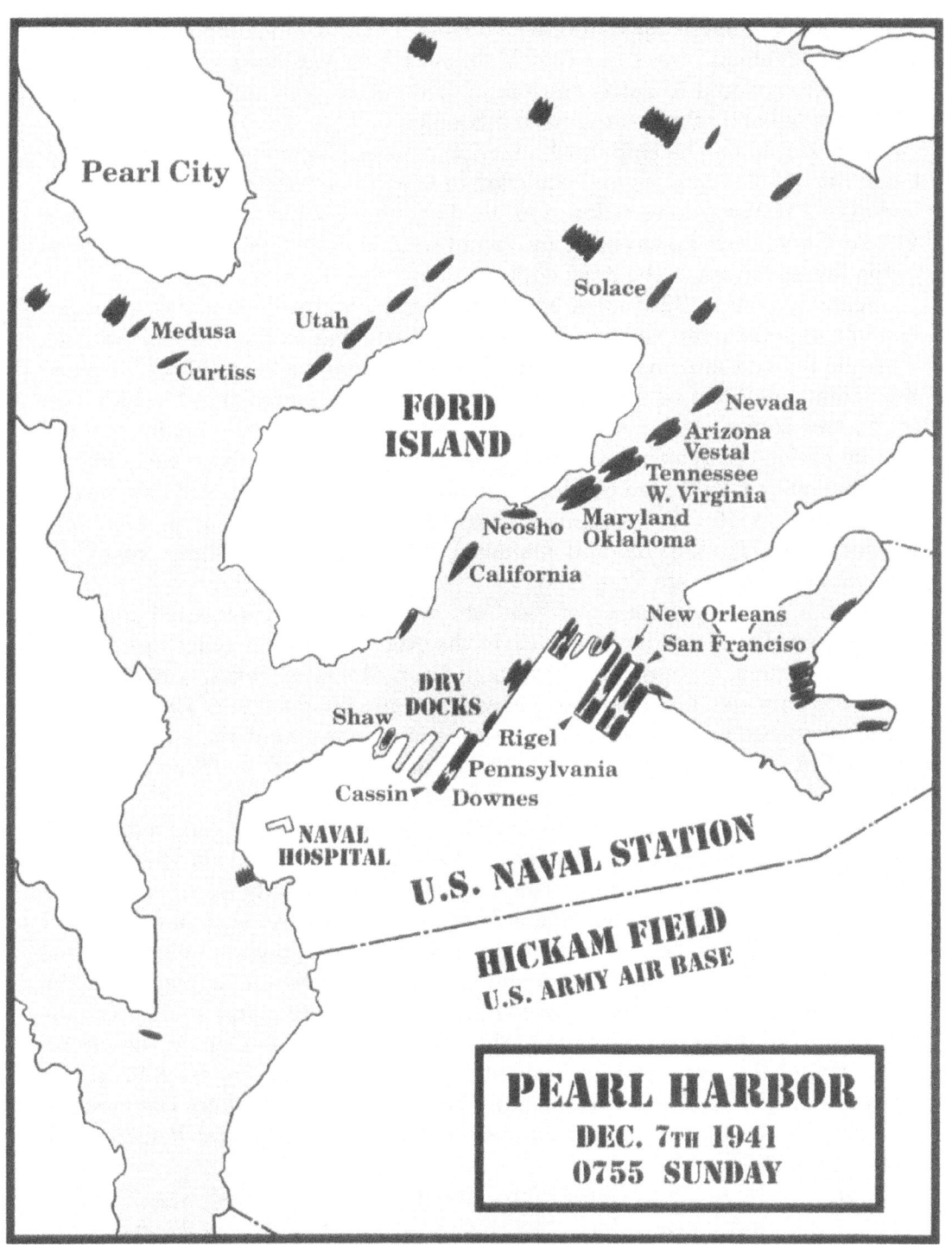

breakfast and was preparing to go into town when the ship first came under attack. A Japanese torpedo swept under the repair ship *Vestal*, which was moored to the starboard, and ripped into the *Arizona*. All hands, including Cory and fellow Texan Seaman First Class Clay H. Musick from Weslaco in the Rio Grande valley, were ordered to battle stations. When bombs pierced the deck, Musick was wounded and taken to the harbor hospital.

Cory stayed on the ship until a terrific explosion occurred when an enemy bomb hit the No. 2 turret and exploded in the forward magazine. The captain and over 1,100 men were killed, and the *Arizona* began settling into the water. Private Cory jumped overboard and swam to the U.S.S. *Tennessee*. He was one of the few survivors of the *Arizona*.[65]

Seaman Jack Kelly, a farm boy from Jones County, Texas, was a powder handler in gun turret No. 4 on the *Tennessee*. He was in the toilet below deck when he felt the ship shake and bounce. At the time, he believed the ship had been rammed. When he reached the top deck, he discovered the ship had been hit by two bombs. As he looked out, he saw the *West Virginia* settling on the bottom beside the *Tennessee*. Looking behind, he saw the *Arizona* covered by a large ball of fire. Up ahead *Oklahoma* had turned upside down with her screws sticking up in the air. Although badly damaged and listing to port, the *Tennessee* did not capsize and managed to pick up a few survivors of the *Arizona* such as Private Cory.[66]

U.S.S. *California*, flagship of Vice Admiral William Pye's Battle Force, was moored near Ford Island to the south of the other vessels in battleship row. Lee Raymond Vrana, a young Czech seaman from Moravia, Texas, was on board when the ship was hit by two torpedoes at approximately 8:15 A.M. Although the crew opened antiaircraft fire at the enemy, a bomb went right through the deck, killing about 100 men. When the last Japanese planes left the scene, the *California* was listing badly because of flooding.[67]

Dan Wentrek from Granger in central Texas was a boiler fireman on U.S.S. *Nevada* when the Japanese attacked. The officers and men on the *Nevada*, moored at the back of battleship row, reacted more promptly than crewmen on some of the other ships. They opened antiaircraft fire and shot down at least one enemy plane. Wentrek and others got the ship's boilers going and the *Nevada* began heading toward the entrance of the harbor. She crept past the *Arizona*, *West Virginia*, and *Oklahoma*, engulfed by fire and smoke. As she moved toward the entrance of the harbor, Japanese dive bombers in the second wave singled her out with several hits. Fearing that she might sink at the entrance and block further use of the harbor, the Naval District Commander ordered the *Nevada* to cut her engines and nose into Hospital Point on the south shore.[68]

Gunner's Mate Third Class Frank Townsend from El Paso was on U.S.S. *Pennsylvania* during the attack. Flagship of the Pacific Fleet, the *Pennsylvania* was in dry dock No. 1 near Hospital Point. Townsend was sleeping on a canvas cot when another sailor woke him to tell him that Japanese planes were bombing Ford Island across the harbor. The *Pennsylvania* was not a target in the first wave but came under heavy attack around 9:00 A.M. Townsend manned an antiaircraft gun but could not elevate it far enough up, so he "just sat there and didn't fire." A bomb hit the ship at 9:07, killing 13 men and wounding 38 others. Although two destroyers (*Cassin* and *Downes*) in the same dry dock and the destroyer U.S.S. *Shaw* in a nearby floating dry dock were badly damaged in the attack, material loss on the *Pennsylvania* was comparatively light.[69]

The heavy cruiser *New Orleans*, berthed with other cruisers on the south side of the harbor, suffered some damage from shrapnel and bomb fragments. Jack J. White, an electrician's mate from Fort Worth, was on board when the enemy attacked. Assigned to a 5-inch antiaircraft gun on the topside, White recalled that the ship was undergoing inspection and all ammunition was stowed away. When an electrical cable was cut during the attack, the men were forced to pass ammunition to the guns by hand.[70]

Although the enemy pilots concentrated their attention upon the battleships and cruisers of the American fleet, they attacked smaller vessels as well. The seaplane tender U.S.S. *Curtiss*, in the harbor on the northeast side of Ford Island, received heavy damage from bomb hits and an enemy plane that crashed into her starboard seaplane crane. In this crash, which may have been the first *kamikaze* (suicide) attack of the war, several seamen including Lee Herwin Duke of Vidor, Texas, were killed.[71]

Machinist Mate Third Class Leon Bennett from Kennard, Texas, was assigned to the tanker *Neosho* at the time of the attack. Carrying a full load of petroleum from California, the *Neosho* arrived at Pearl Harbor on Saturday morning. She had begun pumping aviation gasoline into the tanks at Ford Island just to the south of battleship row. The task had just been completed on Sunday morning when Japanese planes appeared. Bennett had finished duty and walked out on the dock to smoke a cigarette when he saw the Japanese planes. At first he thought they were U.S. planes dropping sandbags as part of a drill. Then he saw the Rising Sun insignia on the planes. "They were so low you could see them grinning," recalled Bennett. Soon bombs were dropping everywhere, and Bennett could see flames on the battleships just to the north.[72]

The seaplane tender *Rigel* was in the repair yard alongside the destroyer *Cummings* when the attack began. Dentist Ed Seiser of San Benito was assigned to the *Rigel* at the time. Seiser had served in the Navy during World War I. When his dental practice in San Benito failed in the late 1930s, he applied for and received a naval commission. At the time of the attack, the *Rigel* was undergoing repairs and without armament. Although the ship was peppered with shrapnel fragments that left a number of holes in her plating, damage was comparatively light. When a call for assistance came from the U.S.S. *Solace*, a hospital ship anchored on the far side of the harbor, Seiser and a physician took a small boat across the harbor to the *Solace*. There they worked for three days and nights without sleeping.[73]

Rudolph P. Zalman from Mart, Texas, was a machinist mate first class assigned to the repair ship *Medusa* on December 7. A 10-year veteran of the Navy, Zalman was in bed in his cottage in the Punch Bowl area when he heard fire engines and sirens. When he looked toward Pearl Harbor he saw smoke, fire, and haze. He hurriedly put on his uniform and headed to the base.[74]

Army Private First Class Melvin Faulkner from Henderson, Texas, was in his barracks in the 24th Infantry quadrangle when the attack began. "I was still in bed, debating whether or not to get up and eat breakfast, when several airplanes flew very low over the barracks," recalled Faulkner. "In a few seconds there was a big explosion." Faulkner ran over to the porch where he saw planes diving and bombs falling. "Big explosions were going off everywhere, one after another." In what was like a nightmare, the young Texan could see pieces of men, planes, trucks, and buildings blasted apart. Everything was in a state of chaos. Gunners on the ground were soon shooting at everything that moved.[75]

Sergeant Emil Matula from Granger in central Texas, a member of the 35th Regiment's football team, had been given a seven day pass after playing in the post championship game on December 6. On the morning of the 7th he was sleeping in Schofield Barracks when awakened by a fellow soldier. There had been a huge explosion that was believed to be an earthquake, and everyone was ordered out of the barracks. Just then, Japanese planes appeared, one dropping a bomb on the flagpole in the quadrangle. Matula and the other soldiers hurriedly dressed and headed to the supply room to get their weapons. The supply sergeant who had the keys was gone, so the men took fire axes, chopped down the doors, and got their weapons and ammunition. Matula had a Browning Automatic Rifle, which was not very effective against airplanes, but he fired it anyway.[76]

Marine Private Leslie Le Fan from Temple arrived in Pearl Harbor only seven days before the Japanese attack. Assigned to the Marine Barracks at the U.S. naval station on Ford Island, Le Fan was shaving when he heard planes and explosions. Believing this to be part of military maneuvers, Le Fan continued shaving. He was almost finished dressing when General Quarters was sounded. He ran down the corridor and grabbed a rifle but had no ammunition. A Japanese Zero fighter strafed the barracks, and a sailor standing in front of Le Fan was killed. A sergeant finally obtained some ammunition, and the men began firing into the air. Le Fan noted that all kinds of weapons were being used; two officers were firing 12-gauge shotguns normally used for skeet shooting.[77]

Le Fan saw the last torpedo hit the *Arizona*. "She just buckled right in the middle," recalled the young Marine. "It just quivered, buckled, and then settled. You could see sailors running around. Many of them were in their whites, some in their skivvy drawers and T-shirts, some of them stark naked."[78]

Chaplain Marcus A. Venta from Sweet Home in south Texas was conducting Sunday services at Schofield Barracks in central Oahu on December 7. He had just finished the second service when the Japanese attacked. He went to nearby Wheeler Field to give sacraments to the dying and those suffering. When Japanese planes bombed the hangars, he returned to Schofield to help with the wounded.[79]

Phillip Willis, a 23-year-old Army Air Corps pilot from Peeltown, south of

Dallas, was on temporary duty with the 86th Observation Squadron at Bellows Field located on the southeast corner of Oahu on the morning of the attack. He had been to a party the night before and still had his tuxedo on when bullets came through the barracks of his quarters. After he hurriedly changed clothes, Willis was helping a fellow pilot get into his P-40 fighter when a Japanese plane strafed the field. Willis' comrade was killed, and bullets riddled Willis' parachute pack. Willis was able to get his own plane airborne but had no ammunition. He flew around to avoid enemy fire until he received a clearance to land. Unfortunately, this was only a lull. Japanese planes soon returned and destroyed his plane. He was then given a pistol, joined Hawaiian National Guard troops, and patrolled the beaches. The group to which he was assigned later captured one of the enemy midget submarine commanders.[80]

Another Texas airman, Major Richard Carmichael, arrived in Oahu with a flight of B-17s from California while the Japanese attack was under way. A member of the Texas National Guard at age 15 and a graduate of the U.S. Military Academy, Carmichael had earlier been stationed at Wheeler Field on Oahu. His squadron had made the flight from Hamilton Field, California. Carmichael was pointing out the sights of the island to fellow airmen when someone noted white puffs ahead. Believing this to be naval practice, Carmichael did not get excited until he drew closer to the scene of devastation. With no ammunition and only skeleton crews, Carmichael led his squadron to an old airfield at Haleiwa on the north side of the island. Although the field was under fire, the B-17s landed and took cover under some trees.[81]

In addition to Doris Miller, two other Texans were awarded the Navy Cross for their actions during the Japanese attack. Seaman First Class Fred Kenneth Moore of Campbell, Texas, remained at his gun station despite orders to take cover and assisted in keeping his antiaircraft gun in operation until killed by an explosion. Boatswain's Mate Paul James McMurtry from Waco was awarded the Navy Cross for assisting "materially in maintaining continuous and effective fire against the enemy" with his 5-inch antiaircraft battery.[82]

When the last Japanese planes left the area around ten o'clock that morning, Pearl Harbor was the scene of great devastation. The mighty battleships, the pride of the American Navy, were a mass of wreckage. The *Arizona* was sunk with over 1,000 officers and men. The *Oklahoma* had capsized, the *West Virginia* was settling in shallow water, the *California* was sunk at her berth, and *Nevada* had run aground near the harbor entrance. The *Pennsylvania*, *Maryland*, and *Tennessee* were all damaged, and even the old target ship *Utah* had been sunk. Three light cruisers suffered moderate damage. Three destroyers had received major damage, a minesweeper capsized, and a repair ship beached. *Curtiss*, a seaplane tender, had been badly damaged. Nearby 200 American airplanes were destroyed and at least another 100 damaged; 2,403 Americans were killed and 1,178 were wounded.[83]

Texans at home and in the nation's capital realized that the Japanese attack was an act of war. That evening President Roosevelt met with Cabinet members and Senate and House leaders to discuss the address he planned to make to Congress the next day. Both Sam Rayburn and Tom Connally attended the meeting. Connally was returning from a relaxing drive in Maryland when he heard about the attack on the car radio. Rayburn had been in Virginia trying to help a young Texan who was in a jam with local police. He did not hear of the attack until he returned to his hotel. The desk clerk ran out to tell him about the attack and inform him that the president wanted to meet with congressional leaders that evening.[84]

The congressional leaders were stunned as the president shared with them what knowledge he had about the Japanese attack. At first the congressmen said little, but when the president attempted to find excuses for the disaster, Tom Connally exploded. According to historian Gordon Prange, Connally "had been slowly coming to a boil during the briefing." Now he lashed out, particularly at Secretary of Navy Frank Knox who had days earlier assured Congress that the Navy was well prepared for any emergency. The Texan berated the Navy for being surprised in light of earlier warnings from Washington. He asked Knox why the ships were all crowded in a neat row and why there were no air patrols to detect an enemy fleet. Knox, who had been shocked by the day's events, did not answer.[85]

The next day President Roosevelt addressed a joint session of Congress. In words heard on radio throughout the nation, the president somberly outlined the Japanese treachery on "a day that will live in infamy," and asked Congress for a declaration of war.[86]

Congress moved quickly to comply with the president's request. The Senate unamiously passed the war resolution introduced by Senator Connally. In the House, the only dissenting vote was cast by Jeanette Rankin of Montana, who had opposed the United States' entry into World War I in 1917. Less than one week later, Japan's allies, Italy and Germany, declared war on the United States. Congress responded by passing a joint resolution that a state of war "which has been thrust upon the United States is hereby formally declared."[87]

For the next three and a half years the United States would be engaged in the greatest war in modern history, a war in which Texas and Texans would play a major role.

CHAPTER TWO

Texas Mobilizes for War

Within a few hours of the attack on Pearl Harbor the Japanese made strikes against other American territories in the Pacific. Guam, Midway, Wake, and the Philippine Islands were all targets of Japanese military assaults. At the same time the Japanese attacked British and Dutch possessions in Malaya and the East Indies. During the next several months Japanese forces were successful in offensive operations that swept across Southeast Asia and the islands of the Pacific.

In the United States, meanwhile, Americans were mobilizing for war. Governor Coke Stevenson, who had become Texas governor when W. Lee O'Daniel was elected to the United States Senate in the summer of 1941, denounced the "cowardly Japanese attack" and issued a plea for a united country. Calling upon all Texans to rally behind state and national leaders, Stevenson declared "Texas will go to the limit in defense of our country."[1]

Support for a united front against the enemy was widespread. Throughout the state, newspaper editors and radio commentators called for an all out effort to avenge the loss of American lives at Pearl Harbor. Thousands of Texans rushed to recruiting stations to offer their services in the great struggle. Governor Stevenson had predicted that Texans would respond enthusiastically to defend their country. Young Texans proved him correct. By the end of January 1942, 148,004 Texans were in the armed forces, nearly two-thirds of them volunteers. The majority of Texas servicemen, 122,693, were in the Army, which at that time included not only the ground forces but also the Army Air Forces (until June 1941 the Army Air Corps). Nearly 20,000 Texans had volunteered for the Navy and slightly over 5,000 volunteered for the Marine Corps. One thousand Texans were in the United States Coast Guard.[2]

While some Texas servicemen were already fighting the Japanese in the Pacific in late 1941 and early 1942, the majority were training at a base or camp in the United States. Texas became a vast training ground for thousands of

Americans as dozens of facilities provided training for ground forces and Army and Navy airmen. During the next three years, 1,250,000 troops were trained in the state.[3]

Some of the troops trained at camps and bases built before 1940, such as Kelly and Randolph fields at San Antonio, Fort Bliss at El Paso, Camp Wolters at Mineral Wells and Camp Hulen at Palacios. Some were trained at bases and camps hurriedly constructed as part of the pre-war military build-up of 1940-1941; others at facilities built or opened after Pearl Harbor.

Fort Bliss at El Paso was the state's oldest major military facility. Established in March, 1854, the post was named for Lieutenant Colonel William W. Bliss, Zachary Taylor's chief of staff during the Mexican War. By the early 20th century, Bliss was the largest cavalry post in the country. The home of the United States 1st Cavalry Division, the fort grew from a few thousand acres to more than one million during the 1940s. By June 1943 Bliss had phased out its horses as the cavalry was mechanized. When the 1st Cavalry was sent overseas, the facility became an artillery post. In 1944, it became the center of antiaircraft artillery training in the United States.[4]

Other cavalry posts in pre-war Texas, Forts Brown (Brownsville), Clark (Brackettville), and Ringgold (Rio Grande City), were older but smaller than Bliss. Established by Zachary Taylor in 1846, Brown was headquarters for the 12th Cavalry Regiment and later the 124th Cavalry Regiment, but was deactivated in 1944. Fort Clark, opened in 1852 near the wagon route from San Antonio to El Paso, was home for the 112th Cavalry until that unit was deployed for combat in the Pacific. Like Brown, the post was deactivated in 1944. Fort Ringgold, once home of the African American 9th Cavalry, was also deactivated in 1944.[5]

Fort D. A. Russell at Marfa and Fort McIntosh at Laredo were pre-World War II cavalry posts that underwent improvements in early 1940. Russell, originally known as Camp Marfa, was renamed in 1930 for D. A. Russell, an officer during the Mexican and Civil Wars. The post was closed in 1933 but occupied by the 77th Field Artillery in 1935. McIntosh, also named for a Mexican War officer, was established at an old Spanish presidio in the aftermath of the Mexican War. Over the years the post had a colorful history. Some new barracks and temporary buildings were erected during the early 1940s. The fort was occupied at different times during World War II by infantry, cavalry, artillery, and engineers.[6]

Fort Sam Houston in San Antonio and Camp Bullis, 17 miles northwest of San Antonio, were both expanded to meet growing military needs in 1940. Fort Sam Houston had been a permanent military post since 1870 and was at one time the largest military post in the United States. Until November 1942 it was the home of the 2nd Infantry Division. Camp Bullis was established as a camp for training World War I troops in 1917. Both Fort Sam (as locals referred to Fort Sam Houston) and Bullis served as reception centers for processing volunteers and draftees as the Army grew in 1940-1941. Fort Sam Houston also served as headquarters for various military commands including Walter

Krueger's Third Army and the Southern Defense Command. Bullis was expanded to provide training for the 2nd, 88th, and 95th Infantry Divisions.[7]

Camp Hulen near Palacois was another Texas training facility that predated World War II. Established in 1926 as a summer training camp for the Texas National Guard, the camp was named for John A. Hulen, commander of the Guard. In 1940 the War Department began to use the camp for antiaircraft training for national guard units across the country. In January 1941, the first draftees arrived at the camp. By 1943 Hulen consisted of 300 semi-permanent buildings, a weather station, fire stations, library, dental clinics, post office, and a 500-bed hospital. At its height, troop capacity was 14,560.[8]

As a consequence of the War Department decision to make Hulen an antiaircraft training facility for all national guard units, the Texas National Guard, federalized in 1940 as the 36th Infantry Division, moved to newly opened Camp Bowie, near Brownwood. Bowie was the first major military base constructed in Texas as part of the nation's pre-war preparedness campaign. Originally, the post consisted of 2,000 acres, but it was expanded to 120,000 acres. In addition to the 36th Division, the 115th Cavalry of the Iowa National Guard, VIII Corps headquarters, and various technical and support units trained at the camp at times during the war. In 1943 a prisoner of war camp was established within the post.[9]

Camp Wolters, four miles east of Mineral Wells, was a pre-Pearl Harbor National Guard facility that was expanded with the approach of war. Opened in 1925 as a summer training camp for the 56th Brigade of the Texas National Guard and named for the brigade commander, Wolters was expanded to 7,500 acres. It became a major infantry replacement training center with a troop capacity of 25,000.[10]

Camp Wallace in Galveston County was a new facility built as part of the pre-Pearl Harbor defense program. Opened February 1, 1941, and named for an artillery officer killed in World War I, Wallace served as an antiaircraft training center for two years. The camp consisted of 161 barracks, almost 400 buildings, and a capacity for 12,000 men. In April 1944 Wallace was transferred to the U.S. Navy as a training and distribution center.[11]

Camp Barkeley, 11 miles south of Abilene, was the another new military camp opened in 1941. Named for a World War I Texas Medal of Honor recipient, Barkeley was originally planned as a small, temporary camp, but became one of the largest military installations in the state. The 45th Infantry Division, made up of national guardsmen from Arizona, Colorado, Oklahoma, and New Mexico, occupied the unfinished camp on February 12, 1941. During the course of the war the 90th Infantry Division and the 11th and 12th Armored Divisions also trained at Barkeley. A medical school was established in May 1942; 12,500 candidates graduated from the school. A prison camp was also activated at Barkeley. At its peak, Barkeley had a total population of 50,000.[12]

Four additional Army training centers opened in Texas during 1942: Camps Hood, Howze, Maxey, and Swift. All four were large posts hurriedly constructed to provide training space for the growing United States Army. Hood, the largest of these, was designed primarily as the Army's Tank Destroyer Tactical and Fire Center but was expanded to include an infantry replacement and basic training center. The selection of Killeen, a small town near Temple, as the site for a major military installation was the result of diligent efforts of Frank W. Mayborn, publisher of the Temple *Daily Telegram* and operator of radio station KTEM. President of the Temple Chamber of Commerce, Mayborn spent considerable time and effort in lobbying for the Center. He enlisted the assistance of Oveta Culp Hobby, a native of Killeen and the wife of former Texas Governor Will Hobby, Jesse Jones of Houston, director of the Reconstruction Finance Corporation, and United States Senator Tom Connally from Marlin.[13]

On January 10, 1942, the War Department announced the new Tank Destroyer Center would be located at Killeen. Land was acquired, and construction began almost immediately. Colonel Andrew D. Bruce, a 1916 graduate of Texas A&M College and a decorated veteran of World War I, was named commander of the post. Colonel Bruce and elements of the tank destroyer command arrived in April 1942. The post, named for Confederate General John B. Hood, was officially opened on September 18, 1942. Bruce, promoted to general officer rank, remained at Hood until May 1943 when he was transferred to command the 77th Infantry Division.

Under the command of Bruce's successor, Major General Orlando C. Ward, a veteran of the North African campaign, Camp Hood continued to grow. It reached its World War II maximum size of 160,000 acres in late 1943. At that time 130,000 officers and men were training at the camp. The War Department expended over $75 million on Camp Hood between 1941-1945.[14]

Camps Howze, Maxey, and Swift, all opened in summer 1942, were primarily infantry training centers. Howze, northwest of Gainesville, was activated on August 17, 1942. Named for a Texas Medal of Honor winner of Indian wars, Howze served as the training ground for over 100,000 men in World War II. The 84th, 86th, and 102nd Infantry Divisions were among the units trained there.[15]

Camp Maxey, activated near Paris in July 1942, was 80 miles to the east of Camp Howze. The 103rd Infantry Division and various Army service units trained at the camp, which had a capacity of slightly over 44,000. Like many camps, Maxey had an artillery range, obstacle course, and infiltration course. A German village created on the post provided realistic training for house-to-house fighting. In 1943, the largest enemy prison camp in the United States, housing over 7,000 German prisoners, was opened at Maxey.[16]

Camp Swift, several miles north of Bastrop, was another large infantry facility opened in 1942. Located on 55,000 wooded acres, the camp was originally designed to accommodate 44,000 troops but eventually had twice that number. At various times the 95th, 97th, and 102nd Infantry Divisions, the 10th Mountain Division, and the 116th and 120th Tank Destroyer Battalions trained at Swift. The camp also housed over 3,000 German prisoners of war before the end of the war.[17]

Camp Fannin, ten miles northeast of Tyler, was the last infantry training center built in Texas during World War II. Construction began on December 1,

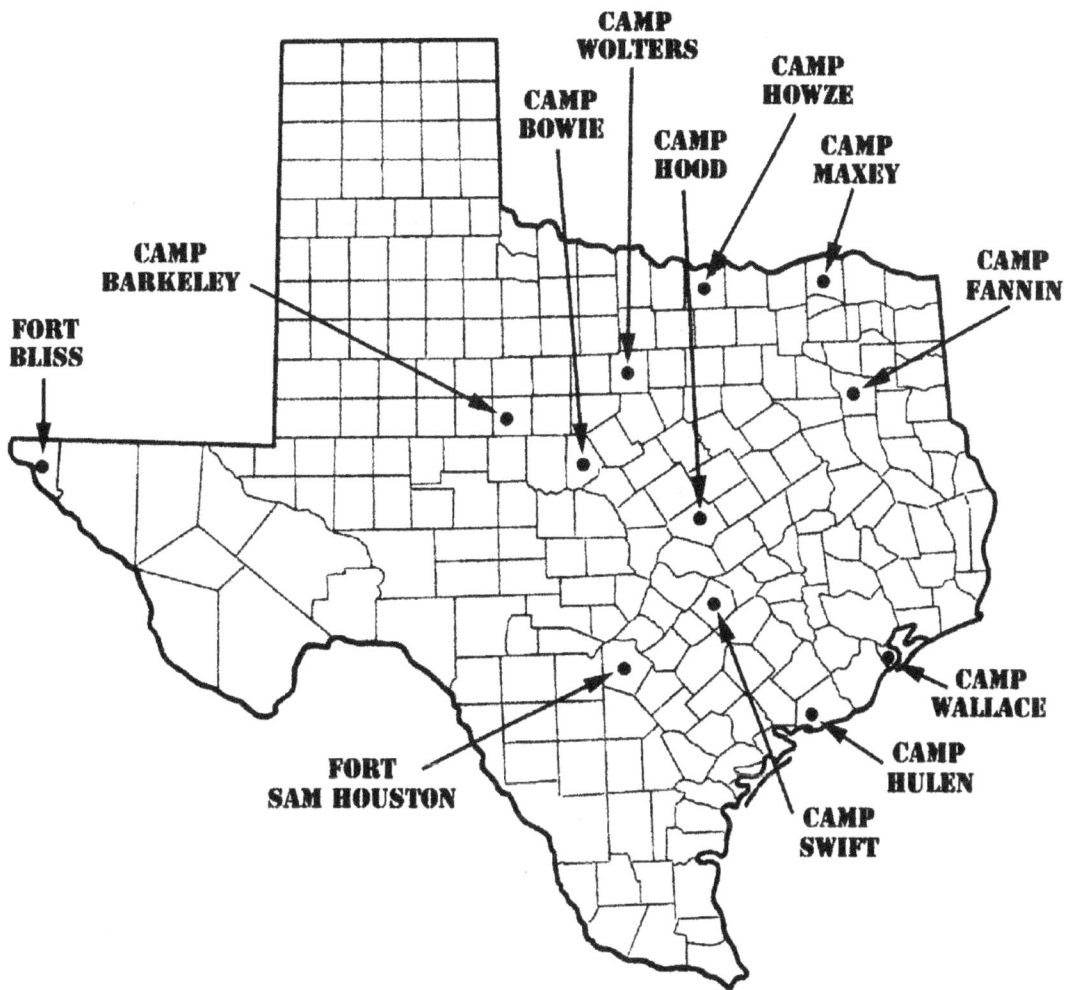

MAJOR ARMY TRAINING CAMPS IN TEXAS WORLD WAR II

1942, and the camp opened in late 1943. By that time the demand for training space had been filled, so no additional training camps for ground troops were opened in Texas.[18]

In addition to the aforementioned camps and forts utilized for training ground troops, the Army maintained and upgraded three coastal artillery posts in Galveston County. All were constructed at the turn of the century. Fort Crockett (1897) and Fort San Jacinto (1901) were on Galveston Island, facing the Gulf of Mexico. Both were in virtual caretaker status until reactivated in 1941. Fort Travis, across the harbor at the southern end of Bolivar Peninsula, was built in 1899. In 1941-43 the Army Corps of Engineers made improvements in the defense capability of these installations, building a casemate for the 12-inch guns at Crockett, new gun batteries at both San Jacinto and Crockett, and instrument towers with detectors to locate enemy vessels and to provide directions for artillerymen manning the guns at all three forts.[19]

The U.S. Army Air Forces (formerly Army Air Corps) operated or maintained even more bases or fields in Texas in World War II than the ground forces. Because of its open spaces and generally favorable weather, the state has always been attractive to aviation. Kelly Field, located at the southwestern edge of San Antonio, is the oldest continuously operating flying base in the country. Captain Benjamin Foulois, "the father of military aviation," selected the site in 1916 and named the field for Lieutenant George Kelly, who was killed in a crash at Fort Sam Houston in 1916. The field grew rapidly during World War I; almost all the American combat pilots in the war earned their wings at Kelly. During the 1920s and 1930s most future leaders of the Army Air Corps passed through Kelly.

Major changes occurred at Kelly during World War II. The War Department expended over $38 million in improvements during 1940-45. Part of Kelly became the Aviation Cadet Reception Center, later to become Lackland Air Force Base. All pilot training was transferred to other fields, but Kelly continued to play a major role in storing, modifying, and repairing aircraft, engines and other equipment.[20]

Brooks Field, seven miles southeast of San Antonio, was opened as a facility for training flying instructors after the United States entered World War I. The field was first named Gosport Field after the Royal Air Force flight instruction method. It was changed to Signal Corps Aviation School, Kelly Field No. 5, in December 1917, but was renamed again in February 1918 to honor Cadet Sidney Johnson Brooks, Jr., killed in a training accident.

From 1922 to1931 Brooks was the primary flight school for the Army Air Corps. More than 1,400 pilots, including Charles Lindbergh, Claire Chennault, and Jimmy Doolittle, trained there. It became the center for aerial observation training during the 1930s. Observation training continued there until 1943, when Brooks began training B-25 bomber pilots.[21]

Like Kelly and Brooks, Ellington Field near Houston was a World War I training facility. Named for Lieutenant Eric L. Ellington, killed in an air accident in California, the field was closed in the 1920s but reopened in April 1941 after extensive modernization. During the first two years of the war, one of every ten Army pilots trained at Ellington. Navigators and bombardiers were also trained at Ellington, receiving instruction in military fundamentals before going elsewhere for specialized flight training. Later in the war, the pilot and bombardier programs were transferred, and Ellington became the location of the Air Forces' Advanced Navigator Training School.[22]

Biggs Army Air Field, located at Fort Bliss, El Paso, was established just after the end of World War I. The field was named for Lieutenant James B. Biggs, a native of El Paso killed in France near the end of the war. It was primarily a refueling stop in the late 1920s and 1930s. With the approach of World War II, extensive improvements were made. In 1942 Biggs became headquarters for the 20th Bombardment Command. During the next three years, hundreds of B-17 and B-24 combat crews were trained at Biggs. In early 1945, runways were enlarged so that B-29 crews could train there.[23]

Randolph Field, 15 miles northeast of San Antonio, became known as "the West Point of the Air" in the late 1930s. Officially opened on June 20, 1930, Randolph Field, named for a Texas Army pilot killed on take-off in 1928, was established to meet the expanding needs of military aviation in the 1930s. Basic flight training at Brooks Field and primary flight training at March Field, California, were both moved to Randolph as those fields took on other responsibilities. Students completing these programs at Randolph could then obtain their final advance training at nearby Kelly Field.[24]

During the 1930s, hundreds of cadets, including young West Point graduates who wished to fly, trained at Randolph. With the buildup of American military strength in 1939-41, the number of cadets trained at Randolph doubled. Randolph continued to grow during the war. In 1943 an instructor's flight training school was added to the field's mission. More than 16,000 pilots were trained at Randolph during World War II.[25]

Even with the improvements, modifications, and program expansions at the pre-1940 military airfields in Texas and elsewhere, the War Department realized that many additional facilities would be required if the United States entered the war. As a part of the buildup of American military strength, construction on a number of new training fields in Texas began in 1940-41. In addition, the War Department made contracts with private flying services to provide flight training at municipal or privately owned air fields. One of the first of these was a contract awarded the Brayton Flying Service located at the Cuero Municipal Airport in January 1941. Under the contract, Brayton provided a nine-week course, which included classes in meteorology, navigation, aircraft identification, Link simulation training, and actual flying time. The instructors and mechanics were all civilians, but the Army rigidly supervised training. Similar contracts were granted to companies for training at Arledge Field at Stamford, Bruce Field at Ballinger, Coleman Field at Coleman, Corsicana Field at Corsicana, Hicks Field at Fort Worth, Victory Field at Vernon, and Garner Field at Uvalde.[26]

The War Department opened seven new Army airfields in Texas during

1940-41. The first of these was at San Angelo. Opened in August 1940 as the San Angelo Air Corps Basic Training School, the base was renamed Goodfellow Field on May 27, 1941, in honor of a former San Angelo resident, John J. Goodfellow, Jr., killed while serving with the Air Service in France during World War I. The first class of cadets arrived for basic flight training in January 1941.[27]

Curtis Field, 3½ miles north of Brady, opened soon after Goodfellow. Construction of the facility began in November 1940 after Mayor Henry C. Curtis of Brady (for whom the field was named) persuaded the War Department to establish a base there. The first class began on March 23, 1941, with 80 students enrolled for primary flight training. Later the size of classes ran as high as 500 students. Several thousand student pilots graduated from Curtis during the war.[28]

Foster Army Air Field near Victoria and Perrin Army Air Field at Sherman were both opened in summer 1941. Foster, an advanced single-engine flying school for fighter pilots, was called Victoria Field until January 1942, when it was renamed for an Army pilot killed in 1925. Perrin, named for a Texan killed while flying the new B-26 bomber at Baltimore, was a basic flying school.[29]

Like Foster Air Field, Moore Field, located 14 miles north of Mission, provided advanced flight training for fighter pilots. Named for a Houstonian killed in World War I, Moore Field was opened in September 1941. Six thousand pilots received training there before the field was closed in October 1945.[30]

Construction of Sheppard Field, named for Texas Senator Morris Sheppard, who died in April 1941, was completed in October 1941. Located just north of the city limits of Wichita Falls, Sheppard provided training for mechanics of medium bombers and gliders and for glider pilots. During the last year of the war, Sheppard became the only helicopter pilot training school in the nation. The base reached it peak strength, 46,304, in 1945, making it the largest concentration of American airmen in the world.[31]

Harlingen Field in the Rio Grande Valley became the home of the Army Aerial Gunnery School. Through the efforts of the Harlingen Chamber of Commerce, the War Department was persuaded to build a new facility for training aerial gunners three miles northwest of the city. Construction began in late summer 1941, and the first classes began the day after Pearl Harbor. During an intensive six-week program, airmen received training in maintaining and firing .30 and .50 caliber machine guns. The base itself was constantly being expanded with new barracks and other facilities. The setting was in a lush tropical background referred to by some as the "Paradise of the Eastern Flying Training Command."[32]

The opening of the seven new airfields in Texas during 1940-41 was the beginning of a flood of building and expanding training fields. Construction of a dozen additional facilities began in early 1942. The first of these were the Midland and Lubbock Army Air Fields, both receiving cadets in February. Midland Army Flying School, popularly known as the "Bombardier College," opened with a class of 119 cadets whose 12-week training employed the highly classified Norden bombsight. New classes continued to arrive thereafter, enlarged to meet the growing need for bombardiers. By the end of the war, 6,627 cadets had gone though the bombardier school.[33]

Lubbock Army Air Field, originally named Lubbock Army Air Corps Advanced Flying School, received its first class in late February 1942. The facility was constructed to teach pilots of twin-engine aircraft, but because of a shortage of twin-engine aircraft, the first three cadet classes were trained in single-engine planes. More than 7,000 pilots were trained at Lubbock during the war.[34]

Two months after the first cadets arrived at Midland and Lubbock, another West Texas town received its first cadets. The city fathers of Sweetwater had made arrangements with the War Department to enlarge the municipal airport, renamed Avenger Field, for training pilots. The first trainees, who arrived in April 1942, were 50 British cadets being trained as pilots for the Royal Air Force. They were soon followed by classes of American cadets. During the next year, 820 aviation cadets received flight instruction at Avenger Field.[35]

The training program for male pilots was terminated in April 1943. For the next 18 months, facilities were used for training experienced female pilots to fly Army planes. Famed aviatrix Jacqueline Cochran convinced the Pentagon that such women pilots could provide invaluable service in ferrying military aircraft from station to station, freeing male pilots for combat duty. Thus was created the Women's Airforce Service Pilots (WASP). The program was originally assigned to Hughes Field in Houston but heavy air traffic and bad weather led to its relocation at Sweetwater. During the next year and half, 1,074 women earned their wings at Sweetwater. When the program ended in December 1944 training for male fighter pilots was resumed at Avenger.[36]

The Army established two flying schools in the Waco area. Construction of the Waco Army Air Field, designed to provide basic pilot instruction, was completed in May 1942. Later that month, the Army opened China Springs Air Field, several miles north of Waco. Established as a glider training school, the base was used later as a two-engine pilot school. The China Springs facility was later renamed Blackland Army Air Field for the black soil on which the field was built.[37]

The Army opened seven new airfields in Texas during summer 1942. Four of these were designed primarily for training fighter pilots. Miller Field at Fort Stockton (later renamed Gibbs Field) provided primary flight instruction; Pecos and Majors at Greenville, provided basic flight instruction; and Eagle Pass Army Field provided advanced single-engine flight training.[38]

The other three fields opened that summer each provided different types of instruction. Lamesa Field in Dawson County was designed for elementary and advanced glider training, Big Spring trained bombardiers, and Hondo Army Air Field trained navigators. The Hondo facility was not only the largest U.S. Air Force navigation school in the world at the time, but was also involved in one of the nation's most interesting, and unsuccessful, military experiments, the use of bomb-bearing bats.[39]

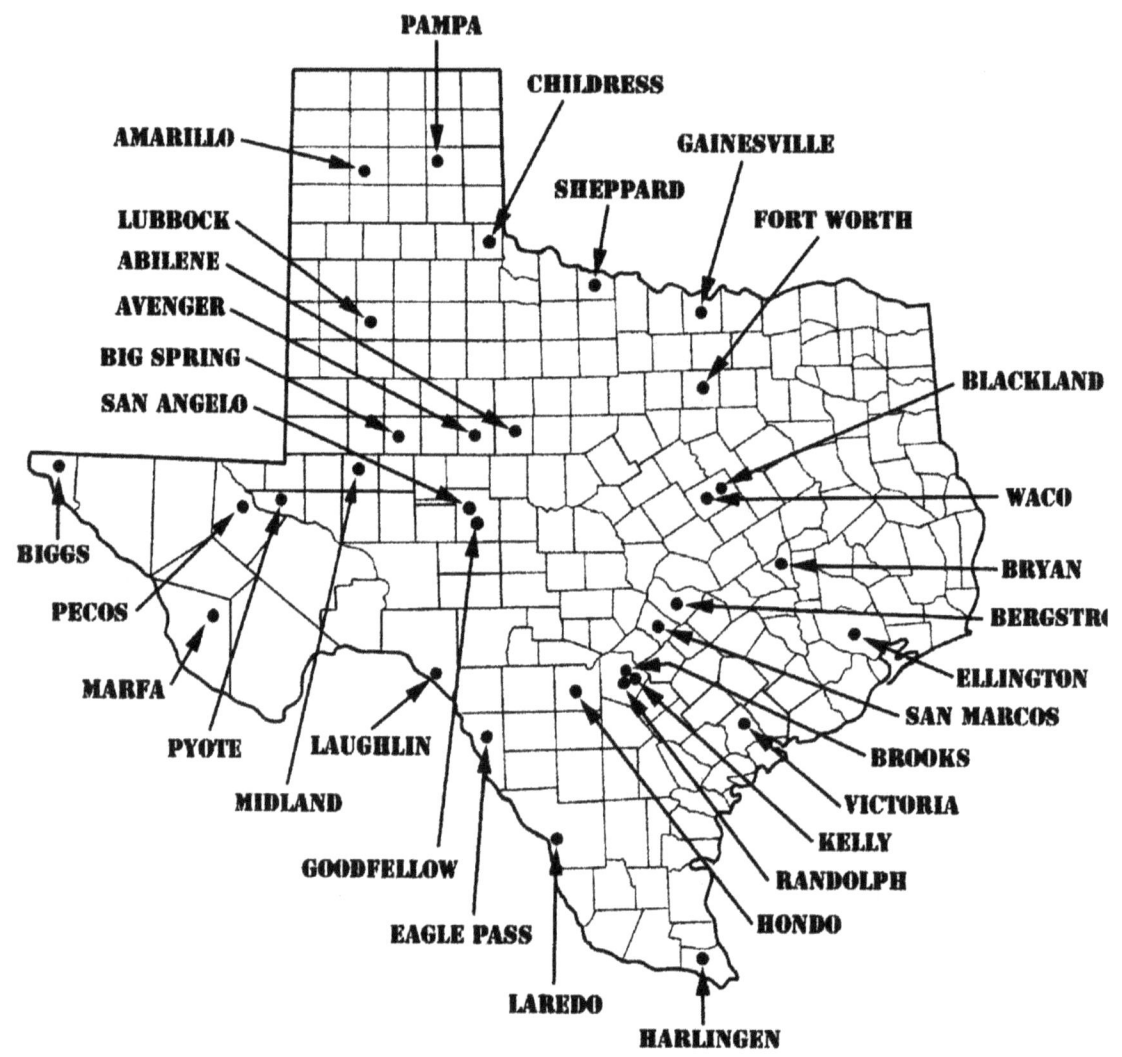

The bat-bomb experiment was conducted on orders from President Roosevelt. A scientist, Dr. Lytle S. Adams, convinced the president that bats with small incendiary bombs clipped to their chests could be dropped over Tokyo and cause great devastation. The bats were collected in the Hondo-Bandera area. The commanding officer of Hondo Field provided a giant block of ice needed to cool the bats on a flight to Arizona, where test-bombing occurred. Some of the bats did destroy a mock Japanese village, but others returned to the Arizona base from which they had been transported and blew up two hangars and ten airplanes. It was then decided the experiment was too risky and the project terminated.[40]

During the autumn of 1942, the Army opened seven additional training fields in Texas. Amarillo Army Air Field began training air crews and ground mechanics for B-17 bombers in September. On September 14 the San Angelo Army Air Field, designed to instruct bombardiers, was opened. During the next two and a half years, more than 5,000 bombardiers received training at San Angelo. Also in September 1942, training for glider pilots began at Dalhart Army Air Field and for pilots of large transport planes at Del Valle Army Air Base near Austin. This base was later renamed Bergstrom Army Air Field in honor of Captain John A. E. Bergstrom, the first Austinite killed in World War II.[41]

Fort Worth Army Air Field, built next to the giant Consolidated Aircraft plant, was activated in July but did not receive its first class of student officers for transition training in B-24 Liberators until October 1942. Laughlin Army Air Field, seven miles east of Del Rio, was activated as a bombardier school that October, but before the first bombardier cadets arrived its mission was changed to transition pilot training for B-26 Marauder bombers. In November Laredo Army Air Field began operations as a gunnery range and flexible gunnery school.[42]

The Army fields at Abilene, Marfa, and Pampa were the last to open in Texas in 1942. The Abilene facility, known originally as Tye Field, later was renamed Dyess Field for pilot William Edwin Dyess of Albany, killed early in the war. Marfa Army Air Field, an advanced flying school, received its first cadets in early December. The mission of Marfa was later broadened to include multi-engine, transport, and mechanic training. Pampa Army Air Field, known as the "Eagle's Nest of the High Plains," received its first cadets for advanced multi-engine instruction that same month.[43]

Several additional airfields opened in Texas in early 1943. Aloe Army Air Field near Victoria, constructed to provide advanced single-engine pilot training, opened in January. That same month the Army activated the Galveston Army Air Field to be used for planes flying antisubmarine patrol. This field would be used later as a school for training overseas veterans as military instructors.[44]

The Pyote Army Air Field, established in a remote West Texas site as a base for bombardment crew training, opened in early 1943. Within a few months of its opening Pyote became "the largest training facility of its kind in the United

States." Because of the thousands of snakes that inhabited the site, Pyote became known as the "Rattlesnake Bomber Base."[45]

The first cadre for the Pyote base were members of the 19th Bombardment Group, which flew directly from the Far East, where they had been the first air group to bomb Japanese targets. These veterans would train less experienced bombardiers, navigators, and pilots for combat.[46]

Construction of Army airfields at San Marcos and Childress began in summer 1942. The first cadets arrived at both fields in February 1943. The San Marcos facility was designed for the instruction of navigators. By the end of the war, several thousand navigators had been trained at the base. Childress was established for training bombardiers, who were also skilled in dead-reckoning navigation. In 3½ years, nearly 5,000 bombardier-navigators graduated from the school. The field was also the site of several "All American Precision Bombing Olympics" in which personnel from seven airfields participated between May 1943 and April 1944.[47]

Bryan Army Air Field was activated in 1943 as a school for instrument flying instructors. A standardized system of instrument flying known as the "Full Panel Attitude System" was developed at Bryan, the only one of its kind in the U.S. Air Forces.[48]

In addition to the numerous training camps and bases, the U.S. Army built and operated five general hospitals in Texas. Each of these was a large multibuilding complex designed to treat various military needs. Asburn General in McKinney specialized in arthritis care; William Beaumont General in El Paso provided plastic surgery, deep X-ray, and psychiatric care; Brooke General and Convalescence in San Antonio, thoracic surgery and psychiatric care; Harmon General in Longview, psychiatry and general medicine; and McCloskey General in Temple amputation, neurosurgery, neurology, and psychiatry.[49]

The United States Navy also opened two hospitals in Texas during World War II, one at Houston and the other at Corpus Christi. The one at Corpus was adjacent to the new Naval Air Training Station at the edge of the city. Construction of the Naval Air Training facility, which ultimately consisted of the main station at Flour Bluff and auxiliary stations Rodd, Waldron, Cuddihy and Cabanis fields in Corpus, the Kingsville Naval Air Station and the Beeville Naval Air Station (also known as Chase Field), was approved in early June 1940. All except the last two were within a few miles of the main station, and all except Kingsville and the main station were named for men who gave their lives in naval aviation.[50]

Groundbreaking for the main station, the largest naval air training center in the country, occurred in late June 1940. The station was commissioned on May 12, 1941 with Secretary of Navy Frank Knox and Texas Governor W. Lee O'Daniel among the speakers. The first cadets arrived a week later. The station trained cadets as pilots, navigators, aerologists, gunners, and radio operators. By the end of the war, 35,000 naval airmen had been trained at the Corpus Christi Naval Air Station. Future President George W. H. Bush was in the third graduating class of pilots at the station.[51]

The Navy also established a naval air station at Hensley Field in Dallas. Named for a Dallas flight instructor who was on the first trans-Atlantic dirigible crossing in 1919, Hensley was established in 1929 as a training field for Reserve pilots. It became a Naval Air Station in January 1943. The basic mission of the station was primary flight training for Navy, Marine, and Coast Guard cadets. Enlisted personnel for aviation duty with the fleet trained there. The Navy also established a radial engine repair facility at the station.[52]

The Navy opened another air station at Hitchcock, between Houston and Galveston. This facility was designed for lighter-than-air, semi-rigid airships, known as "blimps," to be used in protecting shipping facilities and traffic along the Texas coast from submarine attacks. Construction of a massive $10 million wooden hangar to hold six airships began in 1942. Commissioned in May 1943, the Hitchcock Naval Air Station included warehouses, barracks, shops, garages, and administrative offices. One hundred fifty-three officers and men were initially assigned to the station.[53]

While the Army and Navy were building new training camps, airfields, and stations in the state, Texans were expanding and developing industrial resources to support the war effort. In this respect, the oil industry was particularly significant. Since the early days of the Spindletop gusher, Texas had led the nation in oil production, producing 36.5 percent of all the nation's domestic oil in 1940. Prior to Pearl Harbor, most of Texas' refined oil products were consumed by civilians; 98.5 percent of all Texas gasoline went to civilian consumption in December 1941. With the outbreak of war, governmental and military consumption quickly outpaced civilian usage. By 1944 only 28.9 percent of Texas gasoline was used by civilians. In part this was due to gasoline rationing (to be discussed in a later chapter) and in part due to the huge amounts of petroleum products required by American and Allied military forces.[54]

To meet the increasing needs of the nation in wartime, Texas oilmen increased production to record levels. In 1940, the state produced slightly over 491 million barrels of oil. This rose to 505 million barrels in 1941. In 1944, the state produced over 746 million barrels of oil.[55]

The production of 100-octane aviation gasoline became a major function of Texas refineries. The Humble Oil Company's giant refinery at Baytown produced more 100-octane fuel than any other refinery in the world. On December 14, 1944, the Baytown plant celebrated the production of its billionth gallon of 100-octane gasoline. It was the first refinery in the world to hit that mark.[56]

The outbreak of war with Germany brought the threat of enemy submarine attacks on tankers carrying oil and gasoline from Texas to the East Coast. Fearing such a prospect, Secretary of Interior Harold Ickes in 1941 urged the building of a giant pipeline from Texas to East Coast refineries and consumers. The Ickes proposal, however, required massive amounts of steel plating needed for other military projects, especially shipbuilding. As a result, approval was delayed until the sinking of several tankers carrying oil from Texas ports in May 1942 convinced Washington authorities that the pipeline project must go forward.[57]

Work on the pipeline, 24 inches in diameter and called the "Big Inch," began in August 1942. Completed in August 1943 the Big Inch carried Texas crude oil from Longview across the Mississippi to Pennsylvania and New York. Approval for another pipeline, 20 inches in diameter and labeled the "Little Big Inch," to transport refined products, was given in January 1943. This line, completed in March 1944, ran from the refinery complex in the Houston-Port Arthur area to Linden, New Jersey. Together, the two pipelines, built at the cost of $146 million, carried 350 million barrels of Texas crude and refined oil to the East Coast before the war in Europe ended.[58]

Texas chemical and petrochemical industries received a major boost as a result of wartime needs. Dozens of chemical plants were built in the state immediately before and during the war, many to produce materials that were no longer available because of Japanese expansion in the Far East. The Dow Chemical plant was constructed at Freeport in 1940 for the production of magnesium and other products from sea water. With the outbreak of war, the plant was expanded for the production of chemical items such as styrene. The Humble Oil Company received a government contract in 1940 to make synthetic toluene, a basic ingredient of trinitrotoluene (TNT). The Baytown Ordnance Works was built next to Humble's Baytown oil refinery. By late 1941 the plant was shipping synthetic toluene to Karnack, Texas, and other facilities where explosives were made. Shell Oil Company's Deer Park plant also made toluene for the war effort.[59]

The Humble plant at Baytown produced butyl rubber used for insulation and rubberized cloth. Butadiene, a basic ingredient for synthetic rubber, was manufactured by the oil companies at Baytown, Borger, Corpus Christi, Houston, and Port Neches. In June 1943 the General Tire and Rubber Company opened a plant just north of Baytown's Humble refinery to make tires from butadiene produced by Humble and styrene manufactured by Monsanto Chemical Company at Texas City. B. F. Goodrich opened synthetic rubber plants at Borger in July and Port Neches in August. Goodyear's synthetic rubber plant in Houston and Firestone's plant in Port Neches began operations that autumn.[60]

Mineral smeltering and production in Texas took on new importance during the war. Only a handful of metal plants existed in Texas prior to Pearl Harbor. Ten new plants were constructed during the war. Especially important was the world's largest tin smelter built in Texas City for the U.S. government by an American subsidiary of the Dutch Billiton Maatschappy firm. Zinc smelters at Dumas and Amarillo, a copper smelter at El Paso, and an antimony smelter at Laredo provided other materials desperately needed for the war effort.[61]

The iron and steel industry, which had been morbid in Texas prior to 1941, took on new life with the increased need for these products. In 1941 Sheffield Steel of Texas, a division of the American Rolling Mill Company, built a new steel mill in the Houston Ship Channel that used scrap metal. Two years later the mill was expanded with open-hearth furnaces, coke ovens, a blooming mill, and a blast furnace. At Longview the Madaras Steel Corporation built a plant to reduce iron ore to sponge iron. Sponge iron was then converted into steel ingots by the East Texas Electric Steel Company.[62]

In 1943 the Lone Star Steel Company built a blast furnace and coke ovens near Daingerfield in East Texas. An iron smelting plant was also constructed at Rusk.[63]

The small East Texas town Karnack was a center of ammunition production during the war. In December 1941, Monsanto Chemical Company selected the site near Caddo Lake for the manufacture of the explosive trinitrotoluene (TNT). Construction was begun soon after, and in October 1942 the Longhorn Army Ammunition Plant (also called the Longhorn Ordnance Works) began operation. By the end of the war the plant had produced over 400 million tons of TNT.[64]

The B. F. Goodrich Rubber Corporation built an ammunition loading plant for artillery shells, bombs, fuses, and other ordnance items near Texarkana in late 1941. The Lone Star Ammunition Plant (also known as the Lone Star Ordnance Plant) was consolidated with the Red River Ordnance Depot, located adjacent, in April 1943 to form the Texarkana Ordnance Center. Other ordnance plants and depots were located at McGregor, Amarillo, San Antonio, Texas City, and along the Houston and Sabine ship channels.[65]

Production of military aircraft was an early contribution of Texas to the national war effort. Although the Southern Aircraft Corporation had begun aircraft construction at Houston in July 1940, the industry was soon centered in the Dallas-Fort Worth area. The Hall Aluminum Aircraft Corporation and the Bennett Aircraft Corporation began operations near Dallas in the summer of 1940. At the same time the Worth Garment Company bought and moved the equipment of Kansas City's Roos Aircraft Corporation to Fort Worth. In late September 1940 the North American Aviation Corporation broke ground at Dallas' Hensley Field for a $7 million factory to produce P-51 Mustang fighters and AT-6 Texan trainers. In February 1941 Southern Aircraft moved from Houston and began building primary training planes at a new facility near Garland, just northeast of Dallas.[66]

In early 1941 the Consolidated Aircraft Corporation announced plans for a $10 million plant near Fort Worth for the construction of four-motor heavy bombers and cargo planes. Groundbreaking took place in May. The main building, 14 blocks long and more than a block wide, was completed in December 1941. The Consolidated plant became one of the nation's major aircraft builders. More than 3,000 B-24 Liberator bombers and hundreds of C-87 cargo planes were built at the Fort Worth plant during the war. At its peak of production the plant employed 32,000 workers.[67]

Although aircraft construction moved from Houston, the Bayou City still played a role in the aircraft industry. The Hughes Tool Corporation spent over $3 million in expanding its plants to make parts for American bombers. Houston native Howard R. Hughes, Jr., who inherited ownership of the company following his father's death in 1924, was an avid pilot who set a speed record on an around-the-world flight in 1938. Hughes secured a government contract to build three giant flying boats to ferry men and supplies across the ocean. When he was unable to meet the ten month deadline, the contract was canceled. In March 1944 Hughes received a new contract to build one large flying boat. This plane, built out of plywood using a "duramold" process, was constructed by the Hughes plant in California. Dubbed the *Spruce Goose* by the press, the flying boat was not finished until after the war. It was flown only one time, by Hughes himself on November 2, 1947. Hughes received other contracts to build reconnaissance planes, but like the flying boat contract, these were not completed before the end of the war.[68]

Shipbuilding was another Texas industry revived by military needs during World War II. There had been a lively shipbuilding and ship repairing business along the Texas coast in World War I, but it declined appreciably after the war. The need for vessels of all types was greatly accelerated by European and Asian events in 1939-41. In 1941, the U.S. Maritime Commission contracted with the Houston Shipbuilding Corporation, a subsidiary of Todd Shipyards Corporation, to build cargo vessels at Irish Bend on the Houston ship channel near Deer Park. In March 1942 the Irish Bend facility had 6,000 employees; by June 1942, 20,000; by 1943, 40,000. During the war, the Deer Park yard turned out 208 cargo vessels and 14 oil tankers.[69]

At nearby Green's Bayou, contractors Herman and George Brown formed the Brown Shipbuilding Company. Their first contract was for construction of four pursuit vessels. Contracts for destroyer escorts and landing craft soon followed. By the end of the war Brown Shipbuilding employed 25,000 men and women and had built 354 combat vessels. On one occasion, eight ships were launched in one afternoon.[70]

The Beaumont-Orange region was the other Texas major shipbuilding area. The Pennsylvania Shipyard on the Neches River at Beaumont employed 10,000 men and women to build naval vessels and auxiliary ships. By the end of the war the Pennsylvania yard had constructed 109 vessels for the Maritime Commission and the Navy. At Orange, three shipbuilding firms, Levingston, Weaver, and Consolidated Western Steel, all were working around the clock to fill government contracts. The Levingston firm built 157 vessels, including steel tugboats, oil barges, cargo barges, and small tankers. Weaver Shipyards built 26 wooden minesweepers to counter enemy magnetic mines, which were dangerous to steel vessels. In addition, the yard constructed two 110-foot submarine chasers. Consolidated, largest of the Orange yards, built 39 destroyers, 92 escort destroyers, 109 landing craft, and nine amphibious personnel destroyers. At the peak of production over 22,000 workers were employed in the Orange shipyards.[71]

Although the oil, aircraft, and shipbuilding industries were the largest employers and producers of war materials, many other Texas companies and individuals provided items the nation required for war. The Lufkin Foundry and Machine Company, for example, became heavily involved in the war effort. Its 800 employees made drive gears for Sherman tanks, marine gears for cargo vessels and landing craft, artillery carriages, and cast-iron practice bombs. Its trailer division produced truck trailers, mobile laundry units, and gasoline transports. Lukfin historian Bob Bowman points out that the company operated three shifts, including Sunday, and for the first time employed women as welders.[72]

Similarly, the Farah clothing company in El Paso converted its operations to military production. While younger brother William Farah served as a bomber pilot in the Air Forces, older brother James remained in charge of the plant, which manufactured khaki combat pants, fatigues, jungle wear, and uniforms. The plant made 359,000 pairs of pants without a rejection, and its 140 employees worked five consecutive weeks without an absence. As a result, Farah became the first clothing plant west of the Mississippi to earn the coveted Army-Navy E flag.[73]

Industry across the state mobilized for war. Houston's Cameron Iron Works made depth charges and new K-guns for antisubmarine warfare. In the same city Anderson and Clayton, in a joint venture with Brown and Root, made eight-inch shells. Former mayor Oscar Holcombe created a construction company that made huts for the Army, houses for the Navy, and pre-cut structures for overseas shipment. Mattress companies in Waco manufactured cots, mattresses, and barracks bags for the military. The J. M. Haggar factories in Greenville and Waxahachie and the Williamson-Dickie factory in Fort Worth, like Farah, produced combat clothes and uniforms.[74]

One of the more interesting commitments to the war effort was the powdered egg business in Denison. The Henningsen Company of Denison had a small egg drying business in the 1930s. As the market for powdered eggs in those days was limited, the operation had been a seasonal part-time business but with Lend Lease, and later the war, large orders rolled in. Henningsen and another local firm, J. R. Clymer's Denison Poultry and Egg Company, went into full time production. Historian Lee Kennett says that by the end of 1941 Denison could claim itself the "Egg Breaking Capital of the World." He notes that the plants operated day and night and that "shifts of women working around the clock were breaking a million and a half eggs a day, some of the workers so adept that they could break two eggs in each hand."[75]

The need for eggs was only one of many new demands placed upon Texas farmers and ranchers during the war. The previous decade had been a time of agricultural surpluses and government attempts to reduce production. Agricultural historian Rainer Schickele points out that the war changed this: "Surpluses disappeared as demand surged up, and shortages took their place. Instead of output restrictions, production goals and incentives became the order of the day. The 'Food-for-freedom' campaign on the home front carried the banner 'Food will win the war and write the peace.'"[76]

The war had a profound effect on Texas agriculture. Trends that had begun earlier, such as greater diversification, increase in mechanization and size of farms, shifts in labor, decline in tenancy, and greater production efficiency, were accelerated by the needs of war.[77]

The shift from cotton production toward livestock and other crops that had begun in the early 1930s continued. In 1930 Texas produced over 4 million bales of cotton. This had fallen to 3.2 million bales by 1940. Production continued to decline during the war; in 1944 Texas farmers produced only 2.6 million bales. The acreage devoted to cotton also continued to fall, from slightly more than 16 million acres in 1930 to 8.5 million in 1940, and to 7.2 million in 1944, the lowest acreage devoted to cotton in Texas since 1899.[78]

The livestock industry grew as the cultivation of cotton declined. In 1941 Texas had slightly fewer than 5½ million beef cattle. The number increased every year of the war, reaching 6,259,000 in 1945. At the same time the state had the heaviest marketing of cattle and calves in its recorded history, 2,601,001 head in 1943.[79]

The number of milk cows also increased, from 1,470,000 in 1941 to 1,641,000 in 1945. Although Texas dairy cows yielded more milk than ever, the heavy demand for Grade A milk by the large number of troops training in Texas meant that levels of processed dairy products, such as cheese, declined during the war years.[80]

To meet wartime needs, Texans raised more hogs and chickens. In 1944 the state's hog population totaled slightly more than 3 million, nearly 500,000 more than in 1943 and 1.2 million more than the average annual number in the previous decade. The state had over 38 million chickens in 1944, 2 million more than the previous year and 12 million more than the average year in the preceding decade.[81]

Texas grain production also increased during the war. Wheat production, which totaled less than 27 million bushels in 1941, soared to 74 million bushels in 1944. Rice production jumped from 11.5 million pounds in 1941 to slightly over 19 million in 1944. The yield of corn rose from 73 million bushels in 1941 to over 88 million in 1943 but dropped back to 69.9 million in 1944.[82]

The wartime demands for fresh vegetables led to expansion of Texas truck crops. During the ten years prior to Pearl Harbor the state had an annual average of 258,610 acres devoted to truck crops. This rose to 349,800 by 1944. The greatest increases were in production of tomatoes, onions, spinach, and carrots. Tomato production in Texas, the highest in the nation, rose from slightly more than 3 million bushels in 1941 to over 6 million in 1944, onions from 1.5 million bushels in 1941 to 6.8 million in 1944, spinach from 4.9 million bushels in 1941 to 6.1 million in 1944, and carrots from 2,048,000 bushels in 1941 to 2,976,000 bushels in 1944.[83]

The year 1941 was a particularly good one for Irish potatoes, slightly over 6 million bushels harvested in Texas, nearly double the 1940 total. Production increased to 6.3 million bushels in 1943 but dropped to slightly over 5 million in 1944. Sweet potato production was 5.4 million bushels in 1941 (1.4 million more than 1940); 5,025,000 bushels in 1944.[84]

Production of grapefruit, oranges, and pecans increased during the war. Texas growers harvested 16.6 bushels of grapefruit in the September 1941-March 1942 season; this increased to slightly more than 20 million in 1944-45.

Orange production in the 1944-45 season was one million bushels higher than in 1941-42, a 30 percent increase. The Texas pecan yield doubled during the war years.[85]

The Japanese capture of the coconut producing islands of the Pacific early in the war led Texas farmers to increase their peanut production, as peanut oil replaced coconut oil in making glycerin required in munitions manufacturing. In 1942, the first full year in which the United States was at war, Texas harvested 430,000 pounds of peanuts, nearly tripling the 156,000 pounds harvested in 1941. Production slowed somewhat in the following two years but was still double the pre-war figures.[86]

These large increases in production of Texas meat, grains, fruits, and vegetables came in spite of severe labor shortages. Although farmers had a measure of deferment protection under the Tydings amendment to the Selective Service laws, many farmers volunteered or were conscripted into military service. Many others moved to towns and cities to take good paying jobs in defense industries. It is estimated that 500,000 Texans moved from rural to urban locations during the war. Many farm workers left the state, attracted by offers of high wages in Pacific coast defense plants such as Kaiser, Boeing, and Du Pont. Transient, or migratory, labor also decreased appreciably in Texas during the war, perhaps by 150,000 workers.[87]

The loss of farm labor was partially offset by reasonably good weather, greater use of fertilizers, and increased mechanization. In spite of wartime restrictions and shortages, the number of tractors used by Texas farmers and ranchers nearly doubled between 1940 (98,923) and 1944 (195,056). Even so, Texas farmers needed and wanted more laborers.[88]

One apparent way to find additional workers was to bring in more Mexican laborers. Since the late 19th century, farmers in south and west Texas had used Mexican nationals to supplement their labor force, particularly in the harvest season. This seasonal migration of Mexican laborers rose in the 1920s in spite of restrictions on immigration. It declined in the pre-war decade, however, because of low wages, poor working and living conditions, and lack of jobs during the Great Depression. In addition, the Mexican government, under pressure from nationalist interest groups because of discrimination against Mexicans in Texas, discouraged migration.[89]

Texas farmers hoped to increase the number of Mexican laborers to help offset the losses to defense industries. They supported efforts of the American Farm Bureau Federation to persuade the Roosevelt administration to encourage the greater migration of Mexican nationals to the United States as farm workers. An agreement was made between the United States and Mexican governments in August 1942 for such migration. Under this agreement the United States made guarantees to the Mexican workers, or *braceros*, for better housing, health care, sanitation, transportation, and a 30-cent minimum wage.[90]

Most Texas farmers disliked the *bracero* agreement. They favored the system used in World War I in which operations were left largely in the hands of farmers with the government playing only a passive role. Not only did Texas farmers oppose the governmental intrusion, but they objected to the mandatory 30-cent wage. They persuaded Congress to pass legislation suspending all immigration restrictions on workers from the western hemisphere entering the United States for agricultural work. Once the law passed they began hiring more Mexican nationals. The Mexican government protested, however, and the Immigration and Naturalization Service closed the border, "shattering the Texans' hopes for an abundant, and unregulated, cheap labor supply."[91]

With their hopes for unregulated Mexican labor blocked, some Texas farmers turned to the *bracero* program, but they found their efforts blocked by the Mexican authorities. After several months of considering the requests of Texas farmers for documented workers, the Mexican government in June 1943 announced it would not authorize *braceros* in Texas "because of the number of cases of extreme, intolerable social discrimination."[92]

Texas growers, led by Cullen W. Briggs of Nueces County, persuaded Governor Coke Stevenson to use his good offices to secure Mexican workers. Already the Texas Legislature had passed a so-called "Caucasian Race" resolution affirming the right of all Caucasians within the state to equal treatment in public places of business and amusement. Stevenson now issued a proclamation directing Texans to adhere to the policy of non-discrimination in accordance with the resolution. He also agreed to create a Good Neighbor Commission to which complaints of discrimination could be submitted, and accepted an invitation from the Mexican government to visit Mexico City for further discussions.[93]

As a result of the efforts of Governor Stevenson and the U.S. State Department the Mexican government in August 1943 agreed to approve a limited number of *braceros* for work on railroad track in west Texas. The Mexican government refused to permit *braceros* for farm work in Texas until fully assured the state was free from discrimination. As a result, Texas growers finished the 1943 season with student volunteers, prisoners of war, a small number of Mexican nationals still in the state, and an increasing number of illegals, sometimes disparagingly called "wet backs." Wishing to protect itself from domestic criticism and yet not wanting to keep its laborers from finding employment, the Mexican government did little to stop its citizens from entering Texas illegally. The number of illegals continued to grow as "thousands of Mexicans entered Texas surreptitiously, virtually unhindered by Mexican and American border authorities."[94] Although 220,000 Mexican agricultural workers entered the United States under the *bracero* program between 1942-1947, none of these worked in Texas. It was not until the 1950s that Texas farmers participated in the program.[95]

CHAPTER THREE

The Pacific War, December 1941-July 1942

While thousands of Texans were undergoing military training or building military weapons in the United States in late 1941 and early 1942, other Texans were defending American outposts overseas. As the last Japanese planes left the Hawaiian Islands on Sunday morning, December 7, 1941, other Japanese aircraft bombed British installations at Singapore and Hong Kong. Several hours later, Japanese planes attacked American-held Wake and Guam islands. Almost at the same time (6:00 A.M., Philippine time) the first Japanese planes attacked the north coast of Luzon in the Philippines.

There was much confusion in the Philippines on the morning of December 8. Once he learned of the Japanese attacks on Pearl Harbor, Major General Lewis Brereton, commander of the U.S. Far East Air Force, wanted to bomb the Japanese held-island of Formosa with the B-17 Flying Fortresses in his command. Because of delays in receiving approval from Brereton's superior, General Douglas MacArthur, the bombers were still on the ground at Clark Field when a large Japanese bomber force escorted by new Zero fighters attacked. Two squadrons of American B-17s and a squadron of P-40 fighters were almost totally destroyed.[1]

Historian Ronald H. Spector points out that "this catastrophe, which deprived MacArthur of almost half of his best aircraft on the first day of the war, has never been adequately explained." Critics of MacArthur blame the general and his staff for the Clark Field debacle; defenders blame Brereton for failure to move his planes to the southern island of Mindanao where they would be out of enemy range.[2]

Second Lieutenant James T. Drake of Dallas, a pilot in the 20th Pursuit Squadron, was among the casualties in the Clark Field attack. Drake's squadron was one of six assigned to the 24th Pursuit Group, commanded by

Major Orrin Grover of New York. These six squadrons, Headquarters, 3rd, 17th, 20th, 21st, and 34th, were stationed at Nichols, Iba, Nielson, and Clark fields on Luzon. All of the squadrons, with the exception of the small Headquarters squadron, included Texans among their pilots.[3]

The 3rd Pursuit Squadron was commanded by First Lieutenant Hank Thorne, a native of Waco, who had enlisted as a private following high school graduation. The 28-year-old Thorne had been commissioned when he completed flight school in 1937. Four other Texans (all second lieutenants commissioned in 1941), Howard Hardegree of Ben Wheeler, James H. Pate of Tyler, Paul O. Mock of Goose Creek, and Robert J. Hinson of Lufkin, were among the 43 pilots in Thorne's squadron.[4]

The 17th Squadron, commanded by First Lieutenant Boyd D. Wagner of Johnston, Pennsylvania, listed eight Texans among its pilots: Maurice G. Hughett of Waco, A. W. "Dub" Balfanz, Jr., of Abilene, Forrest M. Hobrecht of Dallas, Truett J. Majors of Greenville, Oscar D. Wyatt of Fort Worth, James W. Rowland of Fort Worth, Willis P. Culp III of Elgin, and Earl A. Hulsey of Dallas. All these Texans were commissioned in 1941.[5]

The 20th Pursuit Squadron, of which Lieutenant Drake mentioned above was a member, included four other Texans: First Lieutenant Charles R. Sneed of Hamilton (commissioned 1939), First Lieutenant Hugh H. Marble, Jr., of Houston (commissioned in 1940), Second Lieutenant Robert F. Duncan of Dallas (commissioned 1940), and Second Lieutenant William Tom Atkins of Hillsboro (commissioned 1941).[6]

First Lieutenant William Edwin Dyess of Albany, Texas, commanded the small (12 pilots) 21st Pursuit Squadron. Commissioned in 1937, Dyess, a graduate of John Tarleton Agricultural College of Stephenville, was a skilled pilot, admired and respected by the young men of his squadron. Second Lieutenant John L. McCown of Grandview was the only other Texan in the squadron.[7]

Sam H. Marrett of New Braunfels commanded the 15-man 34th Pursuit Squadron. A rather small man with dark features, Marrett had come up from the ranks, having served as an enlisted man before gaining his wings and his commission in 1938. Although he worked his men hard in preparation for combat, Marrett was highly regarded as a leader. Six of his pilots (all commissioned in 1941) were Texans: Claude Paulger of Lubbock, James C. Nicol of Fort Worth, Charles A. Gaskell of Dallas, James D. Henry of Kingsville, Frankie M. Bryant of Graham, and Don "Shorty" Crosland of Mineral Wells. Bryant and Crosland were best friends, having attended North Texas State Teachers College together and having gone through flight school at Stockton Field, California, together.[8]

The men of the 24th Pursuit Group learned of the Japanese attack on Pearl Harbor early on the morning of December 8 (Philippine time). By noon of the 8th all fighter squadrons, except the 20th stationed at Clark Field, were in the air searching for Japanese planes. Because of confusing orders and poor communication, however, only the 20th Squadron was at Clark Field when Japanese bombers and fighters appeared.[9]

Some of the fighters of the 20th Squadron were able to get in the air during the Japanese attack. Although their P-40 Curtiss and P-35 Seversky aircraft were inferior to the Japanese Zeros, American pilots shot down five of the enemy attackers. Lieutenant Drake was hit by enemy strafing fire while he taxied on the runway. His plane burst into flames, and Drake was killed. The Japanese destroyed 17 bombers and 20 fighters in the raid.[10]

During the next several weeks, the 24th Pursuit Group fought a courageous but hopeless battle against enemy air and naval forces supporting the Japanese invasion of the Philippines. Losses quickly mounted. On December 10, Sam Marrett of New Braunfels, commander of the 34th Squadron, was killed while leading an attack on a Japanese minesweeper. His plane was rocked by an explosion from the minesweeper when Marrett's machine gun fire detonated depth charges on the ship. The enemy ship sank, but Marrett's right wing was blown off and he crashed into the sea.[11]

Lieutenant Forrest M. Hobrecht from Dallas, a member of the 17th Squadron, was also killed on December 10. His plane was hit by fire from a Japanese Zero. He attempted to bail out but hit the stabilizer and fell to the ground, his parachute unopened. Lieutenant Oscar Wyatt of Fort Worth, a member of the same squadron, was hit by "friendly fire" on January 2, 1942, when flying his P-35 to Bataan Field. Wyatt was attempting to land when he was hit by U.S. defenders of the field. He attempted to make it back to his home base, but his plane crashed, killing him instantly.[12]

Following the death of Lieutenant Wyatt, Chuck Page from Spokane, Washington, and Truett J. Majors from Greenville were detached from the 17th Squadron to serve with the 91st Coast Artillery in identifying aircraft. Tragically, an antiaircraft round exploded prematurely, killing both Page and Majors. As noted in the previous chapter, the Army air field at Greenville, Texas, was later named for Majors.[13]

The plane of Jim Rowland of Fort Worth, a member of the same flying class and squadron as Wyatt and Majors, was hit in the gas tank while bombing and strafing a Japanese landing party on December 24. Rowland was forced to make a water landing in Laguna de Bay but was able to swim ashore as his P-40 sank. Charley Sneed from Hamilton, Texas, and another officer from the 20th Squadron were forced to make a water landing while trying to evacuate an Associated Press correspondent. Sneed and his two companions swam to shore and made it to an American outpost on the island of Guimaras but later were captured by the Japanese.[14]

Most of the Texas pilots in the 24th Pursuit Group survived the Philippine campaign. Several, like Sneed, became prisoners of the Japanese when Bataan and Corregidor surrendered. Others were evacuated to Australia before the fall of the Philippines and continued the war from other bases in the Pacific. Several of these Texans were later killed in combat. Of the 27 Texas pilots who were in the 24th Pursuit Group on December 8, 1941, only eight were still alive when the war ended in August 1945.[15]

While Army pilots were continuing to struggle against heavy odds in the skies, the battle for the Philippines was unfolding on the ground. General MacArthur, American commander in the Far East, hoped to defeat the Japanese on the beaches, but major landings in north Luzon on December 22 convinced him that American and Filipino troops had to fall back into the Bataan Peninsula. Here they would continue their resistance until early April.[16]

Meanwhile, other American forces were attempting unsuccessfully to keep the Japanese from gaining control of the entire western Pacific. On December 10 a small American contingent of 430 Marines and Navy men surrendered Guam to a Japanese force of over 5,000 troops. Another Japanese force attempted to land on Wake Island on December 11 but was repulsed by a detachment of the 1st Marine Battalion commanded by Major James P. S. Devereux and a small Marine fighter squadron commanded by Major Paul Putnam. For the next ten days, the defenders of the island atoll were bombed almost constantly from the air. On December 23 the enemy made a successful landing. After several hours of bitter fighting, U.S. forces surrendered.[17]

Two dozen Texans took part in the gallant defense of Wake. Marine Technical Sergeant Charles A. Holmes from West Texas was the garrison's senior antiaircraft fire control technician. Private First Class Erwin D. Pistole from Austin directed a .50 caliber machine gun in one of the island's main batteries. Corporal Jack Hearn of Boerne and Private First Class Wiley W. Sloman of Texas City were among Marine defenders on the beach. Private First Class Jesse E. Nowlin from northeast Texas handled Battery A's communications with Devereux's command post. On the last day of the siege, Nowlin was knocked unconscious by a ricocheting bullet while he helped man a skirmish line.[18]

Private First Class James C. Venable, E Battery, 1st Defense Battalion, was another Texan among the Wake defenders. The surrender was particularly painful to Venable, who remembered "this was the lowest point of our lives because we had been trained to fight, not to surrender." Surrender was a blow to the men's pride and esprit de corps; according to Venable, several Marines cried at the thought of surrender.[19]

The defense of Wake Island, especially a reported (but untrue) response of Major Devereux to "send us more Japs," inspired Americans. Texans at home compared the defense of Wake to the gallant, hopeless stand at the Alamo.[20]

The Wake defenders had hoped for some type of relief coming from Hawaii, but with the heavy losses that had occurred at Pearl Harbor, no relief was forthcoming. Admiral Husband E. Kimmel, commander of the Pacific Fleet at Pearl Harbor, had wanted to commit his aircraft carriers to such a mission. Because of the disaster at Pearl, however, Kimmel was relieved of his command on December 16. His interim replacement, Vice Admiral William S. Pye, reluctant to undertake such a dangerous expedition, canceled the mission and recalled the carriers.[21]

Back in the nation's capital, President Roosevelt and Secretary of Navy Frank Knox passed over a number of senior admirals and appointed Texan Chester W. Nimitz to replace Kimmel as commander of the Pacific Fleet. At the time Nimitz, the descendent of pioneer German settlers in Fredericksburg, was chief of the Bureau of Navigation (later the Bureau of Personnel) in Washington, a post he had held since 1939. As chief of the Navy bureau handling personnel, Nimitz had attracted the attention of Roosevelt, who took keen interest in all naval matters. The president believed that Nimitz could restore confidence in naval personnel and guide American forces to victory. "Tell Nimitz to get the hell out to Pearl and stay there till the war is won," Roosevelt told Knox.[22]

Chester Nimitz was 56 years old at the time of his appointment. Trim and vigorous, with fair complexion, pink cheeks, steel blue eyes, and blond hair that had turned white, Nimitz was a quiet and thoughtful individual who was a good judge of men. Graduating seventh in the Annapolis class of 1905, Nimitz passed through the various commands and schools prescribed by the Navy for senior commanders. Although he had served on cruisers and battleships, the Texan was known as a submariner, having commanded three different submarines, serving as chief of staff to the commander of the Atlantic Submarine Force, and commanding the Submarine Division at Pearl Harbor. Married and the father of three daughters and a son (who became a submarine commander), Nimitz was well respected and highly regarded by the men with whom he served.[23]

Nimitz assumed command of the Pacific Fleet with the rank of admiral on December 31, 1941, on the deck of the submarine *Grayling*. At the time morale in the fleet was extremely low. The devastating raid on Pearl, the loss of Guam, and the failure to relieve Wake had shaken the fleet. Nimitz moved quickly to restore morale. One of his first moves was to inform the staff at Pearl Harbor that he did not blame them for what had happened and that he had complete confidence in them. Although he was under heavy pressure from naval superiors in Washington to take immediate action against Japanese-held islands, Nimitz moved carefully and deliberately to strengthen his forces before engaging in premature action.[24]

Part of the strengthening process included the salvage operations going on in Pearl. In this important but often overlooked activity, Texans played active rolls. Captain Francis H. Whitaker from Tyler served as Salvage Superintendent, for which he was later awarded the Legion of Merit. Three Texas enlisted men, Christian R. Peters from Stanton, Tony G. Vandagriff from Wellington, and Herbert E. Vaughn from Port Arthur, received the Navy and Marine Corps Medal for their work as divers in the salvage operation.[25]

At the time Nimitz assumed command in Hawaii, American, British, and Dutch forces were struggling to stop the Japanese advance in the Far East. Although crippled by the attacks on Clark and other Philippine fields, MacArthur's Far East Air Force continued to carry out missions against Japanese naval and air forces supporting the invasion. American bombers, some flown by Texans, destroyed several Japanese ships. Captain James T. Connally, a Texas A&M graduate and a cousin of Senator Tom Connally, led a B-17 attack on Japanese tankers off Mindanao. He then rescued 23 stranded pilots, earning for himself the Distinguished Flying Cross. Major Cecil E. Combs,

Chester W. Nimitz, Commander Pacific Ocean Area.
—Admiral Nimitz Museum, Fredericksburg, Texas

a West Point graduate from Dallas, received the Distinguished Flying Cross for leading a B-17 attack on Japanese ships in Philippine waters. Another Texan, Captain Alvin Mueller, Jr., from Seguin, earned the Distinguished Flying Cross for bombing a Japanese airdrome and then fighting off enemy fighter planes.[26]

In spite of the heroic efforts by American airmen, the Japanese continued to throw troops and supplies into Luzon, the main island of the Philippines. The American Navy was no more successful than the airmen in stopping the Japanese advance. Although Rear Admiral Tommy Hart had to pull his surface fleet out of Philippine waters to avoid destruction, much was expected from the 29 U.S. submarines on station in the Philippines. The submariners, however, had little success the first month of the war. In December, the U.S. Asiatic submarine force mounted 49 separate attacks in which they fired 96 torpedoes. They claimed to have sunk 11 Japanese ships, but postwar records confirm only three, all freighters.[27]

These early underwater failures were attributable to several factors: poor training, bad maintenance, inadequate deployment, and the defective new Mark-14 torpedoes.[28]

Submariners often believed they had hits and sinkings which later were proven not true. The skipper of the *Sturgeon*, William L. "Bull" Wright of Roby, Texas, whose four torpedoes had missed in his first patrol in December, believed he had sunk a capital ship on his second patrol (as did his third officer, young Chester W. Nimitz, Jr.). He sent a message back to headquarters "*Sturgeon* No Longer a Virgin." Postwar Japanese records, however, show no such sinking. Wright claimed two other sinkings on this patrol, but these are not substantiated by later records.[29]

American submariners did have some successes in early 1942. A classmate of "Bull" Wright in the Annapolis class of 1935, Lieutenant Commander Stanley P. Moseley of Fort Worth, whose *Pollack* was among nine submarines at Pearl Harbor in December 1941, took his boat to the mouth of Tokyo Bay, where he sank two enemy ships. On his second patrol in February, he sank another enemy ship in Formosan waters. Charles C. Fitzpatrick of San Angelo was another successful submarine commander. Commanding the *Triton*, Fitzpatrick, who at age 31 was one of the youngest submarine captains at the time, sank five enemy vessels on his first patrol in April 1942. Both Moseley and Fitzpatrick received the Navy Cross for their successes.[30]

A Texas enlisted man, Herbert Weldon Smith of Wichita Falls, was a torpedoman on the S-37, which had the first confirmed sinking of a Japanese destroyer, *Natushie*, on February 8, 1942. Joining the Navy in August 1937, Smith had been assigned to the S-37 since 1939. He made seven war patrols in the S-37 and obtained the rank of Chief Motor Machinist Mate before receiving a commission in February 1944.[31]

The S-37 sank the *Natushie* during the great sea battle that raged around Java in February 1942. Although a small American naval force inflicted damage upon Japanese transports in Makassan Strait, they were unable to stop the Japanese movement into the Dutch East Indies. The American light cruiser

Marblehead was hit by Japanese bombers on February 4. For their efforts in keeping the ship afloat, two Texans were awarded the Navy Cross. Quartermaster Second Class Lester J. Barre of Orange was cited for his work in freeing the jammed rudder of *Marblehead*. Chief Boatswain's Mate Herman E. Hock of Galveston was commended for taking charge of operations on the upper decks, facilitating the evacuation of the wounded, fighting fires, and clearing debris and wreckage on the ship. Although the efforts of Barre, Hock, and others kept *Marblehead* afloat, she was so badly damaged that she had to return to the United States for repairs.[32]

In this same engagement the heavy cruiser *Houston* was also damaged. The *Houston*, which gained the sobriquet "Galloping Ghost of the Java Coast," because she was reported sunk several times, was the most powerful American warship in Far Eastern waters. She, a British cruiser, and two Dutch cruisers engaged in a bitter battle with larger Japanese forces in Java Sea in late February. Although damaged *Houston* managed to pull away only to encounter additional Japanese warships in Sunda Strait. In a wild night of fighting *Houston* and the British cruiser *Perth* sank or damaged several enemy ships before themselves going down.[33]

The loss of the *Houston*, the favorite ship of President Roosevelt, who had made four cruises on her, was a terrible blow. Of the 1,015 men on board, 655 (including her captain Albert H. Rooks of Washington) were killed in action or drowned; 360 survived but became prisoners of war. Seventy-five of these died in Japanese prisons or work camps.[34]

News of the *Houston*'s gallant struggle stirred the hearts of Americans. In the Texas city for which she was named thousands bought war bonds and stamps to pay for the construction of a new *Houston*. One thousand volunteers to replace those lost on the *Houston* were sworn into the Navy in an impressive ceremony in downtown Houston on Memorial Day 1942. After listening to a written message from President Roosevelt in which the chief executive praised the officers and men of the *Houston*, the new recruits marched through the cheering crowd of thousands to the Union station where special trains waited to take them to the San Diego Naval Training Station.[35]

William J. Wissinger, Jr., of Mooreville, James W. Gee of Howe, Frank H. King of Shamrock, Marvin E. Robinson of Fort Worth, Seldon Reese of Bronson, and Charles C. Pryor of Dickens County were among those who survived the sinking of the *Houston* and made their way to Java. On the island they soon encountered other Texans, members of the 2nd Battalion, 131st Field Artillery of the Texas National Guard.[36]

The 2nd Battalion, later known as the "Lost Battalion," 131st Field Artillery, was made up of men from Decatur, Wichita Falls, Abilene, Jacksboro, Amarillo, Plainview, and Lubbock. The battalion had been detached from the Texas National Guard when the unit was reorganized from a "square" division of four regiments to a "triangle" division of three regiments as part of a general Army reorganization in summer 1941. The 2nd Battalion was assigned to the Philippine Islands to join a new division being formed from other detached units. When the attack on Pearl Harbor occurred, the Texans were on an Army transport, the *Republic*, part of a convoy sailing west of Hawaii. When it became apparent that they would not be able to reach the Philippines because of Japanese aerial and naval activity, the convoy was diverted to Australia. From there the battalion was sent to Java to reinforce Dutch-British-Australian troops.[37]

When the 2nd Battalion landed on Java in mid-January 1942, it found Allied forces there disorganized and confused. Japanese aerial and naval activity soon cut off any additional reinforcements and supplies. In late February, the Japanese landed in strength. Batavia, the island capital, was captured on April 1. A week later all Allied forces on the island surrendered. Among those surrendering were over 400 men of the 2nd Battalion and 360 survivors of the *Houston*. They were brought together as one Prisoner of War unit under the command of Amarillo's Colonel Blucher Tharp of the 2nd Battalion.[38]

For the next seven months the Texans, along with thousands of other Allied troops, remained as prisoners of war on Java. In October 1942, two POW contingents, including most of the men of the Houston and the 2nd Battalion, were taken by boat to Singapore. From there they were sent to Burma, where they worked in building the infamous Burma-Thailand Railroad.[39]

With the fall of Java, the American Army in the Philippines was the only western force resisting the Japanese conquest of the southwest Pacific. Throughout January and February, American troops on the Bataan peninsula beat back repeated enemy attacks. However, Japanese reinforcements, disease and illness, and lack of supplies forced the American and Filipino defenders to slowly fall back toward the south end of the peninsula. Shortages of food became a major concern as rations were cut to 1,200 calories a day. Captain John S. Coleman, a Texas A&M graduate from Wellington in West Texas, recalled that the reduction in rations led the men to kill horses and mules. "We tried [to eat] large red monkey meat," he wrote in his memoirs, "but it was tough and stringy."[40]

In late February President Roosevelt ordered General MacArthur to leave the Philippines and assume command of Allied forces in Australia, leaving Major General Jonathan Wainwright in command. Throughout March, the fighting continued with American forces steadily becoming weaker. In April the Bataan garrison surrendered, but troops on the island of Corregidor, "the Rock," held out several weeks longer. Finally, on May 7, General Wainwright, accompanied by four officers including his adjutant, Captain Tom Dooley of McKinney (A&M class of 1935), surrendered to the Japanese commander, Lieutenant General Masaharu Homma.[41]

Captain Dooley was one of 25 Texas Aggies on Corregidor. Major General George F. Moore of Fort Worth, a 1908 A&M graduate, former commandant of the Corps of Cadets, and commander of the harbor defenses on Corregidor, was the senior officer among the Aggies. He shook General MacArthur's hand when MacArthur left the island on a PT boat. Moore and 24 other Aggies had celebrated San Jacinto Day on Corregidor in the traditional muster in which they drank toasts of water to the Texas heroes of 1836 and sang Aggie songs.[42]

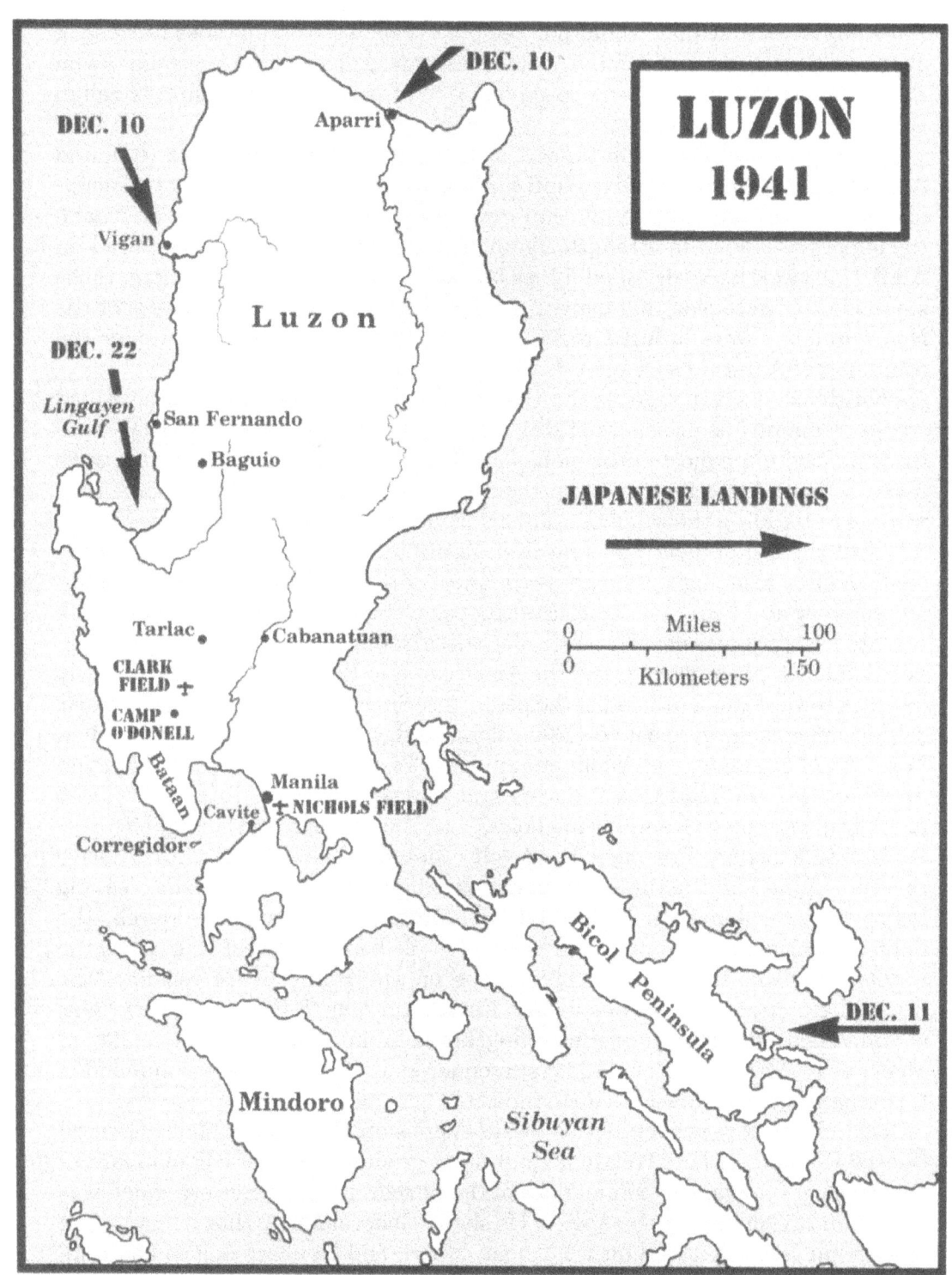

The Texas Aggies were among 22,000 Americans and 60,000 Filipinos captured in the Philippine Islands. The bulk of the troops were surrendered on Bataan. These men, weakened by disease and malnutrition, were subjected to a painful 65-mile march to Camp O'Donnell in northern Luzon. In this journey, known later as the "death march," the prisoners were subjected to beatings, lack of food and water, and various forms of humiliation. Texan Private Tom Blaylock of the 34th Pursuit Squadron remembers the march as "a living nightmare. You had no water, no food. If you dropped to the ground, and you weren't on your feet by the time the Japs got there, they shot you or stuck a bayonet in you." Another Texan, Corporal Louis R. Read of the 31st Infantry, later recalled "the Japs were great about chopping off people's heads, and all the noncoms carried these two-headed swords, and they were allowed to use them. Everywhere you looked almost, you would see somebody who had their head cut off." West Texan John Coleman of the Army Air Forces was hit several times when he failed to give the Japanese information they desired about the Norden bombsight. In his memoirs Captain Coleman describes the killing of an American sergeant by a Japanese guard who, after shooting the prisoner several times, ran his bayonet through the sergeant's chest.[43]

Durwood Joyner of Clarksville, a Marine assigned to the Cavite naval base on Manila Bay, was among those captured on Bataan. "The Bataan March was terrible, so many killed," he later told interviewer Martha Sue Stroud. "Lots of them [prisoners] died along the way, [or] were killed if they tried to help somebody," he recalled. "There's not much that you've heard of about the Japanese that didn't really happen, and it happened to everybody."[44]

In an account of his experiences on the death march, Army pilot Ed Dyess of Albany, Texas, described repeated instances of cruelty and brutality by the Japanese guards. Like Corporal Read, Dyess witnessed a guard chop off a prisoner's head with one blow of his sword. Dyess noted that the guards regularly "beat and slugged prisoners, robbing them of watches, fountain pens, money, and toilet articles." Any Americans who attempted to help fallen or ill comrades were "kicked, slugged, or jabbed with bayonet points by the guards...." Similarly, Filipino civilians who attempted to slip food or water to the prisoners were beaten and clubbed.[45]

The exact number of men who died on the Bataan march is not known. Historian John Toland believes from 7,000 to 10,000 prisoners died. Of these, 2,330 were Americans. Many of those who survived the death march died in Japanese prisoner of war camps.[46]

Seventy-seven Army and Navy nurses were among the Americans taken prisoner in the Philippines. Ten of these, all Army nurses, were Texans: Agnes Barre, Orange; Clara Mae Bickford, Tivoli; Evelyn Black, Groesbeck; Hattie Brantley, Jefferson; Myra V. Burris, San Antonio; Bertha Dworsky, Hallettsville; Dorcas E. Easterling, Abbot; Eula R. Fails, Houston; Verna V. Henson, Trinity; and Frankie T. Lewey, Dalhart. Two other Texans, Eunice C. Hatchitt and Lucy Wilson, were among 22 nurses who were successfully evacuated to Australia before the surrender. Wilson, from Big Sandy, was assisting in the operating room on Corregidor when she received orders to leave. In a later interview she declared "walking out in the middle of an operation, when hundreds were lined under the trees waiting for surgery, was devastating to me."[47]

Wilson and Hatchitt returned to the States following their evacuation. Both received big receptions when they arrived home. The people of Big Sandy bought a new wardrobe for Wilson. About 6,000 people, including local congressman Lyndon B. Johnson, turned out at the Lockhart High School stadium to greet Eunice Hatchett. She later served in an advisory role in Paramount Pictures' *So Proudly We Hail*, a wartime movie starring Claudette Colbert and Veronica Lake. Purported to be a description of the heroism of the Philippine nurses, the movie was filled with romantic scenes and lacked realism. Many of the nurses later blamed Hatchitt, who herself was disappointed with the movie.[48]

The captured Army and Navy nurses spent the next three years as prisoners in Santo Tomas Internment Camp in Manila. During their imprisonment they suffered from a variety of diseases and dietary deficiencies. They were liberated by the American 1st Cavalry when Luzon was retaken in February 1945.[49]

Although they suffered during Japanese imprisonment, the American nurses were treated better than the male captives. Many of the men who survived the death march from Bataan succumbed to diseases and malnutrition at Camp O'Donnell or camps near Cabanatuan in north Luzon or in Manila's old Belibid Prison. Historian D. Clayton James notes that 1,600 Americans and 26,000 Filipinos died during the first seven weeks in these prison camps. Conditions at O'Donnell were particularly bad. Captain Ed Dyess of Albany remembered that "the stench of the place was beyond description." After two weeks 50 Americans died every day at O'Donnell; the Filipino death rate was 350 a day. Conditions were no better at Cabanatuan camps. Thornton Hamby, a Marine POW from Lubbock, described Camp No. 1 at Cabanatuan as "a death hole." There was nothing to eat and everyone was sick. In addition, the guards were abusive and cruel. "Some of the worst brutality I saw in the entire war was at Cabanatuan," remembered Hamby.[50]

In late summer and autumn 1942, many of the surviving Philippine captives were sent to Formosa, Japan, and Manchuria to work in industrial labor camps. There, as in Burma where *Houston*, Lost Battalion, and other Allied prisoners labored on construction of the railroad, thousands of these Americans would die.

While Americans were dying on the battlefield and in prisons, Admiral Chester W. Nimitz was attempting to regain the initiative in the central Pacific. In February 1942 he sent Vice Admiral William Halsey's task force, built around the carrier *Enterprise*, on a raid against Japanese bases in the northern Marshall Islands. Another task force under Rear Admiral Frank Jack Fletcher, including the carrier *Yorktown*, hit the southern Marshalls. Although these raids did not stop the Japanese advance, they did raise morale and give the carrier groups valuable training experience. Two Texans were recognized for their contributions in these early actions: Rear Admiral Spencer S. Lewis from Calvert, chief of staff to Admiral Halsey, was given the Legion of Merit and Ensign Earl Donnell from Temple was awarded the Air Medal posthumously for his gallantry when *Enterprise*'s Scouting Squadron 6 damaged enemy installations in an attack on the Kwajalein Atoll.[51]

The raiding tactics employed by American carriers continued throughout early spring 1942. Ensign Marvin M. Hascke of Austin was among the carrier pilots awarded the Navy Cross for successful aerial attacks against Japanese bases in northeastern New Guinea in early March. Another Texan, Photographer's Mate John A. Pack of Fort Worth, received the Navy and Marine Corps Medal for his part in these same operations.[52]

Texans played a major role in the famous Doolittle Raid on Tokyo in April 1942. The raid was the outgrowth of discussions between President Roosevelt, Admiral Ernest J. King and General H. H. Arnold. King and Arnold concluded that long range Army bombers, with careful planning and training, could take off from the deck of an aircraft carrier, bomb Tokyo, and fly on to friendly bases in China. They selected Lieutenant Colonel James H. "Jimmy" Doolittle, a well known pre-war aviator and aeronautical engineer, to command the operation. Doolittle picked Major John A. Hilger of Sherman, Texas, as his deputy. Hilger, a 1932 graduate of Texas A&M, had previously commanded the 89th Reconnaissance Squadron at Pendleton, Oregon.[53]

Doolittle and Hilger assembled a team of volunteers for the mission. After a month of training with the B-25 bombers at Elgin Field, Florida, the group was assigned to the aircraft carrier *Hornet* on the west coast. From there they sailed to a rendezvous point near Midway, where they joined Admiral Halsey's task force. The task force then headed through rough waters toward Japan.

The original plan called for launching the aircraft at a point 500 miles from Tokyo. However, the task force was spotted earlier by a Japanese picket ship, forcing the planes to take off 150 miles farther from their target than planned. This meant the attack on Tokyo would take place during daylight rather than at night and the bombers would have only a slight chance of reaching airfields in China.[54]

Eleven of the 16 Army planes on the Tokyo raid had a Texan as pilot or co-pilot. Lieutenant Robert M. "Bob" Gray of Killeen, a 22-year-old graduate of Texas A&M, was pilot of the third plane, *Whiskey Pete*, that left the wave-covered deck of the *Hornet*. Dean Hallmark from Robert Lee, Texas, piloted the sixth plane, *Green Hornet*, that took off with much difficulty. Plane 13 was piloted by Lieutenant Edward E. McElroy, 30-year-old aviator from Ennis, followed by plane 14, flown by Major John Hilger, age 33, the deputy commander.[55]

Texas co-pilots on the Doolittle raid included Lieutenants William Fitzhugh, Temple, plane two; Lucian Youngblood, Pampa, plane four; Ross Wilder, Tyler, plane five; James Parker, Houston, plane nine; Kenneth Reddy, Bowie, plane 11; Thadd H. Blanton, Archer City, plane 12; and Robert Hite, Odell, plane 16. Second Lieutenant Nolan Herndon from Greenville was the navigator-bombardier on plane eight and Staff Sergeant Douglas V. Radney of Mineola was the rear gunner on plane two.[56]

Ten of the planes were assigned targets in Tokyo; the other six had industrial targets elsewhere in Japan. The first American bombers reached Japan just as air raid drills were being completed in Tokyo. The raiders swept across the area at low level and released their bombs. Although the last planes to arrive encountered fighter and antiaircraft fire, all the planes continued on toward China after dropping their bombs. All but one of the planes managed to reach the China coast where, with fuel exhausted, they crashlanded. Plane eight, upon which navigator-bombardier Nolan Herndon of Greenville flew, landed in the Soviet Union where crewmembers were interned until they escaped the following May.[57]

Most of the raiders were rescued by Chinese guerrillas and made their way back to the United States. Two members of Dean Hallmark's *Green Hornet*, were killed in the landing. Hallmark, two members of his crew, and the crew of plane 16, *Bat Out of Hell*, piloted by William Farrow from South Carolina and co-piloted by Bob Hite from Odell, Texas, were captured by the Japanese. They were taken to Tokyo, where after being tortured, beaten, kicked, and starved, they were brought to trial. Death sentences were given to all eight Americans, but the sentence of five of them was commuted to life imprisonment.[58]

There was no commutation for pilots Hallmark and Farrow, nor Sergeant Harold S. Spatz of Kansas, engineer-gunner of Farrow's plane. They were found guilty of war crimes and sentenced to execution by firing squad the next day. They were allowed to write letters home to their families, which the Japanese permitted the Red Cross to deliver. In the letter to his mother in Texas, Dan Hallmark expressed disbelief and bewilderment that this was occurring. He had assumed that as a prisoner of war he would not be executed.[59]

The Tokyo raid caused only minor damage, but the psychological effect on the Japanese was profound. The Army and Navy were embarrassed for failing to protect the Emperor and the homeland from attack. Japanese naval leaders had already been debating whether to attack Midway, the suspected staging area for the Tokyo raid. Any opposition to the Midway operation was now dropped. Another operation against Port Moresby on the southeastern side of New Guinea was also pushed forward.[60]

The American Navy was ready to respond to the new Japanese moves. Code breakers at Pearl Harbor were convinced the Japanese planned an offensive against Port Moresby. Admiral Nimitz moved quickly to thwart the Japanese operation. He sent the carrier Lexington from Pearl Harbor to join Jack Fletcher's Yorktown task force in the Coral Sea. There, in early May, a great battle was fought between the American and Japanese fleets.[61]

The battle of Coral Sea, May 4-8, 1942, was the first great naval engagement between aircraft carriers in which all losses were inflicted by air action in which no ship on either side sighted the enemy. On the climactic day of battle, May 8, American carrier planes destroyed an enemy light cruiser, a destroyer, and several smaller ships, and damaged the large carrier *Shokaku*. Both

American carriers, *Lexington* and *Yorktown*, were hit, however. Paul Forsythe, born in Brownwood and reared in Port Arthur, was a Marine aboard the *Lexington*, one of the most beloved ships in the U.S. fleet. Forsythe was assigned to a battery manning one of *Lexington*'s five-inch guns. During the morning of the 8th, the ship was hit repeatedly by Japanese bombs. Seamen put out most of the early fires, but explosions shortly after noon caused fires to rage out of control. Forsythe and other seamen battled the flames, but the fires continued to spread. Late that afternoon, Captain Frederick C. Sherman gave the order to abandon ship. Although 216 of the crew lost their lives, most of the crew, including Forsythe, who gave his life jacket to a fellow Marine who could not swim, were picked up by other American ships.[62]

Because of the loss of the *Lexington*, Coral Sea was a tactical victory for Japan. Admiral Fletcher, the task force commander, now had only one carrier, *Yorktown*, and she was badly damaged. With Nimitz's approval, Fletcher withdrew from the area and headed back to Pearl Harbor. The Japanese were also hurt by the loss of the carrier *Shokaku*, causing their commander to call off the attempted landings at Port Moresby. For the first time, a Japanese offensive operation was negated, a strategic victory for the United States and a tremendous boost to American morale both in the Pacific and at home.[63]

The battle of Coral Sea was an important preliminary to a larger naval engagement that took place the following month near Midway. Admiral Isoroku Yamamoto, commander of the Japanese Imperial Fleet and architect of the Pearl Harbor attack, was determined to strike a powerful blow at the island. As a diversion, Yamamoto planned to attack the Aleutian Islands off the coast of Alaska just before the main blow was delivered at Midway.

Yamamoto assigned an impressive force for the Aleutian-Midway operations: four large carriers, two light carriers, seven battleships, ten heavy cruisers, four light cruisers, 44 destroyers, 16 submarines, 12 transports, and numerous oilers, minesweepers, and auxiliary craft. The main strike force aimed at Midway's defenses consisted of the four big carriers, *Soryu*, *Kaga*, *Akagi*, and *Hiryu*, all veterans of the attack on Pearl Harbor.[64]

Admiral Nimitz was convinced by his intelligence operatives that Midway would be the main Japanese target. He reinforced the island itself with as much strength as possible and sent his carriers *Hornet* and *Enterprise* northwest of Midway to intercept the Japanese fleet. His third carrier, *Yorktown*, was undergoing needed repair. Technical experts insisted it would take 90 days to make the repairs; Nimitz insisted the work be done in three days. Once these repairs were made, *Yorktown* sailed out to join *Hornet* and *Enterprise*.[65]

The major engagements in the battle of Midway occurred on June 4. Early that morning planes from the four Japanese carriers attacked the island. Although they caused considerable damage, they did not destroy all the island's defenses. While the Japanese planes were being refueled and rearmed for a second strike at the island, the Japanese carriers were attacked by U.S. planes. The first American strikes were unsuccessful. High flying Army B-17 bombers from Midway failed to score any hits. Dive bombers from *Hornet* could not find the enemy and missed the battle. Torpedo Squadron 8 from the *Hornet* located the enemy, but all 15 planes in the squadron were shot down by Japanese fighters and antiaircraft fire. The torpedo squadrons from *Enterprise* and *Yorktown* suffered almost a similar fate; 20 of their 26 planes were shot down without damaging the enemy fleet.[66]

Just when it appeared all American efforts would fail, dive bombers from *Yorktown* and *Enterprise*, taking advantage of Japanese fighter preoccupation with the low-flying torpedo planes, attacked the enemy carriers, which were loaded with planes, bombs, and fuel on their decks. *Akagi* was hit first, then *Kaga*, and finally *Soryu*. Soon all three were aflame and sinking. Only *Hiryu* managed to escape.[67]

A Texan, Ensign George Gay from Houston, witnessed much of the destruction by American dive bombers. A former mechanical engineering student at Texas A&M, Gay left college in 1939 because his family was pressed for money. He attempted to join the Army Air Corps but was turned down because of a slight heart abnormality. After working a year as an oil field engineer near Corpus Christi, he was accepted by the Navy for flight training. After completing his training, he joined Torpedo Squadron 8 in November 1941. The squadron, which included two other Texans, J. D. Woodson and Robert B. Miles, was assigned to the carrier *Hornet*.[68]

Gay was the only survivor of the 30 officers and men in Torpedo Squadron 8. Slightly wounded in the arm and leg, Gay managed to hide under his rubber seat cushion in the water, concealed from enemy view until the battle passed him by. Gay floated in the water for 30 hours before finally being picked up by a PBY rescue plane.[69]

The battle of Midway did not end with the destruction of *Akagi*, *Kaga*, and *Soryu*. The fourth Japanese carrier, *Hiryu*, managed to launch her dive bombers and torpedo planes. They fought their way through American defenders to hit the *Yorktown*. Salvage operations to save *Yorktown* were undertaken, but a torpedo from a Japanese submarine was a fatal blow, causing the captain to order abandon ship.[70]

Although their ship was sinking, dive bomber pilots from the *Yorktown* secured some revenge. Along with dive bombers from *Enterprise* they located and destroyed *Hiryu*, the last Japanese heavy carrier.

Following the loss of their carriers, the Japanese abandoned their efforts to occupy Midway. The battle was a major victory for the United States and was the turning point in the Pacific war. Admiral Nimitz is credited with the American success in the battle of Midway. In this engagement, the son of pioneer German Texans clearly demonstrated his intelligence, courage, and ability to delegate authority and responsibility for the execution of his plan of operations. From this moment on, the forces of the United States would move forward toward victory.[71]

CHAPTER FOUR

Expansion of the War, July 1942–December 1943

Three weeks after American victory at Midway, Major General Dwight D. Eisenhower arrived in England to assume command of American forces in Europe. At the time, Eisenhower, a native of Texas who grew up in Kansas, was little known by the American public. A 1915 graduate of West Point, Eisenhower spent the First World War on duty in the United States. After attendance at various Army schools and service on the American Battle Monuments Commission in France, he served as a staff officer in the War Department, 1929-1935. This was followed by several years' service as General Douglas MacArthur's chief of staff in the Philippine Islands. In summer 1941 Eisenhower was appointed as chief of staff for Walter Krueger's Third Army in San Antonio. In this role, Eisenhower performed brilliantly during the 1941 Louisiana maneuvers, earning a promotion to brigadier general.[1]

Five days after Pearl Harbor, Army Chief of Staff George C. Marshall called Eisenhower to Washington to serve in the War Plans Division of the General Staff. In the following weeks Eisenhower so impressed Marshall that he was promoted to major general. In March he was named to head the War Plans Division, now renamed the Operations Division.

As head of the Operations Division, Eisenhower worked to implement American strategy that gave priority to the war in Europe. This Europe-first strategy had been adopted by American military planners on the assumption that Germany was the greatest threat to the survival of the western democracies.

As part of the Europe-first strategy, the War Department began sending American troops and equipment to Northern Ireland and England. A small contingent of American military personnel, including the staff of what became the U.S. Eighth Air Force, arrived in England in early 1942. Bomber and fighter crews, ground support elements, planes, and equipment followed later that spring. Soon American ground troops, some already in Northern Ireland, would be arriving to take part in what American planners hoped would be the invasion of northern Europe. This Second Front against the Germans would support the Russians, who were battling the Germans in a great struggle involving millions of men.[2]

In early June 1942, General Marshall appointed Eisenhower to command the European Theater of Operations with headquarters in London. Eisenhower arrived in England on June 24. His biographer, Stephen Ambrose, notes, "there were no bands to greet him, no speeches at the airport, no ceremonies." Quietly and unobtrusively, Eisenhower set about preparing for the buildup of forces under his command.[3]

At the time Eisenhower assumed command, most of the Americans in England were assigned to the U.S. Eighth Air Force. The Eighth Air Force, later to be labeled "the Mighty Eighth," was created in January 1942 when a headquarters was activated at Savannah, Georgia. Major General Carl "Tooey" Spaatz, a combat veteran of World War I and close friend of Army Air Forces commander H. H. "Hap" Arnold, was head of the Eighth. To command the VIII Bomber Command, Spaatz's major component, General Arnold picked another close friend and veteran pilot, Brigadier General Ira Eaker.[4]

Ira Clarence Eaker was born in April 1896 in Field Creek, a small hamlet in Llano County, Texas. When Ira was ten years old, the family moved by covered wagon to Eden, Texas, one hundred miles north in Concho County. Three years later, they moved to Durant, Oklahoma, where Ira attended Southeastern Normal School. When war with Germany was declared in April 1917, Eaker enlisted in the Army at Greenville, Texas. In August he received a commission as a second lieutenant as a result of a competitive examination. After flight training at Kelly Field, San Antonio, Eaker was transferred to Rockwell Field near San Diego. There he met Colonel H. H. Arnold, later chief of the Army Air Forces, and Major Carl Spaatz, his future commanding officer.[5]

During the 1920s and

Lt. Gen. Ira C. Eaker, Commander of U.S. Eighth Air Force

—Library of Congress

1930s the friendship and professional relationship among Eaker, Spaatz, and Arnold grew through additional schooling, endurance flights, and promotional activities for the Army Air Corps. Eaker was awarded the Distinguished Flying Cross twice, earned a college degree at Southern California, and co-authored (with Arnold) three books on air power during these years. Although he was known chiefly as a fighter pilot, Eaker was given the task of building a bomber command in England when the United States entered the Second World War.[6]

Eaker arrived in England in February 1942 and set up headquarters at High Wycombe near London. The first B-17 bombers arrived in England on July 6. Six weeks later VIII Bomber Command launched its first B-17 raid against the continent of Europe. On that date, August 17, 1942, Eaker himself flew with a small force of 12 B-17s of the 97th Bombardment Group in an attack on the railroad marshaling yards at Rouen, France. While the raid caused only minor damage, this was the beginning of the American bombing campaign against Nazi occupied Europe.[7]

In the next several weeks, other bomber and fighter squadrons arrived in England. By early autumn raids along the French coast were being undertaken on a regular basis. Just as Eaker's crews were gaining experience, however, the first three bombardment groups were siphoned off to take part in the Allied invasion of North Africa.[8]

The decision to invade French North Africa was the result of British pressure on President Roosevelt. British Prime Minister Winston Churchill was convinced that the Allies were not strong enough yet to make a successful landing on the European continent. Landings in North Africa would relieve pressure upon British forces fighting Erwin Rommel in Egypt and at the same time satisfy Roosevelt's desire to get American ground troops, now completing training, in the war against Germany. Although American military leaders, especially General Marshall, who favored a cross channel invasion of Europe, and Admiral Ernest J. King, who wanted increased forces in the Pacific, opposed the move, President Roosevelt gave his approval to the North African invasion, co-denamed TORCH.[9]

Dwight Eisenhower, now a lieutenant general, was called from his post in London to command TORCH. Eisenhower brought with him key members of his staff including Carl Spaatz, who was succeeded as head of the Eighth Air Force by Ira Eaker. Troops for the North African invasion were divided into three components: the western task force commanded by Major General George S. Patton, Jr., which would sail from the U.S. east coast and land near Casablanca on the Moroccan coast; the center task force commanded by Major General Lloyd B. Fredendall to sail from Great Britain and go ashore near Oran in western Algeria; and the eastern task force made up of American and British troops sailing from Britain commanded by Major General Charles W. Ryder to land at Algiers.[10]

The North African landings took place on November 8, 1942. Although it had been hoped that French forces occupying the area would not fire upon the Americans, there was some resistance, especially near Casablanca. At Port

Lyautey, north of Casablanca, American troops commanded by Texan Brigadier General Lucian K. Truscott, Jr., encountered determined enemy defenders. It was in this fighting that the colorful Truscott, later to be regarded as one of the most brilliant and daring combat officers in the American Army, first made his reputation. Born in Chatfield, a small community north of Corsicana, Truscott grew up in northeast Texas and southern Oklahoma. After teaching school several years he enlisted in the Army in 1917, earned a commission, and gradually worked his way up as a cavalry and armored officer. In May 1942 he was assigned to the Allied staff under Lord Louis Mountbatten and participated in the Dieppe raid. He then helped recruit and train U.S. Rangers along the lines of the British commandos.[11]

Although Allied warships, including the battleship U.S.S. *Texas*, shelled their coastal defenses, the French put up formidable opposition to Truscott's troops, primarily the 9th Infantry Division, which landed near Lyautey. After a day of heavy fighting, Truscott put 250 troops on the destroyer-transport *Dallas* which carried the men up the shallow Sebow River through heavy enemy artillery and machine gun fire. Supported by Navy dive bombers, Truscott's men captured the French fortress and the vital airfield nearby.[12]

Elsewhere French resistance was spotty. The American 1st Infantry and 1st Armored Divisions landed near Oran with little opposition. The 34th Division occupied Algiers after overcoming French resistance. Two days later Admiral Jean Darlan, French commander in North Africa, issued orders for a general cease-fire. By November 12 Operation TORCH had achieved its initial objectives.[13]

Once Morocco and Algeria were in Allied hands, Eisenhower turned his forces into Tunisia where during the next several months American and British troops fought a series of battles with German and Italian armies that had been driven back from Egypt and Libya.

Photo of Maj. Gen. Lucian H. Truscott when later serving as Commander, U.S. 3rd Infantry Division
—Library of Congress

Many Texans were involved in the North African campaign. The 36th Division, formerly the Texas National Guard, landed at Oran in April 1943, several months after the initial invasion by the Allies. The division spent the next several months in occupation duties and additional training. Although the division now contained many non-Texans, it maintained a distinctly Texas flavor and preferred to be known as "the Texas Army."[14]

Texans served in other units involved in the North African campaign. Numerous Texans were in the lst Infantry Division, "the Big Red One," which fought its way across Tunisia. Terry de la mesa Allen, the colorful division commander, was born in Utah but had married an El Paso native and considered Texas his home. He was a close friend of 36th Division commander Fred Walker and served for a time as deputy commander of the 36th.[15]

Lieutenant Jack Ilfrey from San Antonio, a Texas A&M graduate of 1942 and P-38 fighter pilot in the U.S. Twelfth Air Force, became the first American ace in North Africa, shooting down two German FW 190s one day, two ME 109s the second day, and a ME 110 several days later. The correspondent Ernie Pyle, who traveled with American troops in North Africa, noted that Ilfrey was lucky to be alive; one day he had 268 bullet holes in his plane. His armor plate stopped at least a dozen bullets that would have killed him.[16]

Pyle met several other Texans in North Africa. One, Lieutenant Davey Williams of Fort Worth, was navigator of the B-17 "Thunderbird," which lost two engines on a bombing run against the Tripoli airdrome. The pilot, Lieutenant John Cronkite of St. Petersburg, Florida, gave Williams credit for getting the plane, low on fuel, back to its base. Among other Texans interviewed by Pyle were rifleman Private Thomas Stewart from Scurry, Sergeant John D. Taylor, former football and baseball player from Temple, nurse Kate Rodgers from Houston, who worked in a tent hospital in the battle area, and Major Ronald "Satch" Elkins of College Station, whose half-track was hit three times by German shells near Sidi-bou-zid. Another Texan, Lieutenant Sam Kesner, a Texas A&M chemical engineering graduate, served in the chemical warfare division. Pyle noted that Kesner had a sign on his door "Sixty-Five Hundred Miles from Deep in the Heart of Texas."[17]

Most of the Texans visited by correspondent Pyle were upbeat about their experiences in North Africa. Charles Clinton Green from Kansas, who became a Texan after the war, was more critical. Landing at Oran three days after the initial invasion, Green remembers that German snipers shot at him several times but that he never fired back because he could not see them. Green later told interviewer Stephen Neal Manning that he never saw a German soldier. "North Africa was one confused mess," according to Green, a sergeant in the 132nd Finance Disbursing Center. He remembered North Africa for its mud, rain, contaminated food, prostitution rings, corruption, fraud, alcoholism, and incompetent officers.[18]

When Green first landed in North Africa, other Americans were battling for control of Guadalcanal, a small island in the south Pacific. The battle of Midway in June 1942 had been the first defeat for the Japanese; American forces were now on the offensive. In early August, two regiments of the lst Marine Division landed on Guadalcanal in the lower Solomon Islands. The Japanese were building an airfield that, when completed, would give them a base for aircraft to operate in Australian waters. American military commanders were determined to prevent the enemy from using the airfield. For the next six months, American marines battled the elements and the Japanese for control of the island.

Private Travis Moore, a former convenience store clerk in Dallas, was a member of the 8th Marine Regiment which landed on Guadalcanal in November. The island was far from secure at the time. The Japanese continued to fight tenaciously. Heat, rain, dysentery, spiders, flies, and mosquitoes, fungus infections and malaria added to the difficulties facing Moore and other American Marines. During November and December, the Marines slowly got the upper hand. In January young Moore took part in a series of daring attacks against the enemy, action for which he received the Silver Star.[19]

Another Texan, First Lieutenant Robert M. LaPrade of San Antonio, received the Navy Cross posthumously for his part in the fighting for Guadalcanal. A 1942 graduate of Rice Institute, LaPrade died from wounds received while leading a combat patrol against the enemy. A destroyer escort was later named for him.[20]

By late January 1943 most of Guadalcanal was controlled by U.S. troops. In early February the Japanese withdrew their remaining troops from the island.[21]

The ground fighting on Guadalcanal had been accompanied by a series of naval engagements for control of the sea lanes around the island. Oscar C. Kilcher from San Benito was a seaman on the destroyer *Wadsworth*, which took part in the action in "Iron Bottom Bay," in which dozens of warships were sunk or destroyed. Kilcher's ship was attacked several times by Japanese airplanes using anti-personnel bombs. On one occasion the man standing next to Kilcher had his head blown away. The *Wadsworth* was hit more than 60 times and had to return to Pearl Harbor for repairs.[22]

The naval engagements in the Solomons were costly for both sides. In one of the battles Leonard R. Harmon, an American African mess attendant from Cuero, Texas, serving on the heavy cruiser *San Francisco*, was killed while shielding a wounded shipmate with his own body. For his "extraordinary heroism," Harmon was the posthumous recipient of the Navy Cross. A naval escort vessel, U.S.S. *Harmon*, was later named for him.[23]

While the fighting for Guadalcanal was taking place, American and Australian troops under the command of General Douglas MacArthur were pushing their way through the jungles and across the mountains of New Guinea in a drive toward Buna on the northeastern side of the island. Although Allied forces suffered heavy casualties, Buna was captured on January 2, three weeks before the end of the struggle in Guadalcanal.[24]

Once in possession of Buna, MacArthur planned a series of operations along the northern coast of New Guinea. To direct these campaigns MacArthur requested and received the appointment of Lieutenant General Walter Krueger, commander of the Third Army at San Antonio. Krueger, born in Germany in 1881, was a veteran officer who first joined the American Army as a private in the Spanish American War. He won a commission soon thereafter and over the years worked his way up to a senior command. As a young officer he had served with MacArthur in the Philippines, and they had attended the Army War College together. Krueger, who regarded Texas as his home, was an excellent trainer of men and knowledgeable concerning amphibious operations. He joined MacArthur in February 1943 and was appointed commander of the newly created U.S. Sixth Army.[25]

While MacArthur and Krueger planned their advance in New Guinea, other American forces under the command of Admiral Chester Nimitz were moving up the Solomon Islands chain. In late June 1943, troops of the Army's 43rd Division landed on the coast of New Georgia. Here they encountered terrain, climate, and Japanese resistance much like that on Guadalcanal. Although the 43rd Division was a former National Guard unit from New England, several Texans had joined the division as replacements. One such replacement, Leonard Hall, a tall rifleman from northeast Texas, wrote an account of his experiences in the division. Hall, later a history teacher in Orange, Texas, mentioned several Texans who served with him on New Georgia. Among these were Willard Mitchell, a former football player at North Texas State Teachers

Lt. Gen. Walter Krueger, Commander, U.S. Sixth Army (on right); Brig. Gen. Carlyle H. Wash on left.
—UT Institute of Texan Cultures at San Antonio

College with whom Hall had trained at Camp Roberts, California; Emit "Tex" Ellison, a big, easygoing farm boy from East Texas who was a leader of machine gun squad; Charles Hampton, another East Texan from Naples, who was a rifle squad leader; Trinidad Borrega from San Antonio, described by Hall as "an exceptional soldier;" and Patricio Torrez from Sugar Land, who was Borrega's partner in a scouting team. Not mentioned by Hall was another Texan in the 43rd Division, Sergeant Eugene M. White from Bogata. White was wounded on New Georgia when a Japanese inflitrator dropped a hand grenade in his foxhole.[26]

Japanese resistance on New Guinea, like that in New Georgia and Guadalcanal, was fierce. The fight for the airfield at Munda was especially costly in casualties. Before the airfield could be taken a Marine regiment and two additional Army divisions had to be called in to assist the 43rd. Slightly over 1,000 Americans were killed and nearly 4,000 wounded in securing the island.[27]

While Army and Marine troops were fighting for control of the Solomons and New Guinea, a small group of Americans were carrying on air raids against the Japanese in China. Claire Chennault's American Volunteer Group, the "Flying Tigers," was officially disbanded in July 1942. Those who wished were inducted into the U.S. Army Air Forces. Chennault returned to active duty as a colonel and was soon promoted to brigadier general commanding U.S. Army Air Forces in China. Most of the Flying Tiger pilots elected to return home, but a few remained as officers in the 23rd Fighter Group.[28]

Claire Lee Chennault, Commander, Flying Tigers, later U.S. Air Forces in Far East
—UT Institute of Texan Cultures at San Antonio

Major David L. "Tex" Hill, one of the Flying Tigers who stayed as officer in the Air Forces, eventually became group commander. Hill, a tall, sandy-haired, 26-year-old fighter pilot, was born of missionary parents in Korea. He grew up in central Texas, attended Texas A&M, and graduated from Austin College. In 1938 he enlisted in the Navy. After qualifying as a pilot, he served on the carriers *Ranger* and *Saratoga* before joining the Flying Tigers. For his role in leading some of the early raids against Japanese installations Hill was awarded the Distinguished Flying Cross. Ill with malaria and dysentery, Hill returned home in late autumn 1942 but was back in China in 1943.[29]

Hill was not the only Texan flying in China in 1942. Another Texan, Major Samuel Richardson, commanded the 75th Squadron in Hill's Group.

Richardson shot down eight Japanese planes in combat over China. Matthew Kuykendall, a 23-year-old pilot from San Saba, was another Texan whose exploits were described in a 1942 *Life* magazine story on the Flying Tigers. Lieutenant Colonel Samuel "Tex" Knowles became commander of the 51st Fighter Group, which arrived in China in 1943 to help protect American transport planes flying over the Himalaya mountains to bring supplies from India to China.[30]

At the same time American pilots were battling the Japanese in skies over China, the bombing campaign against targets in occupied Europe was gaining momentum. Ira Eaker, now commander of the U.S. Eighth Air Force, convinced British Prime Minister Winston Churchill that the American concept of daylight precision bombing and the British policy of nighttime saturation bombing would permit around the clock operations against the enemy. Beginning with attacks against the German naval base at Wilhelmshaven on January 23, 1943, Eaker sent his B-17 and B-24 heavy bombers and his B-26 medium bombers on a series of raids against German coastal installations.[31]

In an attack by Eaker's bombers on the submarine yards at Vegesack, Germany, in March seven enemy U-boats were damaged and two-thirds of the shipyard was destroyed. In this raid, Lieutenant Jack W. Mathis from San Angelo, bombardier in the lead plane *The Dutchess*, gave his life to assure that planes in his squadron hit their target. Mathis was severely wounded by antiaircraft fire as his plane neared the target. Although he was mortally wounded, he dragged himself to his sights and released his bombs. As a result of his action, other planes in the squadron put their bombs directly on the target. For "his conspicuous gallantry and intrepidity above and beyond the call of duty," Mathis was awarded the Medal of Honor posthumously. He was the first Texan in World War II and the first member of the Eighth Air Force to receive this honor.[32]

Another Texan, Captain Vincent Evans, was an officer on one of the most famous bombers in the Eighth Air Force during these early raids against the enemy, the *Memphis Belle*. The 22-year-old Evans, who had run a fleet of trucks in Fort Worth before the war, was bombardier on the *Belle*, the first heavy bomber to complete the required 25 missions over enemy territory. The pilot of the *Memphis Belle*, Captain Robert Morgan from Asheville, North Carolina, described Evans as "a pure-life force always into something," but "one of the best bombardiers I have ever seen." Flying as lead plane in a mission of the German submarine pens at St. Nazaire, the *Memphis Belle* was the first aircraft to employ the dictum of wing commander Curtis LeMay of "no evasive action " over target. To ensure this, the pilot turned the plane over to the bombardier during the moments of the bomb run. Such a procedure did result in greater accuracy; Evans laid his bombs within 10 or 15 feet of the target's epicenter.[33]

The raids against German targets continued into the summer of 1943 reaching their climax in the last week of July in what became popularly known as "Blitz Week." Taking advantage of unusually good weather, the Royal Air Force and the U.S. Eighth Air Force pounded various targets including

Germany's second largest city, Hamburg. It was for action during this week that another Texan, John Clay Morgan of Vernon, received the Medal of Honor.[34]

Morgan, flying as a co-pilot in the 326th Squadron, 92nd Bomb Group, had a varied career. After attending New Mexico Military Institute and Schreiner Institute, Morgan worked as a labor overseer on a pineapple plantation in the Fiji Islands, 1934-1937. Then he returned to Texas, where he worked in the oil fields. He attempted to join the U.S. Army Air Corps but was rejected due to a poor academic record and a work injury. He went to Canada, where he joined the Royal Canadian Air Force. After training there, he was sent to the England as a flight sergeant. After seven months of flying, he transferred to the U.S. Eighth Air Force with the grade of flight officer and rating as a pilot.[35]

In the bombing mission of July 28, for which he received the Medal of Honor, Morgan was co-pilot when his plane, *Ruthie II*, was attacked by a large force of enemy fighters. The pilot, First Lieutenant Robert L. Campbell, was hit in the head by enemy fire and fell over the steering wheel. Morgan grasped the controls and pulled the plane back into formation. For the next two hours, he kept the plane in formation, one hand on the controls and one hand holding off the injured pilot, who was half-crazed from his injury. In the official citation awarding Morgan the Medal of Honor the Texan was praised for his "miraculous and heroic performance" resulting in the "successful completion of a vital bombing mission and the safe return of his airplane and crew."[36]

The "Blitz Week" bombing carried out by the Royal Air Force and U.S. Eighth Air Force in England was followed by a raid on the Ploesti oil refineries in Rumania by the U.S. Ninth Air Force operating out of North Africa. The Ploesti refineries had long been a tempting target but were out of range of Allied planes in Great Britain.

On August 1, 1943, 177 B-14 bombers left Libya, crossed the Mediterranean and headed across Albania, Yugoslavia, and Bulgaria. Unfortunately the leading squadron took a wrong turn because of dense clouds in the mountains. When the bombers arrived over target, the enemy already had been alerted. The attackers encountered heavy enemy fighter and antiaircraft fire, resulting in major losses. Although damage to the refineries was intensive, 54 planes were lost and 532 airmen killed, missing, imprisoned, or interned.[37]

Several Texans were among the casualties. Nineteen-year-old co-pilot Ivan Canfield from San Antonio was killed when his plane *Jose Carioca* rammed through the wall of a refinery building. Canfield's plane was hit and burning five miles from the target but Canfield and pilot Nicholas Stampolis guided their burning plane on to the target.[38]

John Palm, a husky youngster from El Paso, was pilot of the B-24 *Brewery Wagon*, which was hit by an .88 mm shell that destroyed one engine and set two others on fire. Palm's right leg, shattered when the plane crashed, was amputated by his Rumanian captors. Palm was treated well by the Rumanians. Dictator Ion Antonesu visited him in the hospital that night. The next morning the Queen Mother and her son, King Michael, visited him. The Queen Mother, who was sympathetic to Americans, had Palm moved to a private room.

After his recovery he remained her personal hostage until liberated at the end of the war.[39]

Another injured Texan, Richard Britt of Houston, who was navigator of a bomber that crashed near the estate of Princess Catherina Caradja, was taken to a clinic by the princess in her 1939 Plymouth. Britt and four other members of the crew remained as prisoners of Rumania until the end of the war.[40]

Two Texans were awarded the Medal of Honor for their part in the Ploesti raid. Colonel John R. "Killer" Kane, born in McGregor, Texas, directed his 98th Bomb Group on its assigned course and arrived at target on time. Kane led his formation through extensive antiaircraft fire, enemy fighters, fire, smoke, and explosions to bomb the refineries. Kane went in so low that flames singed the hair on his arm. For his heroic actions he was awarded the Medal of Honor on August 9, 1943.[41]

Lieutenant Lloyd H. Hughes, a B-24 pilot in the 389th Bomb Group, was the other Texan to be awarded the Medal of Honor for the Ploesti raid. Born in Alexandria, Louisiana, Hughes graduated from Refugio High School and attended Texas A&M. His squadron, commanded by Captain Philip Ardery, husband of Ann Tweedy of San Angelo, was the last to attack the target. His plane received several direct hits from antiaircraft that seriously damaged his aircraft, "causing sheets of escaping gasoline to stream through the bomb bay and from the left wing." Hughes could have made a forced landing but entered the blazing target area and dropped his bomb load with precision. Only then did he attempt a forced landing, but it was too late. The plane crashed, killing Hughes and all but two crew members. The posthumous Medal of Honor was presented to his widow, Mrs. Hazel Hughes, at Kelly Field on March 5, 1944.[42]

Two weeks after the Ninth Air Force made the Ploesti raid, Ira Eaker's Eighth Air Force launched one of its longest and most costly attacks, on the ball bearing plants at Schwienfurt, Germany, and the Messerschmitt complex at Regensburg. The plan called for the attacks to be carried out by two bombardment wings. The 4th Bomb Wing, consisting of 147 B-17s commanded by Brigadier General Curtis LeMay and escorted part of the way by the 353rd Fighter Group, hit Regensburg, the site of the Messerschmitt factory. Instead of returning to England as the enemy would expect, LeMay's wing flew southward across Italy and the Mediterranean to bases in North Africa. The lst Bomb Wing, consisting of 230 B-17s commanded by Brigadier General Robert B. Williams of Albany, Texas, followed LeMay's wing 15 minutes later, taking the same route to southeastern Germany before turning away to bomb Schweinfurt, where half of Germany's ball bearings were produced. Williams' wing returned to bases in England. The wing was escorted part of the way by RAF Spitfires and part of the way by P-47 fighters of the 78th Fighter Group.[43]

The two wing commanders were already well known personalities. Curtis LeMay, a stocky 35-year-old cigar chewing Ohioan, had the reputation as a stern, demanding officer. Admired for his courage and flying skills, LeMay would come to personify the determined bomber commander who neither asked for nor gave quarter.[44]

Robert B. Williams, commander of the 1st Bomb Wing, was a veteran airman. A 1923 graduate of Texas A&M, Williams was in the Army Air Corps in the days of Billy Mitchell. At Langley Field, Virginia, Williams was operations officer of the first group to fly the B-17s. Williams lost an eye in the London blitz, but still continued to fly. In the Schweinfurt raid he flew in the second lead plane and manned the bombardier's machine gun until the barrel burned out.[45]

Both air wings made it to their targets but suffered heavy losses. German fighter planes attacked from almost every direction, employing conventional methods as well as rockets and air-to-air bombing. At Schweinfurt, the Germans used artificial fog generators to spread a gray haze over the town. As a result, bomb groups dropped their loads everywhere, causing major damage but not destroying all the factories. The Regensburg raid was more successful; nearly 1,000 ME-109s were destroyed.[46]

The Schweinfurt-Regensburg raids were costly. Thirty-six of the 230 B-17s in the Schweinfurt wing were shot down. Over 100 of those that made it back to England were damaged, 27 so badly they could not fly again. LeMay lost 24 of his 147 planes in the Regensburg attack. He had to abandon 60 additional bombers in North Africa. On the return mission to England, he lost another three planes. In all, VIII Bomber Command lost 147 B-17s shot down, badly damaged, or abandoned; 40 percent of the force dispatched.[47]

The heavy loss of aircraft in the August 17 Schweinfurt-Regensburg raids caused only a brief pause in European air operations. In late August Eighth Air Force planes hit "special installations" (later V-1 rocket sites) on the French coast. In early September a major mission was carried out on a roller-bearing factory in Stuggart, but heavy clouds over the city prevented many of the attackers from finding their target. After crossing and criss-crossing the city several times a number of planes, low on fuel, dropped their loads on "targets of opportunity."[48]

Lieutenant Paul W. Scoggins, a navigator from Tioga, a small town north of Dallas-Fort Worth, was on both the "special installations" and Stuggart raids. His plane, *Winning Run*, was one of 12 B-17s that were forced to ditch on their return from Stuggart because of low fuel. His plane was a total loss, but fortunately none of the crew was seriously injured.[49]

In early October, Eighth Air Force bombers made a second attack upon the ball bearing factories at Schweinfurt. Two air divisions consisting of 291 B-17s were assigned the mission. A third air division made up of 60 B-24 bombers was assigned a diversionary mission in northwestern Germany.[50]

Colonel Archie J. Old, a 37-year-old Reserve officer from northeast Texas, was flying in the lead plane of one of the two B-17 air divisions. Commissioned in 1929, Old left active duty in the 1930s to pursue an engineering career. He was recalled in 1940 and developed the 96th Bomb Group into one of the most successful units in the Eighth Air Force. Twenty-six of his original 35 aircrews, including that of the *Memphis Belle*, successfully completed their 25 mission tours. Although his plane aborted in the first Schweinfurt raid, Old was now commander of the 45th Bomb Wing and flew as co-pilot in the division's lead plane, *Fertile Myrtle II*, in the second Schweinfurt raid.[51]

The second Schweinfurt raid, on October 14, 1943, a day that came to be known as "Black Thursday," resulted in heavy losses for the Eighth Air Force. American P-47 fighters accompanied the bombers as far as their fuel capacity would allow. When the American fighters turned back, German fighters attacked with great effectiveness. When the bombers reached their target, they were hit hard by enemy aircraft fire. The first bombers to reach Schweinfurt dropped their loads with considerable accuracy, but those arriving later, hampered by the smoke, fire, and dust, did little damage. Sixty American bombers were shot down, one ditched in the English Channel, six were wiped out in crash landings, and seven others were so badly damaged they could not be repaired.[52]

The heavy losses in the Schweinfurt raid brought a pause in major operations. There were additional missions carried out in October and November but against soft targets along the French and German coasts. It was now realized that long-range fighter escorts were necessary to secure deep penetration inside Germany without unacceptable losses.[53]

The search for long-range fighter escorts culminated in late autumn 1943. Two Texans, Assistant Secretary of War Robert A. Lovett and Deputy Commander of the Air Forces Major General Barney M. Giles, played roles in this effort. Lovett, born in Huntsville and a graduate of Yale University, was a longtime advocate of air power. As a naval pilot in World War I he received the Navy Cross. Highly successful as an investment banker in the inter-war years, Lovett joined the Roosevelt administration as Assistant Secretary of War for Air in 1941. In this position he played a vital role in strengthening the U.S. Air Forces.[54]

Like Lovett, Barney M. Giles from Mincola, Texas, served as a pilot in World War I. He and his twin brother, Benjamin, also an Army pilot, remained in service after the war and took part in the growth of the Army Air Corps. In 1942 Benjamin was commander of the Greenland Air Base and Barney headed the 4th Bomber Command in Colorado. In July 1943 Hap Arnold appointed Barney as his chief of staff and later promoted him to deputy commander of the Army Air Forces.[55]

After a visit to England where he was convinced of the need for greater fighter protection, Secretary Lovett assigned Giles the task of solving the long range escort problem. Giles turned to Brigadier General William Kepner, a veteran fighter pilot who had been experimenting with the use of drop tanks for carrying extra fuel as well the use of fuel tanks in the wings of fighter planes. Kepner had encountered opposition from many airmen, including Air Forces Chief Hap Arnold, who argued that these steps would compromise a fighter's maneuverability. Now with the support of Lovett and Giles, Kepner persuaded North American Aviation to put fuel in the wings of its P-51 Mustang fighter and also to add drop tanks for extra fuel. This move gave the P-51 the needed range to accompany bombers deep inside Germany.[56]

By early 1944, the new long-range fighters would be available for the Eighth Air Force. Unfortunately for Texan Ira Eaker, who had struggled against odds to build the Eighth Air Force into a powerful, strategic weapon, this came too late. In December 1943 a general reorganization of American Air Forces in the Europe Theater occurred. Carl Spaatz was made head of U.S. Strategic Air Forces in Europe. Jimmy Doolittle became commander of the Eighth Air Force, and Eaker was transferred to command a new headquarters in Italy, the Mediterranean Allied Air Forces.[57]

The transfer was a complete surprise and a severe shock to Eaker. Although his new command was an important one, it did not have the potential of his old command. He protested the assignment to his friend General Arnold, but to no avail. Just when it appeared he would have the resources to accomplish his goals, he was sent to Italy; others would harvest the results of his efforts. Historian Richard G. Davis, biographer of Carl Spaatz, says of Eaker, "No one could have done better than, and few as well as, he did as commander of the Eighth Air Force." "Eaker," writes Davis, "was the right man at the right place at the wrong time. He lacked the bombers and crews, the long-range fighter escorts, drop tanks, and H2X radar sets his successor had in abundance."[58]

Although he had every reason to be bitter, Eaker assumed his new job as head of Allied Air Forces in the Mediterranean with good grace. With over 12,000 American and British aircraft and over 500,000 officers and men, it was a substantial command. But by January 1944, the Mediterranean was secondary to Allied planning and preparation for the invasion of northern Europe.[59]

The Allied move into the Mediterranean had followed the surrender of German and Italian forces in Tunisia. From there, American and British forces under General Eisenhower moved into Sicily. Three American infantry divisions, the 1st, 3rd, and 45th, an armored division (2nd), and an airborne division (82nd) took part in the assault on July 10. A fourth American infantry division, the 9th, followed up the initial landings.

The divisions that took part in the Sicily invasion were all experienced units. The 1st Infantry, led by Terry Allen, and the 45th Infantry, commanded by Troy Middleton, had many Texans in their ranks. The 45th, a National Guard Division from Oklahoma, New Mexico, Arizona, and Colorado, had trained at Camp Barkeley near Abilene, Texas, where according to the division historian "a love affair" between the town and the division occurred. The 3rd Division, commanded by Texan Lucian Truscott, also listed many Texans in its ranks, including a young baby-faced 19-year-old soldier from Hunt County who would become the most highly decorated American in the Second World War, Audie Murphy.[60]

Murphy, a farm boy with limited formal education, had been turned down by Marine and Paratroop recruiters before finally persuading the Army to accept him in June 1942. Only 5 feet 5 inches in height and 110 pounds in weight, Murphy looked younger than his 18 years at the time of enlistment. After training at Camp Wolters in Texas and Camp Meade in Maryland, Murphy was sent to North Africa, where he was assigned to the 15th Infantry Regiment, 3rd

Division. Three other Texans, Walter Buck, Avery Dowdy, and Milton Robertson, who trained with Murphy at Camp Wolters, were also in the 15th Infantry. Another Texas buddy from Camp Wolters, Corliss Rowe, was in the 3rd Division, but in a different regiment.[61]

Fortunately for Murphy and his comrades, the Sicilian campaign was brief. Within 38 days, the American and British armies overran the island. Even so, there were many casualties. Young Murphy came to respect the enemy and wrote to his sister, "the Sicilian campaign has taken the vinegar out of my spirit. I have seen war as it actually is, and I do not like it."[62]

Another Texan, novelist George Sessions Perry, was troubled by the death and suffering he witnessed in Sicily. Perry, a native of Rockdale, had established himself as a prize-winning writer before the war. Although he was declared medically unfit for military service, he managed to get an assignment as a war correspondent for several magazines and went ashore in the Sicily landings. What he saw there made a lasting impression on him that he later said "defictionized" him for life. According to one of his biographers, "he found that he could not write much about the war experiences that had moved him so profoundly, nor could he go back to writing lighthearted tales of rural Texas."[63]

The veteran war correspondent Ernie Pyle also covered the Sicilian campaign. As was his custom, Pyle visited with as many front-line units as possible. In his dispatches, later published in book form as *Brave Men*, Pyle described a front-line medical station commanded by Captain Carl Carrico of Houston. Carrico and his fellow surgeons "handled a flow of wounded that would sicken and dishearten a person less immune to it," wrote Pyle.[64]

Pyle also witnessed the efforts of three officers and six MPs who put out a fire while enemy dive bombers were attacking. For their courage under fire, these men, one of whom was Private First Class Barney Swint of Douglasville, Texas, were awarded the Silver Star.[65]

After the conquest of Sicily, Allied forces invaded the Italian mainland. Units of the British Eighth Army commanded by General Bernard L. Montgomery crossed the Messina Strait separating Sicily from Italy on September 3, 1943. A week later, British and American troops of the Fifth Army commanded by Lieutenant General Mark W. Clark landed at Salerno, south of Naples. The first American troops ashore, and the first to land on the European mainland, were members of the 36th Division, formerly the Texas National Guard. The 36th had been training in North Africa for several months. The division was originally scheduled to take part in the Sicilian campaign but George S. Patton, commander of U.S. troops in that campaign, wanted battle-tested troops. As a result the 1st Division was substituted for the 36th.[66]

The 36th was still a green division, but General Clark chose it to spearhead the Salerno landings. The 36th had performed well in training exercises, and the Texans had a good reputation as soldiers. Although the 36th was no longer an all-Texas outfit and included replacements from various states, particularly New York, Pennsylvania, West Virginia, and Michigan, the division still had a distinctive Lone Star flavor. Major General Fred L. Walker, who became commander in September 1941, had made few changes among the division's senior officers, most of whom were Texans. Walker himself had been made an honorary Texas citizen by Governor Coke Stevenson.[67]

The 36th Division had a difficult task at Salerno. All amphibious landings are difficult; this one was particularly challenging because of the terrain. The Paestum beaches where the Texans landed were ringed by a series of hills that gave the enemy excellent observation. Consquently, the inexperienced troops of the 36th faced devastating artillery fire.[68]

General Walker assigned the initial landing assault to the 141st Regimental Combat Team commanded by Colonel Richard J. Werner and the 142nd Regimental Combat Team commanded by Colonel John D. Forsythe. The division's third regiment, Colonel William H. Martin's 143rd, served as a floating reserve. The first two waves of the 141st Regiment, led by Lieutenant Colonel Carlo C. Smith of Gonzales, encountered only light resistance, but the third wave was met by heavy small arms and artillery fire. The 142nd Regiment, which landed to the left of the 141st, was greeted by heavy machine gun and artillery fire. As the Texans moved in from the beaches, the German fire intensified.[69]

In the early morning fighting on the beaches there was considerable confusion. At one time it appeared the Germans might push the Texas division and a British division on the left back into the sea, but by midday the invaders had consolidated their hold on the beaches.

36th Division landing at Salerno

—Texas State Archives

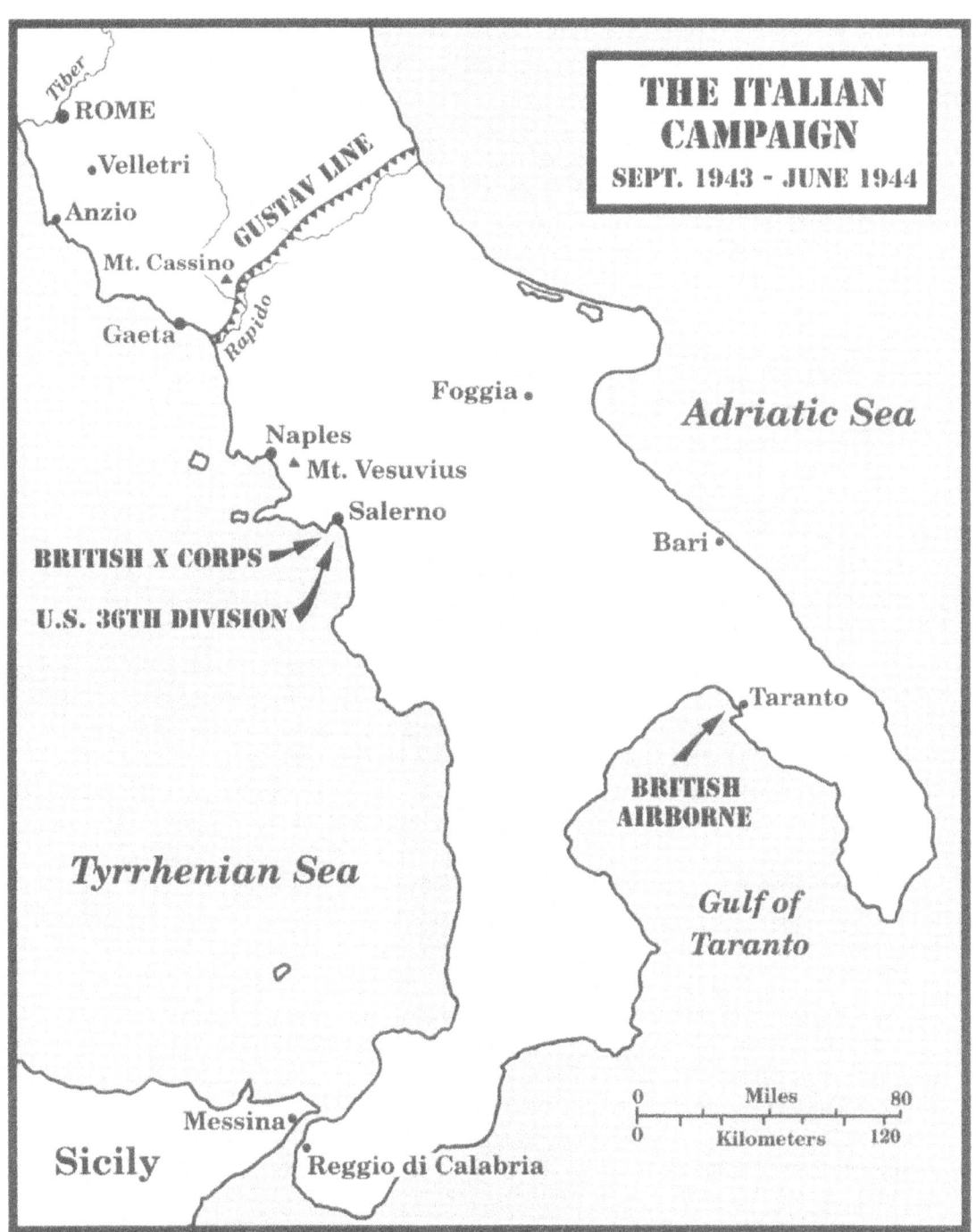

Some individuals distinguished themselves in the fighting that morning.. Sergeant James M. Logan of Luling, a member of the 141st Regiment, displayed particular bravery as he dashed across open terrain to capture a German machine gun and kill the gunners. Later that morning he ran through heavy fire to kill a German sniper. For his actions Logan was later awarded the Medal of Honor.[70]

During the afternoon fighting, the 36th Division slowly pushed the enemy back toward the foothills. By nightfall, the entire division was ashore and in control of all its initial objectives. The division had suffered nearly 500 casualties, including 100 men killed. Many of these men had been with the division since the training days of the Texas National Guard.[71]

For the next two days, the enemy concentrated its attention on the British division to the left of the Texans. The American floating reserve, the 45th Division, came ashore and occupied the gap between the Texans and the British. On September 12 the fighting picked up as the Germans attacked the 2nd Battalion of the 143rd Infantry, commanded by Lieutenant Colonel Charles H. Jones of Austin.[72]

The main German counterattack came on September 13. Reinforced German troops hit the 1st Battalion, 142nd Infantry, and the 2nd Battalion, 143rd Infantry, hard, forcing the Texans to give up some ground. Losses were heavy. At one time General Clark, commander of the Fifth Army, considered withdrawing his troops from the beaches. However, support from British and American naval gunfire and Allied warplanes allowed the division to stabilize its lines and hold. Gradually the tide turned and the Germans began withdrawing into the interior. On September 20 the battle for Salerno was over. Allied troops began moving inland. On October 1 Clark's Fifth Army entered Naples.[73]

The 36th Division sustained slightly over 2,000 casualties in ten days fighting at Salerno. Two hundred sixty-seven members of the division were killed; 132 of these in the 143rd Regiment. Nearly 300 men were missing and presumed captured.[74]

After Salerno was secured, the 36th Division was pulled out of the line and passed into Fifth Army reserve. Although the division was bloodied, General Walker was pleased with the efforts of his men. Four soldiers of the division, including Sergeant Logan, received the Medal of Honor for their part in the fighting. Walker himself was awarded the Distinguished Service Medal with citations praising him "for his exceptional foresight in planning and his superior handling of the forces at his command."[75]

The 36th Division spent the next two months in reserve guarding the beachhead. In mid-November, the Texans replaced the veteran 3rd Division (Audie Murphy's division) on the Winter Line north of Naples. The weather was bitterly cold, and rain turned the ground into a muddy and frozen quagmire. In early December the division captured the fortified town of San Pietro. Losses were again heavy. The division had over 1,500 casualties in December, 290 of whom were killed. Once again the 143rd Infantry, with 855 casualties, suffered the heaviest losses.[76]

The First Special Service Force, an elite organization of American and Canadian troops organized in July 1942 to carry out special operations, joined the 36th Division in the mountain fighting. Commanded by Brigadier General Robert E. Frederick, the Special Service Force had served in the Aleutian Islands campaign earlier in the war. The 3rd Regiment of the Special Force was led by Lieutenant Colonel Edwin A. Walker of Center Point, Texas, a 1931 graduate of the United States Military Academy. Later in 1944, when General Frederick was promoted and assigned command of the First Airborne Task Force, Walker became commander of the Special Service Force.[77]

Toward the end of December, the 36th Division was relieved by the 34th Division and came out of the line. One of the last deaths recorded in 1943 was that of Captain Henry T. Waskow, commander of Company B, 143rd Infantry. Waskow, from Belton, Texas, had been with the company since it left the States. Correspondent Ernie Pyle, who was with the 36th Division at the time, wrote that Waskow was more loved and respected by his men than any officer he had encountered. According to Pyle, Waskow, who was only in his mid-twenties, "carried in him a sincerity and a gentleness that made people want to be guided by him." His loss was especially painful to the men who served with him.[78]

While the Texans of the 36th Division were fighting in Italy during the late autumn of 1943, other Texans were distinguishing themselves in campaigns in the Pacific. Two Texans were awarded the Medal of Honor for their heroism in amphibious operations along the northern coast of New Guinea. Seaman First Class Johnnie David Hutchins of Weimar gave his life during the September landing at Lae. After a bomb hit his LST (Landing Ship, Tank), Hutchins, though mortally wounded, grasped the wheel of the vessel and maneuvered the ship clear of an advancing torpedo, saving the lives of the men on board. For the gallant action Hutchins was awarded the Medal of Honor posthumously.[79]

Colonel Neel E. Kearby, born in Wichita Falls, earned the Medal of Honor in air action over Wewak, New Guinea, on October 11, 1943. While leading a flight of fighter planes to reconnoiter the strongly defended enemy base, Kearby shot down six Japanese aircraft.[80]

Two other Texans were awarded the Medal of Honor posthumously for their part in the bloody battle for Tarawa during November. Lieutenant William Dean Hawkins, born in Kansas but reared in El Paso, and Staff Sergeant William James Bordelon of San Antonio, the two Medal of Honor winners, were veterans of Guadalcanal. Scarred from burns in a childhood accident, Hawkins had been rejected by the Army and Navy because of cosmetic disfigurement but was accepted by the Marines. He received a commission after the Guadalcanal campaign. As commander of a scout sniper platoon he repeatedly risked his life on the first day at Tarawa while leading attacks on enemy pill boxes and installations with grenades and demolitions. On the second day he personally led an assault on a hostile position fortified by five enemy machine guns. Although wounded three times, he destroyed three enemy pill boxes before he was mortally wounded. Reporter Robert L. Sherrod, who accompanied the marines at Tarawa, described Hawkins, or "Hawk" as the men knew him, as "the bravest man I have ever known." The airstrip on Tarawa and a U.S. destroyer were later named for Hawkins.[81]

Staff Sergeant William Bordelon, the other Texan awarded the Medal of Honor posthumously at Tarawa, was a native of San Antonio. Bordelon joined the Marines the day after Pearl Harbor. As a member of the 1st Battalion, 18th Marines, Bordelon was with one of the first assault teams to cross the Tarawa seawall. He personally put two enemy pill boxes out of action and although severely wounded carried an injured comrade to safety. He was killed while assaulting another Japanese machine gun position. His Medal of Honor citation noted that his "great personal valor during a critical phase of securing the limited beachhead was a contributing factor in the ultimate occupation of the island."[82]

Private Jack R. Stambaugh of Bowie, Texas, a 19-year-old rifleman, Company B, 1st Battalion, 6th Marines, was awarded the Navy Cross, posthumously, for his heroism and self sacrifice in the fighting on Tarawa. While helping repulse an enemy night attack he observed four Japanese attacking a wounded and isolated Marine. Without regard for his own safety he went to the aid of his fellow Marine. He killed all four Japanese but was himself wounded and died before aid could reach him.[83]

Lieutenant Colonel Raymond L. Murray, a 1935 graduate of Texas A&M and a former All-Southwest Conference end, received his second Silver Star for bravery against the enemy at Tarawa. Another Texan, Lieutenant Edward Dale of Dallas, used his Sherman tank "China Gal" to batter his way through obstacles and help clear Green Beach from enemy defenders. Although he busted his ankle stepping in a shell hole, Private First Class Adrian Strange, a 20-year-old rifleman from Knox City, Texas, killed six Japanese snipers on Tarawa. Gene G. Seng and Charlie Montague, Texas boyhood friends aged 21, were two of more than 1,000 Marines killed in securing Tarawa.[84]

Air support for ground troop operations continued to be vital in the Pacific campaigns of 1942-1943. Texans played their part in these activities. Wallace Fields of Shamrock, Texas, served with Army Air Forces stationed in Australia. In early 1942 Fields was co-pilot of a B-17 in the 19th Squadron, which helped evacuate key military and civilian personnel from the Philippines. Later that year, Fields piloted his own plane in the 435th Squadron during a series of bombing missions over New Guinea and the Admiralty Islands. Fields flew 51 missions and was awarded the Distinguished Flying Cross. George A. Davis, Jr., from Dublin, Texas, a P-47 pilot in the 342nd Fighter Squadron became one of the early "aces" in the South Pacific, shooting down seven enemy planes. Davis was awarded the Silver Star, Distinguished Flying Cross with oak leaf clusters, and the Air Medal with seven clusters. Lonnie Hood of Beaumont, pilot of a C-47 cargo plane, flew 114 missions in the New Guinea campaign, including several in which he piloted General Walter Krueger. On two occasions he flew General MacArthur's plane. Hood also received the Distinguished Flying Cross and Air Medal with two Oak Leaf clusters. Another Texan, Lieutenant Everett E. Frazier of Jacksonville, a professional engineer, played an important role in locating and preparing air fields for MacArthur's Fifth Air Force. He was awarded the Legion of Merit for his services.[85]

Donald J. Moore flew a series of missions in 1942-1943 with Marine Squadron 214, the Corsair fighter unit later popularized as the "Black Sheep Squadron," commanded by the charismatic and unorthodox Major Gregory "Pappy" Boynington. Described as "a Texan whose infectious grin established him as one of the most likeable pilots in the outfit," Moore was a skilled flyer who had served earlier with the Royal Canadian Air Force. He shot down several enemy planes before disappearing in a raid over Rabaul on December 28, 1943. This was the last the squadron saw of the popular Texan. Officially he was listed as missing in action.[86]

Lieutenant Wayland Bennett from Texarkana was killed while serving with a squadron attached to Boynington's command. Bennett's plane was seen going down in the jungle in October 1943. His body was found, still in the cockpit, by members of his family in 1994. His remains were brought home and buried in a military ceremony in Texarkana.[87]

Navy submarines played an increasingly important role in the Pacific Theater in the latter part of 1942 and 1943. The problems with the magnetic exploders on torpedoes had not been completely resolved, but the addition of new submarines and new officers and men led to increased sinking of Japanese naval and merchant vessels.[88]

Lieutenant Commander Glynn Robert Donaho, from the small town of George (12 miles north of Madisonville), was one of the most successful submarine captains during the summer of 1942. Commanding the submarine *Flying Fish* in waters off Truk Island, Donaho was the first American submarine officer to score hits on a Japanese battleship. He received the Navy Cross for his efforts. This was the first of many awards received by Donaho during the war. In his fifth patrol in early 1943 he was credited with sinking four freighters totaling 43,000 tons. Donaho later became commander of a submarine pack that operated in waters off Luzon during 1944. This "wolf pack" sank 17 Japanese ships and damaged seven others.[89]

Lieutenant Corwin Mendenhall of Anahuac and Winnie was one of the junior officers in submarine service. A graduate of the U.S. Naval Academy in 1939, Mendenhall served on the battleship *Mississippi* before volunteering for submarine duty in early 1941. After attending submarine school at New London, Connecticut, he was assigned as torpedo-gunnery officer on the U.S.S. *Sculpin* (SS-191) commanded by Lieutenant Lucius Chappell. The *Sculpin* was stationed in Manila Bay when the Japanese attacked Pearl Harbor. In the next 19 months, Mendenhall participated in seven war patrols made by the *Sculpin*. As he recorded in his diary, these were months of some success and a great deal of frustration. Although the captain claimed four sinkings, totaling 13,500 tons in the first four patrols, the Joint Army-Navy Assessment Committee (JANAC) credited *Sculpin* with no sinkings over 500 tons on these patrols. *Scuplin* was more successful on the fifth patrol, in the Solomon Islands, in September 1942. The captain claimed three ships, totaling 24,100 tons, sunk; JANAC credited two ships totaling 6,652 tons. Mendenhall listed two tankers, one transport, and one Q-ship sunk on this patrol. The captain and JANAC agreed that no major sinkings occurred on patrols six and seven, November 1942 and May 1943. Mendenhall listed a 10,000 ton tanker sunk on the sixth patrol and two transports and two fishing boats sunk on the seventh patrol.[90]

Seaman George Wade, a cotton farmer from Littlefield, Texas, served on the U.S.S. *Growler* during four submarine patrols between June 1942 and February 1943. In the last of these patrols, in the Solomon Islands, *Growler* (which had sunk five Japanese ships on previous patrols) was on the surface charging her batteries when she was rammed by an enemy ship. The crew of the Japanese vessel opened fire on the deck party of *Growler*. Two American seamen were killed and several, including *Growler* captain Howard W. Gilmore, were wounded. In what became Navy legend, the injured Gilmore ordered his executive officer to take the ship down, leaving the captain and two dead seamen topside. Texan Wade was injured in the ramming, transferred to an Australian hospital, and subsequently discharged.[91]

Another Texan, Arley W. Ewart, who grew up just north of De Kalb, Texas, in a settlement known as Liberty Hill, served on the submarine *Grouper* during two patrols in the latter part of 1942. On these patrols in August and December, *Grouper* sank five enemy ships totaling 19,000 tons.[92]

Samuel D. Dealey, Commander, U.S.S. Harder
—U.S. Naval Institute

Samuel D. Dealey of Dallas was one of the rising stars in the Pacific Submarine Service during summer and autumn 1943. Dealey came from a highly successful Texas family; his uncle was a founder and publisher of the *Dallas Morning News*. After graduating from Oak Cliff High School in Dallas, Dealey studied at Southern Methodist University for two years, then entered the U.S. Naval Academy at Annapolis. He failed to maintain satisfactory grades and was dismissed. However, through the efforts of Congressman Hatton Sumners, Dealey was readmitted the next year and graduated in 1930. After service on several ships, including the ill-fated *Reuben*

James, Dealey became commander of the new submarine U.S.S. *Harder* in September 1942.[93]

Following brief service in the Caribbean, *Harder* joined the fleet at Pearl Harbor. She was sent almost immediately into Japanese home waters. On her first patrol *Harder* sank a Japanese seaplane tender, 7,000 tons, and damaged six other enemy ships. In August Dealey and *Harder* were even more successful, sinking five enemy vessels totaling 15,272 tons. On his third patrol in Marianas waters in October 1943 Dealey sank five enemy ships totaling an almost identical 15,273 tons.[94]

As the year 1943 came to an end American military forces were on the offensive in Europe and the Far East. Texans were playing their part, in the air, on the ground, and on and under the sea. As of December 9, 1943, 541,897 Texans were in military service, many of them serving overseas.[95]

CHAPTER FIVE

The Home front: A People at War

The Second World War brought significant changes to the lives of Texans. While they were not called upon to make the sacrifices required of the half million Texans who were in uniform by 1943, the 6 million Texans who remained at home were affected by the war in many ways. Almost every family had some member who was in military service. Those at home followed closely the movement of American troops in North Africa, Italy, and the islands of the Pacific. They waited anxiously the arrival of the postman with letters from training camps and battle fronts. And they feared the arrival of the Western Union messenger who might be carrying a telegram telling them that their son or husband was killed or missing while serving their country on distant battlefields.[1]

Julia Wingate Bacom of Orange remembers that "when the Western Union boy came to the door everything drained out of you.... If you saw the Western Union boy you stopped to see which house he went in. And it got to where it was like the plague. That uniform or that delivery in that yellow envelope was catastrophe." Ms. Bacom noted that to this day she hates to see a telegram come.[2]

Louis Dugas, Jr., also of Orange, was a telegram messenger boy during the war. If the telegram was bordered in black, a Red Cross worker or some other adult often accompanied the delivery. Dugas recalled that on one occasion he had to read the message to a family that could not read. As he read the telegram reporting that a son had been killed, the mother was crying, the father screaming, and dogs in the yard were barking, but young Dugas, then only 16, finished the task. This was a traumatic experience that he remembered 40 years later.[3]

Not all messages were bad. Sometimes they simply told that a young man or woman was coming home on leave. Occasionally the telegram reported that a son or husband listed as missing had been found or was still alive as a prisoner of war.

A flag with a blue star hanging in the window of a home indicated to passersby that the family had someone in the military. A flag with a gold star meant a family member had been killed. As the war went on, the number of gold stars in windows gradually increased.

The demography of the state changed rapidly as new military bases and defense plants (later called war plants) were constructed. The overall civilian population in the state remained relatively constant, but the influx of thousands of soldiers, airmen, and sailors to training camps and bases resulted in a 550,000, or 8.7 percent, increase in the total number of people in the state. Some areas experienced tremendous population growth. Orange County in southeast Texas, which had a population of 17,382 in 1940, saw its numbers expand to 45,775 by the end of 1943, a 163.3 percent increase, as hundreds of rural East Texans came to find work in Orange's three shipyards. And the growth continued; by 1945 the population was over 60,000.[4]

The population of Brazoria County, farther down the coast, increased from 27,056 people in 1940 to 45,469 by the end of 1943, a 71.8 percent increase brought about by the building of the Dow Chemical Company facility. Moore County, located in the north central part of the Texas Panhandle, had only 4,461 people in 1940, but the expansion of the petroleum industry and government construction of a nitrogen-producing plant near Etter brought in 5,000 new residents by 1943. Hockley, a county on the High Plains, grew from 12,683 to 21,712 (71.1 percent increase), largely because of expansion of irrigation and increased oil production in the area.[5]

All but one of the state's most heavily populated counties experienced population growth in the early part of the war. Jefferson County, with expanded shipbuilding and three major oil refineries, had the largest percentage population growth (22.7 percent) of the heavily populated counties, but Harris, with shipbuilding and a series of oil refineries along the Houston ship channel, had the largest growth in numbers, 72,228 (13.7 percent). The population of Dallas County increased 44,496 (11.2 percent); Bexar, 48,425 (15.3 percent); El Paso, 10,305 (8.2 percent); Tarrant, 42,335 (18.8 percent); McLennan, 1,287 (1.3 percent); and Nueces, 20,759 (22.4 percent). Travis County, which had 4,901 fewer residents in 1943 than in 1940, was the only one of the state's nine most heavily populated counties to experience a decline in civilian population.[6]

As the counties with war-related industries grew in population, many rural counties suffered major declines. One hundred ninety-four of the 254 counties in Texas lost civilian population during the war. Seventeen counties experienced population losses in excess of 30 percent during the early war years. Ten of these were in East Texas, six east of the Trinity River; the other seven counties experiencing major population loss were in West Texas. None of the South Texas counties lost 30 percent of their population, but Duval, which had a 29.5 percent decline, was close. Yoakum County (in extreme West Texas next to the New Mexico state line), which dropped from 5,354 people in 1940 to 2,663 in

1943, had the largest percentage decline, 50.3 percent. Rusk in East Texas (which lost 13,055 people in the three year period), Hidalgo in South Texas (which lost 11,789) and Henderson in East Texas (which lost 11,300) had the greatest declines in total numbers. In all, 20 counties each lost 7,000 or more residents between 1940 and 1943.[7]

In those cities and counties with major population increases, the lack of housing was soon a major concern. The hundreds who moved to work in defense plants or to be near family members stationed at training camps discovered there was little housing available. Constructing new homes was difficult because building materials were being used for the war effort.[8]

In counties such as Orange, where the population doubled almost overnight, local residents attempted to help by taking boarders in a spare room or dividing their homes into small apartments to accommodate families. Harold Harrington, himself a shipyard worker in Orange, recalls that his mother took in workers from rural East Texas. "She had as many as three beds in a big room, and three men stayed in that one room. She even had 'em in a little place in the hall out there she partitioned off." Emma Jane Nies remembers that she and her husband lived in "a little place that we called the black hole of Calcutta," so named because the room was so dark they had to burn lights even in the middle of a sunny day.[9]

Many defense workers lived in trailer houses, but even here there were problems. Smaller communities had no trailer park, or "courts" as they were called then, and those that had parks were already full. Mary Marshall recalls that when she and her family arrived in Orange they could find no place to park their trailer. The Monroe Colburn family allowed them to park at their home, which "was not convenient for them because we had to go in their house to use the bathroom facilites," as most trailers at the time were not equipped with bathrooms.[10]

To help alleviate the housing shortage in Orange, the government constructed over 4,000 houses along the Sabine River. The houses in the project, known as Riverside, were designed as temporary structures with a maximum life span of 10-20 years. Old-time residents scoffed at the Riverside project which was located on a marsh site, but for the workers and their families this was better than sleeping in their vehicles or in tents. C. W. Waggoner, who came to Orange from Nacogdoches when his father found work in the shipyards, remembers that the narrow streets in Riverside were often knee-deep in water. As a 12-year-old, Waggoner resented the move from the Piney Woods to the treeless marshland, but admitted the house in Riverside was "pretty doggone good." It was tight and warm and had indoor plumbing, which was not always the rule in those days.[11]

The Orange story was duplicated in other Texas communities where war industries brought in newcomers. A similar situation existed in towns located near training camps and air bases. In towns such as Abilene, Corpus Christi, Hondo, Lubbock, and San Angelo the need for housing was acute as servicemen and construction workers competed for any available living space. Civic leaders often called upon citizens to share any empty rooms with the influx of newcomers.[12]

While there was some resentment to the newcomers, especially if they were "Yankees," Texans generally were hospitable and often opened their homes to servicemen and their families. In the Wooster community near Baytown, Mrs. Jessie Wooster, a widow with two sons in service, rented the younger son's room and the family living room to the Stuebers from Minnesota. Joe Stueber, an Army draftee from Minnesota, was a member of an antiaircraft battery assigned to guard the Baytown Humble Oil refinery. He and his wife lived with Mrs. Wooster the several months he was stationed in Baytown, and the families maintained a friendship long after the war had ended.[13]

In large cities, the military often took over hotels in which to quarter their personnel. In September 1942 the U.S. Coast Guard converted the fashionable Galvez Hotel in Galveston into a military barracks. The hotel bedrooms were stripped of furniture and only a few chairs and sofas remained in the lobby. The former bridal suite housed a half dozen men, and the ladies' restroom was now the officers' wardroom.[14]

The housing shortage was not just a Texas problem; it was a matter of national concern. Across America, thousands lived in trailers, converted garages, shacks, automobiles, and shared rooms. As in the Orange Riverside project, the National Housing Authority provided some relief through its own building projects or with federally insured mortgage to private builders. By 1942 Federal authorities had let contracts for 42,000 prefabricated housing units throughout the country. Before the end of the war there would be tens of thousands more.[15]

The National Housing Authority was only one of numerous Federal agencies that affected the lives of Texans during World War II. Eighteen months before Pearl Harbor, President Roosevelt created the Office of Civilian Defense by executive order. Headed by the colorful mayor of New York City, Fiorello H. La Guardia (assisted by Mrs. Franklin Roosevelt), the office created state and local civilian defense committees that enlisted thousands of citizens in a variety of programs aimed at preparing Americans for the eventuality of war, including enemy air attacks. By January 1942 over 5.6 million Americans were enrolled as airplane spotters, air raid wardens, ambulance drivers, first aidsmen, messengers, and clerks. National and state committees prepared and distributed thousands of civil defense brochures and pamphlets as well as thousands of white helmets, shovels, buckets and pails (for water and sand), and first aid packets.[16]

The majority of Americans, and Texans, did not take the civil defense program seriously until after Pearl Harbor. The success of the Japanese attack created a new awareness of vulnerability to enemy air attacks. In early January 1942, Texas cities took part in air raid drills in which all outside lights were extinguished. Although there was some confusion and mistakes made as Texans found themselves in a world of darkness, most local councils and committees reported the drills were successful.[17]

In late January the state's first real blackout occurred along the middle

Texas coast. On January 18 the U.S. Navy reported one of its aircraft sighted a German submarine near Port Aransas. The *Rockport Pilot* put out an extra edition that day reporting the sighting and calling for an all-night blackout. That evening all the towns along the coast from Rockport to Corpus Christi turned off their lights. Hospitals and air raid wardens were alerted to be ready in case of an attack.[18]

In her book *Torpedoes in the Gulf*, historian Melanie Wiggins points out the Navy report must have been a false alarm. German naval records indicated that the first U-boat did not enter Gulf waters until the end of April 1942. Several ships departing Texas ports were sunk off the Florida Atlantic coast earlier, however. In late February the tanker *W. W. Anderson*, sailing from Groves, Texas, with a load of gasoline, was torpedoed off Florida with the loss of 45 crewmen. In March the tanker *Gulf Trade* sailing from Port Arthur and the Pure Oil tanker *W. E. Hutton* sailing from Nederland were sunk with the loss of 31 lives. In early April the tankers *Gulfamerica* and *Texaco Oklahoma* from Port Arthur went down off St. Simon's Island, Georgia. Among those killed were Captain Karl Olson of Groves, First Mate C. E. Harker of Port Arthur, and Second Mate D. Anderson of Port Arthur.[19]

The first sinking in the Gulf occurred in May. The Sabine Transportation Company's *Munger T. Ball*, sailing from Port Arthur loaded with gasoline, was sunk on May 4 with the loss of 37 seamen, 13 from Port Arthur. Several days later *Gulfpenn*, sailing from Port Arthur with fuel oil, was torpedoed off the Louisiana coast; fortunately, most of the crew were rescued by a Honduran vessel. On May 14 the tanker *David McKelvy* was sunk near the mouth of the Mississippi with the loss of 27 men. *Cities Service Toledo*, carrying crude oil from Corpus Christi to Portland, Maine, was sunk in early June. Later that month another Sabine Transportation ship, *Rawleigh Warner*, was torpedoed off the Louisiana coast with its entire crew of 33 killed.[20]

Submarine activity in the Gulf caused great concern to Washington policymakers, who feared that the loss of Texas oil and gasoline would seriously jeopardize the war effort. As noted in Chapter 2, it spurred the building of the Big Inch pipeline to carry Texas oil to the East Coast. It also caused the military to increase its antisubmarine activities in Gulf and Atlantic waters. In June 1942, military authorities ordered all lights along the Texas and Louisiana coasts dimmed. Signs, floodlights, stadium lights, and bonfires on the beaches were prohibited. Street lights were to be blackened on the seaward side and wattage reduced. Greater use was made of escort vessels, convoys, air patrols, and radar. A series of blimp stations, including one at Hitchcock near Galveston, were built along the coast. Along the upper Texas coast the U.S. Coast Guard maintained a mounted horse patrol that reported any suspicious activities.[21]

The Civil Air Patrol, created by President Roosevelt's executive order in December 1941, played an active role in the fight against the submarine. Made up of civilian volunteers who received only a small per diem allowance for their work, the CAP maintained 21 coastal patrols from Maine to the Rio Grande. Three of these patrols operated from Texas bases—Beaumont, Corpus Christi, and Brownsville. During 1942-1943 CAP pilots spotted and reported enemy submarines and floating mines, rescued survivors from sinkings, and sometimes dropped bombs on enemy submarines. The duty was hazardous; 26 members of the coastal patrol including Texans John H. Dean from Fort Worth, Alfred Koym from Rosenberg, and Robert D. Ward from Dallas, all flying out of Beaumont, lost their lives.[22]

Gradually, American countermeasures had effect. From September 1942 through February 1943, the Gulf of Mexico was virtually free of enemy submarines. There were sinkings in the spring of 1943 as Germany launched a major submarine offensive, but by late summer this new threat was ended as the American Navy, Coast Guard, and Civil Air Patrol got the upper hand. On August 31, 1943 the coastal patrols of the Civil Air Patrol were ended. In October the dim-out program along the Texas coast came to an end.[23]

Most Texas families worried more about the availability of consumer goods during the war than about air raids and submarine threats. Within the first few weeks of the war shortages of certain products began to occur. In one of its first acts the newly created War Production Board banned the manufacture of new automobiles as factories turned to increased production of military vehicles. In the next several months the Board halted manufacture of commercial trucks, metal office furniture, radios, phonographs, refrigerators, vacuum cleaners, washing machines, and sewing machines for the duration of the war.[24]

When the Japanese overran British and Dutch possessions in southeast Asia, the United States found itself facing a shortage of natural rubber. In order to save rubber for military needs, the Office of Price Administration, created in April 1941 to fight rising prices and inflation, froze the sale of tires except for emergency purposes. To meet these emergency needs, the OPA established rationing boards in all 48 states. These boards, made up of local volunteers, had the task of allotting new and recapped tires.[25]

The expansion of the war necessitated rationing of other consumer goods. In late spring 1942 the Office of Price Administration, which assumed control of the rationing program, announced that sugar, needed for the military, would be rationed. In May, Texans lined up at their local schools where War Ration Book No. 1, containing coupons for each member of the family, was issued. Each coupon was for one pound of sugar. There were two coupons per individual for each month of the year.[26]

Other products soon joined the list of items rationed. In November 1942 rationing of coffee, now in short supply because of a lack of cargo space, was announced with one pound of coffee per month allowed each individual. Meats, cheese, fish, fats, processed foods and canned goods joined the ration list in February 1943. War Ration Book No. 2, issued that month, contained rows of blue and red stamps: blue for processed foods and canned goods, and red for meat, cheese, and fats. Different point values were assigned to different items. The number of points allotted each consumer varied from time to time. In 1943, for example, each consumer received 15 points per week for rationed meat. In 1945 this was down to 12½ points per week.[27]

The shortage of leather led to the rationing of shoes in February 1943. Initially the ration provided coupons for three pair of shoes per year. This was later reduced to two pair. Shoes not requiring leather were not rationed.[28]

While rationing required that consumers plan more carefully before shopping and burdened merchants who had to keep up with point values and expiration dates of coupons, few Texans suffered from rationing. Buck Young, who grew up in Pelly (now Baytown), Texas, recalls "even with rationing our family did all right. We had plenty of butter from our cow, eggs from our chickens, and fresh vegetables from our garden, or from the Mason jars of my mother's canning efforts." Young points out that his family, like many Texans in small towns and rural areas, still butchered their own hogs, which provided bacon, ham, pork chops, and lard for the family.[29]

This is not to say that rationing was ever popular. For the first time in years, most Texans were gainfully employed and making more money than ever before, but rationing and shortages prevented them from purchasing all the items they desired. Although local newspapers and major distributors carried on public information campaigns, many Americans were unconvinced that food rationing was necessary or was being fairly administered.[30]

In addition to rationing of food items Texas faced shortages in obtaining some unrationed commodities. Cigarettes (especially Camels and Lucky Strikes), Coca-Colas, chewing gum (especially Wrigley's), Hershey Bars, Milky Ways, Mr. Good Bars, liquors (especially Scotch), facial tissue, toilet paper, soap, cotton diapers, cotton shirts, and nylon hose were all in short supply. In some parts of Texas there were milk shortages. Mrs. Leona Whitman of Silsbee remembers the shortage of milk. "I heard a store in Kountze got in a carload of milk and I drove to Kountze to get a case of Carnation milk," she recalls.[31]

To provide a measure of fairness, Texas shopkeepers frequently limited the sale of items in short supply. Customers could purchase only one six-pack of Coca Cola, two or three Hershey Bars, or two packs of cigarettes. It was not uncommon for the purchaser to follow a delivery truck from store to store in order to obtain the number of items desired. On the whole, Texans took these restrictions in good spirit, but occasionally misunderstanding or quarrels occurred.[32]

Texans were more willing to accept rationing for food than they were for gasoline. In a state where there existed an abundance of oil and gasoline and where traveling distances were great, Texans failed to see the need for rationing. When shipping shortages forced the federal government to impose gasoline rationing in the states along the East Coast in May 1942, Texans formed a statewide committee of county judges, state officials, and representatives of various organizations to oppose extension of gasoline rationing to Texas.[33]

When informed that gasoline rationing might be necessary to save rubber, state officials urged Texans to participate in a massive scrap rubber drive. This drive in June 1942 was highly successful; in Houston alone over one million pounds of rubber was collected. Nationwide, over 335,000 tons was collected. Former governor W. Lee O'Daniel, running for re-election to the U.S. Senate, predicted gas rationing in Texas would not be necessary.[34]

Senator O'Daniel was wrong. While the massive collection of scrap rubber was helpful, it did not provide enough to meet the nation's needs. In autumn 1942, President Roosevelt ordered nationwide gasoline rationing, a ban on pleasure driving, and a 35-mile speed limit to take effect on December 1. Drivers were issued stickers and coupons that determined the amount of gasoline they could purchase. The average driver received an "A" sticker, which entitled him to four (later three) gallons of gasoline per week. Individuals employed in war work were given a "B" sticker, which allowed them to purchase additional gasoline dependent upon their distance from work. The "C" sticker was given to ministers, doctors, dentists, and police who were engaged in essential work. This entitled them to even more gasoline than holders of the "B" sticker. A "T" stamp was given to truckers, who received virtually all the gasoline they needed.[35]

Although they complained about gasoline rationing most Texans learned to make do with their gasoline allotment. About half of the state's drivers received "B" or "C" stickers, which permitted them to buy enough gasoline to drive to and from work and to take care of family matters. The holder of an "A" sticker, however, had to be more judicious and limit his driving. There was some counterfeiting of ration coupons, and there was some transferring of coupons from one driver to another. The Office of Price Administration estimated 5 percent of all gasoline was purchased with illegal stamps.[36]

Gasoline rationing caused many inconveniences both for car owners and service station operators. Most coupons expired at the end of every three months. At that time there were long lines of cars at service stations as Texans used all their coupons before they expired. On such occasions tempers and dispositions of drivers and station attendants were strained to the limit. But the system did work. Travel by automobile was reduced, and rubber and gasoline were saved for the war effort.[37]

Gasoline rationing meant that most long distance travel was by bus, train, or airplane. Commercial air travel in Texas was still limited to the big cities and was expensive. On the other hand, almost every town in Texas had some type of comparatively inexpensive bus service. This service was expanded by the needs of the war. In 1941 the state had 1,035 operating buses; by 1943 there were 1,713 buses in Texas. The number of passengers increased even more; from 17 million riders in 1941 to 88 million in 1943.[38]

The number of Texans traveling by train also increased dramatically. In 1940 slightly less than 4 million Texans traveled by rail; in 1943 nearly 25 million people boarded the train in Texas.[39]

Even with an airline, bus, or train ticket one was not assured of boarding. Often there were more passengers than seats or standing room. Military travelers were always given priority; if all room was taken, individuals had to wait for the next scheduled conveyance. Waiting rooms were always crowded, and the traveler faced long lines at every stop. Everywhere signs asked travelers "Is This Trip Necessary?"[40]

Most Texans postponed pleasure travel for the duration of the war. Other than a trip to visit a relative or loved one at a training camp (especially before they went overseas) or a journey to find a new job or to transact business, Texans remained at home.

For the first time in recent memory there was full employment for anyone wishing to work. The work hours were long, but the pay was good and Texans had money to spend — if they could find items to buy.[41]

More women were employed in work outside the home than ever before. The expansion of the war effort and the departure of husbands, brothers, and other young men to the military created the need for additional workers. The War Manpower Committee, another Federal agency created by the Roosevelt administration, made major efforts to recruit women for the labor force. Through radio announcements, newspaper stories, motion picture spots, and outdoor billboards, the Manpower Committee appealed to American women to take jobs in shipyards, aircraft plants, munitions factories, and oil refineries as their "patriotic duty."[42]

There were 12 million women in the work force when the United States entered the war. The majority of these women were single, and most were employed in clerical, teaching, secretarial, or nursing positions. The war changed this. The number and percentage of married women in the labor force increased as did the type of jobs women held. By 1944 married working wives outnumbered single working women for the first time in the nation's history.[43]

The majority of females who joined the work force during the war were married women over the age of 35. Most young mothers remained at home performing the traditional roles of wife and mother, although there were exceptions caused primarily by economic necessity.[44]

Nationally, the number of women in the U.S. work force rose from 12 million in 1940 to 19 million in 1944. Donald Nelson, head of the War Production Board, boasted that 36.9 per cent of the total personnel employed by war industry was female. In 1944 112,024 of the 419,659 individuals employed in essential industries and military establishments in Texas were women; ten percent below the national percentage claimed by Nelson.[45]

Although the greater employment of females may have been a major turning point in the emancipation of women as some historians believe, most Texas women did not join the labor force to make a social statement. Many saw this as a way of contributing to the war effort and at the same time making good wages. Most, like Stella Groves, who worked at Beaumont's Pennsylvania Shipyards, realized the job was "only for the duration." Some, like Ila Martin, who worked at the same shipyard, believed her work would help the safe return of her son who was in the military. Mary Walker Eastwood and Mary Carlson Easley, who worked at Humble Oil's Baytown Butyl Plant, took their jobs because of the high wages paid. Sylvia Boyd of Brownwood thought little about wages or the war. She was looking for adventure when she took a job in Fort Worth.[46]

By 1943 women were working at a variety of jobs formerly reserved for men. At the Magnolia Refinery in Beaumont and the Humble Oil Refinery in

Baytown, women served as timekeepers, yard clerks, storeroom helpers, chemists, crane operators, electricians, and machinists. In shipyards from Orange to Corpus Christi, women worked as welders, packers, burners, mold loft workers, tool checkers, and layout workers. In aircraft factories in Dallas and Fort Worth, women operated machines, rivet guns, and welding torches. Ten thousand women, referred to collectively as "Kelly Katies," worked in a variety of jobs at San Antonio's Kelly Field. Their contribution to the war effort was truly significant.[47]

Unidentified female welder, Pennsylvania Shipyards, Beaumont
—Tyrrell Historical Library, Beaumont, Texas

More than 12,000 Texas women served in the armed forces during World War II; 8,000 in the Army and 4,200 in the Navy, Marines, and Coast Guard. The bill creating what was first called the Women's Army Auxiliary Corps (WAAC) was passed by Congress in May 1942. Two and one-half months later, legislation was passed creating the Navy component, Women Accepted for Voluntary Emergency Service (WAVES). In November 1942 the Coast Guard Woman's Reserve, known as SPARS from the Coast Guard motto, *Semper Paratus* ("Always Ready"), was authorized. In early 1943 the Women's Reserve of the Marine Corps was created.[48]

The day after the bill was passed creating the WAACs, Army Chief of Staff George C. Marshall appointed Oveta Culp Hobby, wife of former Texas governor William P. Hobby, as director. Mrs. Hobby, born in Killeen, Texas, on January 19, 1905, was the daughter of a lawyer and state legislator. Educated at Mary Hardin Baylor and the University of Texas, she served as legislative parliamentarian of the Texas House of Representatives, newspaper reporter, and political campaign director before her marriage to her father's friend, William P. Hobby, in 1931. After her marriage she worked on the *Houston Post* newspaper, which she and her husband owned. During the 1930s she was active in Texas civic affairs while continuing to write and fill the role of wife and mother of two children.[49]

In 1941 Mrs. Hobby was asked to head the Women's Interest Section of the War Department's Bureau of Public Relations. As head of the Women's Interest Section she so impressed General Marshall that he asked her to help secure passage of the bill creating the Women's Army Auxiliary Corps. After the bill passed, Marshall asked her to serve as the first director of the Corps with the rank of colonel.[50]

As director of the WAACs Mrs. Hobby worked hard to overcome various obstacles to the success of her organization. In July 1943 she was successful in getting Congress to give Army women full military status. The "auxiliary" was dropped from the name and members of the Women's Army Corps now had the same rank, titles, and pay as their male counterparts.[51]

The WACs and their sisters in the other services overcame considerable suspicion and hostility, both from civilians and male members of the military. Gossip, rumors, dirty jokes, snide remarks, and obscenities were commonplace. Many considered the female soldiers as little more than camp followers. General Marshall, who was outraged at this type of slander, warned military commanders that such remarks and attitudes would not be tolerated. Although Marshall's admonitions helped, women in uniform continued to be subject to some abuse and ridicule throughout the war.[52]

WACs performed a variety of tasks. They did much of the Army's clerical work, releasing men for combat. But they also worked as machinists, radio operators, tailors, projectionists, chemists, toxicologists, control tower operators, airplane mechanics, and weather observers. At the end of the war 90,779 women were serving in the Women's Army Corps. Nearly 17,000 of them were overseas, serving in combat zones.[53]

WAC graduation day, including Col. Oveta Culp Hobby (second from left).
—Center for American History, UT-Austin

The only African American WAC unit to be assigned overseas duty was the 6888th Central Postal Directory Battalion, stationed first in Birmingham, England, and later Rouen, France. Ninety-one of the 855 members of the battalion came from the Eighth Service Command (Texas, Arkansas, Louisiana, Oklahoma, and New Mexico).[54]

Women serving in the Navy, Marines, and Coast Guard were assigned mainly to clerical duties. At the war's end approximately 4,000 WAVES, 1,000 Women Marines, and 200 SPARS were serving in Hawaii. Another 200 SPARS were stationed in Alaska.[55]

Seventy-six thousand American women served in the Army and Navy Nurses Corps during World War II. Some of these women, such as Ruby Edwina McCain from northeast Texas, were in service before Pearl Harbor. Lieutenant McCain, who graduated from nursing school in Paris, Texas, was commissioned in July 1941 and later served in New Guinea, the Philippines, and New Zealand. As noted in a previous chapter, 77 nurses were taken prisoners after the fall of Philippines in 1942; ten of these nurses were Texans.[56]

With the declaration of war, thousands of nurses volunteered for military service. Like those already in service, these volunteers were commissioned as officers and received equal pay and benefits with male officers. Since most of them had little knowledge of military life, four-week orientation courses for the newly commissioned nurses were begun. Helen K. McKee of San Antonio was one of the first nurses to graduate in this special program at Camp Forrest, Tennessee. Lieutenant McKee was then assigned to the 300th General Hospital Unit, first in Tunisia and later Italy. She was later transferred to the 61st Station Hospital in Foggia, Italy. In letters to her parents she described treating patients who were severely wounded in the Anzio and Mt. Cassino campaigns.[57]

Margaret Anderson, a graduate of Texas Tech, was another Texas nurse assigned to duty in Italy. She was working as a civilian dietitian at the Army hospital in El Paso when she was requested to join the service. After commissioning she was assigned to the 300th General Hospital in Naples. She served there from January 1944 to March 1945, when she was transferred to the 16th Evacuation Hospital near Florence, where she remained until the war ended.[58]

Some Texas nurses joined the military after their husbands entered in service. Catherine H. Wiley of Galveston, whose husband Staff Sergeant Estus F. Wiley was in the Army Air Forces in the China-Burma-India theater, volunteered in May 1944 and served with the Army in the Battle of the Bulge later that year. Clarice Ann Dreskin of Longview, whose husband was in the Army Air Forces in the South Pacific and the Philippines, was assigned to duty in Australia, New Guinea, Leyte, and Cebu.[59]

Nearly 2,000 women served in quasi-military programs designed to release male pilots for combat. Two organizations, the Women's Auxiliary Ferrying Squadron (WAFS) and the Women's Flying Training Detachment (WFTD), were established in 1942. The WAFS consisted of experienced female pilots who ferried aircraft for the Air Transport Command. The WFTD provided a training program to supply pilots for the Ferrying Squadron. Florence Miller Watson from West Texas was one of the first 25 women to serve in the Women's Auxiliary Ferrying Squadron. When the two women's programs were later merged into the Women's Airforce Service Pilot (WASP) program, Watson served with this group.[60]

As noted earlier, the Women's Airforce Service Pilot program was the result of efforts by the famed American aviatrix Jacqueline Cochran, who persuaded the Pentagon to establish the program. To qualify for the WASP program candidates had to be licensed pilots with a high school diploma. The first four WASP classes were trained at the Houston municipal airport, but poor weather conditions and heavy air traffic in the area led to the program being transferred to Avenger Field in Sweetwater, Texas.[61]

The first WASP class arrived in Sweetwater in March 1943. During the next 21 months 1,074 women, many of them Texans, completed their training and received their wings. Once graduated, WASPs were assigned to a variety of duties, including ferrying airplanes, towing targets, testing cadet pilots, simulating strafing attacks, and performing test pilot duties. WASP Millie Davidson of Austin flew B-24 and B-17 bombers for the Eastern Training Command at Maxwell Air Base in Alabama. Another Texan, Dora Dougherty Strother, was one of the first pilots to fly the new B-19 Superfortress. The WASPs remained civilian, not military, pilots. They were given only modest pay and few benefits. They received no insurance, uniform allowances, or pensions. Although 38 WASPs died in government service, they received no cost-free burial insurance. Their only reward was to serve their country in wartime.[62]

The training of WASPs at Sweetwater come to an end in December 1944. The war was drawing to a close and there was now a surplus of pilots. General H. H. Arnold, head of the Army Air Forces, came to Sweetwater to address the final class. Although Arnold told the class "If there was a doubt in anyone's mind that women can become skillful pilots, the WASP have dispelled that doubt," it would be over 25 years before the service of women pilots to the nation was fully recognized.[63]

American women served in a variety of other volunteer organizations. Thousands worked for the American Red Cross in knitting garments and rolling surgical dressings for the military. The Red Cross offered courses in first aid, water safety, home health care, nutrition, and accident prevention. The Red Cross also operated canteens and service clubs, both in the States and overseas. Rita Pilkey of Dallas, a graduate of North Texas State Teachers College, set up and managed such a club at a field artillery training station in China, directed by Brigadier Jerome J. Waters, a graduate of Texas A&M.[64]

Sally Craighead Marcus from Dallas was another Red Cross volunteer. She was sent to Europe, where she was taught to drive a 2½-ton mobile canteen truck that provided coffee and doughnuts for American combat troops.[65]

Some Texas women assisted in the activities of service clubs operated by the United Service Organizations (USO). By the middle of the war many Texas towns, particularly those with or near military bases, had USO clubs where service men and women could play games, write letters, eat and drink snacks and beverages, and dance. Under strict rules, young women were recruited to serve as hostesses and dance partners for servicemen.[66]

Various state and local organizations enlisted the services of women for the war effort. In Fort Worth, a women's auxiliary unit of the Texas Defense Guard called the Texas Guardettes was formed. The Guardettes provided administrative support for the Defense Guard created by the legislature to provide internal security after the National Guard was federalized. In San Antonio, Austin, and several other cities women joined the Women's Motor Corps to provide drivers in cases of emergency. In Baytown a local organization, the Woman's Ambulance Corps, was created to train ambulance drivers. The American Women's Volunteer Services in Beaumont opened a nursery for children of women defense workers. Also in Beaumont, Eloise Milam organized a group of teenage girls, known as the Melody Maids, who provided music for bond rallies, military bases, and military hospitals. In several cities women, such as Ruth Coffey of Beaumont, volunteered their services to the Civil Air Patrol.[67]

Texas young people made their contribution to the war effort in various ways. Almost everyone who grew up during the war remembers purchasing savings stamps and war bonds. Hazel Shelton Abernethy of Nacogdoches recalls that Tuesday was Stamp Day at her high school. Students could purchase savings stamps in denominations of 10 and 25 cents. These were pasted in individual booklets that when filled, were worth $18.75. The filled booklet could be exchanged for a defense (later war) bond that in ten years was worth $25.00. Those who consistently purchased stamps received a special certificate recognizing their achievement.[68]

The savings stamp-bond sales in schools were promoted by the U.S. Treasury Department. An advertising campaign featured Bugs Bunny cartoons urging young people to buy defense stamps and bonds. The Department also encouraged competition within and between schools to see which class or school sold the most stamps or had the highest percentage of purchasers. St. Anthony High School of Beaumont claimed a national record of sales of $152,000 in one major campaign. Although only $2 billion of the $131 billion in stamps and bonds were sold in the nation's schools, the campaign fostered a patriotic pride in the participants.[69]

Young people aided adults in a variety of conservation activities for the war effort. Thirty million children participated in the first full scale national scrap metal drive held in October 1941. In this effort, 1.5 million tons of scrap were collected. Subsequent drives involving the Junior Red Cross and the Boy Scouts collected old tires, newspapers and magazines, tin cans, household fats, tin foil, and flashlight batteries.[70]

Texas children found much of their entertainment and recreation geared to the war effort. Playing war games and collecting toy soldiers, common before the war, intensified. Even the noted expert on child care, Dr. Benjamin Spock, saw no connection between war toys for children and violence in adulthood. On their radios Texas boys and girls heard their heroes Jack Armstrong, Little Orphan Annie, the Green Hornet, and Captain Midnight fight the Axis on land and sea and in the air. Newspaper comic strips featured Steve Roper, Jane Arden, Dick Tracy, and Tarzan battling the enemy. An expanding array of comic books (60 different comic books in 1940; 168 by 1941) featuring Superman, Batman, Captain Marvel, and others supported the war against tyranny.[71]

By the latter part of the war, many Texas children were living in homes without the presence of an adult male. Although fathers were exempt from military conscription when the war began, the need for additional manpower forced Selective Service to remove the ban in October 1943. By April 1944 more than half of the inductees (52.8 percent) were fathers. By the end of the war one-fifth of all fathers aged 18-37 were in military service. Many children grew up without the presence of a father. Texas historian Bob Calvert, whose father volunteered for the Army Air Forces shortly after Pearl Harbor, remembered that he, his mother and infant brother moved from Palmer to Port Arthur to live with grandparents for the duration of the war. Like many other children Calvert missed his father and wished for his return.[72]

Texas young people, as well as adults, continued to take an interest in sports during the war. Although some schools suspended their junior high athletic programs and a few small schools dropped sports altogether, most Texas high schools continued to field football teams. The Austin High Maroons won the 1942 state championship with a 20-7 victory over Dallas Sunset. The following year the San Angelo Bobcats, with Milton Rathbone passing for three touchdowns, defeated the Lufkin Panthers 26-13 for the championship. The previous week the Bobcats had defeated Highland Park, led by Bobby Layne and Doak Walker, by 21-20, in one of the most exciting high school football games ever played in Texas. Lufkin had advanced to the state finals by defeating Goose Creek in a hard fought contest.[73]

In 1944 the Port Arthur Yellow Jackets, combining a stout defense with a solid offense, won the state football championship with a 20-0 victory over Highland Park.[74]

On the college level, the University of Texas Longhorns won the Southwest Conference in 1942 and 1943. The Longhorns defeated Georgia Tech in the Cotton Bowl on January 1, 1943, but the following year were tied 7-7 by the powerful Randolph Field team made of many college stars who were now in military service. That same year the Texas A&M team traveled to the Orange Bowl for a New Year's Day game but were defeated by Louisiana State University, 19-14. In 1944 Texas Christian, victors over Texas 7-6, won the conference but lost to Oklahoma A&M in the Cotton Bowl.[75]

While baseball's major professional leagues continued to play during World War II, the Texas League suspended its operations in February 1943. Attendance had been dropping even before Pearl Harbor, but League owners voted to continue play during 1942. Conscription of young players by the military led to a constant turnover in personnel in a season won by the Beaumont Exporters. Continued decline in attendance and a growing conviction that it was unpatriotic to use needed gasoline, food, and hotel rooms for sport in a national emergency led owners in late 1942 to vote 6-2 to suspend play for the duration of the war.[76]

Although it did not have the mass spectator appeal of football and baseball, professional golf attracted increasing interest among Texans during World War II. The state was home to outstanding professional male golfers such as Ben Hogan, Jimmie Demaret, Byron Nelson, and Lloyd Mangrum. During the last year of the war, 1945, Nelson, who as a hemophiliac was rejected for military service, set a record which still stands when he won 11 consecutive Professional Golf Association tour events. For his achievement Nelson was named Athlete of the Year in 1945 by the Associated Press.[77]

Texas also had the outstanding female golfer and Woman Athlete of the Year in 1945, Mildred "Babe" Didrikson Zaharias of Beaumont. Zaharias, who excelled in a variety of sports, won the Texas Woman's Open and the Western Open in 1945. She also played with men in the Los Angeles Open, the Phoenix Open and Tucson Open, finishing ahead of a number of male professional golfers. She also played in a number of charity matches with celebrities Bob Hope and Bing Crosby.[78]

Texans attended the movies in great numbers during the war. Many of the motion pictures had a war theme; one-third of the 1700 feature films made between 1942-1945 were inspired by the war or carried some patriotic message.

The 1942 Academy Award winner *Mrs. Miniver* told the story of a British middle class family that struggled through the 1940 bombing and the early days of the war. Featuring English actress Greer Garson (who later became a Texan) in the lead role, *Mrs. Miniver* played to full theaters across the state and swept the Academy Awards, taking four of the six major awards.[79]

The following year *Casablanca*, a movie set in wartime French North Africa, won the Academy Award for best picture. Paul Lukas was chosen best actor for his work in *Watch on the Rhine*, an anti-German film. That year three movies were released describing the American men and women who fought in defense of the Philippines: *Cry Havoc* and *So Proudly We Hail*, movies about Army nurses, and *Bataan*, with Robert Taylor battling the Japanese. These were followed by a series of war films, including *Air Force*, *Destroyer*, *Guadalcanal Diary*, *Thirty Seconds Over Tokyo*, *This Is The Army*, *Stage Door Canteen*, *The Purple Heart*, and *The Story of GI Joe*.[80]

One war movie, *We've Never Been Licked*, was filmed on the Texas A&M campus in 1943. The film depicted a young cadet (played by Richard Quine) who was falsely accused of being a Japanese agent. He was cashiered out of the Cadet Corps and went to Japan to broadcast anti-American propaganda. In reality he was waiting for a chance to aid a former classmate (Noah Berry, Jr.) in sinking a Japanese aircraft carrier. Five hundred A&M students, joined by 20 coeds from the Texas State College for Women, took part in the filming. According to A&M historian Henry C. Dethloff, the movie was a tremendous success, "at least among Aggies." It continues to be shown on campus and "is a vital and proud part of the Aggie tradition," says Dethloff.[81]

Not all movies made during the war had a military theme. By the later years of the war moviegoers were seeking something lighter. *Going My Way*, starring Bing Crosby as a happy-go-lucky Catholic priest, picked up four of the major Academy Awards for 1944. *Lassie Come Home*, *My Friend Flicka*, *Life with Father*, *Arsenic and Old Lace*, *My Sister Eileen*, *The More the Merrier*, and *A Tree Grows in Brooklyn* were movies popular with Texas audiences. And for the younger viewers the Saturday afternoon matinees featured Gene Autry, Charles Starett, Johnny Mack Brown, Tex Ritter, and Roy Rogers.[82]

Radio continued to be the major source of information and entertainment for most Americans. In a nationwide poll taken at the end of the war, 67 percent of the respondents put radio at the top of all media as doing the best job of serving the public during the war. Newspapers, ranked highest by 17 percent of the respondents, were second, followed by movies and magazines.[83]

Network commentators H. V. Kaltenborn, Raymond Graham Swing, and Gabriel Heatter continued to bring Americans up-to-date on world affairs every evening between 5:00 and 6:30 P.M. Overseas commentators Edward R. Murrow, Eric Severeid, Larry LaSueur, Cecil Brown, Richard Hottelet, and George Hicks described battle scenes for American listeners.[84]

Radio comedians combined pleasure and patriotism in many of their programs. Bob Hope, whose broadcasting career started in September 1938, became the most popular entertainer during the war. Beginning in January 1942,

Hope broadcast almost all of his shows from Army and Navy bases in the United States and overseas. Radio historian Gerd Horton points out Hope "became the commentator on life on military bases, a sounding board for soldier's disgruntlement, and a mediator between the civilian population and America's men and women in uniform."[85]

Jack Benny, Fred Allen, Fibber McGee and Molly, and Red Skelton were the other leading radio comedians during the war years. "The Guiding Light," "The Right to Happiness," "Young Dr. Malone," "Pepper Young's Family," "Ma Perkins," and "Stella Dallas" were the most popular daytime soap operas.[86]

Popular music reflected the mood of the nation, and Texas, at war. Kate Smith's rendition of Irving Berlin's "God Bless America," became a favorite early in the war and was often played before the beginning of baseball games, boxing and wrestling matches, and automobile races. The 1940 hit "Deep in the Heart of Texas" continued to be popular both at home and with Texas soldiers on the battle front. Sentimental songs such as "I Left My Heart at the Stage Door Canteen," "I'll Walk Alone," "I'll Never Smile Again," "Saturday Night Is The Loneliest Night of the Week," and "I'll Be Seeing You" reminded listeners of the separations caused by the war. Although most Texans had no memories of a white Christmas, Irving Berlin's "White Christmas" was one of the most popular songs in the Lone Star State during the war.[87]

Country and western music (sometimes referred to as "honky tonk" music) remained popular with Texans both at home and abroad. Gene Autry, movie and recording star from Tioga, Texas, enlisted in the Army Air Corps but continued to perform. His "Be Honest With Me," "Tears On My Pillow," and "Mail Call Today" were among his most popular wartime melodies. Ernest Tubb from Ellis County recorded his country favorite "Walking the Floor Over You" in 1941. Tex Ritter from Nederland made a series of western movies during the war that included such musical favorites as "There's A New Moon Over My Shoulder" and "Rye Whiskey." Bob Wills' 1940 hit "San Antonio Rose" continued to be a Texas favorite.[88]

Another pre-war song popular at Texas drive-ins and honky-tonks was the rowdy "Beer Barrel Polka." The song was equally popular with troops overseas, including those of our wartime allies. Paul Fussell, author of *Wartime: Understanding and Behavior in the Second World War*, believes "Beer Barrel Polka," or "Roll Out the Barrel" as many called it, was *the* Allied song of the war.[89]

Texans, like other Americans, found both entertainment and information in reading during the war years. Despite severe paper shortages, book and magazine sales increased appreciably. This was made possible by wartime prosperity, which gave citizens more spending money, and by the publication of paperback books. Paperbacks were introduced to American readers by the Pocket Books Company on the eve of war, 1939. Starting with ten titles, the program grew rapidly during the war. For 25 cents, readers could purchase the small, compact book at drug stores and newsstands.[90]

In 1941, Pocket Books sold over 10 million books; in 1942 20 million. Other publishers soon entered the field: Avon Books in 1941, Popular Library in 1942, Dell in 1943, and Bantam in 1945. These portable, inexpensive books were easy to carry and could be read on the bus or train, on break or at lunch, and almost anywhere the reader wished. They were easily mailed to relations, friends, or troops in stateside camps or overseas.[91]

One of the most popular books published in the war was Marion Hargrove's *See Here Private Hargrove*, which described the misadventures of a young civilian thrown into the Army. Readers at home and in service enjoyed the warmth and humor of this civilian's adjustment (and often misadjustment) to military life. By the end of the war more than 2.5 million copies had been sold. Also popular were Wendell L. Willke's *One World*, Ernie Pyle's *Brave Men* and *Here Is Your War*, William L. White's *They Were Expendable*, Lloyd C. Douglas' *The Robe*, Betty McDonald's *The Egg and I*, and Kathleen Winsor's *Forever Amber*.[92]

Texas colleges and universities were adversely affected by the war. The first Selective Service Act set 21 as the minimum age for conscription, but in 1942 the age was lowered to 18. This had a major impact upon Texas colleges. By late autumn of 1942, the enrollment at the University of Texas dropped from 11,627 students in 1941 to 8,794. An estimated 4,000 male students and over 100 faculty members had departed for military or government service. Enrollment at all-male Texas A&M declined from 6,679 students in 1941 to 2,215 in September 1943. By December 1944, only 1,893 students were enrolled, of whom 1,015 were below draft age. At North Texas State Teachers College, enrollment dropped from 2,505 in 1941 to 1,886 in 1944. Only 330 students in 1944 were male. Enrollment at Texas Tech declined from 4,246 in 1941 to 1,927 in 1944.[93]

Smaller schools were hit particularly hard. Lon Morris at Jacksonville, the state's oldest junior college, dropped from 239 students in 1939 to 82 students in 1942. Kilgore Junior College declined from 700 students in 1941 to 330 in 1944. Stephen F. Austin State Teachers College had 1,021 students in autumn 1941, but only 419 in autumn 1944.[94]

Most Texas colleges looked for ways to supplement their enrollment by adding military training programs. Texas A&M secured an Army Air Force preflight training program, an Army Specialized Training Program (ASTP) for engineers, and a program to train Navy and Marine personnel in radar and radio operation and maintenance. Six Texas schools, North Texas Agricultural College (later Arlington State), Rice Institute, Southern Methodist University, Texas Christian University, the University of Texas, and Southwestern University, had V-12 programs for training naval air cadets. Four Texas colleges, Stephen F. Austin State Teachers College, Texas State College for Women, East Texas State Teachers College, and Sul Ross State Teachers College, housed Army administration schools for the Women's Army Corps.[95]

The biggest controversy in Texas higher education during World War II was over the firing of University of Texas President Homer P. Rainey. Rainey, a native of Clarksville, was an ordained Baptist minister, veteran of World War I, and minor league baseball pitcher before receiving his master's and doctor's degrees at the University of Chicago. He served as president of Franklin College in Indiana and Bucknell University in Pennsylvania and director of the American Youth Commission of the American Education Council prior to being appointed president of the University of Texas in 1939.[96]

The composition of the Board of Regents changed dramatically after Rainey became president. As the terms of regents appointed by liberal Governor James V. Allred expired, Governor W. Lee O'Daniel and later Governor Coke R. Stevenson appointed conservatives to the board. Almost immediately the board disagreed with President Rainey on a number of issues. Led by Orville Bullington, Wichita Falls businessman and former Republican candidate for governor appointed by Governor O'Daniel, and D. Frank Strickland, an attorney and corporate lawyer from Mission appointed by Governor Stevenson, the board majority was convinced the University was overrun by politically subversive individuals who threatened the social, political, and economic structure of the state. They pressured Rainey to fire four tenured professors of economics who expressed liberal political views. When Rainey refused to do so, some board members were convinced that the president would have to go.[97]

For the next two years, the president and the board were at odds. Unable to get rid of tenured faculty members, the board fired three non-tenured economics instructors in 1942 and attempted to change the tenure policy at the University. The regents removed John Dos Passos' acclaimed novel *U.S.A.* from a supplementary reading list for sophomore English classes, charging the book was ob-

Homer P. Rainey, President, University of Texas
—Center for American History, UT-Austin

scene and subversive. Efforts were made by leaders of the Ex-Students Association, former board members, and University faculty to resolve some of the differences between the president and regents, but to no avail.[98]

The controversy continued to grow as regents leveled charges against President Rainey and various faculty members. On October 13, 1944, Rainey outlined his differences with the regents in a general faculty meeting, an action that further angered the board majority.[99]

The regents were now determined to get rid of Rainey. At their meeting in Houston on November 1, the board voted 6-1 to fire Rainey. Regent Marguerite S. Fairchild of Lukfin, who had first been appointed to the board by Governor Miriam Ferguson, was the only regent voting against dismissal. Chairman John Bickett abstained from voting.[100]

The firing of Rainey set off a firestorm of protest. University students went on strike, and 8,000 marched in mourning from the campus to the capitol carrying a black coffin labeled "Academic Freedom Is Dead." The Education Committee of the Texas Senate held hearings on the matter. During the hearings, Regent Bullington declared that Rainey had failed to take action against a "nest of homosexuals" at the University. Regent Strickland charged Rainey with protecting campus radicals and having radical opinions about race relations. Rainey and his supporters rebutted these allegations. Former board chairman J. R. Parten, a defender of Rainey, contended that the firing was the result of a conspiracy by conservative businessmen.[101]

The Rainey controversy continued throughout 1945. Governor Stevenson refused to become directly involved, but when three regents resigned and the terms of three others expired, the governor appointed new regents who made some amends by offering to rehire the fired economics instructors. They refused, however, to rehire Rainey. The American Association of University Professors censured the University, and the Southern Association of Colleges and Secondary Schools placed the University on probation for a year.

Memories of the Rainey controversy lingered on for years. Rainey himself was an unsuccessful candidate for governor in 1946, and many of the old charges and counter-charges were brought up again.[102]

Texas weather during the Second World War was sometimes as stormy as the Rainey affair. The year 1941 was the wettest ever recorded in the state. Statewide precipitation was 40.9 inches, almost 14 inches above normal. Unusually heavy rains in west Texas during May and June were partially responsible. A massive hurricane that crossed the Texas coast near Matagorda in late September brought additional moisture and damage exceeding $6 million. Another powerful hurricane with winds in excess of 100 miles per hour hit the middle Texas coast at Matagorda Bay in August 1942. Eight lives were lost and $26.5 million damage was caused by the storm. The following year in late July, a devastating hurricane with over 100-mile-per-hour wind ripped across the Bolivar Peninsula east of Galveston and moved into the Baytown-Houston area, taking 16 lives and destroying $16.6 million in property. The storm was accompanied by extremely heavy rain; nearly 18 inches falling at Port Arthur in 24 hours. Another hurricane hit Port O'Connor in August 1945, causing more than $20 million in damage. Wind gusts in the storm were estimated at 135 miles per hour.[103]

Texas had other bad weather during the war. An ice storm paralyzed Amarillo in April 1942. Another ice storm devastated East Texas in January 1944. Tornadoes hit Crowell (Foard County) in April 1942, Land Hill and Kilgore in May 1943, Freeport and Galveston in November 1944, and Brady in June 1945. Extremely high winds destroyed crops near Wichita Falls and Mexia in June 1945.[104]

Two serious medical epidemics occurred in Texas during the war. In summer 1943, 1,274 cases of poliomyelitis (infantile paralysis) were reported, the largest number in the history of the state. The epidemic was particularly bad in the Texas Panhandle. The threat abated slightly in the next two years but tragically worsened in the post war years.[105]

Influenza, the great killer in the closing days of World War I, made a reappearance in the Second World War but with less deadly results. In January 1944, 126,000 cases were reported in the United States; 24,000 in Texas. Fortunately, the majority of those afflicted eventually recovered.[106]

CHAPTER SIX

Politics, Race, and Prisoners of War

During the second world war the Federal government played a larger role in the lives of Texans than ever before. A host of new Federal agencies created as part of the war effort affected Texans on the home front in various ways. The most important of these were the War Production Board (WPB), the War Food Administration (WFA), the Petroleum Administration for War (PAW), and the Office of Price Administration and Civilian Supply (usually referred to simply as the Office of Price Administration, OPA).

The War Production Board, headed by former Sears, Roebuck executive Donald M. Nelson, was charged with coordinating the wartime economy, including setting production quotas, formulating production schedules, and allocating materials. The War Food Administration, directed originally by Chester Davis and later by former Texas congressman Marvin Jones, was assigned the task of allocating food for both the civilian and military population. Later the WFA was given the added responsibilities of storing food, transporting food to ports and loading on ships, and purchasing all Lend Lease and Allied food. The Petroleum Administration, headed by Secretary of Interior Harold Ickes, had control over all petroleum products. The Office of Price Adminstration and Civilian Supply, directed initially by New Deal economist Leon Henderson, was charged with regulating prices and wages and administering rationing plans for the nation. The operations of these and other agencies, such as the Office of War Information, the Office of Civilian Defense, and the Office of Transportation, frequently touched the lives of Texans.[1]

Many Texans felt the taxing power of the federal government for the first time. Prior to Pearl Harbor, only 4 million Americans had been required to file a federal income tax form. All those with incomes below $1,500 paid no income tax. Since the average wage in 1939 was $1,231, this meant most citizens were exempt. Those with incomes up to $4,000 were required to pay at a rate no higher than 4 percent, and those with dependents paid virtually nothing. The Revenue Act of 1942, providing $7 billion in new individual income taxes, changed that. The personal exemption was lowered from $1,500 to $624, bringing in an additional 13 million taxpayers. As incomes rose during the war, millions more became taxpayers. A new feature of the taxation scheme was the payroll withholding system, whereby taxes were deducted from paychecks throughout the year.[2]

To help pay for the increasing cost of the war, President Roosevelt asked Congress for an additional $10.5 billion in 1943. Congress, feeling pressure from constituents, balked, allocating only an additional $2.3 billion. Even so, the Revenue Act of 1943 increased the rates. By 1945 over 42 million Americans were paying income taxes at rates ranging from 6 to 94 percent.[3]

The new federal tax law brought in seven times as much money from Texans as before the war. In 1938 Texans paid slightly more than $145 million in Federal taxes; in 1944 they paid slightly more than one billion dollars in Federal taxes. The greatest portion of federal taxes paid by Texans was the tax on income; a little more than $800 million in 1944. The federal tax Texans paid on liquor, $16.8 million, was a distant second, and the tobacco excise tax, $117,700, third.[4]

As before the war, Texans continued to play major roles in the federal government. Sam Rayburn of Bonham began his long tenure as Speaker of the House of Representatives in 1940. Generally a supporter of the Roosevelt administration, Rayburn ran the House with firmness but fairness. On some issues, such as lowering the draft age to 18, he put his own personal objections aside and steered measures through a reluctant House. There would be no "dilly-dallying over important war legislation," he told his colleagues. However, like most Texans Rayburn opposed gasoline rationing and delayed its implementation as long as he could.[5]

Tom Connally, who became Texas' senior senator with the death of Morris Sheppard in 1941, gained power and stature as the war continued. Chairman of the Senate Foreign Relations Committee after Walter George resigned to chair the Senate Finance Committee in July 1941, Connally played an increasingly important role in national and international affairs, particularly in debates leading to the creation of the United Nations organization. In the closing days of the war, Connally served as a delegate to the San Francisco conference and helped write the United Nations charter.[6]

Although he supported the president on foreign policy matters, Connally was often a member of the Southern Democrat–Republican coalition opposed to Roosevelt domestic programs. In 1942 he took a leadership role in a ten day filibuster against repealing the poll tax. The following year, he was co-author of the Smith-Connally bill, which gave the president authority to seize strike-bound war plants. The measure also imposed a 30-day cooling off period for strikes, established criminal penalties for leaders of illegal strikes, required majority approval of union members before a strike, and forbade union contributions to political campaigns during wartime. President Roosevelt, opposed to the measure restricting union contributions, vetoed the bill but Congress overrode the veto and the measure became law.[7]

Connally's Texas colleague in the wartime Senate was the popular, but largely ineffective, former governor of the state, W. Lee O'Daniel. Elected to fill the vacancy caused by the death of Senator Sheppard in 1941, O'Daniel shocked fellow senators with his disdain for senatorial custom by delivering his maiden speech on his second day in office. In this address, the former flour salesman and entertainer announced his objection to a bill extending Selective Service, which was scheduled to expire later that year. When the extension bill was passed, O'Daniel was the only Texas congressman to vote against the measure.[8]

During his first year in office, Senator O'Daniel introduced several antilabor bills but all were rejected by large majorities. Even so, he continued to be popular with many Texans, particularly elderly, rural, and low income voters, who regarded him as a sincere, honest businessman fighting professional politicians. In summer 1942, he won the Democratic nomination (which in the first half of the 20th century was tantamount to election in the Solid South) for a full six-year term as senator, defeating two former Texas governors, James V. Allred and Dan Moody.[9]

In the senatorial campaign, O'Daniel declared that rationing was unneces-

Senator W. Lee O'Daniel
—UT Institute of Texan Cultures at San Antonio

sary and merely an attempt to further regulate the lives of Americans. Although he opposed the Roosevelt domestic program, he asserted his support for the war effort and reminded voters that his oldest son was in military service. He charged that his two opponents, whom he referred to as "the Gold Dust Twins," were backed by "Communist labor leader racketeers." Although he was opposed by many Texas newspapers and a number of leading businessmen who believed his attacks on the administration cost the state government contracts, O'Daniel led in the first Democratic primary, receiving 475,541 votes. Allred with 327,501 votes was second and Moody, with 178,471, was third. Allred, who had the support of the Roosevelt administration, and Moody, backed by urban conservatives, did well in the large cities, but O'Daniel swept the rural areas, carrying 220 of the state's 254 counties.[10]

In the August runoff, Moody endorsed Allred. Although this allowed Allred to cut O'Daniel's margin of victory, O'Daniel was renominated, receiving 451,359 votes to 433,203 for Allred. Allred led in the state's 15 largest cities and picked up heavy support from younger voters. Once again O'Daniel was supported by older voters, especially in rural East Texas. With his victory in the Democratic primary, O'Daniel was assured a full six-year term in the Senate, as the Republican Party at that time was no serious threat to continued Democratic dominance.[11]

O'Daniel spent the next two years criticizing the Roosevelt administration and attempting to prevent Roosevelt's re-election in 1944. He had the support of many of the state's business leaders opposed to the Roosevelt New Deal. These Texas conservatives had been disappointed when the president was elected to a third term in 1940. They were particularly unhappy that liberal Henry A. Wallace became Vice President succeeding Texan John Nance Garner, the friend of oil and gas interests.[12]

Texas conservatives, especially independent oil men such as Hugh Roy Cullen, E. B. Germany, Al Buchanan, and Arch Rowan, were unhappy with wartime regulations and price controls, which they believed stifled business and industrial development. They disliked the president's executive orders directing an end to discrimination in war industries and creating the Federal Employment Practices Commission. They hoped to capitalize upon resentment in the state toward the Federal Supreme Court, which in the 1944 Smith v. Allwright decision declared unconstitutional a Texas law preventing African Americans from participating in the Democratic primary.[13]

In their efforts to block Roosevelt's re-election in 1944, Texas conservatives attempted to gain control of the state Democratic convention and select independent presidential electors. When this failed, they left the Democratic Party and formed a third party, the Texas Regulars. In this manner they hoped to pull off enough Democratic votes to keep Roosevelt from carrying Texas and throw the election into the House of Representatives.[14]

The Texas Regulars adopted a platform that called for the return of states' rights, which they alleged had been destroyed by the Communist-controlled New Deal; the restoration of the Bill of Rights, which had been replaced by rule by regimentation; the restoration of government of law instead of government by bureaucracy, and protection of honest labor union from foreign-born racketeers. The platform also demanded the restoration of the supremacy of the white race, which the Regulars claimed had been destroyed by the Roosevelt administration.

The white supremacy issue was a relatively new concern for O'Daniel and other ultraconservatives. "They were responding," writes historian George Green, "to the civil rights movement which seemed to be making inroads in politics and education."[15]

With Senator O'Daniel as their leading spokesman, Texas Regulars conducted a vigorous 1944 campaign. Ignoring Democratic Governor Coke Stevenson, the conservative rancher-banker who was seeking his second full term in office, Texas Regulars aimed their attacks at Roosevelt and the New Deal. They were unsuccessful in every instance. Sam Rayburn, Wright Patman, and Lyndon B. Johnson, three of the Roosevelt loyalists in Texas, were easily re-elected to their seats in Congress. At the same time, two anti-New Deal congressmen from Texas were replaced. King Ranch executive Richard M. Kleberg, a 12-year congressional veteran and critic of the New Deal, was defeated by John E. Lyle, Jr., a Corpus Christ lawyer who was serving as an artillery officer with the Army in Germany. Martin Dies, Jr., veteran Southeast Texas con-

LBJ campaigning for U.S. Senate, 1941.
—UT Institute of Texan Cultures at San Antonio

gressman and opponent of the administration, was so unpopular in his home district that he announced his retirement. He was replaced by Jesse M. Combs of Beaumont, judge of the Ninth Court of Appeals.[16]

Conservative defeats in the primary elections showed that most Texans were content with the administration's conduct of the war. However, Texas Regulars continued to spend money on newspaper advertisements and radio broadcasts criticizing the president. O'Daniel made over 20 broadcasts and numerous public appearances in which he continued his attack on the administration. Some efforts were made to collaborate with state Republicans, but with little success. Though comparatively few in number, Texas Republicans wanted to maintain their party identity, and Texas Regulars would not pledge their support for the Republican nominee Thomas E. Dewey, who represented the moderate wing of the Republican Party.[17]

In November Roosevelt, with Missouri Senator Harry S. Truman as his vice presidential running mate, carried the state with 821,605 votes. Dewey received 191,425 votes; the Texas Regulars, with unpledged electors, 135,439 votes. While the Republicans and Texas Regulars ran well in the silk-stocking districts of the large cities and in the German counties, Roosevelt had strong support elsewhere in the state. Roosevelt's victory demonstrated that Texans had no desire to make a change. Many probably felt like Mary Shadock, a worker in the B-24 assembly plant in Fort Worth who remembers that Roosevelt was a "very good president; we need another like him" or B. B. Majors, an Army private from Liberty County with American forces in Burma, who believed "Roosevelt was the best president we ever had."[18]

The 1944 campaign was a decisive point in O'Daniel's career. He had lost his influence over Texas voters and had none among his senate colleagues. He continued to criticize the administration and to wail at professional politicians, labor racketeers, and Communists, but no one seemed to listen. His approval rate among Texas voters dropped to less than ten percent. When his six-year term came to an end in 1948 he announced he would not seek reelection.[19]

There was little change among Texas membership in the House of Representatives during the war. All but one of the 21 Texans serving in the House when the war began were re-elected in 1942. Charles L. South from Coleman, who had voted against the 1939 naval expansion bill and against arming merchant ships, was defeated in the Democratic primary, losing to O. Clark Fisher of San Angelo, former state legislator and Tom Green county attorney. As noted above, in 1944 Richard Kleberg was defeated in his bid for re-election, and Martin Dies, Jr., chose not to run again; all other Texas congressmen were renominated and re-elected.[20]

Two Texas House members, Lyndon B. Johnson of Johnson City and Francis Eugene Worley of Shamrock, took leaves of absence for service in the Navy in 1941. They returned to their political duties when President Roosevelt issued a directive ordering congressmen in the armed forces to return to Congress.

Johnson's seven month tour of duty as a lieutenant commander later became an issue when he ran for higher office. A member of the House Naval Affairs Committee, Johnson secured a naval reserve commission in spring 1940. Two days after Pearl Harbor, he went on active duty. Because he had no training for combat, the Navy would not assign him to sea duty. After brief service in the office of the Under Secretary of Navy, Johnson was sent on a fact-finding mission to the Southwest Pacific by President Roosevelt. He traveled to Australia where he met, and was impressed by, General Douglas MacArthur. At his request to see action, Johnson was allowed to fly on a B-26 bomber on a raid of a Japanese base on New Guinea. The plane encountered heavy enemy fire and the pilot turned back before completing this mission. Several other American planes on the mission were shot down.[21]

When Johnson, who performed no duties on the flight but was merely an observer, returned to MacArthur's headquarters he was awarded the Silver Star. He was the only one on his plane to receive a medal. Johnson was self-conscious about the award and upon return to the States gave the impression that he had refused the medal. However, he wore the medal in a number of public appearances. Later he began wearing a small silver bar with a star emblematic of the award. His biographer, Robert Caro, notes "he wore it on his lapel for the rest of his life."[22]

Back in Congress from active duty, Johnson was one of the president's most loyal supporters. Unlike many of his Texas colleagues, he endorsed rationing and price controls as necessary wartime measures. He supported the president's request for an additional $10.5 billion in new taxes in 1943 and voted against the smaller $2.3 billion substitute. When Roosevelt vetoed the congressional substitute, Johnson was one of 95 House members who voted to sustain the veto. Deeply concerned over absenteeism and labor strikes and indebted to construction magnate Herman Brown for financial support, Johnson did vote with the majority to override the president's veto of the Smith-Connally Labor Act.[23]

Wright Patman, long time congressman from Texarkana, was the only other Texan to vote with Johnson to uphold the president's veto of the revenue bill. But like Johnson and every other Texas congressman, Patman voted to override the veto of the Smith-Connally Act. A staunch supporter of local businesses independent of chain stores, Patman played a major role in securing passage of the bill creating the Small War Plants Corporation, an agency designed to assist small businesses convert to war production. At the same time, he was highly successful in securing military bases and ammunition plants for his northeast Texas district.[24]

Texans such as Patman held key positions in the wartime Congress. Hatton W. Sumners of Dallas, first elected to Congress the same year as Speaker Rayburn (1912), continued to serve as chairman of the powerful Judiciary Committee. Joseph J. Mansfield, first elected in 1916, chaired the River and Harbors Committee which was extremely important to Texas with its many waterways. Fritz Lanham of Fort Worth, son of a former Texas governor and a House member since 1919, was the author of the National Housing for

Defense Act and the Community Facilities Act and chair of the Committee on Public Buildings and Grounds. Luther A. Johnson of Corsicana was the second ranking member of the House Foreign Affairs Committee. Ewing Thomason, former mayor of El Paso who entered Congress in 1931, was the second ranking majority member of the House Armed Services Committee. Richard M. Kleberg, manager and part owner of the giant King Ranch, came to Congress the same year as Thomason. Known as the "Cowboy Congressman," Kleberg was a senior member of the Agriculture Committee. Like many other Texas congressmen he supported the New Deal at one time but came to oppose some of Roosevelt's wartime measures, particularly price controls on beef. As noted earlier, he was defeated in 1944.[25]

Martin Dies, Jr., of Orange became a member of the House of Representatives the same year as Thomason and Kleberg. Son of a former congressman, Dies also supported the New Deal in its early days but became increasingly conservative in the late 1930s. In 1938 he was named chairman of a new Select Committee on Un-American Activities. The committee was set up initially because of concern over the German-American Bund, but under Dies' leadership it turned to investigate what the chairman believed was the widespread Communist penetration of the Roosevelt administration. Soon the committee was employing tactics that would later be used by Joseph McCarthy in the Cold War hunt for Communists. Allegations of wrong-doing were released to the press with little evidence to support them. Witnesses before the committee were intimidated, harassed, and charged with various offenses with little opportunity to defend themselves. Educational institutions, labor unions, and minorities were particular targets of the Dies committee.[26]

The public eventually tired of Dies and his committee. In 1944 labor leaders in his home county organized a drive to oust him. At the same time, businessmen concluded that Dies had become an embarrassment and was hurting the district. Dies accepted the inevitable and announced his retirement.[27]

Several Texans played key roles in the Roosevelt administration during World War II. None was more powerful that Houston businessman Jesse H. Jones. After a highly successful career in real estate and banking Jones was appointed to the board of the Reconstruction Finance Corporation by President Herbert Hoover on the recommendation of House Speaker John Nance Garner. When Roosevelt became president in 1933 he asked Jones to serve as chairman of the Reconstruction Finance Corporation (RFC). As head of the RFC, and later the Federal Loan Agency, Jones directed millions of dollars in loans to banks, building and loan associations, railroads, and agricultural corporations.[28]

In 1940, as a concession to conservative Democrats displeased with the selection of Henry A. Wallace as the party's vice presidential nominee, Roosevelt appointed Jones Secretary of Commerce. With the approval of Congress, Jones retained his position as Federal Loan Administrator, an office that supervised 30 agencies receiving federal money. Jones' relationship with the president gradually deteriorated during the war. In January 1945, Jones was replaced as

Secretary of Commerce by Henry A. Wallace, a concession this time to party liberals. Jones was offered other positions in the government but declined.[29]

Three other Texans, Tom Clark of Dallas, Robert A. Lovett of Huntsville, and Alvin J. Wirtz of Seguin and Austin, served as assistant cabinet officers in the Roosevelt administration. Clark, a former district attorney, joined the administration in 1937 as an assistant to the Attorney General. He became chief of the Justice Department's West Coast office in 1940. In his position he coordinated and directed the relocation and incarceration of Japanese Americans in 1942, an action he later admitted was a mistake. In 1943, he was named Assistant Attorney General in charge of the department's anti-trust and criminal divisions.[30]

Robert A. Lovett, Yale graduate and World War I pilot, was a successful banker in the inner-war years. As noted earlier in Chapter Four, in 1941 Lovett became Assistant Secretary of War for Air, a post he held throughout the war. In this position he played a key role in revising pilot training and developing new aircraft for the Army Air Forces.[31]

Alvin Jacob Wirtz, former state senator and organizer of the Lower Colorado River Authority, was a staunch supporter of the New Deal and close friend of Lyndon Johnson. He served as Undersecretary of the Interior from January 1940 to May 1941. He resigned at that time to help run Lyndon Johnson's unsuccessful 1941 senatorial campaign. Soon thereafter, he returned to Washington where he served as a consultant to the Secretary of Interior on power matters.[32]

J. R. Parten, a highly successful independent oil man from Madisonville, former chairman of the University of Texas Board of Regents, and a loyal supporter of Franklin D. Roosevelt, served as Director of the Transportation Division of the Office of Petroleum Administration for War. In this role he was responsible for seeing that crude and refined oil were delivered from the Southwest to the East Coast. He managed the construction of the Big Inch and Little Big Inch pipelines from Texas to New Jersey and New York. In the closing days of the war, Parten was appointed chief of staff of the American delegation to the Allied War Reparations Committee.[33]

Former Texas congressman Maury Maverick of San Antonio was another Texan who served in Washington during the war. In September 1941 he was made assistant to his old friend Leon Henderson, who headed the new Office of Price Administration and Supply. Soon thereafter Maverick was named chief of the War Production Board's Bureau of Government Requirements, the office responsible for screening requests made by Allied governments for materials and equipment. In this capacity he recommended organizing scientific research laboratories in a cooperative program to meet problems of material shortages. This recommendation led to the creation of the Office of Production Research and Development.[34]

In December 1943, Maverick was appointed chairman of the Smaller War Plants Corporation, the agency set up to assist small businesses obtain war contracts. Maverick was the third, and most successful, chairman of the SWPC.

Described by one historian as "a human dynamo with a sparkling personality," Maverick brought zeal and enthusiasm to office. He worked closely with fellow Texan Congressman Wright Patman in an effort to divert more government business to small operators. It was during this period that Maverick struck a blow for clear word usage when in a memorandum to SWPC employees he urged them to write in plain English and "stay off gobbledygook language."[35]

As mentioned earlier, another Texas congressman, Marvin Jones, served as War Food Administrator during the last two years of the war. A long time champion of the American farmer, Jones was a member of the House Agriculture Committee for nearly 20 years (chairman the last ten) before resigning in 1940 to take a judgeship on the U.S. Court of Claims. At President Roosevelt's request, he took a leave of absence from the court in June 1943 to serve as War Food Administrator. Jones took a difficult task but met production goals and at the same time kept morale high among American farmers.[36]

While most Texas leaders in Washington, with the exception of Senator O'Daniel and Jesse Jones, continued to support Roosevelt, state government was in the hands of conservatives who opposed the president. Lieutenant Governor Coke R. Stevenson, a pipe-smoking banker-lawyer-rancher from Junction, became governor when W. Lee O'Daniel resigned to become U.S. Senator. A quiet, soft-spoken individual whom newsmen called "Calculatin' Coke," Stevenson served as county attorney and county judge before election to the Texas house of representatives in 1928. He was house speaker from 1933 to 1937, the first individual to hold that post two successive terms. He was elected lieutenant governor in 1938 and reelected in 1940.[37]

As governor during World War II, Stevenson followed a cautious path. A staunch fiscal conservative, he ignored pleas for additional moneys for state services. Because of the increased state revenues accompanying wartime prosperity and tight budgeting by state agencies, Texas eliminated an $18 million deficit in general funds and had a surplus when the war ended. To avoid additional spending, Stevenson refused to call special sessions of the Legislature and supported a pay-as-you-go amendment to the state constitution.[38]

Stevenson's laid back style and reluctance to deal with controversial matters won him much support from wartime Texans. Like many of them, Stevenson saw no need for gasoline rationing nor the numerous regulations and directives coming from Washington. Historian Robert Caro believes that Stevenson's personality "was the embodiment of what Texans like to think of as 'Texian.'" In 1942 Stevenson easily defeated four opponents in the Democratic gubernatorial primary, receiving 650,000 of the 950,000 votes cast. In the general election that autumn he polled 180,735 votes compared to only 9,204 for his Republican opponent, C. K. McDowell of Sulphur Springs. Two years later, liberal Democrats tried to persuade popular attorney general Gerald Mann, a former Southern Methodist University football star, to run against Stevenson, but Mann declined. An effort was then made to enlist Texas folklorist J. Frank Dobie to run, but he, too, declined. Eventually, eight opponents, including suffragist Minnie Fisher Cunningham, entered the

Governor Coke R. Stevenson
—UT Institute of Texan Cultures at San Antonio

Democratic primary. Stevenson was re-elected by an even greater margin, receiving 700,000 of the 823,460 votes cast. Later that year Stevenson polled over one million votes in the general election (nearly 20,000 more than President Roosevelt). His Republican opponent, B. J. Peasley of Tyler, received 100,287 votes.[39]

Stevenson's policies were as conservative as those of his predecessor, W. Lee O'Daniel. Indeed, political scientist Fred Gantt, Jr., in his study *The Chief Executive in Texas* lists O'Daniel and Stevenson as the most conservative Texas governors during the first 60 years of the 20th century. While slightly more friendly to organized labor than O'Daniel, Stevenson allowed a bill forbidding union contributions to politicians and political parties to become law without his signature.[40]

As pointed out earlier, Stevenson showed some concern about discrimination against Mexican Texans. When the legislature passed a resolution assuring all Caucasians equal rights, Stevenson issued a proclamation directing Texans to adhere to a policy of non-discrimination for all Caucasians. He created a Texas Good Neighbor Commission and traveled to Mexico City for discussion with political leaders concerning treatment of Mexican Texans.[41]

Employment opportunities in Texas for Mexican Americans increased during World War II but generally for less pay than Anglos and as common or unskilled labor. At Kelly Field in San Antonio, for example, none of the 10,000 Mexican American workers held a position above laborer or mechanic's helper. The Federal Employment Practices Commission in the Southwest region, directed by Carlos E. Castañeda and Leonard M. Brin, made efforts to end discriminatory practices but encountered resistance. Although modest gains toward equality were made in some refineries in the Houston area, historian Emilio Zamora concluded that the "FEPC did not make an appreciable impact." Discrimination against Mexican American workers continued throughout the war.[42]

Although the League of United Latin American Citizens (LULAC) won several court cases before the war on the issue of segregation, some school districts continued to separate Mexican and Anglo children. Restaurants and cafes were often closed to Mexican Texans in spite of the governor's proclamation. One incident, in which several Texas Latinos, accompanied by the Mexican consul from Houston, were denied service at the Blue Moon Café in Wharton County, resulted in a letter of protest to Governor Stevenson. Such incidents led the Mexican government to keep Texas from participating in the *bracero* program until after the war.[43]

In contrast to farmers seeking additional Mexican workers, many Texas business and industrial firms refused to hire African American workers until late in the war. In Houston, black workers trained at the government-sponsored Negro Training School had difficulty finding employment in the city's large shipbuilding firms. Managers at the Brown Shipyards and the Houston Shipyards were reluctant to hire African Americans because they feared such employment would anger white workers. Most of the African Americans who were hired performed unskilled work and had little opportunity for advancement. Historian Ernest Obadele-Starks points out that "intimidation and threats awaited blacks" who protested discriminatory practices. Some yards, such as Lexington in Orange, refused to hire blacks. Consolidated Shipbuilding in the same town hired blacks but had to keep them separate from white workers.[44]

African Americans were employed in oil refineries but almost always in a non-skilled capacity. In at least one instance, at the Magnolia Oil Refinery in Beaumont, African Americans lost ground. Following a new contract agreement with locals of the Oil Workers International Union in 1943, the company removed all black workers from skilled and non-skilled jobs and put them in a service department as common laborers. African Americans who had been pipefitters and boilermakers "now found themselves digging ditches."[45]

Under prodding from the Dallas Negro Chamber of Commerce, the North American Aviation and Consolidated-Vultee (Convair) plants in the Fort Worth-Dallas area began hiring African Americans late in the war. The number remained small. By June 1944 only 827 African Americans were among the 20,000 workers at Consolidated. Of these only 130 were in skilled or semi-skilled positions.[46]

While Governor Stevenson appeared to have some concern over the discrimination against Mexican Americans, he displayed little interest in the status of African Americans. In July 1942 Willie Vinson, a black Texarkanan accused of raping a white woman, was dragged to a cotton gin by white vigilantes and hanged. When U.S. Attorney General Francis Biddle registered concern over the affair, Stevenson responded that members of the Negro race sometimes furnished the occasion for mob violence by committing outrageous crimes. He added that even a white man would have been lynched for such an offense.[47]

Both Governor Stevenson and Lieutenant Governor John Lee Smith were out of the state when a race riot occurred in Beaumont in June 1943. The riot was touched off when a white woman charged she had been raped by a black man. Tensions in the city had been growing for some time. The expansion of shipbuilding at the Pennsylvania yards and the local oil refinery brought thousands of newcomers to the city. Inadequate housing, transportation problems, and shortages of consumer goods contributed to unrest. In 1942 several incidents occurred involving black passengers in white sections of city buses because of overflow from the Jim Crow sections. Then, in early June 1943, the beating and raping of a young white telephone operator brought tensions to a peak. They eased only slightly when the alleged rapist died from gunshot wounds received when he attempted to flee the scene.[48]

On the afternoon of June 15, a white woman reported to the Beaumont police that she had been raped by a black man. Although she could provide only a vague description of the attacker, the police made a fruitless search of the scene for the rapist. As word of the assault spread, about 2,000 shipyard workers left their jobs and marched on city hall demanding action. When the woman could not identify the rapist among the blacks held in jail, the mob, now numbering over 4,000, began moving through the African American districts of Beaumont. Hundreds of African Americans were assaulted and beaten, homes, stores, and restaurants were broken into, and automobiles and buildings were set afire. Possibly 300 to 400 blacks were injured. One African American, John Johnson, died from gunshot wounds. Another black man, Alex Mouton, was severely clubbed and died several months later. A white carpenter, Ellis C. Brown, was found dead with a crushed skull. Police speculated that he had been killed by blacks.[49]

The Beaumont police chief, Ross Dicky, and the county sheriff, W. W. Richardson, called out all available lawmen who began arresting rioters. Four companies of the 18th Battalion of the Texas State Guard, commanded by Major Fred C. Stone, a local architect, were also called out. Later than night, A. M. Aikin, Jr., president pro tempore of the Texas Senate, who was acting governor while Governor Stevenson and Lieutenant Governor Smith were out of the state, ordered additional units of the Texas State Guard to the city.[50]

The major rioting ended about daybreak on June 16. Later that day Acting Governor Aikin declared martial law in Beaumont to avoid any further violence. By nightfall, approximately 2,400 lawmen, including Texas State guardsmen, city police, state patrolmen, Texas Rangers, and sheriff's deputies, occupied the city. Liquor stores, many restaurants and hotels, downtown stores, and city parks and swimming pools were closed. Greyhound buses were diverted around the city, which was declared off limits to military personnel.[51]

Beaumont remained under martial law the next four days while authorities took steps to bring life back to normal. During this period, Lieutenant Colonel Royal G. Phillips of the Texas Department of Public Safety heard the cases of 206 individuals who had been taken into custody during the riot. All but 29 were released for lack of evidence. Those retained were charged with minor offenses such as loitering, drunkenness and carrying firearms and turned over to civil authorities. After paying fines of $25 plus court costs, these individuals were released. No serious effort was made to find the murderers of the three men killed. Nor was the alleged rapist found. Dr. Banker D. Chunn, a respected Beaumont physician who examined the woman who claimed she had been raped, reported there had been no rape nor had the woman had sexual relations during the previous 24 hours.[52]

There were fears that the violence that occurred in Beaumont might spread elsewhere in the state. There were other riots that summer in Los Angeles, Mobile, Detroit, and New York City, but the only other racial altercation in Texas occurred at El Paso's Fort Bliss, where African American troops retaliated against some white soldiers who had earlier attacked black troops.[53]

Many African American troops stationed in Texas experienced rigid segregation for the first time. This was particularly painful for soldiers from northern states like Jim Williams, who was attending an Officer Candidate School at Camp Barkeley. When he went into nearby Abilene, the local sheriff told him to "get on the other side of town." At the camp post exchange, the waitresses served all the white soldiers before they served him. When he complained, he was confined to barracks for a week.[54]

Jackie Robinson, later to become a famous baseball star, encountered prejudice and discrimination while serving at Camp Hood in central Texas. A star athlete at UCLA in the late 1930s, Robinson was drafted in 1942. He completed officer candidate school at Fort Riley, Kansas and was commissioned second lieutenant. In early 1944 he was assigned as a platoon commander in the 761st Tank Battalion. The battalion, an all black unit except for some white officers, was completing advanced armored training prior to overseas deployment. In July Lieutenant Robinson became embroiled in a dispute while riding a local bus. Robinson took a seat in the middle of the bus rather than going to the section at the back of the bus reserved for African Americans. The bus driver ordered Robinson to the rear. When he refused, the driver called the military police who took Robinson into custody. Brought before the assistant provost marshal, Robinson found himself subjected to abusive language and epithets. When he attempted to respond, he was charged with being disrespectful and refusing to obey an order. When his battalion commander, Lieutenant Colonel Paul L. Bates, refused to endorse the charges, Robinson was transferred to another battalion where the charges were approved.[55]

Robinson's court martial opened on August 2, 1944. The trial lasted several days with witnesses testifying as to the events that occurred. After due deliberation, the court acquitted Robinson of all charges. He returned to duty at Camp Hood but the 761st Battalion had already departed for overseas duty. Robinson was transferred to Camp Breckinridge, Kentucky, where in late November 1944 he was given an honorable discharge and separated from service by reason of "physical disqualification."[56]

The difficulties faced by Robinson were encountered by many African American soldiers. Philip Latimer from Detroit, Texas, one of the white officers in the 761st Tank Battalion, remembers that black troops "were constantly mistreated and verbally abused by some elements of the civilian population." "It is remarkable that they could continue to train diligently," noted Latimer.[57]

Latimer, Colonel Bates, and the other white officers of the 761st Battalion treated their men with dignity and respect. Such was not always the case in other units. John T. Ferguson, an African American from Fort Worth, remembers that most of his white officers were good men "but we always had one or two bad ones." Some white officers, not pleased to be assigned to an African American outfit, abused their rank and insulted their men. Occasionally they were so mean the soldiers took revenge. Ferguson cites one instance where African American troops backed over an abusive officer with a tractor.[58]

African American women in the military were also subjected to abuse. Constance E. Nelson, a black WAC from Texas, complained to the *Houston Informer*, an African American newspaper, that white civilians at Camp Forrest, Tennessee, were particularly abusive. She reported that a white civilian slapped a black WAC and then attempted to pour hot grease over her. Punishment for the white man was two days off with pay and a return to his job at camp.[59]

At some camps African Americans were treated with respect. Black bombardier cadets at Midland Field ate in the same mess as the white cadets. The black cadets at Midland had a separate club, but it was equal to the white cadet club. Black officers utilized the same officers' club as did whites and were apparently treated well. At Hondo Field black navigator cadets lived in their own barracks but ate in the same mess as the white cadets. The black navigators enjoyed equal access to the Cadet Club, the Cadet PX, and the Cadet Day Room. Black officers had the use of the officers' club and the bachelor officers' mess. At Sheppard Field near Wichita Falls, the base commander was particularly receptive to black airmen. Under his command base officials worked to assign each man to the job for which he was best qualified.[60]

While Mexican Texans and African Texans struggled with years of discrimination, many of the 458 Texans of Japanese ancestry experienced a form of prejudice born out of the attack on Pearl Harbor. Although these Japanese Texans were not forced to relocation centers such as were West Coast Japanese, they were subjected to various forms of intimidation and harassment. FBI agents searched the homes and interrogated members of Japanese families in the state. During such raids, agents seized any suspicious items such as cameras, binoculars, and shortwave radios. Anything written in Japanese was suspect. On some occasions, family members were taken to police headquarters for further questioning. Fukutaro Akagi, a 63-year-old farmer from Sheldon in north Harris County, was held for three months after government agents found an old crystal radio receiver that had belonged to his sons when they were children. Akagi was finally released after neighbors signed affidavits testifying as to his patriotism.[61]

In most instances, Japanese Texans were not held as long as Mr. Akagi. In Orange County, Kitimatsu Kishi, head of a pioneering family of Japanese rice farmers, was released after a brief hearing. His son, Taro, a Texas A&M graduate who was working for a Japanese shipping firm in New York City, was interned briefly but then allowed to return to Texas. Another Japanese Texan, Ken Nagai, who lived near the Kishi family, remembered that the war had little effect upon him. He continued working for the Texas highway department until he entered military service in late 1944. "I was never bothered one way or another," he recalled.[62]

Japanese businessmen were often required to close their shops or at least change their names. The Japanese Restaurant in Houston, established forty years earlier, became the U.S. Café. Another Houston eatery, the Japan Café, was renamed Kay's Café after its owner K. Yoshida. In nearby Genoa, Saburo Avai's Japanese Nursery was closed for a month. When it reopened the word "Japanese" was removed. Hideo Muta, a Dallas resident for 42 years, was forced to close his Oriental Art Company but was allowed to reopen after 200 Dallas citizens signed a petition on his behalf.[63]

The Jingu family of San Antonio was less fortunate. The family had lived in and operated a Japanese Tea Garden on city land at Brackenridge Park for over 20 years. Several weeks after Pearl Harbor city officials forced Alice Jingu, whose husband Kim had died four years earlier, and her five children to leave the Tea Garden. The Jingus were replaced by a Chinese couple and the site renamed the Chinese Tea Garden (later changed to Sunken Garden).[64]

Mrs. Jingu and her children had trouble finding a place to live as local citizens were reluctant to rent to Japanese. Finally, through the efforts of their church, Travis Park Methodist, a residence was obtained. The children found enough work to sustain the family. The oldest son, James, who had been a student at the University of Texas when the war began, volunteered for military service. He subsequently served with the all-Japanese 442nd Regimental Combat Team in Italy, where he was wounded and received a Purple Heart.[65]

The Jingu family moved to California in 1948. In 1984 the tea garden was rededicated as the Japanese Tea Garden in a ceremony attended by family members and representatives of the Japanese government. The family has been unsuccessful in efforts to regain control of what had been their home.[66]

During the first year of the war Japanese Americans were not accepted for military service. Japanese men of military age were classified by Selective Service as "4-C," a special category for individuals unacceptable for military service because of ancestry. Most Japanese already in military service were either discharged or assigned non-combat duties.[67]

Frank "Foo" Fujita, a Japanese American of Abilene, Texas, was an exception to the rule. Fujita joined the Texas National Guard before the war. A member of the 2nd Battalion, 131st Field Artillery, Sergeant Fujita was on a troop ship in the Pacific when the attack on Pearl Harbor occurred. Along with other members of the battalion he was captured in the Dutch East Indies and spent three years as a prisoner of the Japanese.[68]

Mutsuo Kawamura was another Japanese Texan who served in the Army during 1942. The son of a Japanese Rio Grande valley farmer, Kawamura attempted to enlist in his home town of San Benito just after Pearl Harbor but was turned down. He traveled to San Antonio, where Army recruiters accepted him for military service in spite of current policy not to induct Japanese Americans. He later served with the 442nd Regimental Combat Team, the all-Nisei (American-born Japanese) unit that distinguished itself in combat in Europe.[69]

In January 1943 the U.S. War Department reversed its policy toward Japanese Americans and began accepting them, both as volunteers and draftees. Benjamin Franklin (Benny) Ogata of Dallas and Saburo Tanamachi of the Rio Grande valley were among Japanese Texans who entered service under the new policy. Both died while serving with the 442nd Regimental Combat Team. Ogata was killed in late summer 1944 in combat south of Leghorn, Italy. Tanamachi, a platoon leader, was killed in heavy fighting in eastern France two months later. Recipient of the Silver Star, Tanamachi was one of the first two Japanese Americans buried in Arlington National Cemetery.[70]

Although Benny Ogata, Saburo Tanamachi, and other members of the 442nd Regimental Combat Team demonstrated that most Japanese Americans were loyal to the United States, thousands of West Coast Japanese remained in relocation centers operated by the War Relocation Authority. While there were no relocation centers in Texas, there were three internment camps in the state. Thee camps, located at Kenedy, Crystal City, and Seagoville, were run by the Immigration and Naturalization Service. They were established to house and control potentially dangerous enemy aliens. These aliens, Germans, Japanese, and Italians, came from different parts of the United States and its territories as well as from Central and South American nations.[71]

The Kenedy Detention Camp, in Karnes County 50 miles south of San Antonio, was established for alien males. The facility received its first internees, 456 Germans, 156 Japanese, and 14 Italians, in April 1942. During the next 30 months, more than 3,500 aliens passed through the camp. Some, such as Minour Okabayashi of a Houston suburb, were released after friends attested to their loyalty in sworn affidavits. Others were repatriated to Germany and Japan in exchange for Americans detained by the enemy. Occasionally, detainees escaped but were recaptured. Best known of these was the notorious Fritz Kuhn, pre-war leader of the German- American Bund.[72]

The internment camp at Seagoville, a small town in southeast Dallas County, was originally built as a model federal correctional institute for women. It was converted into an internment camp in early 1942 to hold female enemy aliens arrested by the FBI after the attack on Pearl Harbor. Later the camp housed internees from Central and South America and married couples without children from the United States. The facility consisted of two-story brick dormitories, a hospital, auditorium, school, and vocational industries. With no fences or barred windows, the Seagoville camp looked more like a college campus than a detention facility. The largest population interned at the camp was 647.[73]

The Immigration and Naturalization Service established a family internment camp at Crystal City in South Texas. Designed primarily for Japanese aliens from Latin American countries (especially Peru), the camp opened in December 1942. The first internees were Germans, but Japanese began arriving in March 1943. By the end of 1944 the camp housed 4,000 men, women, and children, two-thirds of whom were Japanese. The camp came to resemble a small community with its own schools, churches, post office, and newspapers. Individuals could move about freely within the camp, but a fence surrounded the camp.[74]

As the war approached an end, the Texas internment camps were phased out. Kenedy was converted to a prisoner of war camp in October 1944. The Seagoville camp closed in early summer 1945. Internees began departing from Crystal City for Hawaii and Peru in December 1945. Other departures followed during 1946. The Crystal City internment camp was finally closed in late 1947.[75]

In addition to the three internment camps for enemy aliens, there were 74 prisoner of war camps established in Texas during the war. The first of these camps were constructed in 1942; the first prisoners began arriving in early 1943. By the end of the war nearly 50,000 enemy prisoners of war were confined in Texas. This represented about 15 percent of the 372,000 POWs held in the United States during the war.[76]

Texans held more prisoners of war and had twice as many prisoner of war camps as any other state. This was due in part to space and in part to climate. The Geneva Convention of 1929 which outlined conditions for treatment of prisoners of war required that POWs be held in a climate similar to that where the prisoners were captured. Apparently it was believed that the Texas climate resembled that of North Africa, where the first large number of prisoners, members of Erwin Rommel's famed Afrika Korps, were captured.[77]

Historian Richard P. Walker, whose book *The Lone Star and the Swastika* is the most thorough study of prisoners of war in Texas, classifies Texas' 74 prison camps in four categories: (1) six large base camps built especially to house POWs; (2) 16 base camps built on existing military bases; (3) 37 branch camps administered by one of the six large base camps for the purpose of providing agricultural labor for Texas farmers; (4) 15 branch camps located on military bases to provide labor to be used by American military officials.[78]

The six large base camps built specially as prisoner of war facilities were constructed in 1942 and early 1943. Located at Huntsville, Hearne, Mexia, Hereford, McLean, and Brady, these camps were built on land purchased by the War Department, often as a result of community efforts to secure the economic benefits from such facilities. The Huntsville camp, designed to house 4,800 POWs, was one of the first built in the United States. Work began in late spring 1942 and was completed later that year. The first POWs, captured in North Africa, arrived in spring 1943. By October 1943 Camp Huntsville held 4,840 prisoners.[79]

Camp Hearne and Camp Mexia, completed about the same time, received their first prisoners, all Afrika Korps veterans, in spring 1943. At its maximum capacity Hearne housed 4,800 inmates. Mexia could hold 4,800 enlisted men and 1,000 officers.[80]

Camp Hereford, located in Deaf Smith County in the Texas Panhandle, received its first prisoners in June 1943. The Hereford facility was the only camp in Texas established solely for Italian prisoners, many of them dedicated Fascists. The camp usually held about 3,000 officers and enlisted men.[81]

Camp McLean, in Gray County about 40 miles southeast of Pampa, and Camp Brady, in west central Texas, were slightly smaller base camps completed in late summer 1943. McLean, which was temporarily closed in summer 1944, was home to an average of 2,700 POWs, many of them hard-core, pro-Nazi noncommissioned officers. Brady, also on the inactive list for two months during summer 1944, was also a camp for uncooperative NCOs. It housed an average of 1,950 German prisoners.[82]

Sixteen prisoner of war base camps were located on Texas military bases. The POW camp at Camp Maxey (near Paris), the first base camp authorized on an existing military installation, was the largest prisoner of war camp in the United States. Built to accommodate 9,000 POWs, Maxey held 7,458 prisoners by spring 1945. Maxey held a wide diversity of prisoners, including Army, Navy, and Air Force personnel.[83]

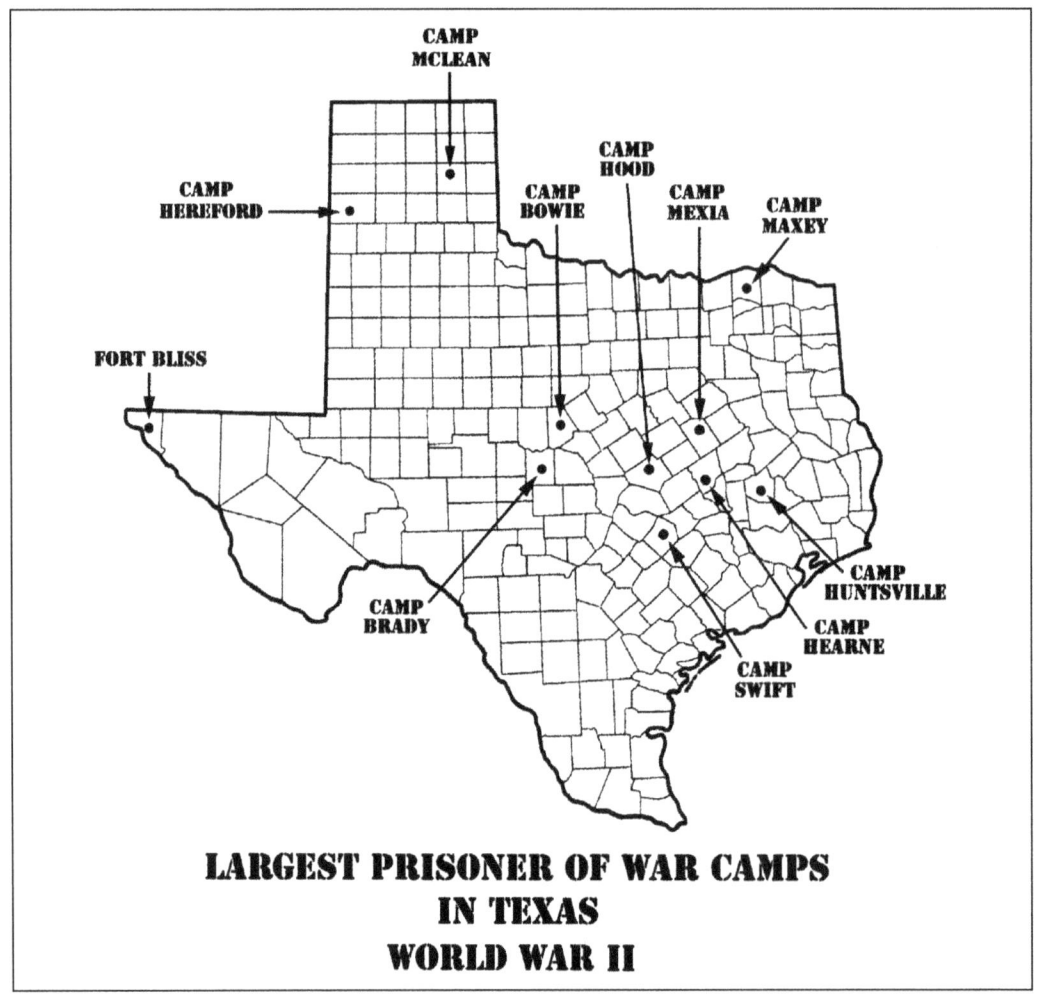

LARGEST PRISONER OF WAR CAMPS IN TEXAS WORLD WAR II

Bowie (Brownwood), Swift (Bastrop), North Hood (Killeen), and Bliss (El Paso) were all designed to hold 3,000 prisoners. None of the other base military camps (Fannin at Tyler, South Hood at Killeen, Howze at Gainesville, Sam Houston at San Antonio, Crockett at Galveston, Hulen at Palacois, Russell at Marfa, Wallace at Hitchcock, Barkeley at Abilene, Wolters at Mineral Wells, and Flour Bluff at Corpus Christi) had capacity for more than 1,000 prisoners of war.[84]

The 35 branch camps established to provide agricultural labor were located in rural areas of the state. Eight of these, administered by Camp Swift, were built in the central Gulf region to meet the needs of rice farmers. Largest of these were the camps at Alvin (400 men) and Bay City (350 men). Camps at Angleton, Eagle Pass, El Campo, Ganado, Rosenberg, and Wharton each housed approximately 200 German prisoners of war.[85]

Twelve branch camps were located in East Texas to provide workers for the area's timber industry. Largest of these was the camp at Center, which at one time had 773 German prisoners. The largest branch camp in the country, the Center facility was a tent camp. Lufkin had two camps with a total of 800 prisoners who worked for the Southland Paper Mills. Camp Liberty, with 300 prisoners, was located on property owned by the Forestry Service. Other POW lumber camps were constructed at Alto, Bannister, Chireno, Milam, Orange, Patroon, Princeton, and San Augustine.[86]

Camp China in Jefferson County was another East Texas facility. The camp, opened in September 1944, was built to provide workers for the county's rice producers. After the rice crop was in, the prisoners became lumberjacks and sawmill workers.[87]

Five branch camps were opened to meet the needs of cotton farmers for laborers. Four of these, Camps El Paso, Fabens, Cantillo, and Ysleta, were in El Paso County. Several hundred Italian prisoners were sent from Lordsburg, New Mexico, to these camps to pick cotton. The fifth branch camp established to meet the request of cotton farmers was Camp Chance Plantation, located 40 miles south of Hearne. Two hundred fifty German POWs worked out of this camp.[88]

Nine branch camps in East and Central Texas provided prisoners of war for general farm work. The first of these, Camp Forney in northwestern Kaufman County, opened in March 1944 but closed two weeks later. Camp Kaufman, 20 miles to the south, opened soon after and remained open until late 1944. Camps at Cleburne, Navasota, Anahuac, Mont Belvieu, and Garwood were established later that year. Camp Corsicana opened in April 1945 and Camp Kirbyville in June 1945. All of these camps were small, none with more than 250 POWs. Prisoners from these camps performed various tasks, including hoeing, weeding, and picking cotton, shocking and thrashing rice, cutting wood, and clearing land.[89]

Branch camps at Dumas and Dalhart, both using Italian POWs from Camp Hereford, were established for non-agricultural purposes. The town of Dumas was furnished 100 POWs for street cleaning and general maintenance work late in the war. Texas Utilities of Dalhart requested use of Italian prisoners to ice down refrigerated railroad cars, but the camp was not established until two months after the war ended.[90]

In addition to the 16 POW base camps on military installations, the U.S. Army operated 15 branch camps providing general labor for its own needs. Three were established at Army general hospitals at McKinney, Longview, and Temple, seven at Army Air Force bases (Amarillo, Big Spring, Childress, El Paso, Galveston, Lubbock, and Pyote), two at Army bases (White Rock Lake near Dallas and Fort Clark near Brackettville), one at the quartermaster depot at Fort Worth, one for the Corps of Engineers (Camp Denison), and one at Camp Kenedy. As noted earlier, Kenedy was originally an enemy alien detention camp. After the detention camp was closed in October 1944 Kenedy became a POW branch camp administered by Camp Sam Houston.[91]

The vast majority of the POWs held in Texas were Germans. As noted earlier, the first arrivals were members of the Afrika Korps. Many of these were ardent National Socialists, or Nazis, who believed Germany would win the war. This was particularly true of junior officers and NCOs, who seemed determined to punish any fellow prisoners displaying anti-Nazi sentiment or cooperating with prison officials. Beatings of non-Nazis often occurred, especially in big camps like Hearne, Mexia, and Huntsville. Several forced suicides and at least one murder of a non-Nazi prisoner took place in Texas prisons. Camp officials attempted to curb this Nazi influence but with only limited success.[92]

Approximately 5,000, or about ten percent, of the POWs in Texas were Italians. Many of these, nearly 4,000, were housed at Camp Hereford at one time or another. Others were scattered at branch camps in El Paso County, Big Spring, Dalhart, Dumas, and Lubbock. Slightly over 1,000 Japanese POWs, one-fourth of all those in the United States, were held in Texas at Hearne, Huntsville, and Kenedy.[93]

Most historians, both American and foreign, agree that Axis prisoners of war in Texas were treated reasonably well. The U.S. government made a serious effort to comply with the provisions of the 1929 Geneva Convention, in part for humanitarian reasons and in part because it feared retaliation upon American prisoners of war if it did not. Indeed, some Texans believed prisoners were treated too well. Historian Arnold Krammer notes that townsfolk often referred to their local German POW camp as the "Fritz Ritz."[94]

For the most part enemy POWs were well fed, adequately clothed and housed, and provided a variety of recreational and educational opportunities. The Geneva Convention stipulated that the food ration provided POWs was to equal in quantity and quality that provided the capturing nation's soldiers. As a result, Axis prisoners in the United States ate well during most of the war. Not only was there sufficient quantity, but there were also efforts made to tailor the food to the national eating habits of the captives. German prisoners preferred and received breakfast with less meat and eggs than Americans and more bread, cereal, fruit, and jelly. Italian prisoners received frequent portions of spaghetti and a diet seasoned with paprika, onions, and olive oil. Certain foods enjoyed by Americans such as peanut butter, corn, canned juices, green peppers, and frozen vegetables were not eaten by the prisoners and removed from menus.[95]

In April 1945 reductions were made in POW rations. These reductions stemmed from several causes: food shortages as the Army attempted to feed liberated people in Europe, complaints in American newspapers that prisoners were treated too well, and discovery of concentration camp cruelties as Allied armies moved into Germany. The amounts of items such as fresh beef were reduced and the calorie content lowered from slightly more than 4,000 calories per day to 3,500 calories for POWs doing active work and 2,500 calories for sedentary prisoners. While such reductions were not threats to health they brought complaints from prisoners and from farmers who argued the reductions left prisoners weak and unable to perform agricultural work efficiently.[96]

Prisoners could supplement their rations with items obtained from canteens established in all camps. These items, such as food, toiletries, clothing, cigarettes, candy, cold drinks and beer, were purchased with coupons. Each enlisted man received $3 in coupons as a gratuity each month. Those who worked received a salary (in coupons) of 80 cents a day. Officers' gratuities ranged from $20 to $40 per month, depending upon their rank.[97]

Various types of recreational and intellectual activities were available for POWs. Indoor and outdoor sports, plays, theatrical performances, choral groups, and camp orchestras provided an outlet for the talents of prisoners. Most camps had a library and a reading room, motion pictures, and a camp newspaper (Camp Maxey had three). Educational opportunities were available through courses taught by prisoners and in extension courses offered by Texas colleges and universities.[98]

Most POW camps had a chapel (sometimes built by prison labor); others used recreation and reading rooms for religious services. American officials encouraged religious observance in the camps, but since the German army had so few chaplains, officials had to depend upon local ministers or priests. Language differences and prisoner distrust limited the success of American clerics in ministering to their POW congregations.[99]

Even under the most pleasant circumstances, some prisoners attempted to escape. Most escapees from Texas camps were caught within a few days. The majority of these escapes were by one or two prisoners who walked off work details. A few were more elaborately planned. The largest single breakout from a Texas camp occurred at Camp Barkeley near Abilene in late March 1944. Twelve prisoners, well supplied with maps and food, escaped through a tunnel that had been dug over a period of several months. Once outside the escapees divided into small groups and headed for Mexico. All were captured within a week; two in downtown San Angelo, two at Winters, three at Ballinger, three in an abandoned ranch house near Bradshaw, and two while walking down the railroad tracks at El Paso.[100]

One of the most successful escapes was made by two Italian POWs, Guiseppe Belfabio and Sirico Bologna, who slipped out of the branch work facility Camp Fabens in El Paso County on the night of July 3, 1944. They managed to elude authorities for over a year before being recaptured.[101]

Texans had mixed feelings toward the thousands of prisoners and dozens of prison camps scattered throughout the state. Many believed the Army pampered prisoners and called for tighter restrictions. Labor union leaders, who saw the prisoners as competitors for jobs, were critical of the use of POWs as cheap laborers. Farmers and businessmen saw the POWs as a solution to the acute shortage of workers and supported expansion of POW worker programs. Other Texans, particularly those who did not live near the camps, expressed little feeling toward the 50,000 POWs in their state.[102]

Most prisoners held in Texas accepted their fate and waited for the war to end. Many later expressed fond memories for their time in the state. Some returned to the United States to live; others came back to take part in reunions at communities that housed prisoners during the war. In his article on prisoners of war in Texas, Professor Arnold Krammer closed with a quotation from one such returning POW, Wilhelm Suerbrei, who stated "if there is ever another war, get on the side that America isn't, then get captured by the Americans—you'll have it made."[103]

CHAPTER SEVEN
Allied Success, 1944

While Texans at home were coping with production schedules, rationing and shortages, and racial and political differences, thousands of Texans were fighting on world battle fronts in 1944. As the year began the 36th Division, the old Texas National Guard, which had been taken out of front line action after suffering heavy losses in December 1943, was preparing to reenter the fighting that would involve the division in an ill-fated attempt to break the enemy defenses along the Rapido River. The 3rd Infantry Division, which included Sergeant Audie Murphy and many other Texans, and the 45th Infantry Division, the New Mexico-Oklahoma National Guard that had completed its training at Camp Barkeley near Abilene, were preparing for landings on the Italian coast at Anzio. The 2nd Infantry Division, a regular Army division that had its home at Fort Sam Houston in peacetime, and the 90th Infantry Division, made up of Texans and Oklahomans, were training for the invasion of France scheduled in early June. Thousands of American airmen, including large numbers of Texans, were carrying on the air war against enemy targets in Europe.[1]

In the Pacific, American Marines were completing the conquest of Bougainville in the upper Solomons. At the same time, Allied forces were taking steps to neutralize the large Japanese garrison at Rabaul on the northeastern tip of New Britain island. In late December, American Marines landed at Cape Gloucester on the northwestern corner of New Britain. Two months later, Los Negroes in the Admiralty Islands was occupied by U.S. forces that included the lst Cavalry Division, formerly stationed at Fort Bliss. By these operations General MacArthur's forces effectively isolated the Japanese garrison at Rabaul.[2]

In April 1944, General Walter Krueger's troops made successful landings at Hollandia and Aitape in northeastern New Guinea. This well-executed move was followed by landings on the small islands of Biak and Noemfoor in May and July 1944, bringing American forces closer and closer to the Philippine Islands.[3]

A small, elite reconnaissance unit, named the Alamo Scouts, played a vital role in the campaigns in the Admiralities and New Guinea. Consisting of 138 men divided into 12 teams, the Scouts performed hazardous missions in obtaining intelligence information that preceded the landings. One small team led by Lieutenant John R. C. McGowen, a 25-year-old Texas A&M graduate from Amarillo, supplied Krueger's forces with valuable pre-invasion intelligence prior to the Los Negros capture. Later, McGowen's team (himself and five enlisted men) landed on the northwest side of Noemfoor and again obtained information needed by the U.S. command.[4]

While General MacArthur's troops were completing the conquest of New Guinea, other American forces under the command of Admiral Chester W. Nimitz moved into the Marianas Islands in the Central Pacific. On June 15, two Marine divisions, the 2nd and 4th, landed on Saipan, one of the three largest islands in the Marianas. Although the island had been subjected to heavy bombardment by the American Navy prior to the landings, the Japanese put up a fierce resistance. Hundreds of Marines, including Travis Moore of Waco and Oscar "Bud" Fowler of Clarksville, both veterans of the Solomons and Tarawa campaigns, were killed in the first two days of fighting.[5]

In spite of heavy losses, the Marines held on to the beaches. Reinforced by the Army's 27th Infantry Division, which landed on the 16th and 17th, the Marines eventually overpowered the Japanese defenders. By the end of the fighting on July 9 when the island was secured 14,000 Americans were killed or wounded and 30,000 Japanese troops were dead. In addition, thousands of Japanese civilians committed suicide by plunging off the cliffs on the island.[6]

While American ground troops fought for control of Saipan, a major naval battle took place to the southwest in the Philippine Sea. The Japanese Combined Fleet attempted to destroy the U.S. Fifth Fleet, which was supporting the Saipan landings. The battle was a major victory for the American Navy. On June 19, the Japanese lost 346 aircraft in four unsuccessful air attacks on the American fleet in what came to be known as the "Great Marianas Turkey Shoot." On the following day, U.S. planes attacked the Japanese fleet, sinking an enemy aircraft carrier, damaging three other carriers, and destroying an additional 80 enemy aircraft. The Japanese lost another 50 airplanes that flew from bases on Guam. American losses in the two days were much less; 120 aircraft lost and several ships damaged. The Japanese lost 450 pilots in the battle; 76 American airmen were lost.[7]

One of the American planes shot down in the Philippine Sea (probably by friendly fire aimed at Japanese dive bombers) was an Avenger torpedo bomber piloted by a young New Englander, George Herbert Walker Bush. Bush already had some Texas connections; he had received his flight training at Corpus Christi Naval Air Station and was assigned to an air group on the light carrier U.S.S. *San Jacinto*. His adoption of Texas as his home state came after the war, but he was already an honorary citizen of the state as a result of action by the Texas Legislature making all crew members of the *San Jacinto* Texas citizens.[8]

His plane hit by shrapnel during the battle of Philippine Sea, Bush was forced to make a water landing. He, his gunner, and his radar-radio operator were taken aboard the U.S.S. *Lexington*, flagship of Marc Mitscher's carrier force, where they remained for several days before being returned to duty on the *San Jacinto*.[9]

American submarines played an important role in the victory at Philippine Sea. One submarine, U.S.S. *Puffer*, sank two Japanese tankers at the Japanese rendezvous site at Tawi Tawi prior to the sea battle. Another U.S. submarine, U.S.S. *Harder*, commanded by Texan Sam Dealey, sank three Japanese destroyers at Tawi Tawi. On the same patrol Dealey's boat sank two other Japanese destroyers, earning the Texan the sobriquet "the destroyer killer," and eventually the Medal of Honor. The submarine U.S.S. *Cavalla* first spotted the movement of the Japanese fleet toward the Marianas and warned the American fleet commander Raymond Spruance of the impending enemy attack. During the battle itself *Cavalla* and U.S.S. *Albacore* sank the Japanese carriers *Shokaku* and *Taiho*.[10]

Once Saipan was firmly in American hands, U.S. naval and ground forces moved to occupy the two other main islands in the Marianas, Guam and Tinian. Landings took place on Guam, an American possession since the end of the Spanish-American War, on July 21. The 3rd Marine Division (which included Captain Joseph D. Jamison of Clarksville, Texas) and the Army's 77th Infantry Division commanded by Major General Andrew D. Bruce, a 1916 graduate of Texas A&M, overcame stubborn enemy resistance, securing the island on August 8.[11]

Landings on Tinian, a smaller island, took place three days after the Guam landings. Resistance here was less determined; within eight days the island was in American hands.

Securing Saipan, Guam, and Tinian provided excellent locations for naval bases and airfields from which the United States could move west to the Philippines or northwest to the Japanese home islands.[12]

By the time Nimitz's forces occupied the Marianas, American troops in Italy had liberated Rome and were slowly moving northward. The advance up the Italian peninsula from Salerno had been costly, as the German defenders fought stubbornly before giving up ground.

The 36th Division, formerly the Texas National Guard, played a major role in the fighting in Italy during the first half of 1944. The division suffered heavy casualties in an attempt to cross the Rapido River in January, a questionable attack that is still shrouded in controversy.

The attempted crossing of the Rapido was part of an overall plan by Lieutenant General Mark W. Clark, commander of the U.S. Fifth Army, to move around the enemy Gustav Line by a landing on the Italian coast at Anzio, 60 miles behind the German defenses, and then march quickly to capture Rome. To pin down German troops and prevent them from moving against the Anzio

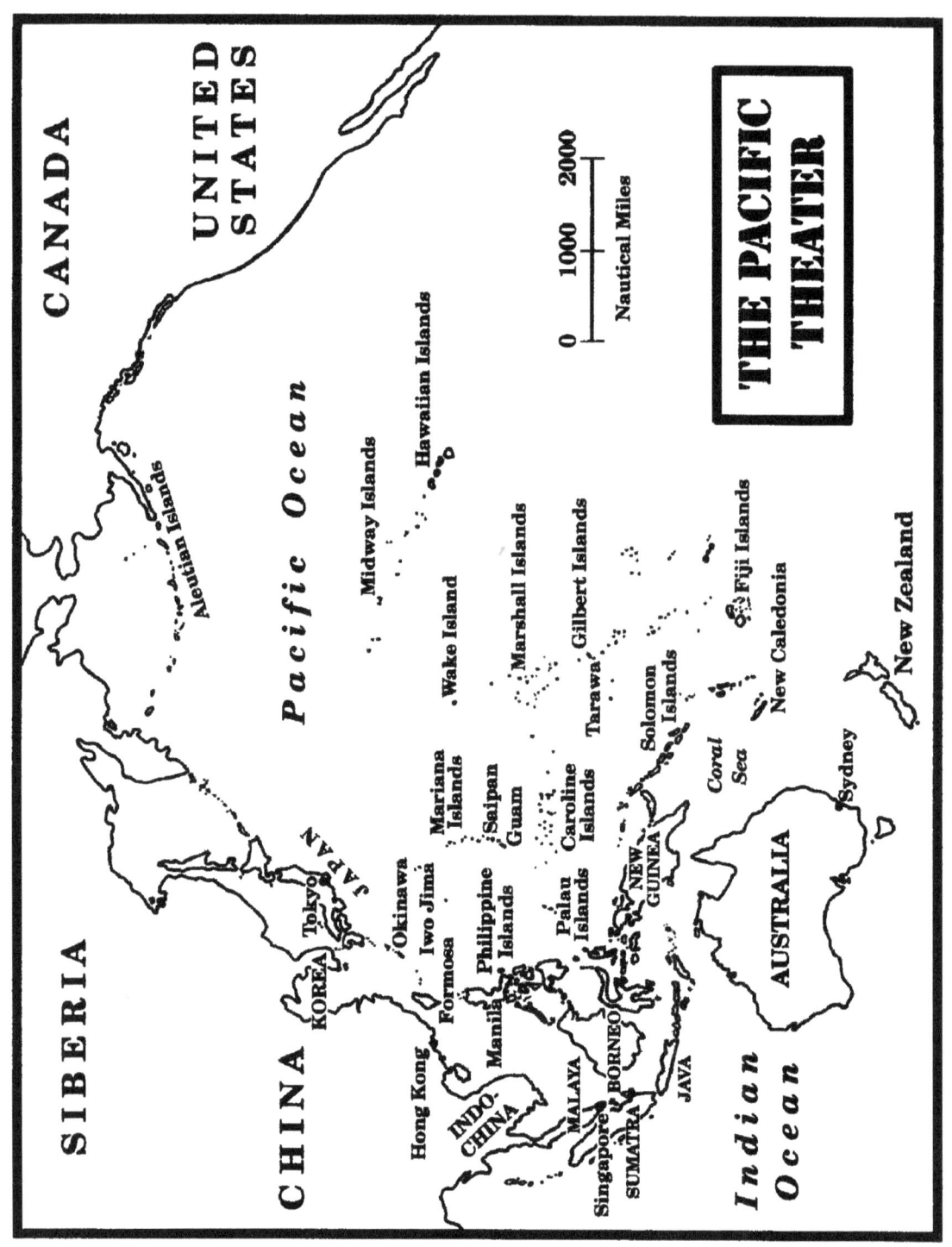

beachhead, General Clark ordered new attacks by British and American troops on the Gustav Line. While other Allied troops opened fighting on the enemy flanks, the 36th Division would cross the Rapido River in the center of the German line. This would be followed up by movement of the 1st Armored Division into the Liri valley.[13]

General Fred Walker, commander of the 36th Division, had misgivings about the Rapido River crossing from the start. Based upon his own experiences in defending against such a river crossing in the First World War and reports from his staff engineer, Walker believed the effort would not be successful. In his diary two weeks before the attack he wrote "... I do not see how we, or any other Division, can possibly succeed in crossing the Rapido River near San Angelo when the stream is included within the main line of resistance of the strongest German position." Four days before the scheduled attack he wrote "we are undertaking the impossible, but I shall keep it to myself...."[14]

Although Walker discussed his reservations about the attack with his superiors, corps commander Major General Geoffrey Keyes and Army commander General Clark, he did not file a formal written protest against the operation. Indeed, historian Martin Blumenson believes "the extent of General Walker's opposition to a crossing of the Rapido was never apparent to his superiors."[15]

In spite of his reservations, General Walker proceeded with plans for the Rapido attack. He assigned two of his three regiments to make the crossing. The 141st Regiment, under the temporary command of Lieutenant Colonel Aaron A. Wyatt, Jr., would cross north of the town of San Angelo, while the 143rd Regiment, commanded by Colonel William H. Martin, would cross south of the town. The division's third regiment, the 142nd, would be held in reserve.

The attack began at 8:00 P.M. on January 20. As one historian notes, "nothing went right from the start." The muddy terrain made it difficult for the men to carry heavy assault boats and equipment to the river. The mist and fog made it hard to find the way in the darkness. Some of the troops marched into an undetected mine field. Then German artillery fire took its toll as the men struggled to cross the river in their boats. Only two companies of the 141st made it to the opposite bank. Colonel Martin's 143rd Regiment fared slightly better on the south, managing to get a battalion across by dawn. When daylight came, however, deadly fire from German artillery forced the battalion to withdraw back across the river.[16]

General Keyes ordered the attack resumed the next morning, but delays in securing boats and equipment caused several postponements. The 143rd Regiment began its second attack at 4:00 P.M. under cover of artificial fog. Several rifle companies made it to the opposite shore but heavy enemy fire prevented engineers from constructing bridges to enable tanks and tank destroyers to cross. Without armor, Colonel Martin's men could not advance. Shortly before noon on the 22nd, Martin ordered his units to withdraw to the American side of the river.[17]

Lieutenant Colonel Wyatt's 141st Regiment made its second attempt at 9:00 P.M. on January 21. The 141st managed to reach the German side of the river, but like Martin's regiment was forced to withdraw on the afternoon of the 22nd.[18]

As conditions deteriorated on the 22nd, corps commander General Keyes ordered General Walker to send his reserve, the 142nd Regiment, into the fighting. After consultation with General Clark, however, Keyes rescinded the order. By nightfall the fighting was over. A few of the men still on the other side of the river managed to swim back to the American side. Others were killed or captured.[19]

The two infantry regiments in the Rapido attack lost heavily. The 141st Regiment reported 1,007 men killed, wounded, and missing (probably captured); the 143rd Regiment, 969 killed, wounded and missing. Some units were particularly hit hard. Guillermo De Leon of Uvalde, who won the Silver Star, Bronze Star, and Purple Heart while serving with E Company of the 141st Regiment, remembered that "it was a slaughter.... We went like pigs to the market. We started with 208 men. When it was over ... there were 26 of us left." Sergeant Harry Moore recalled there were "only three left out of my platoon" in E Company of the 143rd Regiment.[20]

The division commander, General Walker, believed that General Clark was responsible for the failure at the Rapido. Clark himself was convinced that the attack had been necessary to assure the success of the Anzio landing that took place on January 22. Writing several years later, Clark admitted "it was a high price to pay, but to suggest that the brave and able soldiers of the 36th made the sacrifice in vain would be to overlook the fundamental strategy of the drive towards Rome."[21]

The debate over the Rapido crossing was continued for years. Many members of the division agreed with Walker that Clark was responsible for the heavy casualties suffered in attempting the crossing in face of the powerful German defenses. After the war, the 36th Division Association called for a congressional investigation of the "Rapido River fiasco." The military affairs committees of the U.S. House of Representatives and U.S. Senate held preliminary hearings on the matter in January 1946, but following a report by Secretary of War Robert P. Patterson that "General Clark exercised sound judgment in planning it [the Rapido attack] and in ordering it," the investigation was dropped.[22]

The attacks made by the 36th Division and other Allied units along the Rapido probably did make the landings at Anzio on January 22 easier. The British 1st Division and the U.S. 3rd Division, commanded by Texan Lucian Truscott, along with Ranger, Commando, and Special Service Force battalions, landed with little opposition. By nightfall, over 36,000 Allied troops were ashore with fewer than 200 casualties. Within the next several days the Allied forces, commanded by Major General John P. Lucas, were reinforced by men of the 45th Infantry, the National Guard division that had trained at Abilene's Camp Barkeley.[23]

The German army, commanded in Italy by Field Marshal Albert Kesselring, reacted quickly to prevent the Allies from moving inland. Within a week, the Germans had part or all of eight divisions surrounding the Anzio peninsula. An attempt by the Allies to break out of the beachhead was repulsed. During the next four weeks, the American and British troops fought desperately to hold the beachhead against German counterattacks.[24]

Meanwhile, Allied forces continued to pound away at the Gustav Line. The destruction of the Benedictine monastery at Monte Cassino served only to provide the enemy with better defensive positions by which to impede the Allied advance. Although undermanned and crippled from the Rapido attacks, the 36th Division remained on the line until late February when it was pulled out for rest and refitting. In late May it was redeployed to the Anzio region and assigned to VI Corps, now under Major General Lucian Truscott, who replaced General Lucas.[25]

The 36th Division relieved the U.S. 1st Armored Division south of the village of Velletri. The 1st Armored had just taken part in bloody fighting near Carano. In that battle Texas A&M graduate Lieutenant Thomas W. Fowler of Wichita Falls, a tank commander in the 1st Armored, cleared a path through a mine field with his bare hands to enable two infantry platoons to secure their objectives. When one of his tanks was set afire, Fowler attempted to save the lives of the wounded tank crew until enemy fire forced him to withdraw. Even then, he rendered first aid to nine wounded infantrymen at the risk of his personal safety. For his courageous action Fowler, who was killed ten days later, was awarded the Medal of Honor.[26]

The American Army had broken out of the Anzio beachhead when the 36th Division joined VI Corps. General Truscott was planning an assault on the last German defense line south of Rome. The key to the German line was Monte Artesimo, a mountainous ridge overlooking the village of Velletri and the road to Rome. After his patrols discovered a gap in the German line, General Walker convinced Truscott that the 36th Division could move through the gap and capture Monte Artesimo and Velletri.[27]

During the night of May 30-31, men of the 142nd and 143rd Regiments quietly slipped through the gap in the German lines and occupied Monte Artesimo. Division engineers, led by Major Oran C. Stovall of Bowie, hurriedly constructed a road up and over the ridge so that tanks, tank destroyers, and artillery could follow. The 141st Regiment meanwhile moved against Velletri from the west. After some brief fighting the village was firmly in American hands. The following day the Germans decided to evacuate Rome. American patrols entered the city on June 4, and other troops soon followed. On June 5, 1944, Rome was declared officially liberated.[28]

American news correspondent Eric Sevareid, who accompanied the 36th Division in the bold Velletri-Artesimo maneuver, was convinced that Walker's men should receive credit for the liberation of Rome. "If Generals Alexander [the Theater commander] and Clark [Fifth Army commander] received the key to the city of Rome, it was General Walker who turned the key and handed it to them," Sevareid reported.[29]

On the morning of June 5 the 36th Division passed through Rome on its march north. Along with other Allied divisions, the Texans continued in slow pursuit of the retreating Germans. On June 25, the 36th was pulled out of the line along with the 3rd and 45th divisions in preparation for the forthcoming invasion of southern France. General Fred Walker, who had led the 36th Division from Texas to Rome, would not be with the division in that operation. In early July he was ordered back to the States, where he became commandant of the Infantry School at Fort Benning.[30]

By the time General Walker left the 36th Division, major attention in the war had shifted to France. On June 6, 1944, two days after Allied troops entered Rome, a massive Allied force of American, British, Canadian, and Free French troops commanded by Texas-born Dwight D. Eisenhower landed on the Normandy coast, opening a new front in the war.

Texans played various roles in the D-Day landings. Walter Cronkite was one of the war correspondents who flew with a B-17 squadron that carried out a bombing mission on the French coast just before the landings occurred. A graduate of Houston's San Jacinto High in 1933, Cronkite attended the University of Texas and worked for the *Houston Press* before joining United Press as correspondent. Prior to D-Day he had covered the North Africa landings and aerial missions of the American and British air forces.[31]

Several Texans took part in air missions on D-Day. Harry Hodge from Beaumont was top gunner on a B-26 which dropped its bombs on German defenders ten minutes before the troops hit the Normandy beaches. Florian W. "Pete" Piwetz of Fayetteville was flight engineer and gunner on a B-26 bomber that attacked German fortifications just before the D-Day landings. Cooper Hawthorne, a former football star at Port Neches High, flew two missions in his B-26 bomber on D-Day. Elton J. Brownshadel, a graduate of Wharton High and former University of Texas student, was killed when his P-51 fighter crashed on June 6.[32]

Texans were in the American airborne divisions that parachuted into the Cotentin peninsula of Normandy in the predawn hours of June 6. Their assignment was to seize control of roads and causeways in the peninsula to prevent German reinforcement of troops along the Utah beaches where the U.S. 4th Infantry would come ashore. Lieutenant Colonel Julian J. Ewell, a Texas graduate of the West Point class of 1939, commander of the 3rd Battalion, 501st Parachute Infantry Regiment, 101st Airborne Division, landed near St. Marie-du-Mont. He and 60 of his men joined division commander Maxwell D. Taylor and an assortment of headquarters personnel who were wandering around in the darkness. Under Taylor's direction, they headed to the village of Pouppeville, which they captured after a brief fight.[33]

Another Texan, Lieutenant Parker Alford, was an artillery officer with Taylor's group. Alford had been assigned to the 101st as a naval gunfire spotter. When he landed he heard much commotion, which he believed to be enemy troops. He raised his Thompson machine gun into firing position, only to discover he had landed in a herd of cows who were disturbed by the noise of his landing. Alford and his radio operator soon ran into General Taylor and his party. He continued on with them to Pouppeville, where by radio he directed the fire of the U.S.S. *Quincy* on the defenders on the beach.[34]

Lieutenant Colonel Robert G. Cole, a 29-year-old West Pointer from San Antonio, was also among the paratroops landing before dawn. Commander of the 3rd Battalion, 502nd Parachute Infantry Regiment, Cole landed near St. Mere-Eglise. He collected a group of his own men and a few men of the 82nd Airborne and headed toward St. Martin-de-Varreville. From there Cole and his men pushed on to secure two exits to the beaches and await the arrival of the 4th Infantry.[35]

While American paratroopers were groping in the darkness and early morning hours to secure the roadways leading to the beaches, the giant armada of ships bringing thousands of men and machines toward the Normandy coast moved across the English Channel. Just before the ground troops went ashore, a massive naval bombardment blasted away at the German defenses. The battleship U.S.S. *Texas* was the flagship of the naval bombardment group supporting the Allied landings on Omaha beach. Along with another World War I dreadnought, U.S.S. *Arkansas*, and a Pearl Harbor survivor, U.S.S. *Nevada*, the *Texas* used its 14-inch guns to blast the emplacements on Pointe-du-Hoc, the rugged cliff overlooking the landing sites. Later the *Texas* gave fire support to the 29th Infantry Division as it came ashore.[36]

The *Texas* remained off the beachhead until June 9, when she returned to England for supplies and ammunition. She returned to the French coast on June 15 to bombard German installations at Isigng and Carentan. On June 25, the *Texas* joined *Arkansas* in shelling Cherbourg. There the *Texas* received two direct hits from enemy shore batteries, demolishing the conning tower and the bridge, killing the helmsman, and wounding 11 others. The *Texas* was not finished, however. After the damage was repaired, she took part in the landings in southern France, then steamed to the Pacific to support the landings at Iwo Jima and Okinawa.[37]

In spite of the heavy naval bombardment that preceded the landings German defensive positions were still intact when the first Allied troops came ashore. Lieutenant Colonel James Earl Rudder and three companies of the 2nd Ranger Battalion were among the first ashore. Colonel Rudder, a 1932 graduate of Texas A&M with a degree in industrial education and a reserve commission in the infantry, was a former football coach and teacher at Brady High School and John Tarleton Agricultural College. Called to active duty in 1941, Rudder became commanding officer of the 2nd Rangers in June 1943. Rudder and his Rangers were given the task of destroying a battery of six 155 mm. guns on the cliffs at Pointe du Hoc, which overlooked Omaha and Utah beaches, where American infantry were assigned to come ashore. Under heavy enemy fire, Rudder and his Rangers, using ropes and extension ladders, scaled the 100 foot cliffs. When the Rangers reached the top they discovered the big guns were not there. Undaunted, Rudder set up a command post and moved his men inland to secure vital roads along the coast. Around 8:30, one of Rudder's patrols discovered and destroyed the six cannon that had been moved to avoid Allied air strikes. Fighting continued throughout the morning, with Rudder himself twice wounded.[38]

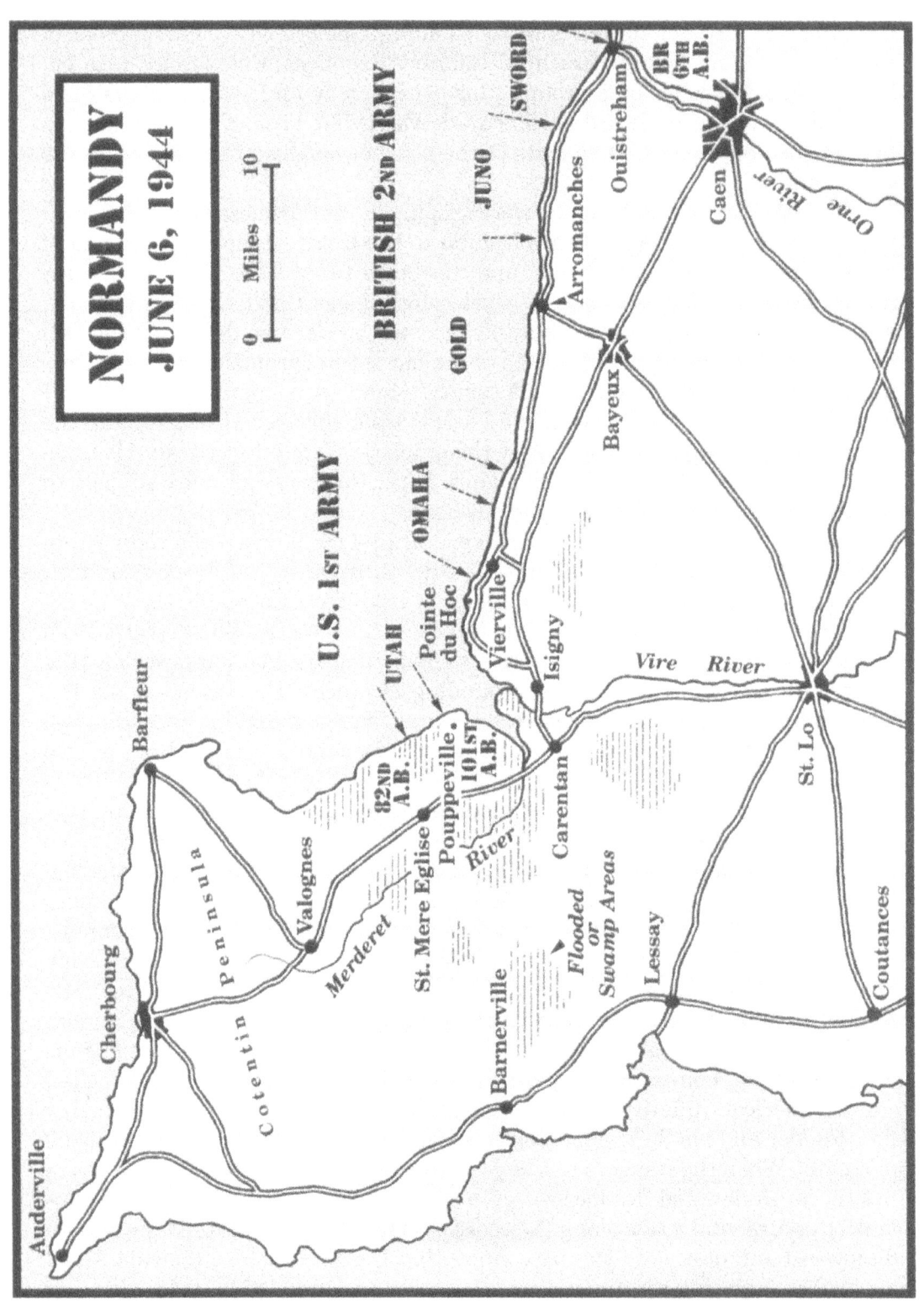

While Rudder and his Rangers were fighting to secure Pointe du Hoc, American, British, and Canadian troops were storming ashore under heavy enemy fire. The British and Canadians, landing on Gold, Juno, and Sword beaches on the east side of the landing area, sustained comparatively light losses in securing most of their D-Day objectives. The United States 4th Infantry Division, led on to Utah beach on the extreme left side of the landing area by assistant division commander Theodore Roosevelt, Jr., encountered only light opposition and quickly achieved its objectives. By noon the division, which included Texans Drate H. Catey of San Angelo, Billy Ward of Beaumont, and Edwin Norris of Tyler, had linked up with the 101st Airborne Division near Pouppeville. Division casualties were fewer than 200 out of 23,000 men who came ashore that day.[39]

The most desperate fighting on D-Day occurred on Omaha, the beach in between Utah and Gold. Historian Stephen Ambrose notes "the Allied planners hated the idea of assaulting Omaha Beach," because it was an ideal defensive position with slopping bluffs overlooking the wide open beach below. German defenses were stronger here than anywhere else in Normandy, with artillery at both ends of the beach, the waters heavily mined with explosives, and protected underground bunkers perched on the bluffs with machine guns, mortars, and field guns.[40]

Regiments of the battle-tested 1st Infantry Division and the inexperienced 29th Infantry Division were assigned the task of moving across the open beach and taking the bluffs. The men who landed at Omaha met a murderous fire and suffered heavy casualties. Arlie Horn of Beaumont, who came ashore with the 29th Infantry, reported there were dead bodies everywhere. When he reached the beach he wanted to hide his face. "There was screaming, hollering, and gunfire," remembered Horn. Corporal Jesse Cantu from the Rio Grande valley, a member of the 1st Infantry, remembered "everybody was pinned down and guys were being hit left and right. Nobody wanted to move."[41]

Captain Joe Dawson from Waco, commander of G Company of the 16th Regiment, 1st Division, came ashore in the second wave. He remembered that he "saw nothing but men and bodies on the shore." But somehow Dawson managed to cross the open beach and reach the top of the bluff, becoming the first man in his area to do so. Soon others in his company followed him. By late afternoon troops on Omaha were moving into the interior.[42]

Although the Allies had control of the beaches by nightfall of June 6, the fighting was far from over. Resistance was light in some areas; in other places was substantial. The 101st Airborne Division, assigned the task of taking the vital road town of Carentan, ran into stubborn opposition. The advance was held up for several hours while Lieutenant Colonel Robert Cole from San Antonio led his men of the 3rd Battalion in a bayonet charge that routed the enemy. For his fearlessness and bravery in leading the attack, Cole, who was later killed in Holland, was awarded the Medal of Honor. Another Texan, Staff Sergeant Bruno Schroeder, a graduate of Texas A&M, was awarded the Silver Star for his role in the capture of Carentan.[43]

As Allied forces slowly moved inland they were reinforced by other divisions. Among those landing during the next two days were the 2nd Infantry Division, which included a large complement of Texans, and the 90th Division, which had trained at Camp Barkeley. The 90th Division, which originally had been made up of Texans and Oklahomans, had adopted the "T-O" insignia for the two states. As it received replacements from other states it came to be known as the "Tough Ombres" Division. The 90th was commanded by Major General Henry Terrell, a native Texan and World War I veteran, from its activation in March 1942 until January 1944, when Terrell was replaced by Jay W. MacKelvie, a native of South Dakota.[44]

The 90th Division fared poorly in the early days of fighting in Normandy. When the division failed to achieve its objectives near the Merderet River in early June, corps commander Joe Colllins relieved MacKelvie and appointed Major General Eugene Landrum, who had commanded the 7th Division in the Aleutians, to replace him. Landrum proved no more successful than MacKelvie and was relieved in late July.[45]

The staff of Army group commander Omar Bradley recommended breaking up the 90th, but Bradley appointed Raymond McLain, former artillery commander of the 30th and 45th divisions, as commander. McLain, a former banker and officer in the Oklahoma National Guard during World War I, was an ideal choice. Under his leadership the 90th Division became one of the finest fighting units in Europe.[46]

American divisions encountered great difficulty as they moved into the hedgerow country of rural France. Allied intelligence had woefully underestimated the advantage these hedgerows gave enemy defenders. Bill Lewis from Wichita Falls, a sergeant in an antitank squad of the 29th Division, remembers that his outfit was "never instructed about them [the hedgerows]," and "never learned a cockeyed thing about blowing up hedgerows." Eventually American troops designed a number of devices (such as lacing steel beams on the front of tanks) to cut through the hedgerows.[47]

Throughout late June and early July, Allied forces slowly expanded their beachhead and pushed the German defenders back. In late July, the American First Army under Courtney Hodges and the newly activated Third Army under George S. Patton, Jr., made a breakout at St. Lo and began a race across northern France. By late August, Allied forces had liberated Paris and were driving toward the German border. Spearheading the Third Army's drive was the XX Corps commanded by Major General Walton H. Walker, a native of Belton, Texas. A 1912 West Point graduate and veteran of the Meuse-Argonne campaign in World War I, Walker was an outstanding commander. Short and heavyset, Walker was a fierce competitor whose nickname was "Bulldog." He was admired by Patton for his fighting qualities and became the model leader of a hard-hitting, rapidly advancing American Army corps.[48]

While American and British armies were moving across northern France, other Allied forces landed in southern France on August 15, 1944. Operation Dragoon was carried out by the U.S. Seventh Army commanded by Lieutenant

General Alexander "Sandy" Patch. The initial assault force consisted of the 3rd, 36th, and 45th Infantry Divisions, units that had been withdrawn from the fighting in Italy. Together they made up VI Corps, commanded by Texan Major General Lucian Truscott. The landings were preceded by massive bombardments by Allied aircraft and warships, including the venerable *Texas*, and a parachute drop by the 1st Airborne Task Force.[49]

John Forrest, a "19-year-old, self-confessed hellraiser" from Houston, was one of the 5,630 paratroopers who took part in the Dragoon air drop. Expelled from Texas A&M for disciplinary reasons, Forrest joined the Army and volunteered for paratroop duty. His 517th Parachute Regimental Combat Team was the largest component of the airborne operation in Dragoon. Another Houston resident, Ernie Kosan, a member of the 596th Airborne Engineer Company, was also among those who parachuted. Kosan was a native of Germany who had migrated to Houston with his family in 1926. Dallas resident Captain James McNamara, Jr., a graduate of Harvard and the Chicago Medical School, was a surgeon with the 517th Parachute Regiment who made the air drop in southern France. McNamara, wounded twice, received the Silver Star, Purple Heart with Oak Leaf cluster, the Combat Badge, and Parachute Badge for his service in Italy, France, and Germany.[50]

Although the airborne task force had been thrown together hastily, the drops were accurate and the paratroopers successfully carried out their missions of blocking roads, seizing coastal towns, and supporting the ground troops. The main landings by the infantry took place without great difficulty. Of the three U.S. infantry divisions, only the 36th, now commanded by John Dahlquist from Minnesota, encountered serious opposition. Once ashore, American troops and the II French Corps, which landed on August 16, occupied Toulon and Marseille, and then moved northward into the interior of France.[51]

Texans figured prominently in the fighting in Europe during the autumn of 1944. In early September a new American Army, the Ninth, became fully operational under the command of Lieutenant General William Hood Simpson from Weatherford, Texas. A West Point classmate of George Patton, Simpson, like Patton, had difficulties at the academy, graduating third from the bottom of his class. He had a steady but unspectacular career in the pre-war Army. Tall, lean, completely bald, Simpson was well liked by all the men who served with him. He was one of the few senior American officers who got along with the difficult British commander Bernard L. Montgomery. Simpson, or "Simp" as his old friends called him, was, in the words of Army group commander Omar Bradley, "a born soldier and leader of men." In his memoirs General Eisenhower described Simpson as "alert, intelligent, and professionally capable . . . the type of leader that American soldiers desire." "If Simpson ever made a mistake as Army commander," wrote Eisenhower, "it never came to my attention."[52]

Seven Texans were awarded the Medal of Honor for their fighting in Europe during autumn 1944. The first of these, Staff Sergeant George D. Keathley of Olney, was awarded the Medal posthumously for rallying platoons of his company of the 85th Infantry to ward off a series of enemy counterattacks at Mt.

Altuzzo, Italy, on September 14. Although he was mortally wounded, Keathley, a former student at Texas A&M, continued to lead his men until the enemy withdrew. Keathley died a few minutes later. His "indomitable courage and incomparable heroism" saved three companies from being annihilated.[53]

First Lieutenant James H. Fields, born in Caddo and a graduate of Houston's Lamar High School, received the Medal of Honor for his heroism while leading his infantry platoon of the 4th Armored Division in action at Rechicourt, France, on September 27. Although rendered speechless by severe wounds to his face and head, Fields continued to lead his men until the objective was taken.[54]

Second Lieutenant James L. Harris of Hillsboro and Staff Sergeant Lucian Adams of Port Arthur were both awarded the Medal of Honor for action in France during October. Harris, who won a battlefield commission near Mt. Cassino, was a member of the 756th Tank Battalion, which was attacked on the night of October 7 at Vagney, France. Although mortally wounded, Harris helped stave off the enemy until reinforcements arrived. He died before he could receive medical attention.[55]

Sergeant Lucian Adams, a member of the 30th Infantry, 3rd Infantry Division, received the Medal of Honor for his action near St. Die, France, on October 28. When his company was stopped in its effort to drive through the Mortagne Forest Adams charged forward, firing a borrowed Browning Automatic Rifle (BAR) from his hip. In the course of his action he "killed nine Germans, eliminated three enemy machine guns, vanquished a specialized force which was armed with automatic weapons and grenade launchers, cleared the woods of hostile elements, and reopened the severed supply lines to the assault companies of his battalion."[56]

Three Texans, First Lieutenant Turney W. Leonard of Dallas, Technical Sergeant Forrest E. Everhart of Texas City, and Staff Sergeant Marcario García of Sugar Land, were awarded Medals of Honor for their heroic efforts in the fighting in Lorraine and the Huertgen Forest in November, 1944. Lieutenant Leonard, a 1942 Texas A&M graduate and member of the 893rd Tank Destroyer Battalion in the First Army, was awarded the medal posthumously for action at Kommerscheidt, Germany, on November 4-6. During a fierce engagement he repeatedly braved enemy fire to direct the fire of his tank destroyer. Although wounded, he continued to direct fire until disabled by a high explosive shell. He was last seen at a medical aid station that was captured by the enemy.[57]

Sergeant Everhart, a native of Ohio, entered military service from Texas City. Assigned to the 359th Infantry, 90th Infantry Division, Everhart rallied his men in face of a major enemy counterattack near Kerling, France, on November 12, 1944. In the course of the fighting Everhart crossed and recrossed the fire-swept terrain and engaged the enemy in a hand grenade duel that forced them to withdraw.[58]

Marcario García of the 22nd Infantry, 4th Infantry Division, received his Medal of Honor for action in the Huertgen Forest on November 27, 1944. Born

in Villa de Castano, Mexico, García grew up working on a farm near Sugar Land. Drafted into the Army in November 1942, Garcia was wounded in Normandy but rejoined his unit to take part in some of the war's most bitter fighting along the French-German frontier. Near Grosshau, Germany, on November 27, García singlehandedly assaulted two enemy machine gun emplacements. Although painfully wounded, he fought on until the objective was taken.[59]

Although he did not win his Medal of Honor until January 1945 young Audie Murphy from Hunt County was gaining recognition for himself and his state in 1944. Murphy, a 20-year-old sergeant in the 3rd Infantry Division, received his first decoration, the Bronze Star, in March when he crippled an enemy tank. He was awarded the Distinguished Service Cross (the Army's second highest award) for his role in the August 15 landings in southern France, when he silenced an enemy machine gun, killed five enemy troops, wounded three others, and forced another five to surrender.[60]

On Ocotober 2, 1944, Murphy won the Silver Star for charging an enemy machine gun, killing four Germans and wounding three others. Three days later he won an Oak Leaf Cluster to his Silver Star for crawling within 200 yards of an enemy machine gun and directing mortar fire that killed 15 Germans and wounded 35 others. In late October, Murphy was seriously wounded and hospitalized. After his return to his unit in January he would win the Medal of Honor.[61]

Many other Texans were involved in the drive across France and into the corner of Germany. Paul Boesch, a professional wrestler and later wrestling promoter in Houston, was a lieutenant in the 121st Infantry Regiment of the 8th Division. Boesch was a company commander in some of the most bitter fighting. He led his men in the house-to-house battle for control of the town of Huertgen. "Never in my wildest imagination had I conceived that battle would be so incredibly impressive," he later wrote, "awful, horrible, deadly, yet somehow thrilling and exhilarating."[62]

The 761st Tank Battalion, the predominately black outfit that had trained in Louisiana and Texas, took part in the drive through French Lorraine. Assigned to the 26th Infantry Division (the old New England National Guard), the 761st gave a good account of itself in assaulting German defenses. One tank commander, Sergeant Warren G. H. Crecy from Corpus Christi, motivated by the death of a close friend, was particularly successful in destroying enemy machine gun emplacements, action for which he received the Silver Star. In early December the 761st, known as the "Black Panthers," crashed through the enemy lines and rolled into Germany, winning the written commendation from XII Corps commander Major General Manton S. Eddy.[63]

The drive across France required vast amounts of supplies to keep the Army moving. To expedite the movement of these materials the Army Quartermaster Corps created the Red Ball Express, a one-way highway using thousands of trucks that traveled around the clock. Organized in early summer 1944 the Red Ball (name derived from railroaders' lingo for fast express) reached its peak of operation in late August. Between August 25 and November 13, quartermaster companies delivered over 400,000 tons of supplies from Normandy ports to troops in Alsace and Lorraine. The hours were long and accidents common. The majority of the drivers in the Express were African Americans. Herman Heard, a native Texan who was one of 15,000 African American drivers, remembered that one would "get so sleepy that you felt like you were drunk." Although the work was vital to the success of the European campaigns most of the Red Ball drivers received little recognition for their efforts. Technical Sergeant Harold Parry of Houston, recipient of the Bronze Star, was one of a few so recognized.[64]

The price for the liberation of France was high. All the combat divisions sustained heavy casualties but the losses were especially high in the 3rd, 4th, 29th, 30th, 36th, 45th, and 90th divisions. One of the units of the 36th Division, the 1st Battalion, 141st Infantry, was cut off from the rest of division in the Vosages Mountains in late October. Described by the press as the "Lost Battalion," the Texans were eventually relieved by the 442nd Regimental Combat Team, the all Neisi outfit. The battalion suffered over 20 percent casualties before the 442nd broke through the German encirclement.[65]

Texans played a major role in the European air war in 1944. Although Jimmy Doolittle replaced Texan Ira Eaker as commander of the Eighth Air Force in January, the Texas presence in Army air forces stationed in England was still strong. Brigadier General Charles P. Cabell from Dallas, a graduate of West Point, commanded the 45th Bombardment Wing of the Eighth Air Force in early 1944. In April he became director of plans for U.S. Strategic Air Forces in Europe. Another Texas West Pointer, Colonel Hunter Harris, Jr., of San Antonio, commanded the 447th Bombardment Group from its activation in May 1943 through September 1944 when he became commander of the Eighth Air Forces' 13th Combat Bombardment Wing. Colonel Archie Old, the northeast Texas engineer and veteran of the Schweinfurt raid, now commanded the 45th Combat Bombardment Wing.[66]

Many Texans were among the fighter pilots who escorted American bombers in raids over the European continent. Lieutenant Jack Jenkins, commander of the 55th Fighter Group, flying his P-38J "Texas Ranger IV," was one of the first American airmen to fly over Berlin. In early March 1944 his group was assigned to provide fighter protection for the first Eighth Air Force bombing raid of Berlin. Because of bad weather the bombers were recalled, but Jenkins and his fighters, who did not receive the recall message, flew on to Berlin.[67]

Lieutenant Colonel Glenn Duncan of Houston, commander of the 353rd Fighter Group, pioneered the use of the P-47 Thunderbolt in dive bombing and ground attack techniques. He also became one of the leading fighter aces in Europe, shooting down 19 enemy planes. Duncan himself was shot down by flak on July 7 but evaded capture and worked with the Dutch underground until Allied armies arrived in spring 1945. He then returned to command his fighter group.[68]

Lieutenant Joseph W. Bennett, a farm boy from central Texas, was a P-47 pilot in the 56th Fighter Group (the "Wolfpack"), which destroyed more enemy planes in aerial combat than any other American unit. Bennett shot down three enemy aircraft in the Berlin raids of March 1944. In May his own plane was rammed by a German ME-109, shearing off the tail section. Bennett parachuted to safety but was captured by German farmers armed with pitchforks, hoes, and clubs. He spent the rest of the war in a German prison camp.[69]

The Eighth Air Force carried out hundreds of missions against strategic enemy targets on the European continent during 1944 and 1945. Occasionally they were so called "milk runs" with little flak or fighter opposition, but more often the attackers ran into heavy enemy fire. Twenty-six thousand of the 350,000 men who served with the Eighth Air Force, or 7.4 percent, were killed. The percentage is much higher for those who actually flew on the B-17s and B-24s. Only 35 percent of those who flew in 1942-1943 survived. The percentage of survivors rose to 66 percent in 1944 after the arrival of P-51 Mustang fighters to provide escort to target and back.[70]

The greatest single loss of aircraft by an Eighth Air Force bomb group took place on September 27, 1944. Part of a 315 B-24 bombing mission aimed at the Henschel engine and vehicle plants at Kassel, the 445th Bomb Group veered off from the main column and was attacked by Focke Wulf 190s and Messerschmitt 109s. In a few moments time, 25 of the 32 planes (four had already aborted) were shot down and several others damaged. Only four of the Liberators made it back to their base south of Norwich. Lieutenant Joe Stewart, 20-year-old bombardier from Port Arthur, was on one of the planes that made it back to base; the co-pilot on his plane was from Ingleside, Texas.[71]

Dan Dennis from Beaumont, navigator in the 834th Squadron, 486th Bomb Group, a B-17 unit, remembers that his first mission over Magdeburg on August 3, was the worst. His plane was hit hard over target, losing one engine and its oxygen supply, forcing the plane to drop to 8,000 feet and fly home alone. "There was no way to survive 29 more trips like that one," Dennis recalls. But survive he did. In February 1945 he completed the required 30 missions and headed home.[72]

The Eighth Air Force had the strategic bombardment of German targets as its primary mission. In 1944 it was joined in England by the Ninth Air Force commanded by Lewis Brereton and later Hoyt S. Vandenberg. Originally stationed in North Africa, the Ninth became a tactical Air Force supporting American ground troops in the march across France. The Ninth was built around four B-26 Martin Marauder bomb groups, one of which was commanded by Colonel William Wood of Chico, Texas.[73]

Although he had been removed from command of the Eighth Air Force, Texan Ira Eaker continued to play a vital role in the European air war. In his new position as commander of the Mediterranean Air Force, Lieutenant General Eaker was responsible for providing tactical air support for ground troops fighting in Italy (Twelfth Air Force) as well as strategic bombing of targets in Italy, France, Germany, and the Balkans (Fifteenth Air Force). It was Eaker's bombers, heavy and medium, that leveled the Italian monastery at Mt.

Cassino and hit railways leading to Anzio and the Gustav Line. His heavy bombers made raid after raid into the Balkans, particularly against Rumania's Polesti oil refineries.[74]

In the summer of 1944, Eaker's Fifteenth Air Force and the Eighth Air Force took part in a series of shuttle bombing missions that took them to remote targets in Germany, Poland, and the Balkans. From there they flew on to airfields in the Soviet Union for refueling and then made a return run, hitting targets again and flying on to fields in Italy. General Eaker himself flew as co-pilot on of one of the first such missions.[75]

The 455th Bomb Group, composed of four squadrons of B-24 bombers, was one of the units in Eaker's Fifteenth Air Force. Commanded by Colonel William Snowden, a Californian who graduated from the University of Texas, the 455th carried out numerous missions in northern Italy and Austria. One of its B-24s was the *Dakota Queen*, flown by Captain George McGovern, later a U.S. Senator and Democratic presidential candidate. McGovern's crew included three Texans: navigator Lieutenant Carroll W. Cooper, a Texas A&M graduate from McCaulley; radio operator Sergeant Ken Higgins from Dallas; and gunner Sergeant William "Tex" Ashlock of Hereford.[76]

McGovern's bomb group often had fighter cover provided by the 332nd Fighter Group, the all-black unit trained at Tuskegee Institute in Alabama consisting of the 99th, 100th, 301st, and 302nd Fighter Squadrons. At first these pilots flew P-40 and P-47 fighters but in July 1944 received the new P-51 Mustangs, whose tails they painted red for distinction. The Tuskegee airmen, as they were often called, proved to be highly competent, boasting that not one bomber they escorted was lost to enemy fighters.[77]

Captain Leonard M. Jackson from Fort Worth was one of the Tuskegee airmen. A member of the 99th Squadron, Jackson shot down three enemy fighters and was awarded the Distinguished Flying Cross. Another African American from Texas, Lieutenant Norman W. Scales from Austin, a member of the 302nd Squadron, also received the Distinguished Flying Cross.[78]

Some American airmen were engaged in special operations. One such mission involved Navy Lieutenant Joe Kennedy, the older brother of future President John F. Kennedy, and Lieutenant Wilford "Bud" Willy, his co-pilot from Fort Worth. Kennedy and Willy participated in a highly dangerous attempt to take out German V-1 launch bunkers on the French coast. Kennedy and Willy were to fly their Liberator bomber loaded with powerful explosives to a point near target, then put their plane on automatic pilot and bail out before the plane reached its objective. Tragically, the plane exploded ten minutes before they were to jump, killing both men.[79]

Several Texans served in the 492nd Bombardment Group of the Eighth Air Force that carried out missions for the Office of Strategic Services. Operating under the code name Carpetbaggers, these airmen flew agents and thousands of tons of arms and supplies to friendly forces in Europe. Sergeant Garrett C. Parnell, Jr., from central Texas, a turret gunner on a B-24, was killed on one such mission in November 1944.[80]

By early December 1944, bad weather, supply problems, and stiffening German resistance slowed both the air and ground war against Germany. Even so, American and British military leaders believed the enemy too weak to halt the continued advance through Belgium and France and into Germany. Therefore, there was great surprise when on December 16 the German army launched a major assault against American lines in the Ardennes Forest.

The attack in the Ardennes, which came to be known in the United States as the Battle of the Bulge, was designed by Adolf Hitler himself, who hoped the German army could break through the American line and push all the way to the Belgian coast. Employing over 200,000 troops in the opening assault against 83,000 American troops, the Germans drove through American defenders along the Schnee Eifel and pushed almost to the Meuse River before their advance was stopped.[81]

Hundreds of Texans took part in the Battle of the Bulge (so named for the bulge in the German line), some in command positions and others in the field as riflemen, artillerymen, and tankers in combat roles. Colonel Hurley E. Fuller, a World War I officer from Texas, commanded the 110th Infantry Regiment (28th Division) which was in the center of the initial German assault. Although Fuller's troops fought gallantly they were overwhelmed by superior German numbers and many of them, including Fuller, were captured.[82]

The 109th Infantry, just south of Fuller's regiment, was commanded by former Ranger leader Texan Earl Rudder. The 109th had a more favorable position in terms of terrain and held its ground a little longer before being forced to fall back. Another Texan, Lieutenant Colonel Sam Hogan, West Point graduate of 1938, was in charge of a task force from the 3rd Armored Division sent to reinforce the beleaguered men of the 106th and 28th Infantry Divisions, but Hogan's forces were cut off by the enemy near the Ourthe River. Efforts made by another Texan, Colonel Jean D. Scott (West Point class of 1924), commanding the 393rd Infantry of the 99th Division, to hold the line were equally futile as his troops were forced to fall back under heavy enemy fire.[83]

As earlier efforts to stop the German advance failed, the 101st Airborne Division, which had recently been in Holland, was ordered to the Belgian town of Bastogne, hub of the roads in the eastern Ardennes. Heading the relief column was the 501st Parachute Infantry, commanded by Colonel Julian J. Ewell, Texan and West Point graduate. Captain Stanfield A. Stach of Milam County, a former Texas A&M football player, commanded A Company, 1st Battalion, in Ewell's Regiment. Another Texan, Lieutenant Colonel Ray C. Allen of Marshall, commanded the 3rd Battalion of the 327th Glider Infantry Regiment, which moved into the defense line west of Bastogne.[84]

For over a week, the men of the 101st Airborne were under constant enemy fire but they refused to surrender. When the German commander asked for capitulation, Brigadier General Anthony McAuliffe offered the classic comment "Nuts." On the day after Christmas the 4th Armored Division broke through the German perimeter and relieved the 101st.[85]

For their role in the fighting to keep the Germans from breaking through, two Texans, both members of the 2nd Infantry Division, were awarded the Medal of Honor. Sergeant Jose M. Lopez, a native of Mission and a member of the 23rd Infantry Regiment, received his award for protecting his company's left flank from being overrun by the enemy on December 17. Carrying a heavy machine gun, Sergeant Lopez moved from position to position under heavy enemy fire, giving cover for the men in his platoon to withdraw successfully. In the fighting Lopez killed at least 100 enemy troops.[86]

Truman Kimbro from Madisonville, Technician Fourth Grade, 2nd Engineer Combat Battalion, was killed while laying mines at the vital crossroads near Rocherath, Belgium, on December 19. Although his body was riddled with rifle and machine gun bullets, Kimbro dragged himself forward and laid his mines across the road. His act of courage prevented the rear of the 2nd Infantry's column from being attacked by the enemy. For this action he was awarded the Medal of Honor posthumously.[87]

The gallantry of men like Kimbro and Lopez gave the American military the time needed to bring up reinforcements to stabilize the line. Although the fighting in the Ardennes continued for several weeks, by the end of December it was obvious that the German offensive had failed. The cost of the Ardennes campaign was high. The German army lost at least 100,000 men killed, wounded, and captured. American casualties totaled 81,000, of which 19,000 were killed and 15,000 captured.[88]

The 15,000 captured Americans joined other Americans held in German prisoner of war camps. Nearly two-thirds of these were ground troops; by the end of the war 60,235 ground troops and 32,700 airmen were prisoners of the German Army and Air Force. Although there were over 50 German prison camps, the majority of American ground troops were held in Stalags II-A, II-B, III-A, IV-A, VII-B, and XII-A. Most airmen were held in four major camps run by the Luftwaffe: Lufts I, III, IV, and VI.[89]

Conditions in the German POW camps varied. Although the German military pledged to abide by the Prisoner of War Code of the 1929 Geneva Convention, shortages of food were commonplace. Most American POWs reported considerable loss of weight while in confinement; this would have been even greater had it not been for American Red Cross packages, which were received on an irregular basis.[90]

Joseph F. Fertitta of Beaumont, a B-17 tail gunner who was shot down on a mission to bomb rocket launching sites, weighed 170 pounds when he enlisted in October 1942; he weighed only 95 pounds when liberated. Matias Rodriquez from Kerrville, a medic with the 110th Infantry Regiment, was captured in the Battle of the Bulge. He spent the rest of the war at a camp near Kassel. Prisoners there received only a piece of black bread and bowl of soup each day. R. H. Peek, Jr., of Gilliam community in Red River County, a rifleman in the 88th Division, was captured in Italy. He lost 40 pounds while living on soup and two or three boiled Irish potatoes each day.[91]

Captured officers generally fared better than enlisted men. David Westheimer of Houston (later the author of *Von Ryan's Express* and other novels), a navigator in the 98th Bombardment Group, was shot down by Italian fighter planes on December 11, 1942. He spent the rest of the war in Italian and German POW camps. The food in German Luftwaffe camps was much better than in the Italian camps. Westheimer reported a variety of food served, including potatoes, bread, turkey, cheese, margarine, pumpkin, blood sausage, sugar, and meat. He did note that the meat was seldom fresh.[92]

Westheimer's experience was probably not typical. Ira Simpson of Dallas, also a navigator, reported that food in his camp near Nuremberg was poor, only hot water in the morning, two slices of bread with a little jam at noon, and soup made of potato peels in the evening. Another officer, B-17 co-pilot Bill Dallas of Austin, remembers that POWs at his camp on the Baltic had only one meal a day, consisting of boiled dehydrated vegetables and one potato. Tommy Lamore, an enlisted airman from Waco, said that POWs in his camps in Poland were "hungry all the time." They were served a turnip soup twice a day and given an "ersatz bread made from sawdust, a little flour, and what tasted like dirt."[93]

Although some Americans were tortured and mistreated by their German captors, most American POWs lived through their imprisonment. Less than one percent of the Americans held by the Germans and Italians died in captivity, about the same percentage of German prisoners who died while in the hands of the Western Powers. This may be contrasted with the much higher death rate among American POWs held by Japan, approximately 40 percent.[94]

The Japanese mistreatment of American and Filipinos who surrendered in the Philippines, Java, Wake, and Guam has been discussed earlier. That mistreatment continued throughout the war. Although the Japanese government expressed its intent to respect the 1929 Geneva Convention for the treatment of prisoners of war (which Japan had not ratified), this policy was seldom observed by area commanders, camp commandants, or prison guards. Historian Van Waterford notes that "contempt for POWs was the natural outcome of the code of bushido, inducted into the Japanese soldier as a part of his basic training." Japanese military doctrine did not recognize or permit a Japanese soldier to become a prisoner of war. Surrender was considered an act of cowardice that brought dishonor and disgrace to oneself and to one's family.[95]

Although Japanese army regulations decreed that POWs be "treated with a spirit of good will and shall never be subjected to cruelties or humiliation," brutal beatings, deliberate starvation, and torture occurred regularly. Descriptions of such treatment are found in most Texas POW accounts. Refugio Medina, an artilleryman from south Texas, remembers "beatings every day." "We lost a lot of people from starvation, hard work, and beatings."[96]

Kyle Thompson from Wichita Falls recalls that guards "would club you with a rifle or anything else within reach." Thornton Hamby, a Marine from Lubbock, had eight ribs broken when a guard beat him with a pick handle for no apparent reason. William J. Weissinger, Jr., a Texas survivor from the *Houston*, noted "once three to four Japanese guards started beating a person, they played no favorites with regard to parts of the body." Robert R. Martindale, a B-24 co-pilot from Brownsville, was knocked down repeatedly during a beating by a guard. Fiske Hanley from Fort Worth, a flight engineer on a B-29 shot down late in the war, reported that he and his fellow crew members were beaten daily with bats and the butt end of a rifle and were kicked with heavy boots. Sergeant Frank Fujita, the Japanese American from Abilene, noted "the harassment and beatings by the guards continued unabated and this inflicted us with our worse torture—the constant mind-bending fear that you would be the next victim. We could not shake this fear. It was with us every waking moment in camp and at work."[97]

In addition to the beatings American POWs held by the Japanese suffered severely from malnutrition. Historian Van Waterford points out that "although many men caught such tropical diseases as malaria, dengue, or dysentery, it was malnutrition from slow starvation that immeasurably increased the deadliness of all the diseases."[98]

Waterford believes that malnutrition was the result of a deliberate Japanese policy to keep captives in a weakened condition so they would give less trouble. Whether deliberate or not, there is little question that Texans in captivity suffered from lack of food. Clyde Fillmore from Wichita Falls later wrote that prisoners in his camp "never had enough to eat" and were always hungry. Fiske Hanley remembered that three rice balls and sometimes a cup of water constituted the daily food ration at his camp. Crayton R. Gordon from Itasca told interviewers that "thinking about food, hell, you'd just go damn near mad." Michael J. Robertson of Beaumont, shot down over Tokyo on his eighth mission in 1945, lost 110 pounds while confined only three months.[99]

The lack of food led prisoners to eat almost anything. Private First Class O. R. Sparkman, a Texas Marine, recalled that at Woosang, near Shanghai, he ate part of a rat that had fallen into the rice gruel he was served. Private Martin Chambers of the 131st Field Artillery stated "we ate every snake we could find." Private First Class William Visage, another Texas artilleryman, told interviewers "you'd eat anything. If a dead fish washed ashore you'd eat it." Frank Fujita recalled that men in his camp killed, skinned, cooked, and ate a dog that had been an RAF mascot.[100]

Most Texas POWs later mentioned the importance of Red Cross food parcels, which were distributed on an irregular basis. "The arrival and distribution of Red Cross parcels had a tremendous effect on morale," Robert R. Martindale wrote in his memoirs. In some camps the food parcels were not distributed at all; in most camps they were ransacked by the Japanese before they reached the prisoners. "You had to give them [the guards] a cut of everything that came in or you didn't get any of it," recalled Marine Private C. Permenter.[101]

Allied prisoners of war were required to perform hard labor for their captors in camps and work sites in Burma, Manchuria, Japan, the Philippines, and the Dutch East Indies. The first Texans captured (survivors of the *Houston* and the 2nd Battalion, 131st Field Artillery) were forced to build the 258-mile railroad connecting Bangkok, Thailand, and Moulmein, Burma. Construction of this road across jungle, mountains, and swiftly flowing rivers ultimately involved 66,000 Allied prisoners (mainly British, Australian, and Dutch) and 270,000 Asian civilians (Javanese, Malays, Burmese, Indian, and Chinese). Over 12,000 Allied prisoners and 72,000 civilians died in building the road. Most of the prisoner deaths were British, Australians, and Dutch; 133 of those who died were Americans.[102]

Many American, and Texan, prisoners of war captured in the Philippines and other islands were taken to Japan and China for work in factories, steel mills, shipyards, and mines. This involved travel in ancient, overcrowded, and poorly ventilated Japanese transports with little food, water, or toilet facilities. In addition, prisoners on these vessels, referred to by captives as "hell ships," faced the danger of U.S. submarine or air attacks. Captain Wilbert A. Calvert, a Texas A&M graduate, was one of thousands of American prisoners of war who died on such ships.[103]

Life for the survivors of the hell ships and other captives consisted of long hours of hard work, inadequate food, a variety of illnesses, poor medical care, and brutal punishments for any infraction of camp rules, real or imagined. Recreation was limited to reading, engaging in a few sports, and conversation with other prisoners, often about food, home, or liberation. News from the outside world was eagerly sought. This was sometimes obtained by outside work crews who smuggled in newspapers or reports from their guards.[104]

Texans in Japanese prison camps looked forward to the day of liberation. For those who did obtain information from the outside, the news in 1944 was encouraging as forces under General MacArthur and Admiral Nimitz drove the enemy back.

Allied advances in the Pacific were often costly. In late August one of the Navy's most successful submarines, U.S.S. *Harder*, commanded by Sam Dealey of Dallas, was fatally depth-charged off Luzon in the Philippines with the loss of all hands. At the time Dealey, known as the "Destroyer Killer" after his fifth patrol, commanded a submarine wolf pack of four boats, including U.S.S. *Haddo* commanded by Lieutenant Commander Chester W. Nimitz, Jr. Prior to his death Dealey received the Navy Cross with three gold stars, the Army's Distinguished Service Cross, two presidential citations and the Purple Heart. He was recommended for the Medal of Honor for sinking five Japanese destroyers on his fifth patrol. This was awarded posthumously in September 1944. He also received the Silver Star posthumously for his actions in his sixth, and final patrol, making him the most highly decorated American seaman in the Second World War.[105]

The loss of *Harder* and her crew, while tragic, did not slow the American submarine war against Japan. During the latter part of 1944, U.S. submarines continued their campaign against Japanese merchant ships, especially oil tankers. In October U.S. boats sank 320,96 tons of Japanese merchant shipping, the highest score in the war. In November another 214,506 tons were sunk.[106]

One of the U.S. submarines that took part in this destruction of Japanese shipping was the U.S.S. *Pintado*, commanded by Lieutenant Commander Bernard A. Clarey (Annapolis, class of 1934) with Lieutenant Commander Corwin Mendenhall (Annapolis, class of 1939) of Anahuac as executive officer.

In two patrols in 1944 and a third in 1945, *Pintado* sank 13 merchantmen and one destroyer, totaling 104,549 tons.[107]

While American submarines were attacking the Japanese merchant fleet in 1944, American airmen were carrying the war to Japan itself. Mass production of the new B-29 bomber, known as the Superfortress, began in autumn 1943. By early 1944 B-29s were available to some commands. The Twentieth Air Force, operating from bases deep inside China, began raids on the Japanese homeland in summer 1944. Once the Marianas were in American hands B-29s based in those islands began bombing Japan.[108]

With a range of 4,100 miles, fully pressurized cabins, and four remote controlled gun turrets mounting 12 machine guns and a 20 mm. cannon in the tail, the B-29 was a formidable weapon but was not invulnerable. Colonel Richard Carmichael, the Texan who had piloted a B-17 approaching Pearl Harbor at the time of the Japanese attack, was commander of the 462nd Bomb Group, which made a series of raids on Japan during summer 1944. On one such raid Carmichael's plane was hit by enemy fire and crashed. Carmichael and most of his crew parachuted to safety but were captured by the Japanese.[109]

Charles Harper, who operated two remote controlled gun turrets on a B-29 in the 444th Bomb Group, was another Texan whose plane was shot down in an early raid. Harper, who apparently shot down four Japanese fighters before he was hit in the chest by a 20 mm. shell, survived the crash at sea and was rescued by the Royal Indian Navy. Another Texan, also a gunner on a B-29, 20-year-old Hubert Roussel, Jr., of Houston, was less fortunate. His plane was shot down over the Marianas in December 1944 with loss of the whole crew.[110]

Major Horace S. Carswell, Jr., from Fort Worth was killed while piloting a B-24 in an attack on a Japanese convoy in the South China Sea on October 26, 1944. Carswell, a former student at Texas Christian University, was deputy commander of the 308th Bombardment Group of the 14th Air Force. After one bombing run, Carswell made a second low-level run that resulted in two direct hits on a larger tanker. His plane was riddled by fire from Japanese guns, puncturing the gasoline tank and wounding the co-pilot. By skillful flying Carswell managed to get his plane over land where he ordered the crew to bail out. When he discovered that one crew member's parachute was too badly damaged to use, he chose to remain with his comrade and attempt a landing. His plane struck a mountain, killing Carswell and the crew member.[111]

Major Carswell was awarded the Medal of Honor posthumously. He was also given the Distinguished Flying Cross, the Distinguished Service Cross, the Air Medal, and the Purple Heart posthumously. The Fort Worth Army Air Field was later renamed Carswell Air Base in his honor.[112]

The operations of American air forces in China were dependent upon vast quantities of supplies, especially gasoline, brought to China from bases in India. Early in the war the Japanese cut the Burma Road over which supplies had been sent to Chiang Kai-shek and the Chinese Nationalists. Until a northern route from Ledo, India, across the mountains to China could be opened supplies had to be flown over the Himalayan Mountains.

Flying over the Himalayas, or "the Hump" as it came to be called, was a horror story. The early cargo planes, C-47s and C-87s, were not designed for the extremely cold temperatures or heights that the Himalayas presented. A new cargo plane, the C-46, was introduced, but fuel problems had to be overcome before the C-46 proved satisfactory.[113]

Otha C. Spencer, a former East Texas State Teachers College student, was one of the pilots who flew the Hump. In his published memoirs, Spencer describes some of the experiences that he, Jim Groce from San Antonio, Henry J. Girad from West, Joseph S. Musil from Stamford, and others faced in flying these dangerous missions. By the end of the war, American airmen had made 167,285 trips across the Himalayas carrying 721,700 tons of supplies.[114]

To provide additional means of supplying forces in China, the Allies worked for over two years to build a new overland route to China. This new road started at Ledo in the Indian province of Assam and crossed the mountains and jungles of northern Burma into southern China. Building the road was a major undertaking requiring thousands of native workers and American engineers and machine operators. Fred O. Garza of Cuero and Buford B. Majors of Liberty County were two Texans who worked on the Ledo Road. In interviews given after the war, both Garza and Majors described the enormous difficulties in building the road. The unbearable heat with temperatures above 110 in summer, the heavy rains in the monsoon season, mosquitoes and other insects, and the terrain itself made this an almost insurmountable task. Finally, in February 1945, the road was open and additional supplies could reach China.[115]

While the air war against Japan intensified in the summer and fall of 1944, American naval and ground forces were moving closer to the liberation of the Philippine Islands. In mid-September, the 1st Marine Division landed on Peleliu, the principal island of the Palaus group about 600 miles east of the Philippines. The belief was that the island, with its airfield, could be occupied quickly without heavy casualties. This assessment proved to be wrong. The occupation of Peleliu, which was honeycombed with coral caves which made ideal defensive positions, was one of the most difficult and bloody operations of the Pacific War.[116]

In spite of heavy pre-invasion shelling and bombing, the three Marine regiments that came ashore on September 115 encountered determined enemy resistance. Even after they secured their principal objective, the airfield, the Marines had great difficulty in driving the Japanese out of the hundreds of caves. In six weeks the Marines lost 6,526 men (1,252 dead and 5,274 wounded). The Army's 81st Infantry Division, which relieved the Marines, lost 3,274 men (542 dead and 2,736 wounded) before the island was finally secured in November.[117]

Texans took part in the capture of Peleliu. Brigadier General Oliver Prince Smith, a native of Menard, was assistant commander of the 1st Marine Division and responsible for operational planning. Author-illustrator Tom Lea of El Paso covered the landings for *Life* magazine. Lea, by this time an experienced correspondent, went ashore 15 minutes after the first wave of Marines. He provided *Life* readers a graphic, visual portrait of some of the war's most bitter fighting. Pharmacist Mate Third Class Charles Victor Porras, Jr., of El Paso, a member of Company l, 3rd Battalion, 1st Marine Division, was awarded the Navy Cross posthumously for his heroism in carrying back four wounded Marines before being hit by enemy machine gun fire.

Marion A. Beall, Jr., of Beaumont, a medical corpsman in the 1st Marine Division, helped set up a forward aid station in a captured enemy blockhouse. Like hundreds of others he was wounded in the fighting. Another Texan, Dr. Edward L. Crain of Houston, was a physician attached to the Marines at Peleliu. Although himself wounded, he attended the dying and wounded while under heavy enemy fire, leaving his post only after 60 hours of continuous work. Crain was awarded the Silver Star for his gallantry under fire.[118]

Twenty-one-year-old Private First Class Charles H. Roan of the 7th Marine Regiment, a native of Claude, was awarded the Medal of Honor posthumously for his heroism at Peleliu. When an enemy grenade landed in the midst of several Marines, the young Texan flung himself on the grenade, absorbing the full impact of the explosion. This prompt and selfless act in face of almost sudden death saved the lives of four other Marines.[119]

Even before the Marines and Army had secured Peleliu, a larger American invasion force had landed on Leyte in the Philippine Islands. Four U.S. Army divisions, the 1st Cavalry, 7th Infantry, 24th Infantry, and 96th Infantry, all part of Lieutenant General Walter Krueger's Sixth Army, participated in the landings in October. In contrast to Tarawa, Saipan, and Peleliu, American troops encountered only moderate opposition as they landed. That afternoon General MacArthur and his party wadded ashore. Many photographers and correspondents, including Stanley Gunn of the Fort Worth *Star Telegram* and *Houston Chronicle*, were there to witness MacArthur's dramatic return.[120]

Captain Paul Austin of Fort Worth, commander of F Company, 34th Regiment, 24th Division, landed on Leyte with the second wave. Unlike many units that landed with little opposition, Austin's company was under fire from the moment it hit the beaches. Snipers, machine guns, mortars, and artillery pinned down Austin's company until an American tank destroyed the enemy pillboxes.[121]

Sergeant William A. Owens, from the small northeast Texas town of Pin Hook, was among those who came ashore on the second day. Owens, a Ph.D. in literature and a college instructor, had enlisted in the Army soon after the fall of Corregidor. Because of his educational background, he was trained in counter and combat intelligence. He and four other college graduates were part of a small counter intelligence team that landed on Leyte. During the next several weeks on Leyte and later on Luzon, Owens worked with Filipino civilians to weed out those who collaborated with the Japanese.[122]

As American troops pushed into the interior of Leyte, they encountered stiffening resistance. For over a month Krueger's Army advanced slowly, much to the dissatisfaction of his superior General MacArthur, who was anxious to move on to Luzon, the most important of the Philippine Islands. Finally, in early December a flanking amphibious movement by Major General Andrew D. Bruce's 77th Infantry Division cut off Japanese reinforcements. Fighting on Leyte continued several more weeks, but American success was now assured.[123]

In the early days of fighting on Leyte a great naval battle occurred in the waters around the island. On October 24 the Imperial Japanese Navy launched its last major offensive against U.S. naval units supporting the Leyte landings. Using nearly empty aircraft carriers to decoy William Halsey and the 3rd Fleet away from Leyte, the enemy then sent two powerful strike forces consisting of battleships, cruisers, and aircraft to attack U.S. transports and other ships in Leyte Gulf. During the next several days the greatest sea battle in naval history occurred as the United States fought off the Japanese attackers.[124]

One of the features of the battle of Leyte Gulf was the Japanese use of suicide, or *kamikaze*, planes to attack the huge American fleet. Roy "Tex" Garner, pilot of a Grumman Hellcat fighter, was one of those assigned to defend the fleet against these Japanese aircraft. On a pre-dawn patrol on October 24, Garner and three other pilots in his squadron shot down four enemy planes. While in the air, however, Garner heard over his radio that his own ship, the escort carrier *Suwannee*, had been hit by a *kamikaze*. Only with some difficulty Garner was able to return to his ship.[125]

The next day a more serious threat to *Suwannee* occurred. An enemy plane crashed into an American torpedo bomber on deck of the *Suwannee*, causing several explosions and tearing a ten-foot hole in her flight deck. Eighty-five crewmen were killed, 58 were missing, and 102 wounded. Garner, who had been sleeping at the time of the explosion, pitched in to aid those injured.[126]

In the same battle in which *Suwannee* was badly damaged, two other American escort carriers, *Gambier Bay* and *St. Lo*, were hit and sank. Lieutenant Leonard E. Waldrop of Liberty was pilot of a Grumman torpedo bomber assigned to the *St. Lo*. In the battle, described by naval historian Samuel Eliot Morison as the "most remarkable of the Pacific war," Waldrop, a graduate of Liberty High School and Lamar Junior College, made several bombing attacks on the large Japanese fleet. When he sighted two torpedoes heading for an American carrier, he dived and hit one of them with machine gun fire. For this action Waldrop was awarded the Navy Cross.[127]

Although the conquest took longer than General MacArthur had wished and the American Navy suffered heavy losses to the *kamikazes*, Leyte was a decisive American victory. The way was now open for the American return to the main Philippine island, Luzon.

As the year 1944 closed, Americans were more confident than ever that final victory was in sight. The battle in the Ardennes (which was still going on) and the taking of Peliliu and Leyte, however, demonstrated that the enemy was still capable of putting up a mighty resistance.

CHAPTER EIGHT

Victory

As the year 1945 began, most Texans believed that the war would soon be over. The German offensive in the Ardennes had been stopped. Although fighting there continued, it was apparent Hitler's attempt to break through had failed. The American Army had given ground but had not broken and was now driving the Germans back.

In the Pacific, the Japanese Imperial Fleet had been destroyed as an effective fighting force. While the *kamikaze* attacks had taken their toll, American naval and ground forces were poised for the invasion of the main island in the Philippines, Luzon. Under the sea and in the air American submariners and airmen were crippling Japan.

On the home front, thousands of Texans were working in aircraft factories, shipyards, munitions plants and oil refineries to produce the weapons needed by the fighting men. Morale remained high although there was the usual grumbling about rationing, price control, and governmental regulations. There was increasing concern over the peace settlements that would follow the end of military hostilities. Already there was evidence that the Russians intended to dominate Eastern Europe and would attempt to promote communism worldwide. While most Texans supported the wartime alliance with the Soviet Union, there was little support for communism. In his inaugural message on January 16, 1945, Coke Stevenson, beginning his second full term as governor, made it clear that Texans did "not want the [national] socialism of Germany, the fascism of Italy, or the communism of Russia." "We want a continuation of the Americanism of our forefathers in the United States," he declared.[1]

Texans at the battle front had little time to worry about rationing, price controls, or communism. While the American Army was gradually pushing the Germans back in the Ardennes Forest, heavy fighting also continued south of Strasbourg, France. The German Nineteenth Army held an area on the west bank of the Rhine in what came to be known as the Colmar pocket. In late

December 1944 and January 1945, several American and French divisions (part of Jacob Devers' Sixth Army Group) fought tenaciously to prevent the Germans from retaking Strasbourg. Eventually, they were able to force the Germans to pull back to the east side of the Rhine.[2]

The U.S. 3rd Infantry Division was in the middle of the fighting to reduce the Colmar pocket. Two Texas members of the division were awarded the Medal of Honor for their part in the campaign. First Lieutenant Eli Whiteley from Georgetown, a 1941 graduate of Texas A&M, was awarded the Medal of Honor for his role in house-to-house fighting in Sigolsheim, France on December 27, 1944. While leading a platoon of the 15th Infantry, Whiteley was severely wounded but charged into a house alone and killed two defenders. Although hit several times, he continued to rush from building to building firing at the enemy. He killed nine Germans and captured 23 more before he was forcibly evacuated.[3]

Audie Murphy, by now a lieutenant in the same regiment as Whiteley, received his Medal of Honor for action near Holtzwihr, France, on January 26, 1945. When his company was attacked by six tanks and waves of infantry, Murphy ordered his men to withdraw to prepared positions in the woods while he remained forward at his command post and gave directions to division artillery. He then climbed on a burning tank destroyer and employed its .50 caliber machine gun against the enemy. Although himself wounded, he killed or wounded 50 German troops before his ammunition was exhausted. He then made his way back to his company and ordered a counterattack that drove the enemy from the field.[4]

Murphy was presented his Medal of Honor at a ceremony in Salzburg, Austria, on June 2, 1945. At the same time he was awarded the Legion of Merit. Presentation of these two medals made the 20-year-old Texas farm boy the most highly decorated soldier in the history of the United States Army. In all, he received 33 medals, decorations, and citations, including French and Belgian medals for valor.[5]

Another Texan, 44-year-old Private First Class George B. Turner, born in Longview, was awarded the Medal of Honor for his role in fighting just north of the Colmar Pocket. Turner, who served in the First World War, was

Audie Murphy after receiving Medal of Honor.
—UT Institute of Texan Cultures at San Antonio

living in California when the attack on Pearl Harbor occurred. He enlisted again and was assigned to the 499th Armored First Artillery, 14th Armored Division. On January 3, 1945, near Phillipsbury, France, Turner was cut off from his artillery battery. He joined an American infantry company that was withdrawing under heavy enemy fire. When he saw two German tanks and infantrymen advancing, Turner seized a rocket launcher and moved to meet the enemy. Under intense enemy fire Turner destroyed one tank and disabled the other. He then seized a machine gun from a nearby half track and opened fire upon the enemy infantry. Then he took part in an American counterattack, firing a light machine gun from the hip.[6]

While Allied armies in Belgium and France were driving the Germans back toward the Siegfried Line on their western border, the American Fifth and British Eighth armies were continuing their movement up the Italian peninsula. In what had become "the forgotten front," Allied soldiers and airmen slowly forced the enemy to give ground. When Mark Clark was promoted to group commander in early 1945 Lucian Truscott, the Texan who had become one of the Army's most successful generals, was named to succeed Clark as Fifth Army commander.[7]

Under Truscott's leadership the Fifth Army pushed the Germans back toward the Po River. In their advance north, Allied infantrymen received close air support from the fighter groups of the U.S. Twelfth Air Force. Flying the rugged P-47 Thunderbolt, these fighter groups made raid after raid, strafing and dive bombing enemy targets. The P-47s caused major damage to the enemy, but flying at low levels they suffered heavy losses from ground fire. Lieutenant Gene Priest of Beaumont was pilot of one of the P-47s hit by enemy ground fire. He was saved only by the heavy iron plate in the rear of his seat. Several missions later Priest was hit again, this time by a 40 mm. shell in his left wing. Somehow he managed to make it back to his field at Pisa, but with most of his controls damaged he hit the end of the runway. His plane was practically demolished, but he was not hurt physically. Priest was later severely injured when flying a mission to support Patton's Army in Germany.[8]

Raymond Knight, a native of Timpson and graduate of Houston's John H. Reagan High, was killed on a mission supporting Allied operations in northern Italy. Flying his P-47 in a series of low level attacks on April 24-25, 1945, Knight destroyed 14 enemy planes on the ground and wrecked ten others. His own plane was hit several times by antiaircraft fire, but he declined to parachute to safety in the hope he could save his plane. While attempting to return to his home field he crashed in the Apennine Mountains. For his gallant action in "eliminating German aircraft which were poised to wreak havoc on Allied forces pressing to establish the firm bridgehead across the Po River," he was awarded the Medal of Honor posthumously.[9]

While Allied troops in northern Italy moved into the Po River valley in the winter and spring of 1945, seven Allied armies (First Canadian, Second British, First French, First U.S., Third U.S., Seventh U.S., and Ninth U.S.) were advancing into Germany on a broad front stretching from Nijmegen, Holland, on the north to Basel on the Swiss border to the south. The fighting continued to be bitter as Allied troops pushed through the heavily fortified Siegfried Line. Large reinforced concrete pyramids (known as "dragon's teeth") prevented tanks from moving through many areas. Concrete pillboxes provided firing windows for artillery and machine guns. Barbed wire and hidden land mines made a nightmare for advancing infantry.[10]

Private First Class Herman C. Wallace, a native of Marlow, Oklahoma, and a resident of Lubbock, was one of the combat engineers assigned to clear German mines for the infantry. On February 27, 1945, Wallace stepped on a well concealed S-type anti-personnel mine. Hearing the characteristic noise that such a mine makes when activated and realizing that if he stepped aside the area would be sprayed with deadly fragments that would kill those men around him, Wallace placed his other foot on the mine to prevent this from occurring. In doing so he saved the lives of other soldiers but was killed himself. For this supreme sacrifice, Wallace was awarded the Medal of Honor posthumously.[11]

Silvestre S. Herrera from El Paso was a rifleman in the 36th Division whose feet were severed by a land mine near the French-German border. Herrera was leading a frontal assault on a German strong point when he stepped on a mine. Despite pain and loss of blood, Herrera pinned down the enemy with accurate rifle fire, allowing other troops to skirt the minefield and capture the German

Barbed wire in deep snow, 36th Division.
—Texas State Library & Archives Commission

machine gun by a flanking movement. He was awarded the Medal of Honor for his courage and self sacrifice.[12]

Extremely cold weather made the fighting even more unpleasant. Lieutenant Colonel Max Lale, born in Oklahoma and later an East Texas journalist and historian, was executive officer of the 401st Field Artillery Group, which provided fire support for several infantry divisions in the Rhineland campaign. In his memoirs Lale recalls that "January was a month of unremembered cold, ice, and snow. The cold was only barely tolerable for those who were prepared for it with adequate clothing, but it was especially miserable for infantry in the line. They bore the brunt of the season and soon were being evacuated from the front at a rate said to be 1,000 a day, suffering from frostbite and frozen feet."[13]

Tom Floyd of Beaumont was a rifleman in one of the divisions supported by the 401st Field Artillery. A native of New Orleans, Floyd joined the 30th Infantry Division, a former National Guard outfit from Tennessee and North Carolina, during the Battle of the Bulge. Floyd recalls the hardships suffered as the division fought its way across France and into Germany. Between January and mid-May 1945 (when the war in Europe ended) his company had a shower only two times. Although food was adequate, it was usually C and K rations while on the move. A particular concern of the infantry was what Floyd called "treebirds." These were explosives the enemy fired into the tall fir trees. They were timed to go off just as American troops entered the forest, causing heavy damage by falling debris from the trees.[14]

Floyd's division, described by military historian Russell Weigley as "the battle-wise, thoroughly reliable 30th Division," crossed the Rhine River south of Wesel on the night of March 23-24. At the time the division was part of Simpson's 9th Army, which was attached to Montgomery's 21st Army Group. The crossing took place after careful preparations and a heavy bombardment by British bombers and American artillery. Floyd and his company crossed the Rhine in small boats about 2:00 in the morning. In the darkness there was considerable confusion as the men came ashore. Floyd was injured by artillery; a close friend was killed in the shelling.[15]

Simpson's Ninth Army, to which Floyd's division was assigned at the time, was the third American Army to cross the Rhine. Two weeks earlier, on March 7, the 9th Armored Division in the U.S. First Army discovered the Germans had failed to blow up the Ludendorff Bridge over the Rhine at Remagen. The 9th Armored quickly moved troops across the bridge. Other nearby divisions were ordered to cross before the bridge could be destroyed by enemy fire. The 78th Infantry Division reached Remagen later that afternoon and began crossing. W. T. Block of Nederland, a radio man in the division, was in a large convoy that crossed that evening. "We crossed in almost total blackness, no headlights except for a few signal flashlights, and only a few soldiers here and there with dimmed lights, guiding the drivers," Block later recalled. "The decks of the bridge and a foot bridge on the side of it were still covered with the bodies of American dead, most killed by exploding shells as they attempted to cross, as well as many Germans who died trying to defend the bridge . . . ."[16]

Montgomery's 21st Army Group was scheduled to make the next crossing of the Rhine. In typical fashion Montgomery had carefully husbanded his resources for such an operation, but the night before (March 22) the 5th Division of Patton's Third Army crossed near Oppenheim and Nierstein, robbing Montgomery of much of the glory.[17]

Harry Haines, a tank officer from Houston, was among Patton's troops who crossed the Rhine at Nierstein. Leader of the 2nd platoon of C Company, 737th Tank Battalion, Haines was in the sixth tank to cross. A German ME-109 fighter strafed Haines' tank as it crossed the small pontoon bridge over the Rhine but failed to seriously damage the vehicle. From Nierstein Haines and his company pushed on to the town of Trebur and later to Frankfurt.[18]

The U.S. Seventh Army, which included the 36th (Texas) Division, the 45th (Oklahoma–New Mexico National Guard), and the 3rd Division (Audie Murphy's division), crossed the Rhine at Worms on March 26. The French First Army made the crossing at Speyer on March 31. All Allied armies under Eisenhower's command were now across the greatest river barrier to the interior of Germany.[19]

During April, Allied armies pushed the enemy back. It now became a contest to see who could capture the most Germans and could advance the fastest. Walton Walker's XX Corps was in the center of Patton's Third Army as it swung south into Bavaria. "The Texas Bulldog," as some referred to the Belton native, pleased the historically conscious Patton when XX Corps captured the famous Ratisbon fortress in late April. From there, Walker pushed on across the Inn River near the Austrian border. By early May Walker's XX Corps was in Czechoslovakia.[20]

Another Texan, Major General Roderick R. Allen, a Texas A&M graduate in 1915, distinguished himself in the drive across Germany. Commander of Seventh Army's 12th Armored Division, Allen led his troops in the successful assault on the ball-bearing city of Schweinfurt in April. The 12th Armored then pushed on deep into southeastern Germany and on April 22 became the first Allied division to reach the Danube River.[21]

As Allied armies moved deeper and deeper into Germany, resistance in some areas weakened. In other instances the enemy continued to fight with determination. Near Untergreisheim in the Neckar Valley, Company A, 232rd Infantry, 63rd Infantry Division, was decimated by heavy machine gun, mortar, and small arms fire. Lieutenant James E. Robinson from Waco, an artillery forward observer attached to the company, rallied the remaining uninjured riflemen and led them to sweep the area of all resistance. Soon thereafter he led the exhausted company survivors in an attack on the town of Kressbach. Although Robinson was seriously wounded in the throat and was losing blood, he continued to direct the attack. Only after the town was taken and he could no longer speak did he walk nearly two miles to an aid station, where he died. For his heroism and bravery, Robinson was awarded the Medal of Honor posthumously.[22]

In early April, American troops of the 4th Armored Division liberated the German concentration camp at Ohrdruf, a small village south of Kassel. In the next several days larger camps at Buchenwald, Dachau, and elsewhere were liberated. The sight of burned bodies, skeletons, and starving inmates made a deep impression upon all who saw them. General Patton became physically ill; General Eisenhower seethed with anger at what he saw. Harrison Frank Ude, an infantryman in Patton's Third Army from south Texas, recalled "it was impossible to believe what we were looking at . . . ovens full of partially and completely burned bodies, uh, dead corpses laying all around, people walking around just skin and bones, didn't know if they were alive or dead."[23]

Bertis C. Henderson from Post, Texas, an infantryman with the 99th Division, expressed horror and disbelief when he saw one of the Dachau subcamps. "We couldn't believe what one human could do to another human," he told an interviewer. Alfredo Garcia, a rifleman in the 20th Armored Division from Brownsville, was so affected by his view of the crematories at Dachau that he could not eat for several days.[24]

Patricia Lockridge, who grew up in Austin, was one of the female correspondents who visited Dachau the day after liberation. She was present for the compulsory visit to the camp by the town's leading citizens. Afterwards she spoke to townspeople who professed ignorance as to what went on at the camp. One German woman attempted to assure Lockridge that most Germans were not involved. "The Fuehrer couldn't have known," the woman declared. "He would never have permitted such suffering."[25]

Most American troops were convinced that the German people did know about the deaths in concentration and extermination camps. The scenes in the camps caused many Americans to fight more tenaciously. Richard Hardison, a Texas A&M graduate from Colorado City, was captain of a field artillery battery in the 8th Armored Division. He had seen heavy fighting in the Roer River campaign and the reduction of the Ruhr pocket but was shocked by the sight of burned bodies and emaciated inmates at the camps. "By this time, I hated the Germans intensely," Hardison later wrote.[26]

A week after Patton's Army first encountered the Ohrdurf concentration camp Franklin D. Roosevelt, the only President many of Patton's younger troops ever knew, died in Warm Springs, Georgia. Roosevelt had been sitting near his desk as an artist painted his portrait when the president put a hand to his head and complained of a severe headache. He then collapsed. He died two hours later without regaining consciousness. On his desk was the *Atlanta Constitution* with the headline "9th–57 Miles from Berlin."[27]

News of Roosevelt's death shocked Americans everywhere. Historian Doris Goodwin points out "for the millions who adored him and for those who despised him, an America without Roosevelt seemed almost inconceivable." At home and on the battle fronts Americans lamented the loss of the man who had led the nation through the Great Depression, the dark days following Pearl Harbor, and was now on the edge of final victory over the enemy. Even Americans held in German prison camps lamented Roosevelt's death. In his memoirs, Kenneth W. Simmons of Dallas, a B-24 bombardier, describes a memorial service held for Roosevelt in his camp near Mooseberg, Germany.[28]

While the nation mourned the death of its president, the war went on. The headlines on the *Atlanta Constitution* had been correct; at the time of Roosevelt's death, April 12, 1945, the 83rd Infantry and 2nd Armored Divisions of Simpson's Ninth Army had reached the Elbe River, 57 miles from Berlin. The next day men of the 83rd Infantry crossed the river just south of Magdeburg. By nightfall they had constructed a bridge which they named for the new President, Harry S. Truman.[29]

Men of the 83rd Infantry and 2nd Armored Division were now poised for the race to Berlin. The 30th Infantry and the 5th Armored Division, also part of Simpson's Ninth Army, were also prepared to move on Berlin. Early in the morning of April 15, however, Simpson was informed by General Bradley that he was not to advance beyond the Elbe. Eisenhower had made the decision to halt at the Elbe in order to avoid the unnecessary loss of thousands of American lives in taking a city and territory much of which would be turned over to the Russians once the war ended.[30]

General Simpson was stunned by the news. He and his division commanders were convinced they could reach Berlin before the Russians. But Eisenhower's orders were clear. For Simpson and his men, the war was over. Both Simpson's Ninth Army and Hodges' First Army stopped at the Elbe. Patton's Third Army and Alexander Patch's Seventh Army drove on into Bavaria, Austria, and Czechoslovakia.

When the final surrender of all German armies became effective on May 8, the 36th Division was at Kufstein, Austria. The division had been in combat for 361 days and had suffered 26,718 casualties. Of these 5,957 had been killed or died of wounds received in action. The 3rd Division, which had many Texans in its ranks (including Audie Murphy), had been in combat 233 days since it landed in France and had 28,400 casualties. The 45th Division, which had fought alongside the 36th and 3rd Divisions in Italy, France, and Germany, had sustained 26,449 casualties. The 45th was at Munich when the Germans surrendered. The "Tough 'Ombres" of the 90th Division, originally a Texas-Oklahoma division, sustained 27,617 casualties.[31]

The news that the war in Europe was over brought great joy, especially to the English people who had struggled against the evils of Nazism for nearly six years. There were major celebrations in the great cities of London, Paris, Rome, Brussels, and New York City. Inside Texas, the celebrations were more subdued. In some towns, civilian defense sirens sounded; in others church bells marked the occasion. Many churches had special services for those who wished to give thanks and to pray that the war in the Pacific would soon be over. Workers in shipyards, airplane factories, and refineries stopped for a moment to give thanks but then went back to work producing the materials needed for victory over Japan. The time for real celebrating would be when Japan surrendered.[32]

When the war in Europe ended, American forces were drawing closer and closer to the Japanese home islands. In early January 1945, the U.S. Sixth Army commanded by Walter Krueger landed on the northern coast of Luzon in the Philippines. Three weeks later, the Eighth Army commanded by Robert Eichelberger made landings on Bataan and south of Manila.[33]

While the naval forces supporting the landings had to withstand a series of *kamikaze* attacks, most troops coming ashore faced little opposition on the beaches. As they moved inland , it was a different story. The Japanese defenders, commanded by Tomoyuki Yamashita, one of Japan's most able generals, followed a shrewd campaign of protracted resistance that resulted in heavy casualties.[34]

Leonard Hall, the tall rifleman from East Texas, was with the 43rd Division on the extreme left flank of Krueger's Army which landed in northern Luzon. Hall's regiment reached the beach without opposition but during the night the Japanese charged in a wild *banzai* attack. When this proved unsuccessful, the Japanese changed their tactics to infiltration. Two nights after the *banzai* attack, they slipped into the American lines, bayoneting two of Hall's comrades to death and wounding several others.[35]

Emil Matula, a young Czech from central Texas, was First Sergeant of D Company, 35th Infantry of the 25th Division, which also came ashore in northern Luzon. A veteran of Guadalcanal, Matula had entered the Army during the Depression when the family lost its farm. Matula's weapons company took heavy casualties in early February as the division broke through enemy defenses at Lupao on the edge of the Caraballo Mountains. Matula himself was wounded by a sniper and spent the next 20 days in hospital.[36]

As Krueger's Army pushed southward there was fear that the Japanese might kill Allied POWs held on the island. One Japanese prison camp was at Cabanatuan, about 25 miles south of Lupao. At one time the camp held several thousand prisoners, most of them survivors of the early fighting in 1942. Late in 1944 the more healthy of these prisoners, including Chaplain Robert P. Taylor, a native Texan and graduate of Baylor University, had been moved to Japan. Five hundred American and British POWs, including 37 Texans, remained in the camp. Lieutenant Colonel Edward Kallus from Caldwell, Lieutenant Colonel Donald Sawtelle from Corpus Christi, and Major Emil Reed from Dallas were the senior ranking Texans still in the camp.[37]

The 6th Ranger Battalion, commanded by Lieutenant Colonel Henry Rucci, a 1932 West Point graduate from New England, was given the assignment of slipping through enemy lines and rescuing the prisoners. The daring operation, described in the best selling *Ghost Soldiers: The Forgotten Epic Story of World War II's Most Dramatic Mission*, was carried out on January 30, 1945. The Rangers killed most of the camp guards. When some of the Japanese attempted to slip away, their trucks were destroyed by a bazooka team headed by Staff Sergeant Manton Stewart of Baytown. Stewart then turned the bazooka on a shed housing Japanese tanks. Stewart's rocket scored a direct hit, destroying two enemy tanks.[38]

Paul Austin of Fort Worth, promoted from company commander to executive officer of the 2nd Battalion, 34th Regiment, 24th Division, was part of Eichelberger's Eighth Army that landed on the northwest corner of Bataan. The regiment encountered heavy resistance as it moved through the Zig Zag Pass. On February 6 Austin's battalion was almost destroyed by enemy mortar fire. "There is nothing more terrifying than those mortar shells," Austin later reported. "You cannot hear them coming. You have no warning. Before you hear anything at all, it has exploded, thrown, or torn your body."[39]

Austin's regiment finally made it through the pass but suffered 325 casualties. Even so, several regimental officers and a division commander were relieved of command for failure to be more aggressive.[40]

While Eichelberger's Army struggled in the mountains on Luzon's west coast, the 37th Infantry Division (formerly the Ohio National Guard) and the 1st Cavalry Division of Walter Krueger's Sixth Army pushed southward towards the capital city, Manila. The 1st Cavalry (formerly stationed at El Paso's Fort Bliss) reached the outskirts of Manila first. On the evening of February 3 a column of the 1st Cavalry broke through the gates of Santo Tomas University, where several thousand Allied civilians and 77 Army and Navy nurses were being held. The Japanese guards were routed and the prisoners liberated.[41]

The battle for control of Manila lasted for a month. General Yamashita had not intended to fight for the city, but Japanese naval units were determined to resist. Much of the fighting was block by block, building by building. To avoid civilian casualties, General MacArthur prohibited air attacks, but thousands of Filipinos died as the Japanese defenders murdered, raped, and burned innocent civilians.[42]

The fighting around public buildings in Manila was bitter. Technical Sergeant Cleto Rodriquez from San Marcos, a member of B Company, 148th Infantry Regiment, 37th Division, was awarded the Medal of Honor for his heroism in the fighting near the Paco Railway Station. Rodriquez, an automatic rifleman, advanced to within 20 yards of the station under heavy enemy fire, killing and wounding Japanese troops as he advanced. Then Rodriquez threw five hand grenades through the doorway of the station, killing seven Japanese, destroying a 20 mm gun, and wrecking a heavy machine gun. Two days later, Rodriquez singlehandedly killed six Japanese soldiers and destroyed another 20 mm gun.[43]

By early March, resistance in Manila ceased. Nearly 100,000 Filipinos died in the battle; almost six times the number of American and Japanese troops killed in the fighting. The city itself was in ruins. General Yamashita, however, continued to resist in the mountains of northern Luzon. The fighting in the north was difficult as American troops pushed their way through the mountain passes toward Yamashita's headquarters at Baquio. The 33rd Infantry Division (formerly the Illinois National Guard), commanded by Major General Percy W. Clarkson, a 1915 graduate of Texas A&M, played a major role in the final capture of Baquio in April. However, Yamashita withdrew much of his army into the northern jungles and continued fighting until the final Japanese surrender in September 1945.[44]

American air power played a major role in Asia and the Pacific during the last year of the war. Rip Collins, a former student at Texas A&M, was a pilot in the first fighter group to fly out of bases in Luzon once American troops landed. Collins' 35th Fighter Group had provided valuable support to MacArthur's troops in New Guinea and Leyte and continued to do so in Luzon. The 35th originally flew the rugged P-47 Thunderbolts, but in spring 1945 exchanged them for the faster, long range P-51 Mustangs. Collins flew 92 combat missions, which included dive bombing, strafing, troop support, and protecting Catalina flying boats as they rescued down American airmen.[45]

R. E. "Peppy" Blount, later a football star at the University of Texas, was a pilot in the 501st Squadron of the 345th Bomb Group which provided low level bombing support for the landings and subsequent fighting in Luzon. A 1943 graduate of Big Spring High School, Blount, who named his B-25 Mitchell bomber *Touch O'Texas*, was only 20 years of age and the youngest man in his squadron. Blount's navigator, Lieutenant Nat Kenney, was a former Baylor student from San Antonio. Staff Sergeant Harold Warnick, engineer-gunner on "Touch of Texas," was, like Blount, a West Texan.[46]

Other Texans played significant roles in American and British operations in China and Burma during 1945. Major General Howard Davidson, a 1911 graduate of Texas A&M, was commander of the Tenth Air Force. Davidson, an enthusiastic and aggressive officer, ran a highly effective campaign that virtually shut down any support for Japanese troops in Burma by water. He then turned his planes to a devastating offensive against railroad marshaling yards, locomotive works, tracks, and bridges.[47]

Another Texan, Colonel John A. Dunning, became commanding officer of the 5th Fighter Group in China. A graduate of San Antonio's Thomas Jefferson High School, Dunning enlisted in the Missouri National Guard while attending Washington University in St. Louis. He received pilot training at Randolph Field under the National Guard quota and was commissioned in the U.S. Army Air Corps in August 1939. As commander of the 5th Fighter Group Dunning led his men in a series of dive bombing and strafing raids against the enemy.[48]

The 112th and 124th Cavalry Regiments, formerly part of the Texas National Guard, took part in ground operations in Asia during 1944 and 1945. The 112th and 124th Cavalry were separated when the Guard was reduced from a square to a triangular division. The 112th, which surrendered its horses in spring 1943, fought in New Guinea, Leyte, and Luzon as an infantry regiment. The 124th did not give up its horses until the next year.[49]

In October 1944, the 124th Cavalry was sent to Burma as part of a two regiment brigade, known as the Mars Task Force. Throughout the latter part of 1944 and early 1945 the Mars Task Force fought alongside Chinese and native partisan forces to help keep open the Ledo-Burma road.[50]

Lieutenant Jack L. Knight from Mineral Wells, a graduate of Weatherford Junior College, led his platoon of F troop, 124th Cavalry, in one of the last battles near the Burma Road. Single-handedly, he knocked out two enemy pill boxes and killed several of the enemy. While attempting to destroy a third pillbox, he was blinded by an enemy grenade. Although he could not see, he led his men in an assault on the third pillbox before falling mortally wounded. For his gallantry he was awarded the Medal of Honor posthumously; it was the only one bestowed in the China-Burma-India Theater.[51]

Several Texans fought alongside Knight. Sergeant Wayne Dale of Santos, a cook for F troop who volunteered to serve as messenger, was killed in the fighting. Knight's brother, Curtis, who was first sergeant of the troop, was severely wounded. Sergeant Richard M. Hatfield of Houston, a mortar platoon leader, was wounded in both legs. A squad of South Texas Mexican Americans, led by Sergeant Clyde Stockton of San Antonio, suffered several casualties while cleaning out an enemy pill box.[52]

While the fighting in Burma and the Philippines was still going on, U.S. Marines landed on the beaches of Iwo Jima, a small volcanic island between Saipan and Tokyo. Capture of the island was important to the success of B-29 bombing raids of the Japanese homeland from the Marianas Islands. To avoid Japanese fighters based on Iwo, American planes had to fly a longer route to their target, consuming valuable fuel and reducing the bomb load. Also, radar on Iwo Jima gave the home islands warning of impending raids. Once Iwo was in American hands B-29 bombers flying the route back from Japan from bases on Saipan, Guam, and Tinian would have an emergency landing field if needed.[53]

Three Marine divisions took part in the Iwo Jima campaign. The initial landings, which took place on the morning of February 19 after a massive naval bombardment, were carried out with precision. The 5th Marine Division landed on the southernmost beaches almost 3,500 yards from the base of Mount Suribachi, a 556 foot high dormant volcano. The 4th Division landed to the immediate right of the 5th Division. The 3rd Division came ashore later as reinforcements in the center of the two assault divisions.[54]

For the first minutes ashore, the Marines encountered little enemy fire. About 30 minutes later, however, the Japanese defenders opened a murderous barrage on the Marines who were struggling in the soft, deep volcanic dust. According to Corporal Alfred R. Stone, a young Marine from Marlin, Texas, "all hell really broke loose." Japanese mortar and artillery shells "started falling all around us, coming from Suribachi [on the southern tip of the island] and the northern tip of island," Stone later wrote. He doubtlessly spoke for other Marines when he recalled "it was frightening to have fire coming at you from two directions."[55]

For the next five weeks, the Marines fought a desperate battle with Japanese defenders for control of the island. Losses were extremely high. When Japanese resistance finally ended in late March, 25,851 Americans were casualties; 6,821 of these were killed. The 22,000 Japanese defenders, including the commander, Lieutenant General Tadamichi Kuribayashi, died almost to a man.[56]

Texans played key roles in the taking of Iwo Jima. John Keith Wells, a tall, dark-haired, 23-year-old West Texan, commanded the platoon that fought its way up Mount Suribachi on February 23. Wells, who carried a Thompson machine gun, was a rather flamboyant but popular leader, known to his men as "J. K." or "Tex." According to one member of the platoon, Wells "liked to tilt his overseas cap forward carelessly and walk around with a don't-give-a-damn look, but was serious minded."[57]

Wells' platoon blasted open the way to the Suribachi's base. Wells himself was severely wounded on the third day of fighting and sent back to a hospital ship. He persuaded the doctor to give him a pack of sulfa and morphine and then hitched a ride back to his platoon. For his actions at Iwo Jima, Wells was awarded the Navy Cross.[58]

Harlan Block from Weslaco, a member of Wells' platoon, was later identified as one of the six Marines in the famous photograph of the raising of the flag over Mount Suribachi. A smaller flag had been raised earlier by Wells and several other Marines including Bernard Holly from Abilene, but was replaced by a larger flag. As the larger flag was placed in the ground, Associated Press photographer Joe Rosenthal snapped a shot. This became one of the most famous photos of the war. Rosenthal received a Pulitzer Prize for the photo, which later inspired the giant bronze monument to the Marine Corps near Arlington Cemetery.[59]

Block, the figure at the far right in the photograph (bending forward, thrusting the base of the flagpole in the ground) was a football star at Weslaco High School in its undefeated season of 1942. He and 12 other players joined the Marines in January 1943. Although they went to boot camp together at San Diego, they were separated thereafter. Block served on Bouganville during the last days of fighting, was given a furlough home, and then joined the newly formed 5th Marine Division in summer 1944.[60]

Flag Raising at Iwo Jima (Harlan Stone on extreme right).
—National Archives

Neither Block nor the other five Marines in the Rosenthal photo had any idea at the time that they would become famous because of the flag raising. On March 1 Block wrote to his mother telling her that he was all right. The next day he was killed.[61]

The capture of Mount Suribachi was only the first step in the fight for Iwo Jima. During the next five days the Marines slowly advanced northward into the interior of the island with the 5th Division on the left, the 3rd in the center, and the 4th on the right. By March 1, the Marines had overrun two of the island's airfields and were moving toward the uncompleted airfield number three. Resistance was especially strong at Hill 362 on the left side of the island, where the 5th Marine Division was fighting.[62]

In the early hours of March 3, the Japanese infiltrated the lines of the 5th Division's 28th Regiment. Sergeant William G. Harrell of Rio Grande City, a former student at Texas A&M, killed several of the infiltrators but lost both hands to grenade explosions. When he was evacuated near dawn, Harrell's body was hedged by the bodies of 12 Japanese, at least five of whom he had personally killed while defending his command position. For his fortitude and valor Harrell was awarded the Medal of Honor.[63]

Another Texan, Lieutenant Jack Lummus from Ennis, was awarded the Medal of Honor posthumously for his gallantry as leader of a rifle platoon of the 27th Marines, 5th Division, in action on March 8. Without rest for two days and nights, Lieutenant Lummus led his men in an attack on a strong enemy position. He was knocked down twice by enemy grenades and severely wounded in the shoulder but continued to move forward until he stepped on a land mine, sustaining fatal wounds.[64]

As the Marines slowly advanced on Iwo Jima the Japanese made full use of the myriad caves, tunnels, and ravines that provided ideal defensive positions. Herman J. Dupont of Port Arthur, first sergeant of I Company, 3rd Battalion, 27th Marines, later recalled that the Japanese were holed up so well in many of the caves "the only way we could dislodge them was by using flamethrowers and heavy demolition charges." "When rifle and machine gun fire or hand grenades, failed," said Sergeant Dupont, "our demolition teams were called up to do the job. It was a slow process, the men had to crawl on their bellies with their tanks long distances to get to the caves and bunkers and not get hit before reaching their target. These men were vulnerable and we lost some of these valuable men."[65]

Organized resistance on Iwo Jima finally came to an end in late March. The Marines began withdrawing, and the Army's 147th Infantry took over garrison duty. Even so, the fighting was not ended as 1,602 Japanese were killed and 867 taken prisoner during April and May, 1945. Corporal Alfred Stone from Marlin, who left the island on March 26, spoke for most of the Marines when he wrote "we were exhausted, saddened from our losses, but glad to be alive."[66]

Okinawa, a 60-mile-long banana-shaped island only 350 miles southwest of Japan, was the next target for American forces in the Pacific. In American hands the island, an independent kingdom until annexed by Japan in 1879, would provide sites for an air base and fleet exchange as well as staging area for the invasion of the Japanese mainland, an operation that was being planned for autumn 1945.[67]

American forces came ashore on the southwestern beaches of Okinawa on April 1, 1945. As usual, the landings were preceded by a massive naval bombardment by American battleships, including the U.S.S. *Texas*, which had steamed half way around the world following the southern France invasion. Four American divisions, the 1st and 6th Marine Divisions, and the 7th and 96th Army Divisions, made up the initial invasion force under the command of Lieutenant General Simon Bolivar Buckner. They would later be supported by the 27th and 77th Infantry Divisions.[68]

Unlike many of the earlier landings, the American troops encountered little opposition as they came ashore on Okinawa. The Japanese commander, Lieutenant General Mitsura Ushijima, believed that defense of the beaches was impossible due to American air and naval superiority. He chose instead to develop a strong interior defense system that made use of the island's caves, mountains, and underground bunkers.

The conquest of Okinawa took months of hard fighting with heavy casualties. Weldon William Havens, a 20-year-old rifleman from Roaring Springs, a small West Texas community in Motley County, was a member of the 5th Regiment, 1st Marine Division, that fought its way across Okinawa. In a letter to his family back home, young Havens, known as Billy, discussed the torrential rains, enemy mortar fire, and air attacks that plagued American forces in securing the island. "We really go through hell up there," Billy wrote his sister in describing action on the front line.[69]

The 96th Division, which pounded away at the enemy Kakazu Ridge defense line for three weeks, sustained particularly heavy losses. Among its dead was the assistant division commander, Brigadier General Claudius Easley, a graduate of Texas A&M. An expert marksman, Easley had a passion for target practice and rifle instruction. Under his proding the 96th Division had become known as the "Deadeyes." Easley was a general who stayed with the troops at the front, a practice that cost him his life. Near the end of the battle for the island, Easley was pointing to an enemy machine gun that wounded his aide when he was hit in the forehead by two bullets from the same weapon.[70]

Major General Andrew D. Bruce, another Texas Aggie, commanded the 77th Infantry Division, which relieved the 96th Division after several weeks of fighting. Bruce had earlier made a reputation for himself and his division in the conduct of an amphibious operation in the Philippines. He further enhanced his standing in early April when the division captured Ie Shima island off the western coast of Okinawa.[71]

It was on Ie Shima that war correspondent Ernie Pyle was killed. Pyle had come to the Pacific in spring 1945. After visiting American airmen in the Marianas he joined the marines for the landing on Okinawa. After two weeks on Okinawa Pyle decided to visit Army troops on Ie Shima. On the second day there, after talking with General Bruce at a regimental command post, Pyle was hit in the temple by fire from a Japanese machine gun and died. The troops put up a memorial to Pyle with an inscription "At This Spot, The 77th Infantry Division Lost A Buddy, Ernie Pyle, 18 April 1945."[72]

While American soldiers and Marines fought their way through the Japanese defenses on Okinawa, Navy personnel in the massive fleet supporting the ground operations suffered from a series of Japanese air attacks, many of them *kamikazes*. Between April 6 and June 22 ten major attacks by several hundred enemy planes were made on the fleet. Sixty-four U.S. ships were sunk or badly damaged. One of the ships damaged was Admiral Raymond Spruance's flagship, U.S.S. *New Mexico*, which was hit by a *kamikaze* on May 12. Joe Beech from Sierra Blanca, Texas, an engineer on a landing craft attached to the U.S.S. *Bowie*, witnessed the attack on the *New Mexico*. The *kamikaze* "swooped right over the top of us, with every ship around us throwing flak at it," Leech later told an interviewer. "It passed less than a hundred feet over us," said Leech, "and hit the *New Mexico*, sending up a big cloud of black smoke and killing 54 men."[73]

Another Texan, Melvin Fenoglio from Montague County, was on the U.S.S. *Little*, which was hit by four *kamikaze* planes and sank on May 5. Fenoglio was thrown into the water but after three hours was rescued by shipmates. Many others were less fortunate than Fenoglio. Nearly 5,000 American sailors were killed and more than 7,000 wounded—more casualties than the Navy suffered in the entire Pacific during the previous two years. Army and Marine losses in taking Okinawa totaled 7,613 men killed, almost 32,000 wounded, and 26,000 in accidents or death from diseases; twice as high as U.S. casualties on Guadalcanal and Iwo Jima combined. Among the last casualties before the island was secured was the young West Texas Marine Billy Havens, killed on June 16, 1945.[74]

The heavy losses suffered in taking Iwo Jima and Okinawa convinced American planners that an invasion of the Japanese home islands would be exceedingly difficult and costly. Most Texans were relieved when the dropping of the atomic bomb on Hiroshima and Nagasaki in early August 1945 made invasion of the Japanese homeland unnecessary. Francis E. Abernethy from Nacogdoches, serving on the minesweeper *Harkness* in the China Sea when the atomic bombs were dropped, expressed the view of most Texas servicemen when he recalled "I don't remember much shipboard philosophizing about the morality of the A-bombs." "We were awed, even frightened by the power unleashed at those holocausts, but we *never* questioned the necessity or morality. We would have been dammed fools to have had it and not used it." Another Texan, Martin Rutledge of Brownsville serving in the 1st Cavalry Division, regretted that the atomic bomb killed old people and children but believed "it was the greatest thing that ever happened" because "it saved millions of lives."[75]

The first atomic bomb was dropped on Hiroshima on August 6, 1945 by the B-29 *Enola Gay* of the 509th Composite Group flown by Colonel Paul W. Tibbets, group commander and veteran pilot from Illinois. The crew of the *Enola Gay* was representative of the entire nation. The co-pilot was from New

Jersey, the bombardier from North Carolina, and the navigator from Pennsylvania. Sergeant Joe Stiborik of Taylor, the radar operator, was the Texan in the crew.[76]

Six other aircraft took part in the mission to drop the first atomic bomb. In addition to the *Enola Gay*, which took off from Tinian at 2:45 A.M., August 6, two escort planes carrying observers and cameras, three planes assigned to report on the weather over the primary and alternate targets, and a fourth plane designated as a spare weather plane took off from Tinian in the pre-dawn hours of August 6. The *Straight Flush*, a B-29 piloted by Texan Major Claude "Buck" Eatherly, was the weather plane assigned to Hiroshima, the primary target. When Tibbets was informed by Eatherly that there was a break in the cloud cover over Hiroshima, Tibbets piloted his plane on to the target. An hour later, at 9:15 A.M., the atomic bomb was dropped over Hiroshima.[77]

Although there was great devastation and nearly 80,000 people killed at Hiroshima, the Japanese government still refused to surrender. Three days later (August 9) a second atomic bomb was dropped at Nagaski by another B-29, *Bock's Car*, piloted by Major Charles Sweeney. Kermit Beahan, a graduate of Rice Institute, was the bombardier.[78]

The dropping of the second atomic bomb, along with the Soviet Union declaration of war against Japan on August 8, finally brought the Japanese surrender on August 14. The formal capitulation was signed on September 2, 1945, on the deck of the U.S.S. *Missouri* before Allied representatives including General MacArthur and Admiral Nimitz.[79]

The end of the fighting caused great rejoicing and celebrating by Americans everywhere. Most Texans at home learned of the Japanese surrender in late afternoon of August 14. Many churches held special services that evening and the next day. In towns and cities people danced in the streets, honked their car horns, and kissed and hugged. In some towns liquor stores passed out free drinks; in others, stores suspended beer and liquor sales. Newspapers ran extras and special editions carrying stories of local servicemen and women. In Houston, the state's largest city, a crowd estimated at between 100,000 and 200,000 people came downtown that evening to shout, sing, weep, exchange drinks, and kiss each other. Similar large crowds assembled in the state's other large cities.[80]

Texas servicemen overseas shared in the joy of victory. East Texan Francis Abernethy was on the minesweeper *Harkness* in a convoy near Okinawa when "the destroyer leading the convoy blew its whistle and ran up the flag spelling 'Victory.'" "We screamed and hollered and jumped around like a bunch of crazies," Abernethy recalled. When someone yelled "unload through the barrels," the men fired off every weapon available from the ship's three-inch gun down through carbines and automatic pistols. Soon there was firing from all the ships in the convoy. "It's a wonder we didn't kill and sink each other and every ship in the East China Sea," wrote Abernethy.[81]

Bruce Aiken, a former University of Texas student who was a naval cryptographic technician stationed on Guam, was on his bunk when someone ran in shouting that Japan had surrendered. "Oh, God," Aiken later old an interviewer, "that was the best news I ever heard."[82]

Fred O. Garza, the aviation engineer from Cuero who had helped build the Ledo Road, was in Mungtze, China, when he learned the war had ended. "We looked over to the town and they were shooting firecrackers," said Garza. "The mess hall was open and we had coffee and all kinds of things. There was singing and crying."[83]

Boatswain Mate James W. Lowry from East Texas was on the U.S.S. *Zeilin* in the Marianas preparing for the invasion of Japan when he received the news. "They let us fire flares off the ship, and shoot tracer shells. The whole sky was lit up," he recalled.[84]

Max Lale, whose 401st Field Artillery Group had fought its way across France and Germany, was in Mourmelon, France, awaiting reassignment, possibly to the Pacific theater, when he learned of the Japanese surrender. "We celebrated the Japanese surrender at a glorious party," he wrote in his memoirs. In a letter to his wife back in Texas he said that he was "anxious to be a civilian all the way."[85]

Lale was not alone in his desire to return to civilian life. After Germany surrendered the Army had begun a partial demobilization and redeployment of troops. Under this plan individuals who had been in service for a couple of years or more would be sent home and separated from service as soon as possible, whether they served in the Pacific or in Europe. Some of those in Europe with less service time would be sent to fight Japan. This plan was based upon a point system. Individuals received one point for each month in service, one point for each month overseas, five points for each campaign star or combat decoration, and 12 points for each child (up to three children). At the time of the German surrender, the minimum requirement for the trip home and discharge was 85 points.[86]

The sudden surrender of Japan brought about reductions in the number of points required for discharge. However, the lack of sufficient numbers of ships meant the return home was often delayed. It was late 1946 before all combat veterans were home. Thousands of other troops with less service time remained in Europe and Asia as occupation forces.[87]

Of the 725,000 Texans who served in the armed forces during World War II, slightly over 600,000 were in military service when the war ended; 592,283 men and 9,403 women. Over two-thirds of the Texans still in service, 416,652, were in the U.S. Army. One-fourth of Texas servicemen and women, 155,554, or 25.9 percent; were in the Navy; 22,442, or 3.7 percent in the Marine Corps; and 7,038, or 1.2 percent, in the Coast Guard.[88]

Nearly 20,000 Texans (19,779) died while in the armed services during World War II. Three-fourths of these (15,764) were in the Army. The U.S. Navy reported 2,966 Texas deaths; the Marine Corps, 1,007; and the Coast Guard, 62.[89]

The thousands of Texas veterans who returned to civilian life in 1945-1946 found a state that had been significantly changed by the war. More Texans now lived in towns or cities as the rural way of live gave way to an urban society. Industry, especially petroleum and chemicals, had replaced agriculture as the main source of livelihood for Texans. Although the aircraft and shipbuilding industries flourished during the war, they were now cutting back production and reducing their work force as the need for planes and ships had been met.

The U.S. Congress had passed the Serviceman's Readjustment Act, better known as the "G.I. Bill," offering educational, housing, employment, and medical benefits to ease the transition of veterans back into civilian life. Thousands of veterans in Texas and elsewhere used benefits under this bill to attend colleges and universities in 1945 and 1946. Within a decade, 8 million American veterans received vocational training or higher education under the G. I. Bill. In addition, many Texas veterans took advantage of the Veterans Land Program created by the state legislature to aid veterans in purchasing farm land.[90]

Returning African American and Mexican American veterans found racial prejudice and segregation had not disappeared in Texas during the war. LuQuincy Bowers, an African American from Fort Worth who had served with the Quartermaster Corps in the Aleutian Islands, was reminded of Texas segregation laws when he stopped in Amarillo on his way home. He was told that he would not be served in a restaurant but that if he went around to the back "we'll get you something," an invitation that Bowers declined. Another Texas veteran, Medal of Honor winner Marcario García, got into a fight when a Richmond restaurant owner refused him service. García was arrested by police but acquitted by a local jury. Discrimination in South Texas led a Corpus Christi veteran, Dr. Hector Garcia, to form the American GI Forum of Texas devoted to securing equal rights for Hispanic Americans. When the undertaker in the town of Three Rivers, Texas, refused the request of the widow to hold a wake in the chapel for her husband Private Felix Longoria killed in fighting in Luzon, Dr. Garcia contacted Texas Senator Lyndon B. Johnson who arranged reburial for Private Longoria in Arlington National Cemetery.[91]

The fight for equal rights for all citizens would be a continuing one that would last longer than the war against Nazi aggression and Japanese imperialism. Meanwhile, Texans would cope with the problems associated with conversion from a wartime to a peacetime society, proud at least that they had played a major role in the victory over tyranny and international disorder. As historian James L. Stokesbury has written "if they [the World War II generation] could not destroy every evil, they destroyed the most vicious of their day. If it is part of the sadness of the human condition that they could not solve the problems of their children's generation, it is part of the glory of it that they so resolutely faced their own."[92]

APPENDIX ONE
After the War

Listed in this appendix are brief sketches of the postwar career and activities of various individuals mentioned in the text and endnotes.

Abernethy, Francis, *crewman on U.S.S. Harkness*. After wandering around a year, attended Stephen F. Austin State College on GI Bill; later received Ph. D., University of Texas. Professor of English, Lamar State College and Stephen F. Austin State University. Long-time secretary-editor of Texas Folklore Society. Member Texas Institute of Letters; Fellow, East Texas Historical Association and Texas State Historical Association.

Abernethy, Hazel Shelton, *school girl, Nacogdoches*. Received bachelor's degree, Stephen F. Austin; married Francis Abernethy in 1948. Twenty years later received master's degree; taught history at Stephen F. Austin for ten years until retirement. Mother of five children and grandmother of six.

Adams, Lucian, *Sergeant, winner of Medal of Honor*. Became benefits adviser for Veterans Administration, San Antonio. Street and park named for him in his native town of Port Arthur. Retired in 1986. Received Heritage Freedom Award aboard U.S.S. *Orleck*, Orange, February 2002. Died April 1, 2003.

Aikin, A. M., Jr., *Texas state senator; acting governor at time of Beaumont riot*. Co-sponsor of Gilmer-Aikin law establishing Minimum Foundation School Program for state of Texas in 1949. Retired from Texas Senate in 1978 after 46 years service in legislature. Died, Paris, Texas, October 24, 1981.

Allen, Roderick B., *Major General, commander of 12th Armored Division*. Remained in the Army; series of commands. In Korean War was chief of staff, Korean Operations. Last assignment, commanding general of New England sub-area. Retired, May 1954. Died February 1, 1970, buried Arlington National Cemetery.

Austin, Paul, *Company commander and battalion staff officer, 24th Infantry, Philippines*. Returned to Texas, worked for telephone company until retirement. Lives in Fort Worth, interviewed by Gerald Astor, *The Greatest War*.

Beaham, Kermit, *Nagasaki bombardier*. Returned to Texas. Employed as engineer by Humble Oil Refinery, Baytown, Texas.

Beall, Marion A., Jr., *Marine, medical corpsman, Peliliu*. Discharged December 15, 1945, returned to Beaumont. Worked for Beaumont Plumbing Company for 17 years, then formed own company, obtained master plumber license. Retired in 1987. Married, three sons, five grandchildren. Lives in Beaumont.

Block, W. T., *Radioman, 78th Infantry Division*. Returned to Jefferson County, worked for postal service. Obtained Master of Arts degree in history. Prolific writer, researcher, historian; author of numerous books and historical column for local newspapers.

Blount, R. E. "Peppy," *Pilot, 35th Fighter Group, South Pacific*. Attended University of Texas; football player in three bowl games, 1946, 1948, 1949. Youngest member of Texas Legislature. Later judge, Gregg County. Married, three children, attorney, oilman, rancher, lives in Longview. Published *We Band of Brothers* (1984), *Mamas, Don't Let Your Babies Grow Up to Play Football* (1985), and *A Time For All Reason* (2002).

Boesch, Paul, *First Lieutenant, Huertgen Forest*. Returned to Houston, became highly successful professional wrestling promoter and television personality. Published account of war experiences, *The Road to Huertgen* (1962). Died in 1980s.

Browning, John Gaitha, *Company Clerk, 592nd Engineer Amphibian Regiment, Leyte, Luzon*. After the war studied at Brooklyn Museum of Art; became successful artist and teacher. Lived in Arizona, New Mexico, and Central Texas. Died November 10, 1992.

Bruce, Andrew D., *Major General, Commander, 77th Infantry Division, Philippines, Okinawa*. Military governor of Hukkaido; returned to U.S. In 1947. Commanded 7th Division in Korea. Retired from Army in 1954, became president and later chancellor, University of Houston. Died, July 28, 1969, buried Arlington National Cemetery.

Bullington, Orville, *Board of Regents, University of Texas*. Active in National Republican Party; worked for nomination of Senator Robert A. Taft in 1952. Died November 25, 1956, in Wichita Falls.

Catey, Drate H., *Sergeant, 4th Infantry, Omaha Beach*. Returned to coaching. Served as coach and teacher in Oklahoma schools for 33 years.

Chennault, Claire, *Commander, Flying Tigers and U.S. 14th Air Force*. Retired from Air Force in July 1945. Organizer and chairman of board, Civil Air Transport. Homes in Taipei, Taiwan, and Monroe, Louisiana. Died, July 27, 1958, buried Arlington National Cemetery. Monuments to him in Taipei, Baton Rouge, and Lake Charles.

Clark, Tom, *Assistant Attorney-General of U.S.* Served as Attorney-General, Truman Administration. Appointed to U.S. Supreme Court in 1949, served 18 years. Retired from the bench in 1967; became first Director of Federal Judicial Center. Died New York City, June 13, 1977.

Coffey, Ruth, *Volunteer, Civil Air Patrol*. Completed university studies, received advanced degrees, taught political science at Lamar University.

Connally, Tom, *Chair, Senate Foreign Relations Committee*. Loyal supporter of President Truman and Democratic Party. Retired from Senate in 1953. Died October 18, 1963.

Cory, James, *Marine Private First Class, U.S.S. Arizona*. One of few Arizona survivors; served rest of the war in the Pacific. After war attended Southern Methodist University, married, and raised a family. Became building director at Nieman-Marcus.

Crecy, Warren G. H., *Sergeant, 761st "Black Panther" Tank Battalion*. Promoted to lieutenant late in the war; stayed in Army in Europe for five years; severely wounded in Korean War, underwent extensive plastic surgery. Promoted to major in 1961. Son, Warren, Jr., graduated from West Point in 1976. Major Crecy died October 26, 1976. Buried Arlington National Cemetery. Street at Corpus Christi Naval Air Station in Corpus Christi named for him.

Davis, George D., Jr., *Fighter Ace in South Pacific*. Served with distinction in Korean War; on 60th mission was shot down by superior enemy forces; awarded Medal of Honor posthumously. Body never recovered. Veteran's memorial in Lubbock dedicated to him.

Dennis, Dan, *Navigator, 486th Bomb Group*. Separated from service in October 1945; recalled briefly during Korean War. Married and children. Worked for Neches Butane ten years; attended Lamar State College in Beaumont at night, received BBA degree in 1957. Certified Public Accountant. Retired. Active in Eighth Air Force Historical Society.

Dies, Martin, Jr. *Congressman*. Retired from Congress in 1945; reelected Congressman-at-Large, 1952. Unsuccessful candidate, U.S. Senate, 1957. Died November 1972.

Dunning, John A., *Colonel, Commander 5th Fighter Group, China*. Stayed on in Air Force after the war, served in China, England, Viet Nam. Died, cardiac arrest while undergoing surgery for ruptured spinal disc in August 1962. Buried in San Antonio.

Dupont, Herman, *Marine 1st Sergeant, Iwo Jima*. Returned to Port Arthur, Texas. Worked at refinery many years. Retired, active in veterans' affairs.

Eaker, Ira, *Commander Eighth Air Force, later CIC, Mediterranean Theater*. Retired from Air Force in 1947. Associated with Hughes Aircraft, 1947-1957. A director with Douglas Aircraft 1957-1961. Syndicated journalist. In 1972 became founding president of U.S. Strategic Institute. Died August 6, 1987. Buried Arlington National Cemetery.

Everhart, Forrest E., *Sergeant and winner of Medal of Honor*. Died August 30, 1986, in Philadelphia. Buried Arlington National Cemetery.

Fairchild, Marguerite, *Board of Regents, University of Texas*. Replaced on Board in 1945. Campaigned for Rainey's election as governor in 1946.

Remained active in civic affairs in Lufkin. Died January 18, 1974. I. D. and Marguerite Fairchild Foundation established in 1977 supports Angelina County projects and University of Texas College of Fine Arts.

Fields, James H., *First Lieutenant, 4th Armored Division, winner of Medal of Honor*. Independent oil operator after war. Wife and three children. Died VA Hospital, June 17, 1970. Buried in Houston.

Floyd, Tom, *Sergeant, 30th Infantry Division*. Moved to Beaumont after the war, employed working on marine engines. Stayed active in Army Reserve. Described his war experiences in "A Walk in Time, 1944-1946."

Fomby, William W., *Seaman First Class, U.S.S. Oklahoma*. Stayed in Navy until December 1946. Attended Odessa College. Worked as sales engineer for same company for 27 years.

Fujita, Frank "Foo," *Sergeant, "Lost Battalion" and POW*. Returned to Texas, had personal and medical problems. Re-entered Army in 1948. Resumed civilian life after Korean War, became illustrator for Air Force, retired on disability because of beatings received while POW. Wrote book describing his experiences. Remarried, traveled extensively in motor home.

Garcia, Marcario. *Medal of Honor, Huertgen Forest*. Refused service in Richmond, Texas, restaurant in September 1945, involved in altercation. Became U.S. citizen, June 1947. Earned high school diploma, 1951. Counselor with Veterans Administration, 24 years. Died in car crash, December 24, 1972. Buried in Houston.

Garner, John Nance, *Vice President of United States, 1933-1941*. Returned to Uvalde, lived in relative seclusion. Died November 7, 1967, few days before 99th birthday. Buried in Uvalde.

Garza, Fred O., *Aviation construction engineer, Burma*. Living in Matamoros, Mexico, when interviewed by son in October 1996 for book *Valley Vets*.

Gay, George, Jr., *Ensign, survivor torpedo attack Midway*. After battle of Midway had celebrity status, cover *Life* magazine, bond drives. Airline pilot after the war.

Giles, Barney M., *Deputy Commander, U.S. Army Air Forces*. Retired July 1, 1946, after 29 years' service. Three years, vice president Air Associates of New York, then for ten years with Lear Jet Corporation, helped perfect automatic pilot. Died May 6, 1984, buried Fort Sam Houston.

Giles, Benjamin, *Commanding General, USAF, Middle East (twin brother of Barney Giles)*. Retired September 1, 1946, after 29 years' service. vice president, Trans World Airways; Board of 20th Century Fox. Died November 30, 1974, buried Fort Sam Houston.

Haines, Harry, *Tank officer, one of first across the Rhine*. Returned to Houston after the war. Later revisited places he passed through in the war. Interviewed May 2000 by Stephen N. Manning for his book *The Courage of Common Men*. Died June 2000.

Hall, Leonard, *Rifleman, 172nd Infantry Regiment, 43rd Division, South Pacific*. After the war moved to southeast Texas, became history teacher. In 1985 published description of his military activities in *Brothers of the Fox*.

Hanley, Fiske III, *B-19 Flight Engineer, POW*. Returned to Texas, employed by General Dynamics for 43 years. In 1997 published *Accused American War Criminal*, account of his experiences as prisoner of war.

Harrell, William G., *Marine Sergeant, Medal of Honor winner, Iwo Jima*. After losing his hands on Iwo Jima, sent to Mare Island for rehabilitation; discharged February 1946. Moved to San Antonio in 1949; chief of prosthetics division, local Veterans Administration; wife and four children. Night of August 9, 1964, Harrell shot and killed Mr. and Mrs. Ed Zumwalt and then killed himself. Cause of killings unknown.

Harris, Lynn, *29th Infantry, POW, Germany, seven months*. Returned to southeast Texas. Proprietor of Harris Florists in Nederland, Texas.

Hite, Robert, *co-pilot and one of Doolittle's Raiders. Survived Japanese imprisonment*. Retired from Air Force in 19555 with rank of Lieutenant Colonel. Operated hotels in Camden, Arkansas, and Enid, Oklahoma. After death of wife, remarried widow of one of the other Doolittle pilots.

Hood, Lonnie, *pilot, C-47 cargo plane, South Pacific*. After war returned to Beaumont, became representative of Southwestern Life Insurance Company and investment counselor. Remained active in flying for many years.

Hobby, Oveta Culp, *Director, Women's Army Corps*. Returned to Houston as director of radio and television station and executive vice president of *Houston Post*. Served on numerous boards. Became first Secretary of Department of Health, Education, and Welfare in 1953. Resigned in 1955 and resumed business duties and civic activities in Houston. Died August 16, 1995, in Houston. Buried in Glenwood Cemetery.

Horn, Arlie, *29th Division, Omaha Beach*. Returned to Beaumont, employed at Mobil Refinery, became maintenance planner department head; retired after 34 years. Returned to Normandy for 50th anniversary in 1994.

Hughes, Howard, *aircraft designer, pilot, head of Hughes Tool*. Continued interest in aircraft design and production; active in commercial aviation and motion pictures; became wealthy recluse; died April 5, 1976, while en route to hospital in Houston. Left estate estimated at $2 billion.

Johnson, Luther, *Congressman, played key role in passage of Lend Lease bill*. Left Congress in 1946 after 23 years' service; appointed Federal tax-court judge by President Truman, held position until 1956. Died on June 6, 1965, buried in Oakwood Cemetery, Corsiciana.

Johnson, Lyndon B., *Congressman, key supporter of Franklin D. Roosevelt*. Remained in U.S. House of Representatives until election to U.S. Senate in 1948; Democratic leader of U.S. Senate, Vice President of United States,1961-1963, President of United States, 1963-1969. Retired to ranch near Stonewall, died January 22, 1973.

Jones, Jesse H., *head of Reconstruction Finance Corporation, later Secretary of Commerce*. Asked to resign as Secretary of Commerce in January 1945; returned to business activities. Broke with Democratic Party, supported Republican ticket in 1948 and 1952. Died June 3, 1956, buried Forest Park Cemetery, Houston.

Jones, Marvin, *Director of War Food Administration*. Returned to U.S. Court of Claims, became chief judge 1947, in 1964 became senior judge, served until death in Amarillo on March 4, 1976.

Kelly, Jack, *seaman, U.S.S. Tennessee*. Remained in Navy until December 1946, discharged as chief boatswain's mate. Became farmer, then construction worker. Retired, lives in Bedford, Texas.

Kleberg, Richard, *Texas Congressman, defeated in 1944*. Returned to King Ranch where he served as chairman. Member of Texas Game and Fish Commission. Died in Hot Springs, Arkansas, May 8, 1955. Buried Chamberlain Burial Park, Kingsville.

Koger, Fred, *bombardier, 326th Squadron, 92nd Bombardment Group*. Studied art at Southern Methodist University, joined Taylor Publishing Company as artist, retired as vice president for sales; president Texas Gun Collectors Association; published *Countdown!* (1990), an account of his 35 daylight missions over Germany.

Lale, Max, *Lieutenant Colonel, 401st Field Artillery Group*. Moved to Marshall, Texas. Served as reporter *Marshall News-Messenger*; later publisher *Greenville Banner*. Public relations officer Longhorn Ordnance Works; Marshall City Council and civic leader. Author of numerous articles and *Max's Memoirs* (2001), an account of his WWII experiences. President of East Texas Historical Association and Texas State Historical Association.

Lanham, Fritz, *Texas Congressman and author of National Housing Act*. Served in Congress until 1947, not a candidate for re-election. Political adviser and lobbyist in Washington. Vice President of Trinity Improvement Association. Returned to Austin in 1963, died July 1965.

Latimer, Philip, *Lieutenant, 761st "Black Panther" Tank Battalion*. Completed graduate degree in mathematics at North Texas State Teachers College after war. Member of Mathematics Department, Lamar University, for more than 30 years, often serving as department head. Remained in Army Reserve, retired with rank of Lieutenant Colonel. President of 761st Tank Battalion & Allied Veterans Association. Lives in Lumberton, Texas.

Lea, Tom, *artist-correspondent, Coral Sea and Peliliu*. Highly successful writer of fiction and non-fiction (*Brave Bulls, King Ranch*, and others) as well as artist and illustrator. Died in 2001.

Le Fan, Leslie, *private, Marine Corps, Pearl Harbor, Guadalcanal, Okinawa*. Returned to Texas, served as circulation manager, *Temple Telegram*. Died October 4, 1986.

Lovett, Robert A., *Assistant Secretary of War for Air*. Resumed partnership with Brown Brothers Harriman banking firm on Wall Street; appointed Under Secretary of State in 1947; succeeded George C. Marshall as Secretary of Defense 1951; returned to Wall Street banking firm; declined invitation of John F. Kennedy to join his Cabinet; continued to be influential advisor in foreign policy matters; died at age 90, May 7, 1986.

Majors, Buford B., *heavy equipment operator, aviation engineers in Burma*. Returned to Southeast Texas; married, raised family, worked at Mobil chemical plant in Beaumont, moved to Arkansas to farm, returned to southeast Texas. Died at age 79, February 7, 2002.

Martindale, Robert R., *co-pilot, B-24, POW, Japan*. Remained in Air Force reserves, retired rank of lieutenant colonel. Air controller, Pan American Airways, teacher Navarro Junior College, staff of Texas Commission on Higher Education. Retired 1986. Published account of experiences as POW, *The 13th Mission* (1998).

Maverick, Maury, *Congressman, Chairman, Smaller War Plants Corporation*. Practiced law, remained active in Democratic Party in Texas, one of liberal leaders against conservative Democrats; active in civil rights and civil liberties matters; died in San Antonio, June 7, 1954.

Mendenhall, Corwin, *submarine officer*. Remained in Navy, retired with rank of Rear Admiral; after retirement wrote *Submarine Diary* (1991), an account of his World War II submarine patrols.

Mitchell, Johnny, *artillery captain, 5th Infantry, 3rd Army*. Highly successful petroleum engineer and wildcatter; president Texas Independent Producers and Royalty Owners; also president of California Independent Producers and Royalty Owners; wrote book *The Secret War of Johnny Mitchell* (1976) describing war experiences.

Morgan, John C., *Lieutenant, B-17 pilot, winner of Medal of Honor*. Left military in 1945, recalled Korean War, retired from military in 1954. Employed by Texaco, retired as division manger International Aviation Sales Department after 39 years service. Died January 17, 1991 in Papillion, Nebraska, buried Arlington National Cemetery.

Murphy, Audie, *3rd Infantry Division, most highly decorated American soldier, World War II*. Discharged August 17, 1945, successful career as motion picture actor, lyric song writer, author, and poet. Joined 36th Division as captain in 1950, later promoted major. Killed in airplane crash in Virginia on May 28, 1971, buried Arlington National Cemetery.

Musick, Clay H., *Seaman First Class, U.S.S. Arizona*. Burned badly at Pearl Harbor, discharged July 1942. Worked in shipyard in Galveston, became dental technician, Veterans Administration Hospital, Temple; retired with medical disability, 1958.

Nimitz, Chester, *Commander, Pacific Ocean Area Command and Pacific Fleet*. Succeeded Admiral Ernest J. King as Commander, U.S. Fleet in December 1945. Went on inactive duty as Fleet Admiral two years later. Died February 20, 1966, buried Golden Gate National Cemetery, San Bruno, California.

O'Daniel, W. Lee, *Governor and U.S. Senator*. Retired from Senate in 1949; involved in Dallas real estate and founded insurance company. Ran unsuccessfully for governor in 1956 and 1958 Democratic primaries. Died, Dallas, May 12, 1969, buried Hillcrest Memorial Park.

Owens, William, *Counter Intelligence officer, Philippines*. Joined faculty, Columbia University. Author of eight books on history and folklore. Retired in early 1970s, continued to be active in folk studies. Now deceased.

Parten, J. R., *oil man, Regent, University of Texas, Director of Transporta-*

tion Division, Office of Price Administration. Political adviser to Homer P. Rainey in governor's race, 1946; founding director, Fund for the Republic, active supporter of Democratic party and University of Texas. Died at home in Madisonville, November 9, 1992, buried there.

Patman, Wright, *Texas Congressman.* Remained in Congress, chair, House Banking and Currency Committee, 1963-1975. During last two terms in Congress was senior member; served 24 terms. Died March 7, 1976, at Bethesda Naval Medical Center in Baltimore

Perry, George Sessions, *novelist, war correspondent.* Depressed by the war, could no longer write lighthearted tales of rural Texas, continued serious writing. Suffered from arthritis and depression. On December 13, 1956, walked into the river; body recovered two months later, verdict accidental death by drowning.

Phillips, O. A. "Bum," *Marine, Guadalcanal.* Returned to southeast Texas, worked briefly at oil refinery, completed college degree. Highly successful high school football coach and later coach of Houston Oilers and New Orleans Saints. Ranching and business interests.

Priest, Gene, *P-47 fighter pilot, Italy, France, and Germany.* Long recovery process from wartime injuries, worked at *Beaumont Enterprise* and Texaco, active in Church of Christ, attended Abilene Christian College, received Master of Arts. Bible Chair director, Lamar State College, studied Johns Hopkins and Pepperdine, received doctorate St. Mary's University (Baltimore). Faculty member Pepperdine, retired in 1988 as full professor, moved back to Beaumont, author of several books. Deceased, 2004.

Rainey, Homer P., *President of University of Texas.* After dismissal as president of University of Texas ran unsuccessfully for governor of Texas in 1946, named president of Stephens College, Missouri, in 1947, joined faculty University of Colorado, 1956. Retired 1964. Died December 19, 1985, at age 89.

Rayburn, Sam, *Speaker of House of Representatives.* Remained as speaker of the House, political advisor Lyndon B. Johnson, died November 16, 1961, at age 79. Buried in Bonham, Texas.

Reddy, Kenneth, *co-pilot, in Doolittle Tokyo raid.* Killed in airplane accident, Little Rock, Arkansas.

Richardson, James O., *Commander, Pacific Fleet 1941.* After relief as CIC, Pacific, in January 1941 transferred to Washington. Executive vice president, Navy Relief Society, 1942-1945. Retired from active duty January 1947. Died, Washington, D. C., May 2, 1974.

Robertson, Michael J., *pilot, prisoner of Japanese.* Returned to Southeast Texas, finished college, taught, and later went to medical school, practiced general medical, Port Arthur. Returned to Air Force as flight surgeon, then returned to family practice. Killed in automobile accident, February 18, 1997, at age 72.

Robinson, Jackie, *1st Lieutenant, 741st Tank Battalion.* After discharge resumed athletic career. Became first African American player in major league baseball as member of Brooklyn Dodgers. After highly successful career elected to Baseball Hall of Fame.

Rodriquez, Cleto L., *Medal of Honor winner, Luzon*. Returned to San Antonio, joined LULAC, 1946, worked for Veterans Administration, member of U.S. Air Force, 1951-1954, U.S. Army, 1955-1970. Died December 7, 1990, buried Fort Sam Houston National Cemetery.

Rudder, James E., *commanded Ranger battalion, later division commander*. Returned to Brady, served as mayor 1946-1952, remained in Army Reserve, became major general, elected Texas Land Commissioner in 1956, became vice president, Texas A&M University, 1958, president in 1959. Died Houston, March 23, 1970.

Seiser, Ed. *Lieutenant commander, dentist on U.S.S. Rigel at Pearl Harbor*. After war served two years in the Philippines, senior dental officer U.S.S. *Boxer* in Korean War. Retired from Navy in 1959, went into private dental practice.

Simmons, Kenneth W., *B-24 bombardier, POW in Germany*. Served four years as chair of Northeast Texas Defense Area Committee, mayor of Avinger, Texas, three times; moved to Texarkana, became national director of sales for Old Rockland Life Insurance Company. Published account of prison experiences, *Kriegie* (1960).

Smith, Oliver Prince, *assistant commander, 1st Marine Division, Peleliu*. Remained in service, commander 1st Marine Division in Korea, conducted Inchon landing, made famous statement concerning Marine withdrawal from Yalu River "We are not retreating. We are merely advancing in another direction." Promoted lieutenant general in 1953, promoted to full general upon retirement. Died in California, December 25, 1977.

Soliz, Felix, *radio operator, Normandy and Germany*. Returned to Port Arthur, chemical operator at manufacturing plant and oil refinery. Retired, resides in assisted living home.

Stark, Luther, *Board of Regents, University of Texas*. Retired from Board of Regents in 1945, continued to be active in charitable organizations. In 1961 founded Stark Foundation. Died September 2, 1965, buried Evergreen Cemetery, Orange.

Stevenson, Coke R., *Governor of Texas*. Defeated in extremely close race for U.S. Senate in 1948 by Lyndon B. Johnson. Resumed ranching, supported Republican candidate for president in 1950s and 1960s. Died June 28, 1975, at San Angelo, age 87. Buried on ranch in Kimble County.

Stewart, Joe, *Bombardier, 445th Bomb Group*. Returned home, stayed in Reserve, recalled in Korean conflict, released because of collapsed lung. Graduated from Louisiana State University, returned to Port Arthur, worked 20 years for pharmaceutical firm, then 16 years with Sears as appliance specialist. Retired, lives in Beaumont.

Stone, Alfred R., *Corporal, 5th Marines, Iwo Jima*. Served in occupation forces in Japan; remained in Reserve, called back in Korean conflict. Highway patrolman, retired after 38 years' service. Published account of experiences *A Marine Remembers Iwo Jima* (2000).

Sumners, Hatton W., *Congressman, Chair House Judiciary Committee, 1932-1946*. Retired from Congress in January 1947. Director of Research in

Law and Government of the Southwestern Legal Foundation, active in civic affairs, received honorary doctorate of laws from Southern Methodist University. Author of *The Private Citizen and His Democracy* (1959). Died April 19, 1962, buried in K. P. Cemetery in Garland.

Taylor, Robert, *Chaplain, captured in Philippines, POW*. Returned home, remarried, remained in Army, retired with rank of Major General.

Townsend, Frank, *Gunner's Mate, U.S.S. Pennsylvania, Pearl Harbor*. Returned to Texas after war, worked as manager for El Paso Gas Sales, then Arrow Butane. Died January 5, 1980, age 60.

Turner, George B., *Private First Class, 14th Armored Division, Medal of Honor winner*. Died on June 29, 1963, in Encino, California, age 64, ashes buried in Arlington National Cemetery.

Valenta, Marcus, *Chaplain, Schofield Barracks, Hawaii*. Stayed in service until 1946. Pastor, El Campo, 1946-1974, St. Mary's Parish, Praha, 1974-1979. Died 1984.

Vrana, Leo Raymond, *Seaman, U.S.S. California, Pearl Harbor*. Joined father in construction business in Corpus Christi, later managed business, retired 1987, lived in Corpus.

Walker, Edwin A., *Brigadier General, Commander 1st Special Service Force*. Remained in Army, commanded artillery unit in Korea. In charge of Arkansas Military District during Little Rock High School integration crisis, later commander of 24th Infantry Division in Europe, admonished for indoctrinating troops with right wing literature. Unsuccessful candidate for governor of Texas, 1962, identified with right-wing causes, went to Mississippi to protest enrollment of James Meredith. Jailed for five days on charges of seditious conspiracy, victim of unsuccessful assassination attempt by Lee Harvey Oswald. Died in relative obscurity in Dallas, October 31, 1993, aged 84.

Walker, Fred L., Jr., *Major General, Commander 36th Infantry Division*. After command of Infantry School retired from Regular Army, April 30, 1946. Appointed lieutenant general and commander of Texas National Guard by Governor Stevenson, held post 14 months. Died October 6, 1969, at Walter Reed Hospital, Washington, buried in Kirkersville, Ohio, where he had his home.

Walker, Walton, *Major General, Commander of XX Corps*. Promoted lieutenant general; in 1948 made commander of Eighth Army, Japan; commander UN forces in Korea, killed in jeep accident December 23, 1950. Before burial in Arlington National Cemetery promoted to full general.

Ward, Billy, *Artilleryman, 4th Infantry, Utah Beach, Normandy*. Returned to Beaumont after the war, wrote article describing his experiences for the 50th anniversary special for *Beaumont Enterprise*.

Wells, John Keith, *Marine platoon leader, Iwo Jima*. Entered Texas Tech, graduated with degree in petroleum geology. Independent oil man, wife, three children, 11 grandchildren, volunteer work with Boy Scout, YMCA, church. Later wrote account of his experiences, "Give Me Fifty Marines Not Afraid to Die" (1995).

Wentrek, Dan, *Fireman, U.S.S. Nevada, Pearl Harbor*. After war farmed and sold farm equipment, maintenance worker, University of North Texas, retired 1986. Lived in Granite Shoals, Texas.

Westheimer, David, *Navigator, 98th Bomb Group, Prisoner of War, 1942-1945*. Resumed writing career. Author of 15 books including the highly popular *Von Ryan's Express* which was made into a movie. Described his own experiences in *Sitting It Out* (1992).

White, Jack, *Electrician's Mate, U.S.S. New Orleans, Pearl Harbor*. Attended University of Texas on GI bill, graduated with degree in business, became purchasing agent, University of North Texas.

Whiteley, Eli, *First Lieutenant, 3rd Infantry Division, Medal of Honor*. Returned to North Carolina State University, completed master's degree, married, two sons and three daughters, received doctorate in soil physics, Texas A&M University. Faculty member, Texas A&M, engaged in plant research and soil management. Died College Station, December 2, 1986, buried in College Station City Cemetery. Memorial Medal of Honor Park at Texas A&M bears his name.

Willis, Phillip, *Fighter Pilot, Bellows Field, Pearl Harbor*. Later co-pilot, B-17, Midway, Guadalcanal, wounded several times, medical discharge when war ended. Served two terms Texas legislature. Realtor in Dallas.

Wirtz, Alvin Jacob, *Under Secretary of Interior*. Represented oil and construction clients. Died heart attack, October 27, 1951, buried in Texas State Cemetery. Granite Shoals Dam renamed Alvin Wirtz Dam in 1951.

Young, Buck A., *Pelly teenager*. Served in Air Force, college degrees Colorado State University and Boston University; retired as major. Active in local writing groups. Wrote history of Baytown and numerous articles describing World War II experiences.

Zaharis, Mildred Didrikson "Babe," *Woman Athlete of Year 1945*. Helped found Ladies Professional Golf Association. Leading LPGA money winner. Named Woman Athlete of Half Century by Associated Press in 1950. Died from cancer on September 27, 1956, at age of 45. Buried in Beaumont. Memorial museum in her honor in Beaumont.

Zalman, Rudolph, *Machinist mate, U.S.S. Medusa, Pearl Harbor*. Remained in Navy until 1954, 23 years' service. Employed Phillips Petroleum and Hercules Power Company. Died September 1, 1957, at home near Waco.

 APPENDIX II

Texas Medal of Honor Recipients, World War II

The Medal of Honor, the nation's highest military award, was created by the United States Congress during the American Civil War to recognize outstanding achievements of Union soldiers and sailors in combat. Since its inception 3,408 Americans have been selected as recipients of the award, often referred to as the "Congressional" Medal of Honor. Nineteen individuals have received the award twice; thus there have been 3,427 Medals of Honor issued.

Four hundred forty Americans were awarded the Medal of Honor for service in World War II, 250 posthumously. Three hundred one of these went to members of the U.S. Army (including the Army Air Forces), 138 to Navy personnel (81 of whom were Marines) and one to a member of the U.S. Coast Guard.

Thirty-four of the 440 Americans awarded the Medal of Honor in World War were either born in Texas or entered military service from Texas (28 born in Texas and six born outside the state but entering service in Texas).

Nineteen of the Texas Medal of Honor recipients were commissioned officers; 15 were enlisted men. Colonel John R. Kane, born in McGregor but entering service in Louisiana, and Colonel Neel Kearby, born in Wichita Falls and entering service in Dallas, both airmen, were the highest ranking officers in the group. Commander Samuel Dealey, skipper of the submarine U.S.S. *Harder*, and Lieutenant Colonel Robert C. Cole, a battalion commander in the 101st Airborne Division, were the next highest ranking Texans to be awarded the Medal of Honor. Fourteen of the Texas Medal of Honor winners were lieutenants; eight were sergeants. Five privates first class and a seaman first class also received the Medal of Honor.

Twenty of the Texas award winners served in the ground forces of the U.S.

Army; seven others were in the Army Air Forces. Seven Texas Medal of Honor recipients were in the U.S. Navy; five of these in the Marines, one a submarine commander, and one a Seaman 1st Class serving on a Landing Ship Tank (LST).

Twenty-three of the Medal of Honor awards were made to Texans for action in the European Theater of Operations; 10 for service in the Pacific Theater, and one for service in Burma. Four of the European awards went to Texas airmen (two on the Ploesti raid); 19 to ground troops (ten for service in France, four for service in Italy, three for service in Germany, and two for service in Belgium).

Private First Class Cleto Rodriquez from San Antonio was the only Texan among Army ground troops to be awarded the Medal of Honor in the Pacific Theater. Five of the Texas Medal of Honor recipients in the Pacific were Marines; two for action in Tarawa, two for service on Iwo Jima; and one for fighting on Peleliu. Two Texas Army airmen (Horace S. Carswell, Jr., and Neel Kearby) and two Navy men (Samuel Dealey and Johnnie Hutchins) were awarded the Medal of Honor for service in the Pacific (all but Kearby posthumously). First Lieutenant Jack Knight of Weatherford, a member of the 124th Cavalry Regiment, was the only Texan (and American) to be awarded the Medal of Honor for ground action in the China-Burma-India Theater.

First Lieutenant Jack W. Mathis from San Angelo, lead bombardier in the 359th Squadron of the 303rd Bombardment Group, Eighth Air Force, was the first Texan awarded the Medal of Honor in World War II. His award, presented posthumously 12 July 1943, was for action over Vegesack, Germany, on 18 March 1943. Although badly injured by enemy antiaircraft fire, Mathis dragged himself to his sights, released his bombs, and died at his post of duty. As a result of his courageous action the planes of his squadron placed their bombs directly on the assigned target.

Eight other Texans were awarded the Medal of Honor for their actions in 1943; 15 for service performed in 1944; and 10 others (including the nation's most highly decorated soldier, Lieutenant Audie Murphy from Hunt County) for action in 1945. Several of the awards were made after the war had ended. Major Horace S. Carswell, Jr., who died when his plane crashed after receiving heavy enemy artillery fire over the South China Sea on 26 October 1944, was the last of the Texans to be recognized; his award was made in February 1946.

The service of each of the 34 Texas Medal of Honor recipients is described earlier in the appropriate chapters of this book. They are all listed on the following pages with rank, unit, place of birth or residence, and place where action occurred leading to Medal of Honor. An asterisk* indicates award posthumously.

Adams, Lucian, S/Sgt., 3rd Inf. Div., Port Arthur, action near St. Die, France, 28 Oct. 1944.

Borderlon, W. J.,* S/Sgt., 2nd Marine Div., San Antonio, action on Tarawa, 23 Nov. 1943.

Carswell, Horace S., Jr.,* Major, 399th Bomb Group, born Fort Worth, entered service San Angelo, action South China Sea, 26 Oct. 1944.

Cole, Robert G.,* Lt. Col., 101st AB Div., San Antonio, action near Caretan, France, 11 June 1944.

Dealey, Samuel D.,* Commander, U.S.S. *Harder*, Dallas, action in Philippine waters, June 1943.

Everhart, Forrest, T/Sgt., 90th Inf. Div., born Bainbridge, Ohio, entered service Texas City, action near Kerling, France, 12 Nov. 1944.

Fields, James H., 1st Lt., 4th Armd. Div., born Caddo, entered service Houston, action near Rechicourt, France, 27 Sept. 1944.

Fowler, Thomas W., 2nd Lt., 1st Armd. Div., Wichita Falls, action near Carano, Italy, 23 May 1944.

Garcia, Marcario, S/Sgt., 4th Inf. Div., born Villa de Castano, Mexico, entered service Sugar Land, action near Grosshau, Germany, 27 Nov. 1944.

Harrell, William G., Sgt., 5th Marine Div., Rio Grande City, action on Iwo Jima, 3 March 1945.

Harris, James L.,* 2nd Lt., 756th Tank Bn, Hillsboro, action near Vagney, France, 7 Oct. 1944.

Hawkins, William,* 1st Lt., 2nd Marine Div., born Fort Scott, Kansas, entered service El Paso, action on Tarawa, 20-21 Nov.1943.

Herrera, Silvestre S., PFC, 36th Div., born El Paso, entered service Arizona, action near Mertzwiller, France, 15 March 1945.

Hughes, Lloyd H.,* 2nd Lt., 389th Bomb Group, born Alexandria, Louisiana, entered service Corpus Christi, action in Ploesti raid, 1 Aug. 1943.

Hutchins, Johnnie D.,* Seaman 1st Class, LST, US Navy, Weimar, action at Lae, New Guinea, 4 Sept. 1943.

Kane, John R., Col., 98th Bomb Group, born McGregor, entered service Louisiana, action in Ploesti raid, 1 Aug. 1943.

Kearby, Neel E., Col., 5th Air Force, born Wichita Falls, entered service Dallas, action near Wewak, New Guinea, 11 Oct. 1943.

Keathley, George D.,* S/Sgt., 85th Inf. Div., born Olney, entered service Lamesa, action Mt. Altuzzo, Italy, 14 Sept. 1944.

Kimbro, Truman,* Techn. 4th Grade, 2nd Inf. Div., born Madisonville, entered service Houston, action near Rocherath, Belgium, 19 Dec. 1944.

Knight, Jack L.,* 1st Lt., 125th Cav. Rgt., born Garner, entered service Weatherford, action near Loi-Kang, Burma, 2 Feb. 1945.

Knight, Raymond,* 1st Lt., 350th Fighter Group, Houston, action Po Valley, Italy, 24-25 April 1945.

Leonard, Turney W.,* 893rd Tank Destroyer Bn., Dallas, action Kommerscheidt, Germany, 4-6 Nov. 1944.

Logan, James M., Sgt. 36th Inf. Div., born McNeil, entered service Luling, action Salerno, Italy 9 Sept. 1943.

Lopez, Jose M., Sgt., 2nd Inf. Div., born Mission, entered service Brownsville, action near Krinkelt, Belgium, 17 Dec. 1944.

Lummus, Jack,* 1st Lt., 5th Marine Div., Ennis, action on Iwo Jima, 8 Mar. 1945.

Mathis, Jack W.,* 1st Lt., 303rd Bomb Group, San Angelo, action over Vegesack, Germany, 18 March 1943.

Morgan, John C., 2nd Lt., 92nd Bomb Group, Vernon, entered U.S. service London, England, action over Germany, 28 July 1943.

Murphy, Audie, 1st Lt., 3rd Inf. Div., Hunt County, action near Holtzwihr, France, 26 Jan. 1945.

Roan, Charles H., PFC, 1st Marine Div., Claude, action on Peleliu, 18 Sept. 1944.

Robinson, James E., Jr.,* 1st Lt., 63rd Inf. Div., born Toledo, Ohio, entered service Waco, action near Untergriesheim, Germany, 6 April 1945.

Rodriquez, Cleto, PFC, 37th Inf. Div., born San Marcos, entered service San Antonio, action in Manila, Philippine Islands, 9 Feb. 1945.

Turner, George, PFC, 14th Armd. Div., born Longview, entered service Los Angeles, action Phillipsbourg, France, 3 Jan. 1945.

Wallace, Herman C.,* PFC, 76th Inf. Div., born Marlow, Oklahoma, entered service Lubbock, action near Prumzurley, Germany, 27 Feb. 1945.

Whiteley, Eli, 1st Lt., 3rd Inf. Div., born Florence, entered service Georgetown, action Sigolsheim, France, 17 Dec. 1944.

Sources of Data: *Texas Medal of Honor Recipients* (Austin: Texas Veterans Commission, 1993); Mike Kingston, "Courageous Texans," in *Texas Almanac, 1992-1993* (Dallas: A. H. Belo Corporation, 1992), 321-324; Ron Tyler, ed., *New Handbook of Texas*, 6 vols. (Austin: Texas State Historical Association); Joseph L. Schott, *Above and Beyond: The Story of the Congressional Medal of Honor* (New York: G. P. Putnam's Sons, 1983); Committee of Veterans Affairs, U.S. Senate, *Medal of Honor Recipients, 1863-1973* (Washington: Government Printing Office, 1973); "Medal of Honor Breakdown (By War and Service as of 13 May 1997)," http://www.army.mil/cmh-pg/mohstats.htm.

Endnotes

CHAPTER ONE
1. Kent Bowman, "Remember Pearl Harbor," in James Ward Lee, et al., *1941: Texas Goes to War* (Denton: University of North Texas Press, 1991), 1-4.
2. U.S. Department of Commerce, Bureau of the Census, *Sixteenth Census of the United States: 1940, Population* (Washington: Government Printing Office, 1942), 1039.
3. *Texas Almanac and State Industrial Guide, 1941-1942* (Dallas: A. H. Belo Corp., 1941), 94. New York, Pennsylvania, Illinois, and Ohio were the four most heavily populated states.
4. *Sixteenth Census of the United States*, 1039.
5. *Ibid.*, 1039.
6. *Ibid.*, 1039-1041.
7. *Texas Almanac, 1941-1942*, 95, 97.
8. *Texas Almanac and State Industrial Guide, 1943-1944* (Dallas: A. H. Belo Corp., 1943), 63.
9. *Ibid.*, 62-63.
10. *Ibid.*, 279.
11. *Texas Almanac, 1941-1942*, 322. Approximately one-sixth of Texas school children were African Americans, a ratio slightly above the percentage of African Americans in the total population.
12. *Ibid.*, 321. Male teachers' salaries ($1,235 average) were slightly higher than female salaries ($1,086 average). Teacher salaries in independent school districts averaged nearly $400 higher than in common school districts.
13. *Ibid.*, 326-328.
14. *Ibid.*, 331.
15. *Ibid.*, 203-204, 217.
16. *Texas Almanac, 1943-1944*, 170-171; Diana Davids Olien and Roger M. Olien, *Oil In Texas: The Gusher Age, 1895-1945* (Austin: University of Texas Press, 2002), 139-212; Bobby Weaver, "Black Gold: Oil Development in Texas," in Donald W. Whisenhunt, ed., *Texas: A Sesquicentennial Celebration* (Austin: Eakin Press, 1984), 272-278.
17. *Texas Almanac, 1941-1942*, 257; Richard Schroeder, *Texas Signs On: The Early Days of Radio and Television* (College Station: Texas A&M University Press), 12, 95-96.
18. *Texas Almanac, 1941-1942*, 257; Michele Hilmes, *Radio Voices: American Broadcasting, 1922-1952* (Minneapolis: University of Minnesota Press, 1997), 257.
19. Charles R. Townsend, "Light Crust Doughboys," Ron Tyler, et al., eds., *New Handbook of Texas*, 6 vols. (Austin: Texas State Historical Association, 1996), 4: 195; Bill Malone, *Country*

Music, USA: A Fifty-Year History (Austin: University of Texas Press, 1968),173-175. See also John Mark Dempsey, *The Light Crust Doughboys Are On the Air* (Denton: University of North Texas Press, 2002).

20. Schroeder, *Texas Signs On*, 111.
21. Hilmes, *Radio Voices*, 110-111.
22. Ibid., 111-113, 214, 223.
23. Schroeder, *Texas Signs On*, 102-103.
24. Richard Schroeder, *Lone Star Picture Shows* (College Station: Texas A&M University Press, 2001), 59-66, 70.
25. Dawn Duncan, "Entertainment at Home & Abroad," in Lee, ed., *1941: Texas Goes to War*, 202-203; *Time*, March 9, 1942, p. 68.
26. Schroeder, *Lone Star Picture Shows*, 173.
27. Ibid., 132-133; Kerry Segrave, *Drive-In Theaters: A History from Their Inception in 1933* (Jefferson, NC: McFarland & Co., 1992), 17-18.
28. Bill O'Neal, *The Texas League, 1888-1987: A Century of Baseball* (Austin: Eakin Press, 1987), 90-92.
29. Bowman, "Remember Pearl Harbor," 13; *Time*, October 13, 1941, p. 72. In 1941 DiMaggio's famous teammate, Lou Gehrig, who at the time held the record for most consecutive games played, died.
30. Kern Tips, *Football–Texas Style: An Illustrated History of the Southwest Conference* (Garden City, NY: Doubleday & Co., 1964), 96.
31. *Life*, November 17, 1941, pp. 110-116.
32. Tips, *Football–Texas Style*, 96-101; Joe B. Frantz, *The Forty-Acre Follies* (Austin: Texas Monthly Press, 1983), 192-193.
33. Howard V. Ratliff, *Autumn's Mightiest Legions: History of Texas Schoolboy Football* (Waco: Texian Press, 1963), 89-91; Bill McMurray, *Texas High School Football* (South Bend, IN: Icarus Press, 1985), 18.
34. Ratliff, *Autumn's Mightiest Legions*, 90-91. Ty Cashion, *Pigskin Pulpit: A Social History of Texas High School Football Coaches* (Austin: Texas State Historical Association, 1998), 4-5, points out that the state was divided into three classes of schools. Only in Class A, districts with the largest enrollment, did schools play for a state championship prior to the Second World War. Basketball, today one of the most popular sports in the state, attracted much less interest in Texas prior to the Second World War.
35. Bowman, "Remember Pearl Harbor," 6-11.
36. Richard Bailey, "Morris Sheppard," in Kenneth E. Hendrickson, Jr., and Michael L. Collins, eds., *Profiles in Power: Twentieth Century Texans in Washington* (Arlington Heights, IL: Harlan Davidson, Inc., 1993), 29-42. For more on Sheppard see Bailey, "Morris Sheppard of Texas: Southern Progressive and Prohibitionist" (Ph. D. dissertation, Texas Christian University, 1980) and Eschal F. Duke, "The Political Career of Morris Sheppard, 1875-1941" (Ph. D. dissertation, University of Texas, 1958).
37. Tom Connally and Alfred Steinberg, *My Name Is Tom Connally* (New York: Thomas Y. Crowell, 1954), 228-231; George N. Green, "Thomas Terry Connally," in Tyler, ed., *New Handbook of Texas*, 2: 270; Janet Schmelzer, "Tom Connally," in Hendrickson and Collins, eds., *Profiles in Power*, 95.
38. C. Dwight Dorough, *Mr. Sam* (New York: Random House, 1962), 271-298; D. Clayton Brown, "Sam Rayburn," in Hendrickson and Collins, eds., *Profiles in Power*, 105-119; Anthony Champagne and Floyd F. Ewing, "Samuel Taliferro Rayburn," in Tyler, ed., *New Handbook of Texas*, 5: 458-459; "A Congress to Win the War," *New Republic*, May 18, 1942, pp. 683-711. For more on Rayburn see Anthony Champagne, *Congressman Sam Rayburn* (New Brunswick, NJ: Rutgers University Press, 1984); Alfred Steinberg, *Sam Rayburn: A Biography* (New York: Hawthorne Books, Inc., 1975); and D. B. Hardeman and Donald C. Bacon, *Rayburn: A Political Biography* (Austin: Texas Monthly Press, 1981).
39. Anthony Champagne, "Hatton Sumners and the 1937 Court-Packing Plan," *East Texas Historical Journal* 3 (Spring 1988): 46-49; Mary Catherine Monroe, "Hatton William Sumners,

in Tyler, ed., *New Handbook of Texas* 6: 149-150; Nancy Beck Young, *Wright Patman: Populism, Liberalism, & the American Dream* (Dallas: Southern Methodist University Press, 2000), 102; Richard Henderson, *Maury Maverick: A Political Biography* (Austin: University of Texas Press, 1970), 3-4, 164-169; George N. Green, *The Establishment in Texas Politics: The Primitive Years, 1938-1957* (Westport, CT: Greenwood Press, 1979), 69-73.

40. Sheppard speech, *Congressional Record*, 9 (August 1940), 10097, quoted in J. Garry Clifford and Samuel R. Spencer, Jr., *The First Peacetime Draft* (Lawrence, KS: University of Kansas Press, 1986), 179.

41. Clifford and Spencer, *The First Peacetime Draft*, 212-221.

42. *Selective Service in Peacetime: First Report of the Director of Selective Service, 1940-41* (Washington: Government Printing Office, 1942), 557-558. Lee Kennett, *G. I.: The American Soldier in World War II* (New York: Charles Scribner's Sons, 1987), 3-23, provides an excellent discussion of selective service operations.

43. The Texas National Guard had previously used Camp Hulen at Palacois for its summer training but the War Department decided to use Hulen for antiaircraft training for national guard units across the country. Bruce Olson, "Texas National Guard," in Tyler, ed., *New Handbook of Texas*, 5: 369; Joseph C. Dawson III, "Thirty-Sixth Infantry Division," *Ibid.*, 5: 461; Rachael Jenkins, "Camp Hulen," *Ibid.*, 1: 939; Tessia Martin, "Brownwood, Texas In World War II," *West Texas State Historical Association Yearbook* 43 (October 1967): 32-33.

44. In the 1940 presidential elections the Republicans carried only Comal, Gillespie, Guadalupe, Kendall, Kenedy, Lee, and Washington counties. With the exception of Kenedy these were all counties with sizable German populations; they had voted consistently for the Republican Party since the Civil War. *Texas Almanac, 1941-42*, 400-401. In the special Senate election O'Daniel received 175,590 votes, Johnson 174,279, Gerald Mann 140,807, and Martin Dies 80,551. For more on the senatorial contest see Seth S. McKay and Odie B. Faulk, *Texas After Spindletop* (Austin: Steck-Vaughn Co., 1965), 168-174, and Green, *Establishment in Texas Politics*, 32-37.

45. Warren F. Kimball, *The Most Unsordid Act: Lend-Lease, 1939-1941* (Baltimore: Johns Hopkins Press, 1969), 152-206; *Congressional Record*, 77th Congress, 1st Session, Vol. 87, Pt. 1, 815. Kimball points out that Sol Bloom of New York, chair of the House Foreign Relations Committee, was highly unpopular; Luther Johnson of Corsicana, second ranking member of the committee, was much more popular with committee members.

46. Kimball, *Most Unsordid Act*, 19-216; Connally, *My Name Is Tom Connally*, 243-244; *Congressional Record*, 77th Congress, 1st Session, Vol. 87, Pt. 2, 1154-1155, 1157-1159, 2097. Both Connally and Sheppard voted for passage. Connally succeeded Walter George as chairman of the Senate Foreign Relations Committee on July 31, 1941.

47. David M. Kennedy, *Freedom from Fear: The American People in Depression and War, 1929-1945* (New York: Oxford University Press, 1999), 505; Gordon W. Prange, *At Dawn We Slept: The Untold Story of Pearl Harbor* (New York: McGraw-Hill Book Co., 1981), 37-48. For Richardson's own story see *On the Treadmill to Pearl Harbor: The Memories of Admiral James O. Richardson, USN (Retired) as told to Vice Admiral George C. Dyes* (Washington: Naval History Department, 1973).

48. John Toland, *The Flying Tigers* (New York: Random House, 1983); Martha Byrd, *Chennault: Giving Wings to the Tiger* (Tuscaloosa, AL: University of Alabama Press, 1987); Daniel Ford, *Flying Tigers: Claire Chennault and the American Volunteer Group* (Washington: Smithsonian Institute, 1991). The exploits of the Tigers will be discussed more fully in a later chapter.

49. Kennedy, *Freedom from Fear*, 510-511; Robert Dallek, *Franklin D. Roosevelt and American Foreign Policy, 1932-1945* (New York: Oxford University Press, 1995), 510-511.

50. President Roosevelt had declared a national emergency on May 27, 1941. George O. Flynn, *The Draft, 1940-1973* (Lawrence, KS: University Press of Kansas, 1993), 49.

51. *Ibid.*, 50-51; Hardeman and Bacon, *Rayburn: A Biography*, 261; George F. Gallup, *The Gallup Poll: Public Opinion, 1935-1971*, 8 vols. (New York: Random House, 1972), 1: 291-292. Support for extension was strongest in the South, 63 percent favoring, 32 percent opposing, and 5 percent no opinion.

52. *Congressional Record*, Vol. 87, Pt.6, 6881, 7074. Soon after Pearl Harbor Congress extended the tour of duty until six months after the end of the war and lowered the induction age for draftees to twenty years. This was later lowered to eighteen. Flynn, *The Draft*, 50-51, 55, 72; Dorough, *Mr. Sam*, 313-314; Steinberg, *Sam Rayburn*, 170-172.

53. G. Patrick Murray, "The Louisiana Maneuvers: Practice for War," *Louisiana History* 13 (No. 2, 1972): 117-138; Christopher Gabel, *The U.S. Army GHQ Maneuvers of 1941* (Washington: Center of Military History, U.S. Army, 1991), esp. 64-95; Geoffrey Perret, *There's A War To Be Won: The United States Army in World War II* (New York: Random House, 1991), 42-45.

54. Charles A. Lockwood and Hans Christian Adamson, *Through Hell and Deep Water: The Stirring Story of the Navy's Deadly Submarine, the U.S.S. HARDER, under the Command of Sam Dealy, Destroyer Killer!* (Philadelphia: Chilton Co., 1956), 72, 90-91; Dallek, *Franklin D. Roosevelt and Foreign Policy*, 267-268; Kennedy, *Freedom from Fear*, 510-511.

55. Quote, Schroeder, *Texas Signs On*, 119; author interview with Dan Dennis, Beaumont, January 9, 2002; transcript of interview Lindsey M. Siewert with Betty and Vito Dimiceli, July 1, 2001, in Special Collections, Lamar University Library, Beaumont, Texas; Valeta Crow, in Ava C. Mills, *West Texans Remember the Home Front* (San Angelo: Doss Books, 1997), 46-47.

56. Martha Sue Stroud, *For Love of Country: The Price of Freedom* (Austin: Nortex Press, 2000), 116; Hazel Shelton Abernethy, "The Home Front in East Texas," in Joyce Gibson Roach, ed., *Collective Hearts: Texans in World War II* (Austin: Eakin Press, 1996), 85; William L. Adams, *Valley Vets: An Oral History of World War II Veterans of the Lower Rio Grande Valley* (Austin: Eakin Press, 1999), 31.

57. Philip Ardery, *Bomber Pilot: A Memoir of World War II* (Lexington: University Press of Kentucky, 1978), 41-42.

58. Gerald Astor, *Crisis in the Pacific: The Battles for the Philippine Islands by the Men Who Fought Them* (New York: Donald I. Fine Books, 1996), 197.

59. Quote by Bill Dallas in Stephen Neal Manning, *The Courage of Common Men: Texans Remember World War II* (Plano: Republic of Texas Press, 2001), 89.

60. Adams, *Valley Vets*, 27-28.

61. Interview, author with Philip Latimer, January 20, 2002, Beaumont, Texas.

62. George Gay, *Sole Survivor: The Battle of Midway and Its Effect on His Life* (Midway, private printing, 1979), 51.

63. Neil Sapper, "Aboard the Wrong Ship in the Right Books: Doris Miller and Historical Accuracy," *East Texas Historical Review* 18 (Spring 1980): 3-11; Vickie Gail Miller, *Doris Miller: A Silent Medal of Honor Winner* (Austin: Eakin Press, 1977), 46-55; Walter Karig and Welbourne Kelley, comp., *Battle Report: Pearl Harbor to Coral Sea*, 6 vols. (New York: Reinhart and Co., 1944), 1: 72-73.

64. Quote, William W. Fomby, in Robert S. La Fonte and Ronald E. Marcello, *Remembering Pearl Harbor: Eyewitness Accounts by U.S. Military Men and Women* (Wilmington, DL: SR Books, 1991), 42. Events of the attack are described fully by Gordon W. Prange, *At Dawn We Slept: The Untold Story of Pearl Harbor* (New York: Mc-Graw Hill Book Co., 1981), 509-513.

65. La Fonte and Marcello, *Remembering Pearl Harbor*, 53-56; Prange, *At Dawn We Slept*, 513-514. Gunner's Mate Jim Lawson of Pasadena, Texas, was another survivor of the *Arizona*. See his account in Coral Rust, "Teen Was Last Man off Sinking *Arizona*," *Houston Chronicle*, Dec. 6, 1991.

66. La Fonte and Marcello, *Remembering Pearl Harbor*, 53-56; Gordon Prange, et al., *Dec. 7, 1941* (New York: McGraw-Hill Book Co., 1988), 146-147.

67. Czech Heritage Society of Texas, *Texas Veterans of Czech Ancestry* (Austin: Eakin Press, 1999), 309; Prange, *Dec. 7, 1941*, 106, 128-129, 153.

68. La Fonte and Marcello, *Remembering Pearl Harbor*, 69-72; Walter Lord, *Day of Infamy* (New York: Bantam Books, 1958), 138-139.

69. Quote, Frank Townsend, in La Fonte and Marcello, *Remembering Pearl Harbor*, 265. Joe McKinley of Nederland, Texas, was one of the survivors of the destroyer *Cassin*. Andrea Wright, "Infamy Survival," *Beaumont Enterprise*, Dec. 7, 2001.

70. La Fonte and Marcello, *Remembering Pearl Harbor*, 112-113; Lord, *Day of Infamy*, 146.

71. Lord, *Day of Infamy*, 142; Andrea Wright, "SE Texas' First WWII Casualty Died on Ship at Pearl Harbor," *Beaumont Enterprise*, Dec. 6, 2001.

72. Quote, Leon Bennett, in La Fonte and Marcello, *Remembering Pearl Harbor*, 79. Paul Howell, founder and CEO of the Howell Corporation, a Houston-based oil exploration company, was an officer on *Neosho*. His story of the attack may be found in Steven Long, "Fighting Tanker," *Houston Chronicle*, Dec. 6, 1991.

73. Paul Joseph Travers, ed., *Eyewitness to Infamy: An Oral History of Pearl Harbor*, (New York: Madison Books, 1991), 168-173.

74. La Fonte and Marcello, *Remembering Pearl Harbor*, 206-209.

75. Quote, Melvin Faulkner, in Travers, ed., *Eyewitness to Infamy*, 256.

76. La Fonte and Marcello, *Remembering Pearl Harbor*, 233-235.

77. *Ibid.*, 154-156.

78. Quote, Leslie Le Fan, in *Ibid.*, 158.

79. *Ibid.*, 242-243.

80. *Ibid.*, 284-286. The submarine, manned by Kazu Sukamaki, had engine trouble and was stranded on a reef and captured.

81. Gerald Astor, *The Greatest War: Americans in Combat, 1941-1945* (Novato, CA: Presidio Press, 1999), 5-6; Donald Goldstein, Katherine V. Dillon, and J. Michael Wenger, *The Way It Was, Pearl Harbor, The Original Photographs* (Washington, D.C.: Brassey's, 1991), 81.

82. Citations given in Karig and Kelley, *Battle Report: Pearl Harbor to Coral Sea*, 332-333. Names of their ships are not given in the citation.

83. Walter J. Boyne, *Clash of Titans,: World War II at Sea* (New York: Simon & Schuster, 1995), 140; Karig and Kelley, *Battle Report: Pearl Harbor to Coral Sea*, 93-94.

84. Connally, *My Name Is Tom Connally*, 248; Hardeman and Bacon, *Rayburn*, 273-274.

85. Prange, *At Dawn We Slept*, 558-559; Connally, *My Name Is Tom Connally*, 248-249.

86. In many Texas schools children heard the address over radio in their classes or school assemblies. The author, a student at Baytown Junior High, heard the address in a school assembly.

87. Quote, A. Russell Buchanan, *The United States and World War II*, 2 vols. (New York: Harper & Row, 1964), 2: 79; *Congressional Record*, 87: 9506, 9536-37, 9652-53.

CHAPTER TWO

1. Coke Stevenson, quoted in *Beaumont Enterprise*, December 8, 1941.

2. *Selective Service in Wartime: Second Report of the Director of Selective Service, 1941-42* (Washington: Government Printing Office, 1943), 587.

3. *Texas Almanac, 1947-1948*, 117.

4. Leon Metz, "Fort Bliss," in Tyler, ed., *New Handbook of Texas*, 2: 1089; W. H. Timmons, *El Paso: A Borderland History* (El Paso: Texas Western Press, 1990), 241.

5. Elizabeth P. Davenport, "Fort Brown," Ben E. Pingenot, "Fort Clark," and Garna L. Christian, "Fort Ringgold," in Tyler, ed., *New Handbook of Texas*, 2: 1089-1091, 1116; Shelby L. Stanton, *Order of Battle, U.S. Army World War II* (Novato, CA: Presidio Press, 1984), 314-315, 317-318.

6. Lee Bennett, "Fort D. A. Russell," and Garna L. Christian, "Fort McIntosh," in Tyler, ed., *New Handbook of Texas*, 2: 1096, 1109.

7. Art Leatherwood, "Camp Bullis," and "Fort Sam Houston," *Ibid.*, 1: 930-931, and 2: 1117.

8. Rachael Jenkins, "Camp Hulen," *Ibid.*, 1: 939.

9. Lonnie J. White, "Camp Bowie," *Ibid.*, 1: 929-930; Tessia Martin, "Brownwood, Texas in World War II," *West Texas Historical Association Year Book* 43 (1967): 31-43.

10. David Minor, "Fort Wolters," in Tyler, ed., *New Handbook of Texas*, 2: 1121-1122.

11. (Unsigned), "Camp Wallace," *Ibid.*, 2: 948; David G. McComb, *Galveston: A History* (Austin: University of Texas Press, 1986), 10-11.

12. James M. Myers, "Camp Barkeley," in Tyler, ed., *New Handbook of Texas*, 1: 923-24. See also Myers, "World War II as an Instrument of Social Mobilization: The Social and Economic Influence of Camp Barkeley at Abilene" (M. A. thesis, Hardin-Simmons University, 1981); Myers,

"The Army Comes to Abilene," *West Texas Historical Association Year Book* 65 (1989): 101-110; John J. Hatcher, "Camp Barkeley," *Texas Military History* 3 (Winter 1963): 219-227.

13. Odie B. Faulk and Laura E. Faulk, *Fort Hood: The First Fifty Years* (Temple, TX: Frank W. Mayborn Foundation, 1990), 17-29.

14. *Ibid.*, 34-79; Frederick L. Brieur, "Fort Hood," in Tyler, ed., *New Handbook of Texas*, 2: 1104-1105. The Hood expenditures were the second highest for military installations in the war; only the building of the Pentagon ($78 million) exceeded the expenditures for Hood. See R. Elberton Smith, *The Army and Economic Mobilization* (Washington: Center of Military History, U.S. Army, 1991), 449.

15. Brian Hart, "Camp Howze," in Tyler, ed., *New Handbook of Texas*, 1: 938-939. For more on Camp Howze see Barbara K. Burns, "World War II and Camp Howze: The Impact Upon Gainesville and Cooke County, Texas" (M. A. thesis, Texas Woman's University, 1984).

16. (Unsigned) "Camp Maxey," in Tyler, ed., *New Handbook of Texas*, 1: 942; Stanton, *Order of Battle*, 179-180.

17. Art Leatherwood, "Camp Swift," in Tyler, ed., *New Handbook of Texas*, 1: 946-947; Stanton, *Order of Battle*, 92, 170, 172, 179.

18. (Unsigned) "Camp Fannin," in Tyler, ed., *New Handbook of Texas*, 1: 936; Lawrence C. Walker, "Camp Fannin: A Reminiscence," *East Texas Historical Journal* 37 (Fall 1999): 64-67.

19. Maury Darst, "Fort Crockett," "Fort San Jacinto," and "Fort Travis," in Tyler, ed., *New Handbook of Texas*, 2: 1095-1096, 1117-1118, 1121; Melanie Wiggins, *Torpedoes in the Gulf: Galveston and the U-Boats, 1942-1943* (College Station: Texas A&M University Press, 1995), 118-122, 131-132; Lynn M. Alperin, *Custodians of the Coast: History of the United States Army Engineers of Galveston* (Washington: Government Printing Office, 1977), 195-196.

20. Art Leatherwood, "Kelly Air Force Base," in Tyler, ed., *New Handbook of Texas*, 3: 1052; Smith, *Army and Economic Mobilization*, 419.

21. Edward B. Alcott, "Brooks Air Force Base," in Tyler, ed., *New Handbook of Texas*, 1: 752.

22. Thomas E. Alexander, *The Stars Were Big and Bright: The United States Army Air Forces and Texas During World War II*, 2 vols. (Austin: Eakin Press, 2000-2001), 2: 263-270.

23. *Ibid.*, 2: 143-147. See also C. Forrest Wilson, *A History of Biggs Field and Early Border Aviation* (El Paso: Texas Western University, 1952).

24. Alexander, *Stars Were Big and Bright*, 1:117-127.

25. *Ibid.*, 1: 127-130; Timothy M. Brown, "Randolph Air Force Base," in Tyler, ed., *New Handbook of Texas*, 5: 440-441.

26. For a good description of the Army's acquisition of new bases for the Air Forces see Wesley Frank Craven and James Lea Cate, *The Army Air Forces in World War II*, 7 vols. (Chicago: University of Chicago Press, 1948-58), 6: 119-168. An overview of training in Texas is provided by Robert E. Hays, Jr., "Air Force Pilot and Instructor Training in Texas, 1940-1945," *Texas Military History* 4 (Summer 1964): 95-117. For Texas bases discussed above see Craig H. Roell, "Cuero Field," in Tyler, ed., *New Handbook of Texas*, 2: 433; (Unsigned) "Arledge Field," *Ibid.*, 1: 238; Art Leatherwood, "Bruce Field," *Ibid.*, 1: 782; Leatherwood, "Coleman Field," *Ibid.*, 2: 203; Leatherwood, "Corsicana Field," *Ibid.*, 2: 340; Leatherwood and Chris Cravens, "Hicks Field," *Ibid.*, 3: 588; Ruben C. Ochoa, "Garner Army Air Field," *Ibid.*, 3: 96; (Unsigned) "Victory Field," *Ibid.*, 6: 743; and Tommy Stringer, "Air Activities of Texas: A Small Town's Contribution to the Big War," *East Texas Historical Journal* 36 (Fall 1998): 10-21.

27. Sangeeta Singg and William A. Allen, "Goodfellow Air Force Base," in Tyler, ed., *New Handbook of Texas*, 3: 238.

28. Robert W. Stewart, "Curtis Field," *Ibid.*, 2: 457-458, notes that 85 percent of the instructors and students were native Texans.

29. Craig H. Roell, "Foster Army Air Field," *Ibid.*, 2: 1135; Art Leatherwood, "Perrin Air Force Base," *Ibid.*, 5: 157.

30. Lucy H. Wallace, "Moore Air Force Base," *Ibid.*, 4: 825-826.

31. David Minor, "Sheppard Air Force Base," *Ibid.*, 5: 1017.

32. Thomas Alexander, *The Wings of Change: The Army Air Force Experience in Texas During*

World War II (Abilene, TX: McWhiney Foundation Press, 2003), 93-97; Alexander, *Stars Were Big and Bright*, 1: 161-166.

33. Alexander, *Stars Were Big and Bright*, 2: 103-116; James L. Colwell, "Hell from Heaven! Midland Army Air Field in World War II," Permian Basin Historical Annual 25-27 (1985-1987): 11-42, 51-90, 95-128.

34. Steven G. Gamble and Ruedele Turner, "Reese Air Force Base," in Tyler, ed., *New Handbook of Texas*, 5: 507. Alexander, *Stars Were Big and Bright*, 2: 221, points out that the South Plains Army Airfield Glider School was later opened north of town.

35. James L. Colwell, "Sweetwater Army Air Field," in Tyler, ed., *New Handbook of Texas*, 5: 174-175; Alexander, *Stars Were Big and Bright* 1: 29-37.

36. Harry F. Snapp, "Pioneer Women in West Texas Skies: Women Airforce Service Pilots of World War II," *West Texas Historical Association Year Book* 70 (1994): 19-39; Alberta Fitzpatrick Head, "General Arnold Comes to Avenger Field," *Ibid.* 50 (1974): 92-103; Anne Noogle, *For God, Country, and the Thrill of It: Women Airforce Service Pilots in World War II* (College Station: Texas A&M University Press, 1990); Bennet Monde, "A History of Avenger Field, Texas" (M. A. thesis, Hardin-Simmons University, 1981). Additional description of the WASP program is provided in chapter five of the present work.

37. Alexander, *Stars Were Big and Bright*, 1: 103; Art Leatherwood, "Blackland Army Air Field," and "James Connally Air Force Base," in Tyler, ed., *New Handbook of Texas*, 1: 570; 3: 907.

38. Majors Field was named for Lt. Truett Majors, the first serviceman from Hunt County to die in the war; Gibbs Field for local resident Major David R. Gibbs, killed in the Philippines. James L. Colwell, "Pecos Army Air Field," in Tyler, ed., *New Handbook of Texas*, 5: 119-120; Glenn Justice, "Gibbs Field," *Ibid..*, 3: 150; David Minor, "Majors Field," *Ibid.*, 4: 471; Art Leatherwood, "Eagle Pass Army Air Field," *Ibid.*, 2: 752; James L. Colwell, "Wings Over West Texas: Pecos Army Air Field in World War II," *West Texas Historical Association Year Book* 63 (1987): 42-62; Alexander, *Stars Were Big and Bright*, 1: 2-24, 86-95.

39. Several thousand navigators (including 132 African Americans) and flight engineers were trained at Hondo. Ruben E. Ochoa, "Hondo Army Airfield," in Tyler, ed., *New Handbook of Texas*, 3: 681-682; Claudia Hazelwood and Mark Odintz, "Big Spring, Texas," *Ibid.*, 1: 538; Alexander, *Stars Were Big and Bright*, 2: 38-47.

40. Robert D. Thompson, *We'll Find the Way: The History of Hondo Army Air Field During World War II* (Austin: Eakin Press, 1992), 63-67. For more on the bat-bomb experiment by one of the men involved in the project see Jack Couffer, *Bat Bomb: World War II's Other Secret Weapon* (Austin: University of Texas Press, 1992).

41. Ross Phares and Paul O. Cormier, "Amarillo Air Force Base," in Tyler, ed., *New Handbook of Texas*, 1: 142; H. Allen Anderson, "Dalhart Army Air Field," *Ibid.*, 2: 471; Art Leatherwood, "Bergstrom Air Force Base," *Ibid.*, 1: 499; Alexander, *Stars Were Big and Bright*, 2: 231-242. The author wishes to thank Suzanne Campbell, archivist of the West Texas Collection, Angelo State University, for providing information on San Angelo Army Air Field.

42. Laughlin was named for Lt. Jack T. Laughlin of Del Rio, who was killed in the crash of his B-17 in Java on January 19, 1942. Art Leatherwood, "Carswell Air Force Base," Laredo Air Force Base," and "Laughlin Air Force Base," in Tyler, ed., *New Handbook of Texas*, 1: 997; 4: 77, 104.

43. Art Leatherwood, "Dyess Air Force Base," in Tyler, ed., *New Handbook of Texas*, 2: 747-748; Lee Bennett, "Marfa Army Air Field," *Ibid.*, 4: 504; H. Allen Anderson, "Pampa Army Air Field," *Ibid.*, 5: 34; Alexander, *Stars Were Big and Bright*, 2: 20-29. Alexander notes that both actor Jack Palance and U.S. Senator George McGovern learned to fly multi-engine aircraft at Pampa.

44. Craig Roell, "Aloe Army Air Field," in Tyler, ed., *New Handbook of Texas*, 1: 129; Maury Darst, "Galveston Army Air Field," *Ibid.*, 3: 53.

45. Quote, Alexander, *Stars Were Big and Bright*, 1: 175.

46. *Ibid.*, 177. See also Thomas E. Alexander, *Rattlesnake Bomber Base, Pyote Army Air Field in World War II* (Abilene, Tx: McWhiney Foundation Press, 2003).

47. Shirley Ratisseau, "Gary Air Force Base," *Ibid.*, 3: 104; James L. Colwell, "Childress Army Air Field," *Ibid.*, 2: 80-81.

48. Art Leatherwood, "Bryan Air Force Base," *Ibid.*, 1: 794. The total number of army airmen trained in Texas during World War II has not been determined. *The Texas Almanac, 1945-1946*, p. 78, gives figures for the period Jan. 1, 1941–May 1, 1944 as 44,958 pilots, 12,534 bombardiers, 12,706 navigators, 45,248 flexible gunners, 74,022 airplane and engine mechanics, 12, 247 pilot instructors, 1,275 bombardier instructors, 1,372 instrument trainer instructors, and 7,500 glider pilots.

49. Ray Dery, "Brooke Army Medical Center," *Ibid.*, 1: 748-749; Ken Durham, "Harmon General Hospital," *East Texas Historical Journal* 38 (Spring 2000): 35-42; *Texas Almanac, 1945-1946*, 78.

50. Art Leatherwood, "Naval Air Station, Beeville," "Naval Air Station, Corpus Christi," and "Naval Air Station, Kingsville," in Tyler, ed., *New Handbook of Texas*, 4: 951-953; *Texas Almanac, 1945-1946*, 80.

51. NAS, Corpus Christi, internet, www.globalsecurity.org/military/facility/corpuschristi.htm; *Texas Almanac, 1945-1946*, 60.

52. Art Leatherwood, "Naval Air Station, Dallas," in Tyler, ed., *New Handbook of Texas*, 4: 952; *Texas Almanac, 1945-1946*, 80.

53. Art Leatherwood, "Hitchcock Naval Air Station," in Tyler, ed., *New Handbook of Texas*, 3: 634; Wiggins, *Torpedoes in the Gulf*, 184-185.

54. *Texas Almanac, 1945-1946*, 237; Diana Davids Olien and Roger M. Olien, *Oil in Texas*, 219.

55. *Texas Almanac, 1945-1946*, 237; Roger M. Olien, "Oil and Gas Industry," in Tyler, ed., *New Handbook of Texas*, 4: 1124-1125.

56. Henrietta M. Larson and Kenneth Wiggins Porter, *History of the Humble Oil & Refining Company: A Study in Industrial Growth* (New York: Harper & Brothers, 1959), 589, 595.

57. Wiggins, *Torpedoes in the Gulf*, 14, 81-84; Jerrell Dean Palmer and John J. Johnson, "Big Inch and Little Big Inch," in Tyler, ed., *New Handbook of Texas*, 1: 532-533.

58. Palmer and Johnson, "Big Inch and Little Big Inch," 532-533; Olien and Olien, *Oil in Texas*, 826.

59. James A. Creighton, *A Narrative History of Brazoria County* (Waco: Brazoria County Historical Commission, 1975), 359-367; Margaret S. Henson, *The History of Baytown* (Baytown: Bay Heritage Society, 1986), 125; Donna Brewer, "Baytown Humble Refinery's Contribution to World War II: The Development and Production of 100-Octane Aviation Fuel and Toluene and Its Impact on Allied Victory," *Touchstone* 14 (1995): 2-15.

60. Charles F. Phillips, Jr., *Competition in the Synthetic Rubber Industry* (Chapel Hill: University of North Carolina Press, 1961), 43; James A. Clark and Mark Odintz, "Exxon Corporation, U.S.A.," in Tyler, ed., *New Handbook of Texas*, 2: 928-930; H. Allen Anderson, "Borger," *Ibid.*, 1: 650; Henson, *Baytown*, 125-126; W. T. Block, *Sapphire City of the Neches: A Brief History of Port Neches, Texas From Wilderness to Industrialization* (Port Neches: Port Neches Historical Committee, 1987), 356.

61. *Texas Almanac, 1943-1944*, 184; (Unsigned) "Tin Smeltering," in Tyler, ed., *New Handbook of Texas*, 6: 504; Clay Reynolds, "Gearing Up for Total War," in Lee, ed., *1941: Texas Goes to War*, 34.

62. Wayne Gard and Diana J. Kleiner, "Iron and Steel Industry," in Tyler, ed., *New Handbook of Texas*, 3: 872.

63. *Ibid.*, 3: 872; Clara H. Lewis and John R. Stockton, "Manufacturing Industries," *Ibid.*, 4: 494.

64. Mark Odintz, "Longhorn Army Ammunition Plant," *Ibid.*, 4: 279.

65. Christopher Long, "Lone Star Army Ammunition Plant," "Red River Army Depot," and "San Antonio Arsenal," *Ibid.*, 4: 270-271; 5: 493, 799: Carter Barcus, "San Jacinto Ordnance Depot," *Ibid.*, 5: 859; Vicki L. Kelly, "In the Shadow of Fame: The San Jacinto Ordnance Depot, 1939-1964," *Military History of Texas and the Southwest* 13 (No. 2, 1977): 39-54; *Texas Almanac, 1945-1946*, 255.

66. Michael V. Hazel, *Dallas: A History of "Big D"* (Austin: Texas State Historical

Association,1997), 46; Charles C. Alexander and E. C. Barksdale, "Aeronautics and Aerospace Industry," in Tyler, ed., *New Handbook of Texas* 1: 38.

67. Thomas A. Hill-Aiello, "Fort Worth's Economy and Defense Spending to 1945," paper presented at East Texas Historical Association meeting, Nacogdoches, Texas, September 28, 2001; Alexander and Barksdale, "Aeronautics and Aerospace Industry," in Tyler, *New Handbook of Texas*, 1: 38; Diana J. Kleiner, "Consolidated Vultee Aircraft Corportion," in *Ibid.*, 2: 281.

68. Walter F. Pilcher, "Howard Robard Hughes, Jr.," *Ibid.*, 3: 771-772; Marguerite Johnston, *Houston: The Unknown City, 1836-1946* (College Station: Texas A&M University Press, 1991), 69; Donald L. Bartlett and James B. Steel, *Empire: The Life, Legends and Madness of Howard Hughes* (New York: W. W. Norton & Co., 1979), 105-134. Labor problems at Hughes Tool are discussed fully in Ernest Obadele-Starks, *Black Unionism in the Industrial South* (College Station: Texas A&M University Press, 2000), 91-100.

69. McComb, *Houston*, 187. Todd Shipbuilding also constructed tankers and concrete barges at its Galveston Dry Docks after taking over Gray's Iron Works. According to David G. McComb, *Galveston: A History* (Austin: University of Texas Press, 1986), 168, Todd employed 4,510 people at its peak. Another contract for concrete barges was given to San Jacinto Shipbuilders, Inc., at Houston. This firm, however, was engaged in what maritime historian Frederic C. Lane says was some "funny business" in the award of subcontracts and in real estate arrangements. The company was sold to McCloskey & Company in September 1942. Four barges were delivered in November-December 1943 and the contracts for other barges canceled. For more on the issue of concrete barges see Frederic C. Lane, *Ships for Victory: A History of Shipbuilding Under the U.S. Maritime Commission in World War II* (Baltimore: Johns Hopkins Press, 1957), 627-634.

70. Joseph A. Pratt and Christopher J. Castaneda, *Builders: Herman and George R. Brown* (College Station: Texas A&M University Press, 1999), 77; Johnston, *Houston*, 370-371; Robert H. Peebles, "Shipbuilding," in Tyler, ed., *New Handbook of Texas*, 5: 1030.

71. Peebles, *Ibid.*, 1030; Howard C. Williams, "U.S. Naval Inactive Ship Maintenance Facility," *Ibid.*, 6: 633; Rita Green, Joe Walker, Marcus Robbins, *Beaumont at War: The Home Front* (Beaumont: Tyrrell Historical Library, 1992), 13-15; William T. Faucett, *The Shipyard at Beaumont* (Beaumont, priv. printed, 1991); Frank Karrpi, "Shipbuilding in Orange," in Howard C. Williams, ed., *Gateway to Texas: The History of Orange and Orange County* (Orange: Heritage House Museum of Orange, 1988), 155.

72. Bob Bowman, "A Century of Entrepreneurs: The Lufkin Industries Story, 1902-2002," *East Texas Historical Journal* 40 (Spring 2002): 21-22.

73. Myrna Zantell, "Farah, Incorporated," in Tyler, ed., *New Handbook of Texas*, 2: 949-950. To boost morale and production the military awarded pennants and badges bearing an "E" (for Excellence) to plants and workers achieving exceptional records.

74. Johnston, *Houston*, 369-370; Roger N. Conger, "Waco," in Tyler, ed., *New Handbook of Texas*, 6: 778; Dorothy D. De Moss, "Looking Better Every Year: Apparel Manufacturing in Texas," in Donald W. Whisenhunt, ed., *Texas, A Sesquicentennial Celebration* (Austin: Eakin Press, 1984), 286-287.

75. Lee Kennett, *For the Duration . . . The United States Goes to War: Pearl Harbor-1942* (New York: Charles Scribner's Sons, 1985), 123.

76. Quote, Rainer Schickele, *Agricultural Policy: Farm Programs and National Welfare* (Lincoln: University of Nebraska Press, 1954), 241. See also Walter W. Wilcox, *The Farmer in the Second World War* (Ames, Iowa: Iowa State College Press, 1947).

77. *Texas Almanac, 1945-1946*, 179; Henry C. Dethloff and Garry L. Nall, "Agriculture," in Tyler, ed., *New Handbook of Texas*, 1: 64-67.

78. *Texas Almanac, 1945-1946*, 190.

79. *Ibid.*, 213.

80. *Ibid.*, 214; *Texas Almanac, 1947-1948*, 230.

81. *Texas Almanac, 1945-1946*, 216-217.

82. *Ibid.*, 196.

83. *Ibid.*, 202-203.

84. *Ibid.*, 201.

85. *Ibid.*, 207-208. Texas produced 45 million pounds of pecans in 1944, compared with 22.6 million in 1941.

86. *Ibid.*, 199.

87. *Ibid.*, 179. Charles D. Chamberlain III, "'On the Train and Gone': Worker Mobility in the Rural Southwest During World War II, 1939-1945," *Southwestern Historical Quarterly* 103 (April 2000): 427, 444-445, 451. For a discussion of matters relating to manpower needs by farmers see Wilcox, *The Farmer in the Second World War*, 83-101.

88. *Texas Almanac, 1945-1946*, 179; Dethloff and Nall, "Agriculture," in Tyler, ed., *New Handbook of Texas*, 1: 64.

89. Johnny M. McCain, "Texas and the Mexican Labor Question, 1942-1947," *Southwestern Historical Quarterly* 85 (July 1981): 45-47.

90. *Ibid.*, 90. The term "bracero" means one who works with his arms; the nearest English equivalent is "field hand." Richard B. Craig, *The Bracero Program: Interest Groups and Foreign Policy* (Austin: University of Texas Press, 1971), ix.

91. Quote, McCain, "Texas and the Mexican Labor Question, 1942-1947," 51.

92. Quoted in Otey M. Scruggs, "Texas and the Bracero Program, 1942-1947," *Pacific Historical Review* 32 (August 1963): 254.

93. Scruggs, "Texas and the Bracero Program, 1942-1947," 255; McCain, "Texas and the Mexican Labor Question, 1942-1947," 52-53.

94. Quote, McCain, "Texas and the Mexican Labor Question, 1942-1947," 62. Scruggs, "Texas and the Bracero Program, 1942-1947," 154-155, takes a slightly different view. He says that because of Mexican pressure, the Immigration Service stepped up efforts to deal with "wet backs." Between June 2 and December 1, 1944, over 45,000 illegals were apprehended and deported.

95. McCain, "Texas and the Bracero Program, 1942-1947," 64 fn. For more on the later program see Craig, *The Bracero Program* cited above.

CHAPTER THREE

1. The early Japanese successes in the Far East are described by John Toland, *But Not In Shame: The Six Months After Pearl Harbor* (New York: Random House, 1961). See also John B. Lundstrom, "The Pacific Boils: The Japanese Juggernaut," in *1942: "The Issue in Doubt": Symposium of the War in the Pacific by the Admiral Nimitz Museum* (Austin: Eakin Press, 1994), 28-35.

2. Quote, Ronald H. Spector, *Eagle Against the Sun: The American War with Japan* (New York: Free Press, 1985), 107. See also Walter Edmonds, "What Happened at Clark Field," *The Atlantic* (July 1951): 20-23; Lewis H. Brereton, *The Brereton Diaries* (New York: William Morrow and Co., 1946), 36-45; Douglas MacArthur, *Reminiscences* (New York: McGraw-Hill Book Co., 1964), 120-121; Geoffrey Perret, *Old Soldiers Never Die: The Life of Douglas MacArthur* (Holbrook, MA: Adams Media Corp., 1996), 247-252; D. Clayton James, "The Other Pearl Harbor," in Robert Cowley, ed., *No End Save Victory: Perspectives on World War II* (New York: G. P. Putnam's Sons, 2001), 144-154, and William H. Bartsch, *December 8, 1941: MacArthur's Pearl Harbor* (College Station: Texas A&M University Press, 2003).

3. William H. Bartsch, *Doomed at the Start: American Pursuit Pilots in the Philippines, 1941-1942* (College Station: Texas A&M University Press, 1992), 79.

4. *Ibid.*, 27, 435-436.

5. *Ibid.*, 436-438.

6. *Ibid.*, 438. Joseph H. Moore commanded the 20th Squadron. He describes actions of the squadron in *1942: "Issue in Doubt,"* 87-93.

7. Bartsch, *Doomed at the Start*, 46, 439-440; Martine Anderson, "William Edwin Dyess," in Tyler, ed., *New Handbook of Texas*, 2: 747; William E. Dyess, *The Dyess Story: The Eye-Witness Account of the Death March from Bataan and the Narrative of Experiences in Japanese Prison Camps and of Eventual Escape* (New York: G. P. Putnam's Sons, 1944). *The Dyess Story* has been republished recently by the University of Nebraska Press under the title *Bataan Death March: A Survivor's Account*, ed. Charles Leareele (Lincoln, 2002).

8. Bartsch, *Doomed at the Start*, 50-51, 440.
9. *Ibid.*, 61-72; Toland, *But Not In Shame*, 48-49.
10. Toland, *But Not In Shame*, 50-51; Bartsch, *Doomed at the Start*, 77-80.
11. Bartsch, *Doomed at the Start*, 134, 450n; Dyess, *The Dyess Story*, 33.
12. Bartsch, *Doomed at the Start*, 151, 222.
13. *Ibid.*, 235-236.
14. *Ibid.*, 178, 189, 405-409.
15. Based upon Appendix B, Roster of Flying Officers of the 24th Pursuit Group, Bartsch, *Doomed at the Start*, 434-440. Ed Dyess of Albany, Texas, commander of the 26th Pursuit Squadron and later of the Bataan flying detachment, was taken prisoner by the Japanese but escaped. He returned to the United States but lost his life in a P-38 accident on December 22, 1943. The flying field at Abilene was later named for him. The story of his capture, imprisonment, and escape is told in *The Dyess Story*.
16. Spector, *Eagle Against the Sun*, 108-111. John W. Whitman, *Bataan: Our Last Ditch, The Bataan Campaign, 1942* (New York: Hippocrene Books, 1990), 39-50, describes the "scramble into Bataan."
17. Spector, *Eagle Against the Sun*, 101-106; Toland, *But Not In Shame*, 88-89, 102-118; Walter J. Boyne, *Clash of Titans: World War II at Sea* (New York: Simon & Schuster, 1995), 151-152; Arthur Poindexter, "The Battle of Wake Island," *1942: "Issue in Doubt"*, 109-121.
18. Gregory J. W. Urwin, *Facing Fearful Odds: The Siege of Wake Island* (Lincoln: University of Nebraska Press, 1997), 195-199, 493-495; Chet Cunningham, *Hell Wouldn't Stop: An Oral History of the Battle of Wake Island* (New York: Carroll & Graf, 2002), 54, 108-109; Bill Sloan, *Given Up for Dead. Heroic Stand at Wake Island* (New York: Bantam Press, 2003), 10-11, 100, 134-136. Hearn, who was wounded in the head by a Japanese bullet, recalled that the rifle ammunition he used was made in 1918. However, he reported that it never misfired.
19. Quote, Private First Class Venable, in Robert S. La Fonte, Ronald E. Marcello, Richard L. Himmel, eds., *With Only the Will to Live: Accounts of Americans in Japanese Prison Camps, 1941-1945* (Wilmington, DL: SR Books, 1994), 9. Venable is identified as a Texan on page xiv of this work.
20. Spector, *Eagle Against the Sun*, 103.
21. Gordon W. Prange, et al., *Miracle at Midway* (New York: McGraw-Hill Book Co., 1982), 5-7.
22. Roosevelt quote, E. B. Potter, *Nimitz* (Annapolis: Naval Institute Press, 1976), 9.
23. Naval historian Dan van der Vat, *The Pacific Campaign: World War II, The U.S.–Japanese Naval War, 1941-1945* (New York: Simon & Schuster, 1991), 150, says "Nimitz has a claim to be considered the most important military leader in the war against Japan, the greatest admiral in American history, and the outstanding naval officer of the Second World War."
Biographical information on Nimitz taken from Potter, *Nimitz*; Frank A. Driskell, *Admiral of the Hills* (Austin: Eakin Press, 1983); Ronald Brink, *Nimitz: The Man and His Wars* (New York: D. I. Fine/Dutton, 1996); and Robert W. Weddle, "Chester William Nimitz," in Tyler, ed., *New Handbook of Texas*, 4: 1015-1017.
24. Eric Larrabee, *Commander in Chief: Franklin Delano Roosevelt, His Lieutenants, and Their War* (New York: Harper & Row Publishers, 1987), 358.
25. Karig and Kelley, *Battle Report: Pearl Harbor to Coral Sea*, 335-336. For more on the salvage work see Homer N. Wallin, *Pearl Harbor: Why, How, Fleet Salvage and Final Appraisal* (Washington: Naval History Division, 1968), 175-284.
26. *Life*, March 16, 1942, p. 45; July 6, 1942, p. 54; Henry C. Dethloff, *A Centennial History of Texas A&M University, 1876-1976*, 2 vols. (College Station: Texas A&M University Press, 1975), 2: 454.
27. Clay Blair, Jr., *Silent Victory: The U.S. Submarine War Against Japan* (Philadelphia: J. B. Lippincott Co., 1975), 135-155; Spector, *Eagle Against the Sun*, 129-130.
28. Blair, *Silent Victory*, 156-160.
29. *Ibid.*, 166-168. Wright did receive the Navy Cross for his patrol. Karig and Kelley, *Battle Report: Pearl Harbor to Coral Sea*, 172-173, 344.

30. Blair, *Silent Victory*, 107, 112-113, 224-225, 901, 907, 908; Karig and Kelley, *Battle Report: Pearl Harbor to Coral Sea*, 344; *Life*, July 6, 1942, p. 54.

31. Blair, *Silent Victory*, 178; *United States Submarine Veterans of World War II* (Dallas: Taylor Publishing Co., 1990), 188.

32. Spector, *Eagle Against the Sun*, 131-132; Karig and Kelley, *Battle Report: Pearl Harbor to Coral Sea*, 182-189, 342.

33. Samuel Eliot Morison, *The Rising Sun in the Pacific, 1931–April 1942* (Boston: Little, Brown, and Co., 1948), 367-369.

34. Art Leatherwood, *U.S.S. Houston*, in Tyler, ed., *New Handbook of Texas*, 3: 714. Captain Rooks was awarded the Medal of Honor (posthumously) "for extraordinary heroism, withstanding courage, gallantry in action and distinguished service." The *U.S.S. Houston* received a presidential unit citation. Karig and Kelley, *Battle Report: Pearl Harbor to Coral Sea*, 488. For more on the *Houston* see Walter Winslow, *The Ghost of the Java Coast* (New York: Laurel Books, 1973) and *The Ghost That Died at Sunda Strait* (Annapolis: Naval Institute Press, 1984).

35. *Life*, June 15, 1942, pp. 32-33; Karig and Kelley, *Battle Report: From Pearl Harbor to Coral Sea*, 246; Leatherwood, U.S.S. *Houston*, in Tyler, ed., *New Handbook of Texas*, 3: 714.

36. Names of these Texans taken from William J. Weissinger, Jr., *Attention Fool!* (Austin: Eakin Press, 1998); H. Robert Charles, *Last Man Out* (Austin: Eakin Press, 1988), 45; Clyde Fillmore, *Prisoner of War: History of the Lost Battalion* (Wichita Falls: Nortex Press, 1973), 98; Robert S. La Fonte, et al., eds., *With Only the Will to Live*, xii-xiii; Robert S. La Fonte and Ronald E. Marcello, eds., *Building the Death Railway: The Ordeal of American Prisoners of War in Burma, 1942-1945* (Wilmington, DL: SR Books, 1993), 91, 158.

37. Ronald E. Marcello, "Lone Star POWs: Texas National Guardsmen and the Building of the Burma–Thailand Railroad, 1942-1944," *Southwestern Historical Quarterly* 95 (January 1992): 293-296. There are numerous published accounts of the 2nd Battalion. Among these are Hollis G. Allen, *The Lost Battalion* (Jacksboro, TX: Herald Publishing Co., 1963); Horace G. Teel, *Our Days Were Years: History of Texas' Lost Battalion* (Quannah, TX: Nortex Press, 1978); Fillmore, *Prisoner of War*, cited above; Elmer R. Milner, "The Lost Battalion: Second Battalion, 131st Field Artillery, 1940-1945" (M. A. thesis, University of North Texas, 1975); Frank Flicklin, "The Lost Battalion," in *1942: "Issue in Doubt*, 31-74; and Kyle Thompson, *A Thousand Cups of Rice: Surviving the Death Railway* (Austin: Eakin Press, 1994).

38. Marcello, "Lone Star POWs," 296-297; E. R. Milner, "Lost Battalion," in Tyler, ed., *New Handbook of Texas*, 4: 297-298; Spector, *Eagle Against the Sun*, 134; Thompson, *Thousand Cups of Rice*, 27-43. Fifty-one of the survivors of the 2nd Battalion, 131st Field Artillery, were interviewed (primarily by Professor Ronald E. Marcello) for the University of North Texas Oral History Program. Their names with a brief description of their experiences may be found in Christopher N. Koontz and Ronald E. Marcello, *Heroes: Oral History Interviews With World War II Veterans* (2nd ed., Denton: University of North Texas, 2002).

39. Marcello, "Lone Star POWs," 206, points out that the men of E Battery of the 2nd Battalion were in a separate prison camp. They were sent to Japan and did not work on the Burma-Thailand Railroad.

40. Quote, John S. Coleman, *Bataan and Beyond: Memories of An American POW* (College Station: Texas A&M University Press, 1978), 33. An excellent description of the fighting on Bataan by a Texan, Louis Read of Dallas, is in Stephen Neal Manning, *Texans Touched by World War II* (Plano, TX: Republic of Texas Press, 2002), 6-11.

41. Toland, *But Not In Shame*, 375-378; Dethloff, *Centennial History of Texas A&M*, 453, 475; John A. Adams, Jr., *Keepers of the Spirit: The Corps of Cadets of Texas A&M University, 1876-2001* (College Station: Texas A&M University Press, 2001), 142-145.

42. Dethloff, *Centennial History of Texas A&M*, 452-454. Dethloff, 453, provides the names, class, and hometown of the Corregidor Aggies. According to John Toland, *But Not In Shame*, 291, MacArthur's parting words to Moore were "George, keep the flag flying." Adams, *Keepers of the Spirit*, 169, notes that since 1946 the General George F. Moore Trophy is presented to the best cadet company at Texas A&M.

43. First quote, Private Tom Blaylock, in La Fonte, et al., eds., *With Only the Will to Live*, 114; second quote, Corporal Louis R. Read, *Ibid.*, 82; Coleman, *Bataan and Beyond*, 74-75, 82.

44. Quote, Durwood Joyner, in Martha Sue Stroud, *For Love of Country: The Price of Freedom* (Austin: Nortex Press, 2000), 225. For more on the march see Stanley L. Falk, *Bataan: The March of Death* (New York: W. W. Norton & Co., 1962); Gerald Astor, *Crisis in the Pacific: The Battles for the Philippine Islands by the Men Who Fought Them* (New York: Donald I. Fine Books, 1996), 145-167.

45. Quote, William E. Dyess, *The Dyess Story*, 71, 75.

46. Toland, *But Not In Shame*, 355. C. Bartlett Kerr, *Surrender and Survival: The Experience of American POWs in the Pacific, 1941-1945* (New York: William Morrow & Co., 1985), 339-340, reports that 25,600 Americans were captured by the Japanese in the Pacific Ocean area (includes Philippines, Wake, Jave, Japan, Celebs, Guam, and China). Kerr states that 10,650 of these were killed or died after capture.

47. Quote, Lucy Wilson, in Elizabeth N. Norman, *We Band of Angels: The Untold Story of American Nurses Trapped in Bataan by the Japanese* (New York: Random House, 1999), 87. Names of nurses and hometowns are given in Appendix II of this work.

48. *Ibid.*, 123, 125-129. It was years, and in some cases decades, before the Bataan nurses forgave Hatchitt. Hatchitt was later named chief nurse of the 53th Army Field Hospital in the European theater. On July 16, 1944 she landed with her unit in Normandy and followed Patton's Third Army across France and Germany. *Ibid.*, 245-246.

49. Evelyn M. Monahan and Rosemary Neidel-Greenlee, *All This Hell: U.S. Nurses Imprisoned by the Japanese* (Lexington: University Press of Kentucky, 2000), 98-153, provide a detailed description of the nurses' imprisonment. In an appendix the authors list each of the nurses with her age, height, weight at capture, and weight at liberation. Each of the Texas nurses lost at least 17 pounds and most lost over 20 pounds while in prison. Frankie T. Lewey of Dalhart, who lost 33 pounds, had the largest weight loss of any Texas nurse. For more on the nurses in the Philippines see Hattie Brantley, "The Philippine Ordeal," in *1942: "Issue in Doubt,"* 99-133; Barbara Brooks Tomblin, *G. I. Nightingales: The Army Nurse Corps in World War II* (Lexington: University Press of Kentucky, 1996), 13-67; Abbie C. Ratledge, *Angels in Khaki* (San Antonio: Naylor Press, 1975); "Hattie Brantley," in Dede Weldon Casad, *Texans of Valor: Military Heroes in the 20th Century* (Austin: Eakin Press, 1998), 74-81; "Heroic Nurses of Bataan and Corregidor," *American Journal of Nursing* 42 (March 1942): 187-198; "Army Nurses Released from Manila Prison Camp," *Ibid.*, 45 (March 1945): 238; Mary Jose, "Army Nurses Return from the Pacific," *Ibid.*, 45 (October 1945): 810.

50. D. Clayton James, ed., *South to Bataan, North to Mukden: The Prison Diary of Brigadier General W. W. Brougher* (Athens: University of Georgia Press, 1971), 41; first quote, Dyess, *The Dyess Story*, 101; second quote, Thornton Hamby, in Stephen Neal Manning, *The Courage of Common Men: Texans Remember World War II* (Plano, TX: Republic of Texas Press, 2001), 236. For more on the terrible conditions at Cabanatuan see Forrest Byron Johnson, *Hour of Redemption: The Heroic WWII Saga of America's Most Daring POW Rescue* (Orig.pub. 1978; New York: Warner Books, 2000), 51-59; and Manning, *Texans Touched by World War II*, 19-20.

51. Karig and Kelley, *Battle Report: Pearl Harbor to Coral Sea*, 255-256, 338, 340.

52. *Ibid.*, 290, 348.

53. Carroll V. Glines, *The Doolittle Raid: America's Daring First Strike Against Japan* (New York: Orion Books, 1988), 9-15; Craig Nelson, *The First Heroes: The Extraordinary Story of the Doolittle Raid – America's First World War II Victory* (New York: Viking, 2002), 107-112.

54. Spector, *Eagle Against the Sun*, 154-155; Nelson, *First Heroes*, 117-125.

55. Glines, *Doolittle Raid*, 83, 93, 117, 120, 210-216; Nelson, *First Heroes*, xv-xviii.

56. Glines, *Doolittle Raid*, 210-216.

57. *Ibid.*, 103-105, 155-156; Nelson, *First Heroes*, 136-155, 169-172, 308-314. Doolittle describes the raid in his *I Could Never Be So Lucky Again* (New York: Bantam Books, 1991), 240-256. One of the pilots, Captain Ted W. Lawson of New York, wrote a popular account, later made into a movie, entitled *Thirty Seconds Over Tokyo* (Cutchoque, NY: Buccaneer Books, 1943). For more on the crew that landed in Soviet territory see Otis Hays, Jr., *Home From Siberia: The*

Secret Odysseys of Interned American Airmen in World War II (College Station: Texas A&M University Press, 1990), 28-54.

58. Glines, *Doolittle Raid*, 129-131, 159-160, 162-163, 174; Nelson, *First Heroes*, 240-246, 264-267, 280-281, 290-292, 302-305, 321-325.

59. Nelson, *First Heroes*, 281-282. One of the five whose sentence was commuted, Lieutenant Robert J. Meder of Cleveland, Ohio, the co-pilot on Hallmark's "Green Hornet," died in prison from starvation and dysentery in December 1943.

60. Spector, *Eagle Against the Sun*, 155.

61. John B. Lundstrom, *The First South Pacific Campaign: Pacific Fleet Strategy December 1941–June 1942* (Annapolis: Naval Institute Press, 1976), 79-88; Spector, *Eagle Against the Sun*, 157-158; Potter, *Nimitz*, 63-77.

62. Samuel Eliot Morison, *Coral Sea, Midway and Submarine Actions, May 1942–August 1942* (Boston: Little, Brown and Co., 1961), 33-60; W. T. Block, "Local Veteran Fired Famous Carrier's Guns," *Beaumont Enterprise*, March 13, 2002. Derrill Thompson from Dallas was a radio operator on the destroyer *Hamman* which helped pick up survivors of the *Lexington*. Author interview, January 11, 2003, Beaumont, Texas. Harold Placette of Port Arthur was on the destroyer *Phelps* which also assisted in the rescue mission. W. T. Block, "Port Arthuran saw first hand Day of Infamy," *Beaumont Enterprise*, December 7, 2001.

63. Morison, *Coral Sea, Midway and Submarine Actions*, 63-64; Potter, *Nimitz*, 75-76.

64. Boyne, *Clash of Titans*, 179-180.

65. *Ibid.*, 182; Potter, *Nimitz*, 78-90.

66. The most complete account of the battle is Prange, et al., *Miracle at Midway*.

67. Boyne, *Clash of Titans*, 189-192; Spector, *Eagle Against the Sun*, 173-175.

68. George Gay, *Sole Survivor: The Battle of Midway and Its Effects on His Life* (priv. printed, 1979), 20-75; Ronald J. Drez, *Twenty-Five Years of War: The Extraordinary Courage of Ordinary Men in World War II* (New York: Hyperion, 2001), 27-40.

69. Gay, *Sole Survivor*, 140-141; Drez, *Twenty-Five Years of War*, 49-53. Gay was flown to Pearl Harbor, where he was hospitalized. While there he was visited by Admiral Nimitz, who awarded him the Navy Cross. Gay was returned to the states for a war bond drive and public appearances supporting the war effort. He was featured on the cover of *Life* magazine, August 31, 1942. He later returned to active duty and served in the Solomon Islands. Gordon Prange, *Miracle at Midway*, 248, describes Gay as "handsome, articulate, with considerable charm and humor, of proven courage and resourcefulness," and as "a public relations officer's dream come true."

70. Boyne, *Clash of Titans*, 191-193; Spector, *Eagle Against the Sun*, 175. Yeoman 2nd Class Jack Adams, from Dayton, Texas, was one of the crewmen on *Yorktown* forced to abandon ship. He and others were picked up by the destroyer U.S.S. *Benham*. *Fifty-Five Years Later*, 2 vols. (Liberty, TX: Rotary Club, 1995), volume 2, unnumbered pages.

71. Boyne, *Clash of Titans*, 197.

CHAPTER FOUR

1. Although Eisenhower moved with his family to Kansas soon after his birth, historian David Reynolds, *Rich Relations: The American Occupation of Britain, 1942-1945* (London: Phoenix Press, 2000), 385, 388-389, points out that British newspapers often focused upon his Texas origin because that fit in with stereotypes of America. Eisenhower's early career is discussed in two works by Stephen Ambrose: *The Supreme Commander: The War Years of General Dwight D. Eisenhower* (Garden City, NY: Doubleday & Co., 1969) and *Eisenhower: Soldier, General of the Army, President-Elect, 1890-1952* (New York: Simon & Schuster, 1983); and Carlo D'Este, *Eisenhower: A Soldier's Life* (New York: Henry Holt and Co., 2002). A good brief summary of Eisenhower's career, written by his son John, may be found in Tyler, ed., *New Handbook of Texas*, 2: 808.

2. Ambrose, *Supreme Commander*, 54-60.

3. Quote, Ambrose, *Eisenhower*, 171.

4. Richard G. Davis, *Carl Spaatz and the Air War in Europe* (Washington: Smithsonian Institute Press, 1993), 22-33; James Parton, *"Air Force Spoken Here:" General Ira Eaker and Command of the Air* (Bethesada, MD: Adler & Adler, 1986), 128; Roger A. Freeman, *The Mighty Eighth: A History of the Units, Men, and Machines of the US 8th Air Force* (London: Cassell & Co., 1970), 4-5.

5. Parton, *"Air Force Spoken Here,"* 17-30; Art Leatherwood, "Ira Clarence Eaker," in Tyler, ed., *New Handbook of Texas*, 2: 753-754.

6. Parton, *"Air Force Spoken Here,"* 52-128.

7. Brian D. O'Neill, *Half A Wing, Three Engines and A Prayer: B-17s Over Germany*, New York: McGraw-Hill, 1999),15-16; Freeman, *Mighty Eighth*, 11-12.

8. O'Neill, *Half A Wing*, 16-17; Freeman, *Mighty Eighth*, 13-19. General Eisenhower paid several visits to Eaker's headquarters during this period. Eisenhower admired the uniform jacket worn by Eaker. This short, khaki jacket had been designed by a British tailor modeled on the battle jacket worn by British troops. Just before Eisenhower left to take command of the North African invasion Eaker sent him a similar jacket. Eisenhower loved it and it became known as the "Eisenhower jacket" worn by the American army. D'Este, *Eisenhower*, 346.

9. For an excellent discussion of the decision to invade North Africa see Charles B. MacDonald, *The Mighty Endeavor: American Armed Forces in the European Theater in World War II* (New York: Oxford University Press, 1969), 57-70.

10. MacDonald, *Mighty Endeavor*, 77-78. The most complete accounts of the North African campaign are George F. Howe, *Northwest Africa: Seizing the Initiative in the West* (Washington: Center of Military History, United States Army, 1991), and Rick Atkinson, *An Army at Dawn: The War in North Africa, 1942-1943* (New York: Henry Holt and Co., 2002).

11. Theodore J. Conway, "Lucian King Truscott," in Roger J. Spiller, ed., *Dictionary of American Military Biography* (Westport, CT: Greenwood Press, 1984), 3: 1110-1112; *Webster's American Military Biographies* (Springfield, MS: G. & C. Merriam Co.,, 1979), 441-442. Atkinson, *An Army at Dawn*, 141, describes Truscott as "almost foppish" in dress, wearing an enameled helmet, silk scarf, red leather jacket, and ridding breeches.

12. Howe, *Northwest Africa*, 150-169; Geoffrey Perret, *There's A War To Be Won: The United States Army in World War II* (New York: Random House, 1991), 140-141; L. K. Truscott, Jr., *Command Missions: A Personal Story* (New York: E. P. Dutton and Co., 1954, reprinted Novato: CA: Presidio Press, 1990), 108-123; Hugh Power, *Battleship Texas* (College Station: Texas A&M University Press, 1993), 23.

13. MacDonald, *Mighty Endeavor*, 141-144. Major General Mark W. Clark, Eisenhower's deputy, negotiated an agreement with Admiral Darlan. This agreement, endorsed by Eisenhower, was unpopular in the United States and Great Britain because of Darlan's connection with the pro-German Vichy government. Eisenhower's recent biographer, Carlo D'Este, notes the deal with Darlan was a blow to Eisenhower's record but believes Eisenhower had little other choice. *Eisenhower*, 358.

14. Robert L. Wagner, *The Texas Army: A History of the 36th Division in the Italian Campaign* (Austin: State House Press, 1991), 4. Division commander Major General Fred L. Walker describes the movement of the division in his memoir *From Texas to Rome: A General's Journey* (Dallas: Taylor Publishing Co., 1969), 183-188. Walker notes that the Texas citizen soldiers sometimes destroyed private property. On one occasion a French farmer and three Arabs complained that the Texans had damaged their watermelon fields. "Texas soldiers just can't resist watermelons," Walker explained. "They carried away all kinds—green, ripe, large, small. I required the 143rd Infantry to pay for them." *From Texas to Rome*, 209.

15. Walker, *From Texas to Rome*, 50, 71, 83; Ernie Pyle, *Here Is Your War* (Cleveland: World Publishing Co., 1943), 154; *Time*, Aug. 9, 1943, pp. 32-36.

16. Pyle, *Here Is Your War*, 87-88; also in David Nichols, ed., *Ernie's War: The Best of Ernie Pyle's World War II Dispatches* (New York: Random House, 1986), 77-78. Pyle was struck by the lonely lives of fighter pilots. When not flying they hung around the field much of the day with little to do. Pyle noted "I walked into his [Ilfrey's] room late one afternoon, after he had come back

from a mission, and found him [Ilfrey] sitting there at a table, all alone, killing flies with a folded paper." *Ibid.*, 78.

17. *Ibid.*, 54-55, 76, 103, 132.

18. Quote, Charles Clinton Green, in Stephen N. Manning, *The Courage of Common Men: Texans Remember World War II* (Plano: Republic of Texas Press, 2001), 132.

19. Robert J. Robertson, "A Texan At War: Sergeant Travis Moore, U.S. Marine Corps, 1942-1944," *Military History of the West* 30 (Fall 2000): 135-139.

20. *A History of the Second World War: A Memorial, A Remembrance and An Appreciation*, 5 vols. (Dallas: Historical Publishing Co., 1948), 2: 750.

21. Richard B. Frank, *Guadalcanal: The Definitive Account of the Landmark Battle* (New York: Penguin Books, 1990), 612-614; Samuel B. Griffith II, *The Battle for Guadalcanal* (Philadelphia: Lippincott Co., 1963), 243-245. Freddie Donatto, an African American bulldozer operator from the Ames community in Liberty County, was a member of the 34th Seabee Battalion providing military construction workers on Guadalcanal. While there Donatto met Eleanor Roosevelt on one of her overseas tours. *Fifty-Five Years Later*, Vol. 1, unnumbered pages.

22. Oscar C. Kilcher, interviewed by Diana Gonzales, in William L. Adams, *Valley Vets: An Oral History of World War II Veterans of the Lower Rio Grande Valley* (Austin: Eakin Press, 1999), 132-133.

23. Richard Allan Burns, "Leonard Roy Harmon," in Tyler, ed., *New Handbook of Texas*, 3: 464.

24. Geoffrey Perret, *Old Soldiers Never Die*, 310-327. For more on this campaign see Evan H. M. Barnet and James Kincaid (two veterans of the Buna campaign), "The Worst of All Possible Worlds," in *1942: "Issue in Doubt*," 221-229; Samuel Milner, *Victory in Papua* (Washington: Center of Military History, United States Army, 1985).

25. Stephen R. Taaffe, *MacArthur's Jungle War: the 1944 New Guinea Campaign* (Lawrence: University Press of Kansas, 1998), 36-37. D. Clayton James, *The Years of MacArthur* 2 vols. (Boston: Houghton-Mifflin Co., 1975), 2: 312, points out that MacArthur soon created an independent tactical organization known as the Alamo Force, which was commanded by Krueger and contained the same units that made up the Sixth Army. This was a move by MacArthur to withdraw American army units from control by Australian General Thomas Blamey who was Allied Land Forces commander in the Southwest Pacific. Krueger's own story is found in his *From Down Under to Nippon: The Story of the Sixth Army in World War II* (Washington: Combat Forces Press, 1953). Lonnie Hood of Beaumont, who piloted General Krueger's plane on several missions, has fond memories of Krueger whom he remembers as a "courageous soldier." Interview, author with Lonnie Hood, Beaumont, Texas, October 30, 2002.

26. Leonard G. Hall, *Brothers of the Fox: Company F, 172nd Infantry, 43rd Division* (Orange, TX: priv. printed, 1985), 1, 3, 4-6, 8-9, 45; Stroud, *For Love of Country*, 165.

27. John Miller, Jr., *Cartwheel: The Reduction of Rabaul* (Washington: Center of Military History, United States Army, 1984), 67-188.

28. Toland, *Flying Tigers*, 116-118; Carl Molesworth, *Sharks Over China: The 23rd Fighter Group in World War II* (Washington: Brassey's, 1994), 9-11.

29. Molesworth, *Sharks Over China*, 14-15, 166-168; Toland, *Flying Tigers*, 124-128, 145-146; *Life*, March 30, 1942, p. 30.

30. Molesworth, *Sharks Over China*, 127, 146, 171-174; *Life*, March 30, 1942, p. 30.

31. O'Neill, *Half A Wing*, 16-17.

32. Quotes from G. O. No. 38, 12 July 1943, in *Texas Medal of Honor Recipients*, compiled by the Texas Veterans Commission Headquarters (Austin, 1993), 55; Freeman, *Mighty Eighth*, 27-28, 267. Lieutenant Mathis' brother, First Lieutenant Rhode M. Mathis, was lost in a raid on Kiel, Germany, two months after the raid over Vegesack. *History of the Second World War, A Memorial*, 4: 1703.

33. Robert Morgan, *The Men Who Flew the Memphis Belle: Memoir of a WWII Bomber Pilot* (New York: Dutton, 2001), 107-108, 148-149.

34. Freeman, *Mighty Eighth*, 63-66.

35. *Ibid.*, 268; Art Leatherwood, "John Clay Morgan," in Tyler, ed., *New Handbook of Texas*, 4: 836-837.

36. Quotes from G. O. No. 85, 17 December 1943, in *Texas Medal of Honor Recipients*, 61. Morgan returned to duty after the July mission. He was later transferred to the 482nd Bomb Group, commissioned second lieutenant, and was shot down over Berlin in March 1944. He parachuted to safety, was captured by the Germans and spent fourteen months in Stalag I. Freeman, *Mighty Eighth*, 268.

37. Craven and Cate, *Army Air Forces in World War II*, 2: 477-483; Buchanan, *United States and World War II*, 1: 266-267. Geoffrey Perret, *Winged Victory: The Army Air Forces in World War II* (New York: Random House, 1993), 218, argues the Ploesti raid "made no appreciable difference." Because of transportation problems the Ploesti refineries had been operating at only 50% capacity. Facilities destroyed by the raid were replaced by bringing unused or underused plants into production.

38. James Dugan and Carroll Stewart, *Ploesti: The Great Ground–Air Battle of 1 August 1943* (London: Jonathan Cape, 1963), 121-122.

39. *Ibid.*, 133-136, 228-229, 257.

40. *Ibid.*, 189-191.

41. General Orders No. 54, 9 August 1943, in *Texas Medal of Honor Recipients*, 38; Perret, *Winged Victory*, 216-217.

42. Quote, General Orders No. 17, 26 February 1944, in *Texas Medal of Honor Recipients*, 38; Perret, *Winged Victory*, 217; Ardrey, *Bomber Pilot*, 103-105; Art Leatherwood, "Lloyd H. Hughes," in Tyler, ed., *New Handbook of Texas*, 3: 773. Ardrey points out that Lieutenant Robert Lee Wright of Austin was one of the pilots who made it successfully through the Polesti raid. When Ardrey became group operations officer in December 1943 Wright became squadron operations officer. Charles S. "Bubba" Young of Liberty was another Texan who successfully completed the Ploesti mission. Lieutenant Young, who had earlier served with the Eagle Squadron of the Royal Air Force, received the Distinguished Flying Cross for his role in the mission. Young was later killed on D-Day. *Liberty Vindicator*, June 19, 1944; John A. Young, *The Lejeunes of Acadia and the Youngs of Southwest Louisiana* (priv. printed, 1991), 712-713.

43. Thomas M. Coffey, *Decision Over Schweinfurt: The U.S. 8th Air Force Battle for Daylight Bombing* (New York: David McKay Co., 1977), 1-3; Perret, *Winged Victory*, 264-265.

44. Perret, *Winged Victory*, 255.

45. Coffey, *Decision Over Schweinfurt*, 24-25, 54, 74; Elmer Bendiner, *The Fall of Fortresses: A Personal Account of the Most Daring—and Deadly—American Air Battles of World War II* (New York: G. P. Putnam's Sons, 1980), 167; Perret, *Winged Victory*, 262.

46. Perret, *Winged Victory*, 267-269.

47. Coffey, *Decision Over Schweinfurt*, 76; Perret, *Winged Victory*, 219. In his *Mission with LeMay* (Garden City, NY: Doubleday, 1965), 293, LeMay says he did not see any friendly fighter escorts in the Regensburg raid. "Our fighter escorts had black crosses on their wings," he wrote.

48. O'Neill, *Half A Wing*, 61-65, 71-75; Perret, *Winged Victory*, 272.

49. O'Neill, *Half A Wing*, 22-23, 61-63, 71-93; Perret, *Winged Victory*, 272-273.

50. O'Neill, *Half A Wing*, 126-127.

51. Perret, *Winged Victory*, 88, 253, 276; Gerald Astor, *The Mighty Eighth: The Air War in Europe as Told by the Men Who Fought It* (New York: Donald I. Fine Books, 1997), 125-127, 162-164; Gerald Astor, *The Greatest War: Americans in Combat, 1941-1945* (Novato, CA: Presidio Press, 1999), 358-360.

52. Astor, *Mighty Eighth*, 164-166; O'Neill, *Half A Wing*, 123-124; Coffey, *Decision Over Schweinfurt*, 294-325; Perret, *Winged Victory*, 276-279. The official Air Force history, Cate and Lea, *Army Air Forces in World War II*, 2: 703, says "the bombing [at Schweinfurt] was unusually effective."

53. Perret, *Winged Victory*, 281.

54. "Robert A. Lovett," in Charles D. Bright, ed., *Historical Directory of the U.S. Air Force* (Westport, CN: Greenwood Press, 1992), 354.

55. Anna Giles Kimbrough, "Barney McKinney Giles," and "Benjamin Franklin Giles," in Tyler, ed., *New Handbook of Texas*, 3: 160-161. For a description of his early training see Barney M. Giles, "Early Military Aviation Facilities in Texas," *Southwestern Historical Quarterly* 54

(October 1950): 143-158. Benjamin Giles became commander of the U.S. Air Forces in the Middle East in 1944.

56. Perret, *Winged Victory*, 106, 261.

57. *Ibid.*, 282; Freeman, *Mighty Eighth*, 104.

58. Quote, Richard Davis, *Carl H. Spaatz*, 593.

59. Parton, *"Air Force Spoken Here,"* 351.

60. Quote, Flint Whitlock, *The Rock of Anzio: From Sicily to Dachau, A History of the 45th Division* (New York: Westview Press, 1998), 22; Donald G. Taggart, *History of the Third Infantry Division in World War II* (Washington: Infantry Journal Press, 1947), 37-56; Albert N. Garland and Howard M. Smyth, *Sicily and the Surrender of Italy* (Washington: Chief of Military History, Department of the Army, 1965), 93-94.

61. Harold B. Simpson, *Audie Murphy, American Soldier* (Hillsboro, TX: Hillsboro Junior College Press, 1975), 45-69; Don Graham, *No Name on the Bullet: A Biography of Audie Murphy* (New York: Viking, 1989), 1-31. In his autobiography *To Hell and Back* (New York, Henry Holt and Co., 1949), 6-7, Murphy recalled "we were share-crop farmers. And to say that the family was poor would be an understatement." Of his father, who left the family in 1940 and never returned, Murphy wrote "he was not lazy, but he had a genius for not considering the future." *Ibid.*, 7.

62. Quote, Audie Murphy, *To Hell and Back*, 15.

63. Quote, Maxine Hairston, "George Sessions Perry," in Tyler, ed., *New Handbook of Texas*, 5: 158-159. See also Truman McMahan, "Remembering George Sessions Perry," *Southwestern Historical Quarterly* 95 (January 1992): 369-376; Garner L. Christian, "George Perry's War," *Ibid.* 102 (October 1998): 187-209; Christian, "A Brief Peace: The Post War Years of George Sessions Perry," *Ibid.* 106 (July 2002): 57-74; Hairston, *George Sessions Perry, His Life and Works* (Austin: Jenkins, 1973); Stanley G. Alexander, *George Sessions Perry* (Austin: Steck-Vaughn Co., 1967); and Curt Riess, ed., *They Were There: The Story of World War II and How It Came About by America's Foremost Correspondents* (Freeport, NY: Books for Libraries Series, 1971), 566-571.

64. Ernie Pyle, *Brave Men* (reprint, Lincoln: University of Nebraska Press, 2001), 60-61.

65. *Ibid.*, 86-87.

66. Garland and Smythe, *Sicily and the Surrender of Italy*, 57.

67. Walker, *From Texas to Rome*, 19-35, 80-82,145; Martin Blumenson, "The 36th Infantry Division in World War II," in Joseph C. Dawson III, ed., *The Texas Military Experience: From the Texas Revolution Through World War II* (College Station: Texas A&M University Press, 1995), 129-130.

68. Blumenson, "The 36th Infantry Division," 131.

69. James D. Padgift, "That Long Day at Salerno," *Texas Military History* 5 (Summer 1965): 45-63, is a description of the fighting by the executive officer of the 2nd Battalion, 142nd Infantry. See also Wagner, *Texas Army*, 7-17; Bruce L. Brager, *The Texas 36th Division: A History* (Austin: Eakin Press, 2002), 126-132; Eric Morris, *Salerno: A Military Fiasco* (New York: Stein and Day, 1983), 90-96, 127-141; and Martin Blumenson, *Salerno to Cassino* (Washington: Office of the Chief of Military History, United States Army, 1969), 73-117.

70. General Orders No. 54, 5 July 1944, in *Texas Medal of Honor Recipients*, 51. Captain Ross Ayers of Lubbock, who may have fired the first shot at Salerno, was awarded the Silver Star for gallantry. "Texas Collection," *Southwestern Historical Quarterly* 47 (July 1944): 124.

71. Morris, *Salerno*, 147. Morris believes that all things considered these were relatively low numbers. Most Texans would probably not agree. There is an excellent description of the fighting at Salerno in a letter by Major James T. Taylor of the 131st Field Artillery published in the "Texas Collection" of the *Southwestern Historical Quarterly* 48 (October 1944): 281-285.

72. Wagner, *Texas Army*, 25-32.

73. Walker, *From Texas to Rome*, 255; Blumenson, "The 36th Infantry Division," 131; Blumenson, *Salerno to Cassino*, 118-132; Brager, *Texas 36th Division*, 135-142.

74. Wagner, *Texas Army*, 53.

75. Citation quoted in Martin Bluemenson, *Bloody River: The Real Tragedy of the Rapido* (reprint, College Station: Texas A&M University Press, 1998), 11.

76. Wagner, *Texas Army*, 60-89; Walker, *From Texas to Rome*, 177-288; Brager, *Texas 36th Division*, 144-157.

77. This is the same Edwin A. Walker, who later was associated with extreme right wing activities and unsuccessfully ran for governor of Texas. For more on Walker see Cris Cravens, "Edwin A. Walker," in Tyler, ed., *New Handbook of Texas*, 6: 793-794; *New York Times*, September 25, 1957, p. 18. For more on the First Special Force (which came to be known as the "Devil's Brigade), see Fred Pusties, et al., *American's Counterterrorist Forces* (New York: Barnes & Noble Books, 2001), 17-18; Robert H. Adleman and George Walton, *The Devil's Brigade* (Philadelphia: Chilton Books, 1996), 95, 98, 161-162, 187, 233-234; and Joseph A. Springer, *The Black Devil Brigade: The True Story of the First Special Service Force in World War II* (New York: I Books, 2003).

78. Quote, Pyle, *Brave Men*, 164; Walker, *From Texas to Rome*, 191-192; Jay A. Matthews, Jr., "Captain Henry T. Waskow, Peerless Leader," *Military History of Texas & the Southwest* 16 (no. 1, undated): 3-4.

79. Citation, undated, in *Texas Medal of Honor Recipients*, 39. Art Leatherwood, "Johnnie David S. Hutchins," in Tyler, ed., *New Handbook of Texas*, 3: 804, points out that a destroyer escort, U.S.S. *Johnnie Hutchins*, was named for him.

80. General Orders No. 3, 6 January 1944, in *Texas Medal of Honor Recipients*, 41. Kearby was shot down six months later and reported missing in action. He had just claimed his twenty-second victory and at the time was one of the highest ranking American aces. His body was not recovered. Leatherwood, "Neel E. Kearby," in Tyler, ed., *New Handbook of Texas*, 3: 1043.

81. Citation, undated, *Ibid.*, 33; Art Leatherwood, "William Dean Hawkins," in Tyler, ed., *New Handbook of Texas*, 3: 511; Robert L. Sherrod, *Tarawa: The Story of A Battle* (New York: Duell, Sloan, and Pearce, 1944), 47.

82. Citation, undated, in *Texas Medal of Honor Recipients*, 10. See also Casad, *Texans of Valor*, 82-87; Michael B. Graham, *Month of Heroism: Tarawa and the Struggle for the Gilberts, November 1943* (Novato, CA: Presidio Press, 1993), 317.

83. Graham, *Month of Heroism*, 184, 318-319.

84. John A. Adams, *We Are the Aggies: The Texas A&M University Association of Former Students* (College Station: Texas A&M University Press, 1979), 155; Graham, *Month of Heroism*, 160, 203-204, 247, 267; Sherrod, *Tarawa*, 95, 128n.

85. Casad, *Texans of Valor*, 97-101; author interview with Lonnie Hood, October 30, 2002, Beaumont, Texas; Art Leatherwood, "George Andrew Davis, Jr.," in Tyler, ed., *New Handbook of Texas*, 2: 528. For Frazier's story see *Saga of Tsili Tsili* (San Antonio: priv. printed, 1992), Volume II.

86. Quote, Bruce Gamble, *The Black Sheep: The Definitive Account of Marine Fighting Squadron 214 in World War II* (Novato, CA: Presidio Press, 2000), 254. See also pp. 189, 243-244, 325-337, 430.

87. Gamble, *Black Sheep*, 243-244.

88. See Blair, *Silent Victory*, 361-362, 551-554.

89. Blair, *Silent Victory*, 253, 313-314, 487, 702-706; "Biographical Information on Vice Admiral Glynn Robert Donaho," Operational Archives Branch, Naval Historical Center. Richard F. Newcomb, *Abandon Ship! The Saga of the U.S.S. Indianapolis, the Navy's Greatest Disaster* (New York: Perennial, 2002), 239, describes Donaho as "a peppery little Texan whose submarine exploits in the war earned him no less than the Navy Cross, four times, Silver Star, twice, and Bronze Star, twice."

90. Blair, *Silent Victory*, Appendix F, 900-983, lists all submarine patrols and ships/tonnage credit. Mendenhall's figures are found in his *Submarine Diary* (Annapolis: Naval Institute Press, 1991), 116, 133, 157. For more on Mendenhall see W. T. Block, "Winnie Native," *Beaumont Enterprise*, January 12, 2001.

91. *U.S. Submarine Veterans of World War II* (Dallas: Taylor Publishing Co., 1990), 201; Blair, *Silent Victory*, 373-374.

92. *U.S. Submarine Veterans of World War II*, 133; Blair, *Silent Victory*, 378-379, 917, 919.

93. Art Leatherwood, "Samuel David Dealey," in Tyler, ed., *New Handbook of Texas*, 2: 549; Lockwood and Adamson, *Through Hell and Deep Water*, 70-93.

94. Lockwood and Adamson, *Through Hell and Deep Water*, 141-167; Blair, *Silent Victory*, 444-445, 931, 933, 939. Another Texan, John Paul (Bettle) Roach from Paris, a 1932 Annapolis graduate, commanded the submarine U.S.S. *Haddock* on patrol in Marianas waters during this period. He later commanded a submarine pack during the battle of Leyte Gulf. Blair, *Silent Victory*, 546-547, 770-772; I. J. Galantin, *Take Her Deep! A Submarine Against Japan in World War II* (Chapel Hill: Algoniun Books, 1987), 130-131, 206.

95. *Selective Service as the Tide of War Turns: The 3rd Report of the Director of Selective Service, 1943-1944* (Washington: Government Printing Office, 1945), 552. The *Texas Almanac, 1945-1946*, 76-77, says that approximately 530,000 Texans were in military service on January 1, 1944. According to the *Almanac* 372,000 Texas men and 4,306 Texas women were in the U.S. Army (including the Army Air Forces).

CHAPTER FIVE

1. Mail to and from troops overseas came in reduced photographic form to save shipping space. Known as "V-mail," letters written on specially designed stationery were photographed and the film then shipped. The developed film was then distributed as a letter in the form of a 4 by 5½ inch photograph. Richard R. Lingeman, *Don't You Know There's A War On: The American Home Front, 1941-1945* (New York: G. P. Putnam's Sons, 1970), 120.

2. Julie Wingate Bacom, "Our Way Of Life Is Ended Right Now," in Louis Fairchild, ed., *They Called It The War Effort: Oral Histories From World War II Orange, Texas* (Austin: Eakin Press, 1991), 177.

3. Louis Dugas, Jr., "Delivering Death Messages," in *Ibid.*, 165-166.

4. *Texas Almanac, 1945-1946*, 109-110; Fairchild, ed., *They Called It The War Effort*, xxv. The estimated civilian population in Texas actually dropped by 123,279 during the 1940-1943 period.

5. *Texas Almanac, 1945-1946*, 109-110; Donald R. Abbe, "Moore County," and John Heffler, "Hockley County," in Tyler, ed., *New Handbook of Texas*, 3: 645-646; 4: 826.

6. *Texas Almanac,1945-1946*, 109-110. These figures are estimates of "civilian" population by the Bureau of Census. They do not include military personnel who were not stationed in Texas on a somewhat permanent basis.

7. *Ibid.*, 109-110.

8. John T. Smith, "Use It Up–Wear It Out," in Lee, ed., *1940: Texas Goes to War*, 85; Tessica Martin, "Brownwood, Texas in World War II," *West Texas Historical Association Year Book* 43 (October 1967): 32-35.

9. First quote, Harold Harrington, "People in the United States Had Too Much," in Fairchild, ed., *They Called It The War Effort*, 32; second quote, Emma Jane Nies, "The World Turned Upside Down," in *Ibid.*, 26.

10. Quote, Mary Marshall, "People at the Trailer Court," in *Ibid.*, 70.

11. Quote, C. W. Waggoner, "They Called Us Drifters," in *Ibid.*, 112.

12. Alexander, *Stars Were Big and Bright*, 2: 10-11.

13. Mrs. Jessie Wooster was the author's grandmother.

14. Wiggins, *Torpedoes in the Gulf*, 159-160.

15. Lingeman, *Don't You Know There's A War On*, 80; Geoffrey Perret, *Days of Sadness, Years of Triumph* (Baltimore: Penguin Books, 1974), 241, 342-343.

16. *Ibid.*, 33-36; Kennett, *For the Duration*, 30-36; Ronald H. Bailey, *The Home Front: USA* (Alexandria, VA: Time-Life Books, 1977), 104. Kevin Ladd, director of the Wallisville Heritage Museum, points out that organization of the Aircraft Warning Service in Chambers County was completed by August 1941. Eleven observation posts in the county were manned by local volunteers. See *The Progress* (Anahuac), August 14, 1941.

17. Lee, ed., *1940: Texas Goes to War*, 76; Wiggins, *Torpedoes in the Gulf*, 15-16; Stroud, *For Love of Country*, 158, 176.

18. William Allen and Sue Hastings Taylor, *Aransas: The Life of a Texas Coastal County* (Austin: Eakin Press, 1990), 310-311; Wiggins, *Torpedoes in the Gulf*, 16-17.

19. Wiggins, *Torpedoes in the Gulf*, 17; W. T. Block, "Other Gulf War Claimed Many from SE Texas," *Beaumont Enterprise*, September 6, 2000; W. T. Block, "World War II Heroes At Last Are Recognized," *Ibid.*, December 5, 2001.

20. Wiggins, *Torpedoes in the Gulf*, 53, 55, 91-95, 98-100; Block, "World War II Heroes;" Block, *Sapphire City on the Neches*, 352.

21. *Houston Post*, June 1, 1942; Samuel Eliot Morison, *The Two-Ocean War: A Short History of the United States Navy in the Second World War* (Boston: Little, Brown and Co., 1963), 122-136, 376-380; Wiggins, *Torpedoes in the Gulf*, 147-156, 184-185. The author thanks Kevin Ladd, director of the Wallisville Historical Park, for information on the Mounted Coast Guard.

22. Lieutenant James Taylor of Baton Rouge, also flying with the Beaumont Civil Air patrol, lost his life in a rescue mission. Another Texan, John T. Burke of Fort Worth, was killed while flying on a mission for the Replacement Center in Fort Worth. Robert E. Neprud, *Flying Men: The Story of the Civil Air Patrol* (New York: Duell, Sloan, and Pearce, 1948), 54, 70-71, 75, 233-234, 236. See also Louis E. Keefer, *From Maine to Mexico: With America's Private Pilots in the Fight Against Nazi U-Boats* (Reston, VA: COTU Publishing, 1997).

23. Wiggins, *Torpedoes in the Gulf*, 176, 224. Several naval officers from Texas played significant roles in the campaign against German U-boats. Vice Admiral Adolphus "Dolly" Andrews from Galveston was commander of the Eastern Sea Frontier, 1941-1943; Rear Admiral William R. Munroe from Waco was commander of the Seventh Naval District and Gulf Sea Frontier, 1943-1944; and Rear Admiral Samuel M. Robinson from Eulogy was Chief of the Naval Bureau of Ships. Samuel E. Morison, *History of U.S. Naval Operations in World War II*, 15 vols. (Boston: Little, Brown, 1947-1962), 1: 189n, 208, 208n; 10: 33, 135n, 178.

24. Kennett, *For the Duration*, 105, 124.

25. Lingeman, *Don't You Know There's A War On*, 235-237; Kennett, *For the Duration*, 134-135.

26. Bailey, *Home Front: U.S.A.*, 110; Barbara McLean Ward, "A Fair Share at a Fair Price: Rationing, Resource Management, and Price Controls during World War II," in Barbara McLean Ward, ed., *Produce and Conserve: Share and Play Square* (Portsmouth, NH: Strawbery Banke Museum, 1994), 83-84.

27. Rationing of coffee was ended in July 1943 when additional shipping space became available. Bailey, *Home Front: U.S.A.*, 110; Lingeman, *Don't You Know There's A War On*, 246-247; *Houston Post*, February 22, 1943. Detailed studies of rationing of coffee, food, dairy products, and fats may be found in *The Story of Wartime Rationing* (Washington: Office of Price Administration, 1945) and Judith Russell and Renee Fantin, *Studies in Rationing* (Washington: Office of Price Administration, 1947).

28. Lingeman, *Don't You Know There's A War On*, 243. Since the average American purchased 3.43 pairs of shoes before the war it was believed this would be no hardship. However, individuals interviewed by the author always remembered the inconveniences of shoe rationing.

29. Quote, Buck Young, "Memories of World War II," *East Texas Historical Journal* 30 (Spring 1992): 14.

30. Ward, "A Fair Share at a Fair Price," 88-89. For an early work explaining the need for rationing see Caroline F. Ware, *The Consumer Goes to War: A Guide to Victory on the Home Front* (New York: Funk & Wagnalls Co., 1942).

31. Quote, Mrs. Leona Whitman, interview with Phyllis Jordan, March 27, 1989, in Special Collections, Gray Library, Lamar University, Beaumont, Texas. Lingeman, *Don't You Know There's A War On*, 260, describes a critical milk shortage around Beaumont and Port Arthur. The shortages of milk was nationwide. In the spring of 1943 when it appeared that milk would be rationed the Office of Price Administration drafted plans and procedures for administering a fluid milk rationing program. Objections by the industry, however, led the government to abandon the plan. See "Plans for Fluid Milk Rationing," in Russell and Fantin, *Studies in Food Rationing*, 265-311.

32. Personal experience of the author. Gladys Price of Nederland, owner of a wholesale candy and tobacco store in Port Arthur, remembers this as well. She gives the example of demands and shortages of a chewing tobacco (Copenhagen), purchased by refinery workers who could not smoke on the job. Interview, Gladys Price, by Jan Street, November 6, 1990, Special Collections, Gray Library, Lamar University, Beaumont, Texas.

33. *Houston Post*, June 5, 1942.

34. Lingeman, *Don't You Know There's A War On*, 237; *Houston Post*, June 11, 19, 20, 1942.

35. Lingeman, *Don't You Know There's A War On*, 238-239; *Liberty Vindicator*, October 19, 1942.

36. Lingeman, *Don't You Know There's A War On*, 242-243. The author's father, who operated a Humble service station, always found extra ration stamps for servicemen home on leave.

37. Author's personal experience as a teen-age service station attendant during the war years. *Time* magazine, November 30, 1942, p. 20, reported that some Texans drove across the Mexican border, registered their cars there, paid $180 in duties and got Mexican tires and gas.

38. *Texas Almanac, 1944-1945*, 299.

39. *Ibid.*, 281.

40. Smith, "Use It Up–Wear It Out," 86.

41. Seth S. McKay and Odie B. Faulk, *Texas After Spindletop* (Austin: Steck-Vaughn Co., 1965), 186-187.

42. *Texas Almanac, 1945-1946*, 274; Julia Kirk Blackwelder, *Now Hiring: The Feminization of Work in the United States, 1900-1995* (College Station: Texas A&M University Press, 1997), 136-138.

43. Blackwelder, *Now Hiring*, 123-124.

44. William L. O'Neill, *A Democracy at War: America's Fight at Home and Abroad in World War II* (New York: Free Press, 1993), 242.

45. David M. Kennedy, *Freedom From Fear: The American People in Depression and War, 1929-1945* (New York: Oxford University Press, 1999), 776-777; George Q. Flynn, *The Mess in Washington: Manpower Mobilization in World War II* (Westport, CT: Greenwood Press, 1979), 172; *Texas Almanac, 1945-1946*, 273-274.

46. William H. Chafe, *The American Woman: Her Changing Social, Economic, and Political Roles, 1920-1970* (New York: Oxford University Press, 1972) believes the war was a major turning point for women. For reasons for entering the labor force see Charlotte A. Holliman, "Beaumont Women During World War II," *Texas Gulf Historical and Biographical Record* 31 (November 1995): 59-60; Cynthia Guidici, "Women at War," in Lee, *1941: Texas Goes to War*, 149-150; Donna Bonin, "Baytown's 'Rosie the Riveter'," in *From Humble Beginnings* (Exxon Baytown, 75th Anniversary), 51-52.

47. Guidici, "Women at War," 152-153; Holliman, "Beaumont Women During World War II," 55-59; W. T. Block, "Women Pitched In To Help Industry in Wartime Beaumont," *Beaumont Enterprise*, May 18, 2003; Alexander, *Wings of Change*, 36-37. Although the increase in numbers is impressive, D'Anne Campbell, *Women at War with America: Private Lives in a Patriotic Era* (Cambridge, MS: Harvard University Press, 1984), 73, argues that nearly half of the new entrants in the work force probably would have entered in any event..

48. *Texas Almanac, 1945-1946*, 81-82; Jeanne Holm, *Women in the Military: An Unfinished Revolution* (Novato, CA: Presidio Press, 1982), 23-24; Judy Barrett Litoff and David C. Smith, eds., *We're In This War, Too: World War Letters from American Women in Uniform* (New York: Oxford University Press, 1994), 29; Victoria Sherrow, *Women and the Military* (Denver, CO: ABC-CLIO, 1996), 285-291.

49. William P. Hobby, Jr., "Oveta Culp Hobby," in Tyler, ed., *New Handbook of Texas*, 3: 637-638. See also Al Shire, comp. and ed., *Oveta Culp Hobby* (Houston: William P. Hobby and Jessica Hobby Cato, 1997); Casad, *Texans of Valor*, 20-26.

50. Mattie E. Treadwill, *The Women's Army Corps* (Washington: Office of the Chief of Military History, 1954), 24-25; Hobby, "Oveta Culp Hobby," 3: 638; Holm, *Women in the Military*, 29-30.

51. Treadwill, *Women's Army Corps*, 220-221.

52. Holm, *Women in the Military*, 53. Perret, *There's A War To Be Won*, 458-462, has a good discussion of the problems and inequities faced by women in the military. See also Leisa D. Meyer,

Creating GI Jane: Sexuality and Power in the Women's Army Corps During World War II (New York: Columbia University Press, 1996), 33-50.

53. Bettie J. Merden, *The Women's Army Corps, 1945-1978* (Washington: Center of Military History, United States Army, 1990), 25; Guidici, "Women at War," 165-166; Clarice F. Pollard, "WAACs In Texas During the Second World War," *Southwestern Historical Quarterly* 93 (July 1989): 74; Holm, *Women in the Military*, 94; Aileen Kilgore Henderson, *Stateside Soldier: Life in the Women's Army Corps, 1944-1945* (Columbia, SC: University of South Carolina Press, 2001), 57-66.

54. Brenda L. Moore, *To Save My Country, To Serve My Race: The Story of the Only WACs Stationed Overseas During World War II* (New York: New York University Press, 1996), 94. Corporal Johnnie Walton from Hempstead, Texas, was one of the members of the 6888th interviewed by Ms. Moore.

55. Guidici, "Women at War," 165; Holm, *Women in the Military*, 94; Stroud, *For Love of Country*, 443-444.

56. Litoff and Smith, eds., *We're In This War, Too*, 29; Stroud, *For Love of Country*, 459-460.

57. Lifoff and Smith, eds., *We're In This War, Too*, 46-48, 130-131.

58. *Ibid.*, 136-142.

59. *History of the Second World War, A Memorial*, 5: 1529, 1855.

60. Anne Noggle, *For God, Country, and the Thrill of It: Women Airforce Service Pilots in World War II* (College Station: Texas A&M University Press, 1990), 3-4; *Corpus Christi Caller-Times*, March 7, 2002; Amy Nathan, *Yankee Doodle Gals: Women Pilots of World War II* (Washington: National Geographic Society, 2001), 23-24, 57.

61. Noggle, *For God, Country, and the Thrill of It*, 4-5; Nathan, *Yankee Doodle Gals*, 31;

Ann B. Carl, *A WASP Among Eagles: A Woman Military Test Pilot in World War II* Washington: Smithsonian Institution Press, 1999), 41-46.

62. Cindy Weigand, "Yankee Doodle Gals: Women Pilots of World War II," *Texas Co-Op Power* (June 2002), 12-15; Melinda Rice, "The Sky Was No Limit: On the Wings of A WASP," *Texas Highways* 49 (November 2002): 43-49; Henry F. Snapp, "Pioneer Women in West Texas Skies: Women Airforce Service Pilots of World War II," *West Texas Historical Association Year Book* 70 (1994): 19-39; Alexander, *Stars Were Big and Bright*, 2: 8-46; Nathan, *Yankee Doodle Gals*, 73.

63. General Arnold quoted by Alberta Fitzpatrick Head, "General Arnold Comes to Avenger Field, "*West Texas Historical Association Year Book*, 50 (1974): 102. For more on the WASPs see Sally Van Wagenen Kiel, *Those Wonderful Women in Their Flying Machines* (New York: Four Directions Press, 1990); Doris Brinker Tanner, comp., *Who Were the WASP?* (Sweetwater, TX: Sweetwater Daily Reporter, 1989); Molly Merryman, *Clipped Wings: The Rise and Fall of the Women Airforce Service Pilots* (New York: New York University Press, 1998); Marianne Verges, *On Silver Wings: The Women Airforce Service Pilots of World War II* (New York: Ballantine Books, 1991); Marion Hodgson, *Winning My Wings* (Annapolis, MD: Naval Institute Press, 1996). The Texas Woman's University in Denton maintains the archives of the Women Airforce Service Pilots.

64. Litoff and Smith, eds., *We're In This War, Too*, 210-218.

65. Guidici, "Women at War," 156-157. American servicemen had mixed reactions to the work of the Red Cross. While many appreciated the efforts of the organization others resented that the Red Cross sometimes asked troops to pay for coffee, doughnuts, and cigarettes.

Contrasting views of the Red Cross are shown by two Texans who later became highly successful football coaches. Houston Oiler and New Orleans Saint coach O. A. "Bum" Phillips, who served with the Marines on Guadalcanal, refused to give to the Red Cross when employed by the Magnolia Refinery Company after the war. High school coach Bill Carter of Weatherford, who went ashore at Normandy on D-Day, was so pleased with the reception that the Red Cross gave him after crossing the Atlantic on a troop ship he contributed to the Red Cross the rest of his life. See Cashion, *Pigskin Pulpit*, 136, 148-149.

66. Guidici, "Women at War," 156; Mills, *West Texans Remember the Home Front*, 24.

67. *Ibid.*, 152, 154-155; Valentine J. Belfiglio, *Honor, Pride, Duty: A History of the Texas State Guard* (Austin: Eakin Press, 1995), 59-60; Henson, *History of Baytown*, 128; Holliman,

"Beaumont Women During World War II," 61; Mamie Bogue, "Melody Maids," in Tyler, ed., *New Handbook of Texas*, 4: 608; Keefer, *From Maine to Mexico*, 236-239, 289-290, 368-376.

68. Hazel Shelton Abernethy, in Roach, *Collective Hearts*, 85-86; Buck Young, "Memories of World War II," 12.

69. Rita Green, Joe Walker, Marcus C. Robbins, "Beaumont at War: The Home Front, 1941-1945" (typescript manuscript, Beaumont, Tyrrell Historical Library, 1992), 10; Robert W. Kirk, *Earning Their Stripes: The Mobilization of American Children in the Second World War* (New York: Peter Lang, 1994), 80-82, 95, 98.

70. Kirk, *Earning Their Stripes*, 55-74.

71. *Ibid.*, 35-40. Superman, a favorite comic strip hero since his appearance in 1938, was classified as 4F for failing his eye test at the induction center. Because of his X-ray vision, he absent-mindedly reported letters on the eye chart on the wall of an adjoining examining room. *Ibid.*, 37.

72. William M. Tuttle, Jr., *"Daddy's Gone to War": The Second World War in the Lives of America's Children* (New York: Oxford University Press, 1993), 31; Sally Strange, "Love, Marriage & The Family," in Lee, ed., *1941: Texas Goes to War*, 190.

73. The Lufkin-Goose Creek game was tied 7-7 but Lufkin won the game by having the greater number of penetrations inside the 20-yard line. Bill McMurray, *Texas High School Football* (South Bend, IN: Icarus Press, 1985), 18-19.

74. *Ibid.*, 20.

75. Kern Tips, *Football–Texas Style*, 104-108. Texas A&M had beaten LSU earlier in the season. Coach Homer Norton attributed the Aggie defeat to the long train ride. Because of crowded conditions on trains during the war his players were unable to get Pullman cars. They failed to get much sleep riding in the day coach to Miami.

76. Bill O'Neal, *The Texas League*, 93-97. Although Beaumont won the regular season title, the Exporters were beaten by the Shreveport Sports four games to three in the league playoffs.

77. Curt Sampson, *Texas Golf Legends* (Lubbock: Texas Tech University Press, 1984), 98-100; Donald Steel and Peter Ryde, *Encyclopedia of Golf* (New York: Viking Press, 1975), 269-270; Al Barlow, *The History of the PGA Tour* (New York: Doubleday, 1989), 79-81; Herbert Warren Wind, *The Story of American Golf: Its Champions and Its Championships* (New York: Simon & Schuster, 1956), 422-437.

78. The author wishes to thank W. L. Pate, Jr., president of the Babe Zaharias Foundation, Beaumont, Texas, for information on Zaharias' 1945 activities. Of numerous biographies of Zaharias *Babe: The Legend and Life of Babe Didrikson Zaharias*, by Susan Cayleff (Urbana: University of Illinois Press, 1998) is the most satisfactory. See also "Brash Babe Showed the World," *USA Today*, May 20, 2003, for the 1945 tours.

79. Kirk, *Earning Their Stripes*, 91; Dawn Duncan, "Entertainment At Home & Abroad," in Lee, ed., *1941: Texas Goes to War*, 203-204.

80. Duncan, "Entertainment at Home & Abroad," 205; Lingeman, *Don't You Know There's A War On*, 198-205.

81. Quote, Henry C. Dethloff, *Centennial History of Texas A&M*, 462. John Keith Wells, an A&M student who later distinguished himself as a marine platoon commander on Iwo Jima, played a bit part in the movie. Although he never saw the movie he was not impressed with the filming. He was of the opinion that the school did not care for it either. Wells, *"Give Me Fifty Marines Not Afraid to Die": Iwo Jima* (Abilene, TX: Ka-Well Enterprises, 1995), 13.

82. Lingeman, *Don't You Know There's A War On*, 180-181.

83. Gerd Horton, *Radio Goes to War: The Cultural Politics of Propaganda during World War II* (Berkeley: University of California Press, 2002), 89-90.

84. Lingeman, *Don't You Know There's A War On*, 223-224; Horton, *Radio Goes to War*, 22-38.

85. Quote, Horton, *Radio Goes to War*, 140.

86. *Ibid.*, 147-175.

87. Lingeman, *Don't You Know There's A War On*, 213-220; Duncan, "Entertainment at Home and Abroad," 198.

88. Duncan, "Entertainment at Home and Abroad," 199-200.

89. Paul Fussell, *Wartime: Understanding and Behavior in the Second World War* (New York: Oxford University Press,1989), 187.

90. *Ibid.*, 140.

91. *Ibid.*, 140-141.

92. Lingeman, *Don't You Know There's A War On*, 274-278.

93. Kennett, *G. I.: The American Soldier in World War II*, 22-23; Dethloff, *Centennial History of Texas A&M*, 459; *Time*, November 30, 1942, p. 64; *Texas Almanac, 1945-1946*, 373-375; James L. Rogers, *The Story of North Texas: From Texas Normal College, 1890 to North Texas State University* (Denton: North Texas State University, 1965), 312-313.

94. Glendell A. Jones, Jr., *Mid the Pine Hills of East Texas: The Methodist Centennial History of Lon Morris College* (Jacksonville: Progress Publishing Co., 1973), 79-80; *Texas Almanac, 1945-1946*, 373-375. Trinity University, another comparatively small college, was an exception to declining enrollment but this was because of a move from Waxahachie, where 1942 spring enrollment was 181 students, to a much larger city, San Antonio. Enrollment at San Antonio was 503 in fall 1943 and 871 in fall 1944. Only 101 of the 1944 students were male. Donald E. Everett, *Trinity University: A Record of One Hundred Years* (San Antonio: Trinity University Press, 1968), 111, 144-148.

95. Dethloff, *Centennial History of Texas A&M*, 456, 461; *Time*, November 30, 1942, p. 64; Fredericka Meiners, *A History of Rice University: The Institute Years, 1907-1963* (Houston: Rice University Studies, 1982), 134-135; *Texas Almanac, 1945-1946*, 81; Karen Kaemmering, "The Training of WAACs at Stephen F. Austin State Teachers' College," *East Texas Historical Journal* 35 (Spring 1997): 74-80.

96. Don E. Carleton, *A Breed So Rare: The Life of J. R. Parten, Liberal Texas Oil Man, 1896-1992* (Austin: Texas State Historical Association, 1998), 210-211. Parten was chairman of the Board of Regents that employed Rainey. He remained a supporter of Rainey after his term of appointment expired.

97. *Ibid.*, 138, 244-245, 301-302; George H. Green, *The Establishment in Texas Politics: The Primitive Years, 1938-1957* (Westport, CN: Greenwood Press, 1979), 83-84.

98. Carleton, *A Breed So Rare*, 302-306; Green, *Establishment in Texas Politics*, 86-87.

99. Carleton, *A Breed So Rare*, 303-304; Frantz, *Forty-Acre Follies*, 82-83.

100. One board member, Dr. K. H. Aynesworth of Waco who was ill at the time, did not attend the meeting. Mrs. Fairchild, wife of former state senator I. D. Fairchild, was the second woman to serve on the University of Texas Board of Regents. Carleton, *A Breed So Rare*, 306; Debbie Mauldin Cottrell, "Marguerite Gibson Shearer Fairchild," in Tyler, ed., *New Handbook of Texas*, 2: 934. In his own book describing the events, *The Tower and the Dome: A Free University Versus Political Control* (Boulder, CO: Pruett Publishing Co., 1971), Rainey states that Chairman Bickett also voted against his firing. The student newspaper *The Daily Texan*, November 2, 1944, also reported the vote as 6-2. The motion to fire Rainey was made by Lutcher Stark of Orange, wealthy lumberman and veteran member of the board. Stark was angry with Rainey for refusing to fire three members from the Division of Extension who presided over a change in Interscholastic League rules that affected the eligibility of Stark's two sons. Frantz, *Forty-Acre Follies*, 82.

101. George N. Green, "Homer Price Rainey," in Tyler, ed., *New Handbook of Texas*, 5: 416; Carleton, *A Breed So Rare*, 312-316; "Trouble in Texas," *Time*, November 13, 1944, p. 54; "In the Lone Star State," *Time*, November 27, 1944, p. 44.

102. Joe B. Frantz, long time faculty member at the University of Texas, writing a history of his school in 1983, declared "the university has never fully recovered from the unfavorable publicity surrounding Rainey's firing." Frantz, *Forty-Acre Follies*, 85.

103. John T. Carr, Jr., *Hurricanes Affecting the Texas Coast* (Texas Water Development Board, Report 49, 1967), 17; John F. Griffiths and Greg Ainsworth, *One Hundred Years of Texas Weather, 1880-1979* (College Station: Office of State Climatologist, 1981), 105-108, 110-113.

104. Griffiths and Ainsworth, *One Hundred Years of Texas Weather*, 108-113.

105. Chester R. Burns, "Epidemic Diseases," in Tyler, ed., *New Handbook of Texas*, 2: 877.

106. *Ibid.*, 2: 877.

CHAPTER SIX

1. Lingeman, *Don't You Know There's A War On*, 104-105, 234-235, 240, 335.
2. Kennedy, *Freedom From Fear*, 624-625.
3. *Ibid.*, 624-625. Kennedy points out that because the 1943 Revenue Act contained many special interest benefits President Roosevelt vetoed the bill. Congress, however, overrode the veto and the bill became law, "the first time in national history that a revenue law was enacted without presidential approval."
4. *Texas Almanac, 1945-1946*, 401.
5. Rayburn quote, Dorough, *Mr. Sam*, 328; Steinberg, *Sam Rayburn*, 212.
6. Connally and Steinberg, *My Name is Tom Connally*, 263-285; Janet Schmelzer, "Tom Connally," in Kenneth E. Hendrickson, Jr., and Michael L. Collins, *Profiles in Power: Twentieth-Century Texans in Washington* (Arlington Heights, IL: Harlan Davidson, 1993), 83-102.
7. Kennedy, *Freedom From Fear*, 643-644; Connally and Steinberg, *My Name is Tom Connally*, 252-253; George N. Green, "Tom Connally," in Tyler, ed., *New Handbook of Texas*, 2: 270.
8. McKay and Faulk, *Texas After Spindletop*, 175.
9. George Norris Green, *Establishment in Texas Politics*, 39-43.
10. *Texas Almanac, 1943-1944*, 249; McKay and Faulk, *Texas After Spindletop*, 176-179; Green, *Establishment in Texas Politics*, 41-42; Seth S. McKay, *W. Lee O'Daniel and Texas Politics, 1938-1942* (Lubbock: Texas Technological Press, 1944), 565-580.
11. Green, *Establishment in Texas Politics*, 42. Roger M. Olien, "The Republican Party of Texas, 1920-1961" (Ph.D. dissertation, Brown University, 1973), 124, says that in November 1942 a Texas Republican leader wrote Senator Robert A. Taft that the Texas group was "dead from the bottom up."
12. Green, *Establishment in Texas Politics*, 45-47.
13. *Ibid.*, 47-49; Seth S. McKay, *Texas Politics, 1906-1944* (Lubbock: Texas Technological Press, 1952), 434-438. For more on *Smith v. Allwright* see Darlene Clark Hine, "The Elusive Ballot: The Black Struggle Against the Texas Democratic White Primary, 1932-1945," *Southwestern Historical Quarterly* 81 (April 1978): 371-392; Hine, *Black Victory: The Rise and Fall of the White Primary in Texas* (Millwood, NY: KTO Press, 1979); Lucille Davis, "Negro Voting in the Democratic Primaries in Texas, 1901-1945" (M.A. thesis: Texas Southern University, 1976); Walter Lindsey, "Black Houstonians Challenge the White Democratic Primary, 1921-1944" (M.A. thesis, University of Houston, 1969).
14. Green, *Establishment in Texas Politics*, 54-55. For more on the strategy of the Texas Regulars see Stanley Schneider, "The Texas Regular Party of 1944" (M. A. thesis, University of Chicago, 1948).
15. Quote, Green, *Establishment in Texas Politics*, 50.
16. *Texas Almanac, 1945-1946*, 537; Green, *Establishment in Texas Politics*, 70-75; Robert Dallek, *Lone Star Rising: Lyndon Johnson and His Times, 1908-1960* (New York: Oxford University Press, 1991), 260-263; Hardeman and Bacon, *Rayburn: A Biography*, 297-300; *Biographical Directory of the American Congress, 1774-1949* (Washington: Government Printing Office, 1950), 1006, 1419, 1484. For more on Martin Dies see Dennis K. McDaniel, "Martin Dies of Un-American Activities: His Life and Times" (Ph.D. dissertation, University of Houston, 1988); Patience Couch Evans, "A Political Mystery: Martin Dies' Withdrawal from the 1944 Texas Democratic Primary" (M. A. thesis, University of Houston, 1984).
17. Green, *Establishment in Texas Politics*, 51-55; Olien, "The Republican Party in Texas," 126-128.
18. Mary Shadock interviewed by Richard Howard, November 11, 1991, in Special Collections, Gray Library, Lamar University, Beaumont; B. B. Majors interviewed by Valerie Majors Domingue, October 6, 1997, printed copy in author's possession. Election returns taken from *Texas Almanac, 1945-1946*, 531-532. Dewey led in only seven counties; the Texas Regulars car-

ried only one county, Washington. Roosevelt led in all other counties but in seven of these had only a plurality, not a majority.

19. Green, *Establishment in Texas Politics*, 55; Kenneth E. Hendrickson, Jr., *The Chief Executives of Texas, from Stephen F. Austin to John B. Connally, Jr.* (College Station: Texas A&M University Press, 1995), 201-202.

20. *Biographical Directory of the American Congress*, 718, 730, 1159, 1842; Mills, *West Texans Remember the Home Front*, 42-43.

21. Robert A. Caro, *The Years of Lyndon Johnson: Means of Ascent* (New York: Alfred A. Knopf, 1990), 32, 45; Dallek, *Lone Star Rising*, 231-241; Ronnie Dugger, *The Politician: The Life and Times of Lyndon Johnson, The Drive for Power, from the Frontier to Master of the Senate* (New York: W. W. Norton & Co., 1982), 238-253. The Lae raid is described more fully by Martin Caidin and Edward Hymoff, *The Mission* (Philadelphia: Lippincott, 1964). But for the call of nature Johnson would have been on a plane shot down. He initially boarded the B-26 "Wabash Cannonball," but left the plane briefly to urinate. When he returned he found his seat taken by a senior officer, so Johnson flew with the crew of the "Heckling Hare." The "Wabash Cannonball" was shot down with everyone on board, including the army colonel who took Johnson's seat, killed.

22. Quote, Caro, *Means of Ascent*, 52.

23. *Congressional Record*, Vol. 89, Part 5, 6548-6549; Vol. 90, Part 2, 2013-2014.

24. Nancy Beck Young, *Wright Patman: Populism, Liberalism & The American Dream* (Dallas: Southern Methodist University Press, 2000), 107, 111-112, 125-126.

25. Information on Texas congressmen found primarily in Tyler, ed., *New Handbook of Texas* and *Biographical Directory of American Congress*.

26. *The Nation*, March 21, April 4, 11, 18, 1942; David Brinkley, *Washington Goes to War* (New York: Alfred A. Knopf, 1988), 198-200; Perret, *Days of Sadness, Years of Triumph*, 87-88, 90, 93, 94, 101, 114, 223. Dies' own accounts are *Trojan Horse in America* (New York: Dodd, Mead, 1940) and *Martin Dies' Story* (New York: Bookmailer, 1963).

27. Green, *Establishment in Texas Politics*, 74-76. Dies reentered politics in 1952, winning a new seat as congressman-at-large. He retired once again in 1958 after losing election for the U.S. Senate.

28. Lionel V. Patenaude, "Jesse Holman Jones," in Tyler, ed., *New Handbook of Texas*, 3: 984-985.

29. *Ibid.*, 985; Walter Buenger, "Jesse Jones," in Hendrickson, ed., *Profiles in Power*, 61-81; Kennedy, *Freedom From Fear*, 457. For more on Jones see Bascom N. Timmons, *Jesse Jones* (New York: Henry Holt, 1956) and Jesse Jones (with Edward Angly), *Fifteen Billion Dollars: My Thirteen Years with the R. F. C., 1932-1945* (New York: Macmillan, 1951).

30. Paul Finkleman, "Thomas Campbell Clark," in Tyler, ed., *New Handbook of Texas*, 2: 137-138.

31. Charles D. Bright, *Historical Directory of the U.S. Air Force* (Westport, CT: Greenwood Press, 1992), 359; Larrabee, *Commander in Chief*, 215-222. For more Lovett's role during the war see Walter Isaacson and Evan Thomas, *The Wise Men: Six Friends and the World They Made* (New York: Simon & Schuster, 1966), 21, 61-62, 90-93, 183-185, 203-209; and Jonathan F. Fanton, "Robert A. Lovett: The War Years" (Ph.D. dissertation, Yale University, 1978).

32. Michael Gillette, "Alvin Jacob Wirtz," in Tyler, ed., *New Handbook of Texas*, 6: 1027-1028.

33. Carleton, *A Breed So Rare*, 253-349.

34. Henderson, *Maury Maverick*, 236; Bruce Catton, *The War Lords of Washington* (New York: Harcourt, Brace and World, 1948; reprinted Greenwood Press, 1969), 124-137.

35. First quote, Gerald D. Nash, *World War II and the West: Reshaping the Economy* (Lincoln: University of Nebraska Press, 1990), 17; second quote, Henderson, *Maury Maverick*, 240; Catton, *War Lords of Washington*, 138, 252, 289-290; Young, *Wright Patman*, 121-122.

36. Irvin M. May, *Marvin Jones: The Public Life of an Agrarian Advocate* (College Station: Texas A&M University Press, 1986), 226; Joseph M. Ray, ed., *Marvin Jones Memoirs* (El Paso: Texas Western Press, 1993), 157-162.

37. Caro, *Means of Ascent*, 145-169; Eldon S. Branda, "Coke Stevenson," in Tyler, ed., *New*

Handbook of Texas, 6: 96-97. A full length biography is Booth Mooney, *Mister Texas: The Story of Coke Stevenson* (Dallas: Texas Printing, 1947).

38. Caro, *Means of Ascent*, 169-170; Hendrickson, *Chief Executives of Texas*, 204; *Texas Almanac, 1945-1946*, 321.

39. Quote, Caro, *Means of Ascent*, 173; Carleton, *A Breed So Rare*, 303-304; Patrick E. Cunningham, "Minnie Fisher Cunningham," in Tyler, *New Handbook of Texas*, 2: 450-451; *Time*, November 1, 1943, p. 18; Paul Casdorph, *The Republican Party in Texas, 1865-1965* (Austin: Pemberton Press, 1965), 155-160. Roger M. Olien, "The Republican Party of Texas, 1920-1961," p. 119, points out that the Republican nominee B. J. Peasley nearly doubled the vote the Republican candidate received in 1940.

40. Fred Gantt, Jr., *The Chief Executive in Texas: A Study in Gubernatorial Leadership* (Austin: University of Texas Press, 1964), 327; Green, *Establishment in Texas Politics*, 81.

41. McCain, "Texas and the Mexican Labor Question," 52-53.

42. Quote, Emilio Zamora, "The Failed Promise of Wartime Opportunity for Mexicans in the Texas Oil Industry," *Southwestern Historical Quarterly* 95 (January 1992): 349; David J. Montejano, *Anglos and Mexicans in the Making of Texas, 1836-1936* (Austin: University of Texas Press, 1987), 269. See also Felix D. Almaráz, Jr., *Knight Without Armor: Carlos Eduardo Castaneda, 1896-1958* (College Station: Texas A&M University Press, 1999), 213-262; Richard A. Garcia, *Rise of the Mexican Middle Class: San Antonio, 1928-1941* (College Station: Texas A&M University Press, 1991), 202, 298-299, 312-212.

43. Donald M. Dozer, *Are We Good Neighbors? Three Decades of Inter-American Relations, 1930-1960* (Gainesville: University of Florida Press, 1959), 180; Tuttle, *Daddy's Gone to War*, 166-167. For more on issues of discrimination of Mexican Texas seen Everett Ross Clinchy, Jr., *Equality of Opportunity for Latin Americans in Texas* (New York: Arno Press, 1974); Ozzie G. Simmons, *Anglo-Americans and Mexican Americans in South Texas* (New York: Arno Press, 1974); Neil Foley, *The White Scourge: Mexicans, Blacks, and Poor Whites in Texas Cotton Culture* (Berkeley: University of California Press, 1997).

44. Quote, Ernest Obadele-Starks, *Black Unionism in the Industrial South*, 105. Obadele-Starks, 101-111, provides a detailed discussion of discriminatory practices in the shipyards.

Merl Reed, "The FEPC, the Black Worker, and the Southern Shipyards," *South Atlantic Quarterly* 74 (Autumn 1975): 462, says "The Todd Shipbuilding Company in Galveston probably had one of the worst records of discrimination in the South." See also Charles D. Chamberlain, *Victory at Home: Manpower and Race in the American South during World War II* (Athens: University of Georgia Press, 2003), 63-66; and Lester Rubin, *The Negro in the Shipbuilding Industry* (Philadelphia: University of Pennsylvania Press, 1970).

45. Quote, Marcus Robbins, "'Our Unalienable Rights': A Brief History of Locals 229 and 243 Oil Workers International Union, Magnolia Refinery, 1937-1945," *Texas Gulf Historical and Biographical Record* 39 (1993): 63. The author wishes to thank Robert Robertson of Beaumont for calling his attention to this article.

46. Chamberlain, *Victory at Home*, 136-137, 140.

47. Hendrickson, *Chief Executives of Texas*, 205-206; Green, *Establishment in Texas Politics*, 79-80.

48. James A. Burran, "Violence in an 'An Arsenal of Democracy' : The Beaumont Race Riot, 1943," *East Texas Historical Journal* 14 (Spring 1976): 39-42.

49. *Ibid.*, 42-44; James S. Olson and Sharon Phair, "Anatomy of a Race Riot: Beaumont, Texas, 1943," *Texana* 11 (No. 1, 1973): 66-71.

50. Burran, "Violence in an 'Arsenal of Democracy'," 45; James S. Olson, "Beaumont Riot of 1943," in Tyler, ed., *New Handbook of Texas* 1: 448; Valentine C. Belfiglio, *Honor, Pride, Duty: A History of the Texas State Guard* (Austin: Eakin Press, 1995), 64.

51. *Beaumont Enterprise*, June 16, 17, 18, 1943; Interview, J. T. Mattox with Donald W. George, July 31, 1992, and interview, Abby Cormier with Allen Fruge, March 3, 1999, both in Special Collection, Gray Library, Lamar University, Beaumont, Texas.

52. Burran, "Violence in an 'Arsenal of Democracy'," 46-47. Merline Pitre, *The Struggle Against Jim Crow: Lulu B. White and the NAACP, 1900-1957* (College Station: Texas A&M

University Press, 1999), 40-41, points out that black leaders in Beaumont were divided on the issue of bringing suit to recover damages. Most favored accepting donations from wealthy white businessmen who raised over $3,000 to compensate African American businessmen. Lulu White, executive secretary of the Houston NAACP, persuaded at least one man, Frank Hadnott, to seek redress in the courts.

53. John M. Blum, *V Was For Victory: Politics and American Culture During World War II* (New York: Harcourt, Brace, Javanovich, 1976), 202-206; Harvard Sitkoff, "Racial Militancy and Interracial Violence in the Second World War," *Journal of American History* 58 (December 1971): 672-674; Alwyn Barr, *Black Texans: A History of Negroes in Texas, 1528-1971* (Austin: Pemberton Press, 1982), 108.

54. Maggi M. Morehouse, *Fighting in the Jim Crow Army: Black Men and Women Remember World War II* (Lanham, MD: Rowman & Littlefield Publishers, 2000), 122-123.

55. Arnold Rampersad, *Jackie Robinson: A Biography* (New York: Alfred A. Knopf, 1997), 102-106; Jackie Robinson (as told to Alfred Duckett), *I Never Had It Made: A Biography* (New York: G. P. Putnam's Sons, 1972), 24-33; Joe Wilson, Jr., *The 761st "Black Panther" Tank Battalion in World War II* (Jefferson, NC: McFarland & Company, 1999), 39-42.

56. Robinson had been injured earlier playing in an army softball game. The "physical disqualification" was apparently the army's way of ridding itself of Robinson.

57. Quote, Philip Latimer, *The 761st "Black Panther" Tank Battalion*, 38. See also Latimer, "When the Black Panthers Prowled," *Army* (January 1992), 45.

58. Quote, John Ferguson, in Manning, ed., *Courage of Common Man*, 180.

59. Litoff and Smith, *We're In This War, Too*, 74-75.

60. Alan M. Osur, *Blacks in the Army Air Forces During World War II* (New York: Arno Press, 1980), 53, 105; Stanley Sandler, *Segregated Skies: All-Black Combat Squadrons of WWII* (Washington: Smithsonian Institution Press, 1992), 78.

61. Thomas K. Walls, *The Japanese Texans* (San Antonio: Institute of Texan Cultures, 1987), 151-153, 176.

62. Quote, Ken Nagi, in Fairchild, ed., *They Called It The War Effort*, 31. See also Walls, *Japanese Texans*, 6-7, 95-96; Gwendolyn Wingate, "The Kishi Colony," in Francis E. Abernethy, ed., *The Folklore of Texan Cultures* (Austin: Encino Press, 1974), 327-337.

63. Walls, *Japanese Texans*, 154-155.

64. *Ibid.*, 158; Kimi E. Jingu to U.S. Department of Justice, May 15, 1992 (and attachments). The author expresses his thanks to Howard Peacock, formerly of Woodville and now living in San Antonio, for providing copies of this letter and attachments.

65. Kimi E. Jingu to U.S. Department of Justice, May 15, 1992; Walls, *Japanese Texans*, 157.

66. Kim E. Jingu to U.S. Department of Justice, May 15, 1992.

67. Walls, *Japanese Texans*, 163.

68. See his account, *FOO, A Japanese-American Prisoner of the Rising Sun: The Secret Prison Diary of Frank "Foo" Fujita* (Denton: University of North Texas Press, 1993).

69. Walls, *Japanese Texans*, 164. The 442nd Regimental Combat Team consisted of the 442nd Infantry Regiment, the 552nd Field Artillery Battalion, and the 232rd Combat Engineer Company. The 442nd RCT was an elite unit. Its average strength was 3,000 men. It became the most highly decorated unit in the army with one Medal of Honor winner, fifty-two Distinguished Service Crosses, 560 Silver Stars, and hundreds of Purple Hearts. Perret, *Days of Sadness, Years of Triumph*, 365.

70. Walls, *Japanese Texans*, 167-173.

71. Emily Brosveen, "World War II Internment Camps," in Tyler, ed., *New Handbook of Texas*, 6: 1082.

72. Robert H. Thonhoff, "Kenedy Alien Detention Camp," in Tyler, ed., *New Handbook of Texas*, 3: 1066-1067. For more on Fritz Kuhn see Sander A. Diamond, *The Nazi Movement in the United States, 1924-1941* (Ithaca, NY: Cornell University Press, 1978).

73. Brosveen, "World War II Internment Camps," 6: 1082.

74. Walls, *Japanese Texans*, 187-100; Brosveen, "World War II Internment Camps," 6: 1082-1083. Karen Lea Riley, *Schools Behind Barbed Wire: The Untold Story of Wartime Internment* *and the Children of Arrested Enemy Aliens* (Lanham, MD: Rowan and Littlefield Publishers, 2002) describes the schools at the Crystal City facility.

75. Walls, *Japanese Texans*, 199-203, notes that many of the Japanese Peruvians fought deportation, thus accounting for the delay in closing Crystal City. In August 1954 the U.S. Congress passed legislation granting any alien brought to the United States from other American nations for internment the right to remain in the United States and become a naturalized citizen. For more on the plight of the Peruvian Japanese see C. Harvey Gardiner, *Pawns in a Triangle of Hate: The Peruvian Japanese and the United States* (Seattle: University of Washington Press, 1981).

76. I have used the number of POWs provided by Richard P. Walker, *The Lone Star and the Swastika: Prisoners of War in Texas* (Austin: Eakin Press, 2001), 1; Robert Tissing, "Stalag Texas, 1943-45," *Military History of Texas and the Southwest* 13 (Fall 1976): 24; and Richard P. Walker, "The Swastika and the Lone Star: Nazi Activity in Texas POW camps," *Ibid.* 19 (Spring 1989): 39-40. Arnold P. Krammer, "When the Afrika Korps Came to Texas" *Southwestern Historical Quarterly* 80 (January 1977): 252, states that 78,982 POWs were held in Texas. Walker and Krammer, who states there were 130 camps in Texas, are at variance on the number of POW camps. Walker, *Lone Star and Swastika*, points out that Krammer apparently included temporary or mobile camps. Walker believes these were merely work detachments and not separate camps. Walker, p. 2, states there were seventy prisoner of war camps in Texas and shows these on maps vi-ix. However, in Chapters One and Two of his text he mentions seventy-four camps by name.

77. Arnold P. Krammer, "German Prisoners of War," in Tyler, ed., *New Handbook of Texas*, 3: 141.

78. Walker, *Lone Star and Swastika*, 2-3.

79. *Ibid.*, 3-7.

80. *Ibid.*, 8-15; Tissing, "Stalag Texas, 1943-45," 24. See also Michael R. Waters, *Lone Star Stalag: German Prisoners of Camp Hearne* (College Station, Texas, A&M University Press, 2004).

81. Walker, *Lone Star and Swastika*, 16-17. Lucielle Henegar, "Hereford Military Reservation and Reception Center," in Tyler, ed., *New Handbook of Texas*, 3: 569-570, and Donald Mace Williams, *Interlude in Umbarger: Italian POWs and a Texas Church* (Lubbock: Texas Tech University Press, 1992), 4, state that Hereford received its first prisoners in April 1943. For more on Hereford see Joe D. Robbins, "Camp Hereford: Italian Prisoners on the Texas Plains, 1942-1945," *Panhandle Plains Historical Review* 62 (1989): 57-110.

82. Walker, *Lone Star and Swastika*, 7-8, 18.

83. *Ibid.*, 18-19.

84. *Ibid.*, 20-30.

85. *Ibid.*, 5-36.

86. *Ibid.*, 37-38. The work of German prisoners in the timber industry is described by Mark Choate, *Nazis in the Piney Woods* (Lufkin: Best of East Texas Publishers, 1989) and Jeanie Carmody, "German Prisoners of War–the Liberty Experience," *Touchstone* 6 (1987): 59-65.

87. Walker, *Lone Star and Swastika*, 38-39.

88. *Ibid.*, 39-41.

89. *Ibid.*, 41-43.

90. Walker, *Lone Star and Swastika*, 44.

91. *Ibid.*, 47-49.

92. Arnold P. Krammer, *Nazi Prisoners of War in America* (Reprint, Lanham, MD: Scarborough House, 1996),148-188; Krammer, "When the Afrika Korps Came to Texas," 274-277. Walker, *Lone Star and Swastika*, 107, points out that most Texans knew nothing about this pro-Nazi activity. Because of secrecy regulations Texas civilians had little knowledge of conditions within the prison camps.

93. Krammer, "When the Afrika Korps Came to Texas," 274; Tissing, "Stalag Texas, 1943-45," 26. For more on the Italian POWs see James Richard Keen,"The Captive Enemy: Italian Prisoners of War in Texas during World War II" (M. A. thesis, University of Texas of the Permian Basin, 1988).

94. Krammer, "When the Afrika Korps Came to Texas," 252.

95. Walker, *Lone Star and Swastika*, 53-55.

96. *Ibid.*, 56-59; Krammer, *Nazi Prisoners of War in America*, 240-243. Local camp commanders were given much discretion in the handling of ration reductions. The commandant at Camp Hereford appears to have been particularly zealous. Inspectors for the Eighth Service Command reported reduction of food at Hereford in the summer of 1945 was excessive. One American soldier resorted to smuggling carcasses of wild animals into camp for POWs to eat. See Williams, *Interlude in Umbarger*, 87-92, 145.

97. Walker, *Lone Star and Swastika*, 62-64; Krammer, "When the Afrika Korps Came to Texas," 258. American POWs received similar monetary payments in German prison camps. See Walter Rundell, Jr., "Paying the POW in World War II," *Military Affairs* 22 (Fall 1958): 121-134.

98 Krammer, "When the Afrika Korps Came to Texas," 260-263, names Abilene Christian College, Howard Payne College, the University of Texas, Southern Methodist University, Texas Christian University, Rice Institute, Texas School of Mines, and West Texas State Teachers College as those offering courses to POWs in Texas.

99. Walker, *Lone Star and Swastika*, 72; Krammer, *Nazi Prisoners of War in America*, 72-73. In some instances POWs performed services for local churches. At Umbarger, twenty-six miles from Camp Hereford, Italian POWs used their talents as painters and carvers to provide murals, carvings, and paintings at St. Mary's Catholic church. Williams, *Interlude in Umbarger*, 49.

100. Walker, *Lone Star and Swastika*, 115-126; James Myers, "Prisoners of War at Camp Barkeley," *West Texas Historical Association Year Book* 61 (1985): 137-138.

101. Walker, *Lone Star and Swastika*, 115-116.

102. *Ibid.*, 162-185.

103. Krammer, "When the Afrika Korps Came to Texas," 282. Krammer is quoting from Norman L. McCarver and Norman L. McCarver, Jr., *Hearne on the Brazos* (San Antonio: San Antonio Century Press of Texas, 1958), 79.

CHAPTER SEVEN

1. Excellent descriptions of the European theater of operations may be found in Williamson Murray and Allan R. Millett, *A War To Be Won: Fighting the Second World War* (Cambridge, MA: Belknap Press of Harvard University Press, 2000), and Gerhard L. Weinberg, *A World at Arms: A Global History of World War II* (Cambridge, England: Cambridge University Press, 1994).

2. The 1st Cavalry Division included the 12th Cavalry Regiment which had trained at Fort Clark near Brackettville. Walter Krueger, *From Down Under to Nippon: The Story of the Sixth Army in World War II* (Washington: Combat Forces Press, 1953), 45-55; *The Admiralties: Operations of the 1st Cavalry Division, 29 February–18 May 1944* (Washington: Center of Military History, U.S. Army, 1990); *Texas Almanac, 1945-1946*, 76; Stanton, *Order of Battle*, 71-72, 315.

3. The 43rd Infantry Division, which included a number of East Texans, took part in the occupation of Aitape. Hall, *Brothers of the Fox*, 75-91. The Biak and Noemfoor operations are described in Daniel E. Barby, *MacArthur's Amphibious Navy: Seventh Amphibious Force Operations, 1943-1945* (Annapolis, MD: Naval Institute Press, 1969), 185-216.

4. Lance Q. Zedric, *Silent Warriors of World War II: The Alamo Scouts Behind Japanese Lines* (Ventura, CA: Pathfinder Publishing of California, 1995), 93-103, 118.

5. Robertson, "A Texan At War," 149-152; Stroud, *For Love of Country*, 400.

6. Spector, *Eagle Against the Sun*, 313-317. For more details on the conquest of Saipan see Carl W. Hoffman, *Saipan: The Beginning of the End* (Washington: Historical Division, Headquarters, U.S. Marine Corps, 1950) and Philip A. Crowl, *Campaign in the Marianas* (Washington: Office of the Chief of Military History, 1960).

7. Samuel Eliot Morison, *New Guinea and the Marianas* (Boston: Little, Brown, and Co., 1953), 320-321; William T. Y'Blood, *Red Sun Setting: The Battle of Philippine Sea* (Annapolis, MD: Naval Institute Press, 1981), 220-221. O. C. "Buck" Bailey of Aransas County was one of the naval pilots participating in the battle of Philippine Sea. Bailey received the Distinguished Flying Cross, the Silver Star, and five Air Medals during the war. Allen and Taylor, *Aransas*, 317.

8. Robert B. Stinnett, *George Bush: His World War II Years* (Washington: Brassey's Inc.,

1992), 10-15, 18-29, 75-96. By order of Admiral Nimitz the *San Jacinto* flew a Lone Star flag under the Stars and Stripes.

9. Sinnnett, *George Bush*, 73-83. The U.S.S. *Lexington*, now a museum moored in Corpus Christi harbor, has a display concerning Bush's part in the battle. Bush later participated in the Peleliu campaign and carrier strikes against other Japanese-held islands. He was shot down by antiaircraft fire on September 2, 1944, and forced to parachute to safety. He was rescued by an American submarine three hours later. *Ibid.*, 138-161.

10. Blair, *Silent Victory*, 637-638; Y'Blood, *Red Sun Setting*, 29-30; Charles A. Lockwood and Hans Christian Adamson, *Through Hell and Deep Water: The Stirring Story of the Navy's Deadly Submarine, the U.S.S. Harder, under the Command of Sam Dealey, Destroyer Killer* (Philadelphia: Chilton Co., 1956), 141-163.

11. Stroud, *For Love of Country*, 487-488; Diana J. Kleiner, "Andrew Davis Bruce," in Tyler, ed., *New Handbook of Texas*, 1: 781-782. Ronald H. Spector, *Eagle Against the Sun*, 320, describes Texan Andrew D. Bruce as "an aggressive, intelligent commander." Another Texas Aggie, Brigadier General John T. Walker, class of 1917, was chief of staff of the 1st Provisional Marine Brigade during the Guam campaign. Dethloff, *Centennial History of Texas A&M University*, 474.

12. Spector, *Eagle Against the Sun*, 319.

13. Bruce L. Brager, "Rapido and Velletri: Problem Solving in World War II," *Military History of the West* 31 (Fall 2001): 98, points out that the river was actually the Gari, a tributary of the Garigliano, but was generally called the Rapido. For a brief discussion of the planning for Anzio-Rapido see Martin Blumenson, *Bloody River: The Real Tragedy of the Rapido* (originally published, 1970; College Station: Texas A&M University Press, 1998), 49-55; Lee Carraway Smith, *A River Swift and Deadly: The 36th "Texas" Infantry Division at the Rapido River* (Austin: Eakin Press, 1997), 10-19; and Brager, *Texas 36th Division*, 159-165.

14. First quote, Walker, *From Texas to Rome*, 296; second quote, *Ibid.*, 300.

15. Quote, Martin Blumenson, *Salerno to Cassino* (Washington: Office of Chief of Military History, U.S. Army, 1969), 327. Blumenson points out General Keyes was sure that at a meeting of division commanders on January 18 he heard Walker say he could do the job. According to Brager, "Rapido and Velletri," 100, Walker objected verbally to Clark and Keyes about the planned crossing.

16. Quote, W. G. F. Jackson, *The Battle for Italy* (New York: Harper & Row, 1967), 180; Smith, *A River Swift and Deadly*, 32-48; Blumenson, *Bloody River*, 82-92; Clifford H. Peck, Jr., *Five Years, Five Countries, Five Campaigns: An Acccount of the One-Hundred-Forty-First Infantry in World War II* (Munich, Germany: F. Bruckmann, 1945), 35-41.

17. Blumenson, *Bloody River*, 100-106; Smith, *A River Swift and Deadly*, 67-83; Brager, *Texas 36th Division*, 171-172.

18. Blumenson, *Bloody River*, 107-109.

19. Brager, "Rapido and Velletri," 105-106.

20. Quote, Guillermo De Leon, in Roach, ed., *Collective Hearts*, 63; Harry R. Moore quoted in Smith, *A River Swift and Deadly*, 86. Total casualties taken from Wagner, *Texas Army*, 121. Company E, 141st Regiment, of which Guillermo De Leon was a member, was a company made up primarily of Mexican Americans. One of its officers, Lieutenant Gabriele Navarrete from El Paso, was very critical of regimental and battalion leadership for ordering the attack. Paul Morin, *Among the Valiant: Mexican-Americans in World War II and Korea* (Alhambra, CA: Borden Publishing Co., 1960), 59-76.

By the time of the Rapido fiasco the majority of men in the ranks were not Texans. This is illustrated in the casualty reports provided by Lee Smith, *A River Swift and Deadly*, 107-124. Most of the casualties were non-Texans; 65 Texans were among the casualties for the 141st Regiment and 92 Texans among casualties for the 143nd Regiment. Smith provides the names of 11 Texans killed in action at the Rapido: Captain Selsar R. Harmonson of Wharton, Private Jess Hudson of Denison, Sergeant Alejandro R. Serna of Harlingen, Captain John L. Chapin of El Paso, Staff Sergeant Roque O. Segura of El Paso, Captain James R. Glenn, Jr., of San Benito, Private First Class Adam R. Garcia of Kingsville, Private First Class Natividad S. Garcia of Abraham, Captain

Carl R. Bayne of Yoakum, Sergeant Angel G. Acevodo of El Paso, and Sergeant Dudley O. Henry of Mosheim.

21. Mark Clark, *Calculated Risk* (London: George G. Harrop & Co., 1951), 265.

22. For more on the controversy see Lee Carraway Smith, *A River Swift and Deadly*, 96-105, which is critical of Clark, and Martin Blumenson, *Bloody River,* 125-135, which places more blame on General Walker. Robert L. Wagner, *The Texas Army*, 127, faults both Clark and Geoffrey Keyes, the corps commander. "It was a cockamamie idea conceived by two mediocrities, Clark and Keyes," he writes. See also Wagner's "The Rapido River Controversy: A Review," *East Texas Historical Review* 38 (Fall 1990): 49-51. Bruce Brager, *Texas 36th Division*, 175-177, while faulting Walker for not objecting to the attack more strongly, believes there was no way the attack could have succeeded.

23. Flint Whitlock, *The Rock of Anzio: From Sicily to Dachau, A History of the 45th Infantry Division* (Boulder, CO: Westview Press, 1998), 137-151.

24. *Ibid.*, 152-258; Wick Fowler of the *Dallas Morning News*, the first Texas reporter to go overseas, was at Anzio. He received a Purple Heart for an injury received when the press hut was bombed. Alice M. Shukala, "Homer Thomas Wilson (Wick) Fowler," in Tyler, *New Handbook of Texas*, 2: 1143-1144. A team of medical personnel from the Baylor College of Medicine at Dallas provided valuable medical support for troops during the Anzio operation. See Lawrence D. Collins, *The 56th Evac Hospital: Letters of a WWII Army Doctor* (Denton: University of North Texas Press, 1995), esp. 155-196.

25. Brager, "Rapido and Velletri," 107; Wagner, *The Texas Army*, 128-153.

26. Citation, General Order No. 28, October 28, 1944, in *Texas Medal of Honor Recipients*, 23; Art Leatherwood, "Thomas W. Fowler," in Tyler, ed., *New Handbook of Texas*, 2: 1144.

27. Walker, *From Texas to Rome*, 375-376; Wagner, *The Texas Army*, 159-161.

28. Robert H. Ableman and Colonel George Walton, authors of *Rome Fell Today* (Boston: Little, Brown, and Co., 1968), 22, write "Velletri was Walker's moment in history." The Velletri-Artesimo campaign is discussed fully in their work, 14-30; Brager, *Texas 36th Division*, 178-191; Wagner, *The Texas Army*, 154-181; Ernest F. Fisher, Jr., *Cassino to the Alps* (Washington: Center of Military History, U.S. Army, 1977), 184-202. For more on Wagner's chief of engineers, Oran C. Stovall, see Robert L. Wagner, "The Odyssey of a Texas Citizen Soldier," *Southwestern Historical Quarterly* 72 (July 1968): 60-87.

29. Eric Sevareid, quoted in Wagner, *The Texas Army*, 181. For a very critical view of Mark Clark in the Italian campaign see Murray and Millett, *A War To Be Won*, 377-386.

30. Fisher, *Cassino to the Alps*, 260; Walker, *From Texas to Rome*, 398-407. General Clark was convinced that Walker's mental attitude had been a decisive factor in the failure at the Rapido. Charles W. Ryder, formerly commander of the 34th Division, succeeded Walker in command of the 36th Division. Wagner, *The Texas Army*, 214-224.

31. Walter Cronkite, *A Reporter's Life* (New York: Alfred A. Knopf, 1996), 50-82, 94-99, 102-104; M. L. Stein, *Under Fire: The Story of American War Correspondents* (New York: Julian Messner, 1968), 117-120; Robert W. Desmond, *Tides of War: World News Reporting, 1931-1945* (Iowa City: University of Iowa Press, 1984), 295-297, 339, 350.

32. *Beaumont Enterprise*, June 5, 1994; Czech Heritage Society, *Texas Veterans of Czech Ancestry*, 22, 218-219; W. T. Block, "Local Vet Had Many Missions Over Europe," *Beaumont Enterprise*, January, 17, 2001. For more on the role of the Air Force in the Normandy invasion see John J. Sullivan, *Overlord's Eagles: Operations of the United States Army Air Forces in the Invasion of Normandy in World War II* (Jefferson, NC: McFarland & Co., 1997).

33. Leonard Rapport and Arthur Norwood, Jr., *Rendezvous with Destiny: A History of the 101st Airborne Division* (Old Saybrook, CT: Konecky & Konecky, 1948), 95-99, 393; Stephen E. Ambrose, *D-Day June 6 1944: The Climatic Battle of World War II* (New York: Simon & Schuster, 1994), 299-300; Patrick O'Donnell, *Beyond Valor: World War II's Ranger and Airborne Veterans Reveal the Heart of Combat* (New York: Free Press, 2001), 139-140.

34. Ronald J. Drez, *Voices of D-Day: The Story of the Allied Invasion Told by Those Who Were There* (Baton Rouge: Louisiana State University Press, 1994), 86; Ambrose, *D-Day*, 201, 207,

306. Private First Class Lawrence W. Kirby, Jr., of Texarkana was one of the paratroopers killed in the landings. *History of World War II, A Memorial*, 3: 1063.

35. S. L. A. Marshall, *Night Drop: The American Airborne Invasion of Normandy* (Boston: Little, Brown, and Co., 1962), 211-215; Rapport and Norwood, *Rendezvous With Destiny*, 105-107; Cornelius Ryan, *The Longest Day: June 6, 1944* (New York: Simon and Schuster, 1959), 232-233; George Koskimaki, *D-Day With the Screaming Eagles* (Havertown, PA: Casemate, 2002), 187-190; Mark Bando, *101st Airborne: The Screaming Eagles at Normandy* (Osceola, WA: MBI Publishing, 2001), 112.

S. L. A. Marshall, author of *Night Drop* cited above, a former El Paso newspaper reporter, and veteran of World War I, was a combat historian who landed in Normandy a week after D-Day. He later became chief of the Army Historical Division. See his memoir, *Bringing Up the Rear* (San Rafael, CA: Presidio Press, 1979).

36. Millard Cloutman of Beaumont was a crewman on the *Nevada* during the Normandy shelling. "We fired so much the rifling was gone on our gun barrels," reported Cloutman. *Beaumont Enterprise*, June 5, 1994. See also Power, *Battleship Texas*, 24-26; Ambrose, *D-Day*, 120, 170, 268-269; William E. McMahon, *Dreadnought Battleships and Battle Cruisers* (New York: University Press of America, 1978), 108.

37. Power, *Battleship Texas*, 27-30; Art Leatherwood, "Texas," in Tyler, ed., *New Handbook of Texas*, 6: 273.

38. Ronald L. Lane, *Rudder's Rangers* (Manassas, VA: Ranger Associates, 1979), 67-170, 179-185; Gerald Astor, *The Greatest War: Americans in Combat, 1941-1945* (Novato, CA: Presidio Press, 1999), 507-514; David H. Hogan, Jr., *U.S. Army Special Operations in World War II* (Washington: Center of Military History, Department of the Army, 1992), 41-43; Ambrose, *D-Day*, 398-399, 405-417; Gordon A. Harrison, *Cross-Channel Attack* (Washington: Office of the Chief of Military History, Department of the Army, 1957), 322; Ronald J. Drez, *Twenty-Five Yards of War: The Extraordinary Courge of Ordinary Men in World War II* (New York: Hyperion, 2001), 127-136.

39. Francis X. Bradley, ed., *4th Infantry "Ivy" Division* (Paducah, KY: Turner Publishing Co., 1987), 83; Billy Ward, "A Landing Craft Exploded," *Beaumont Enterprise*, June 5, 1994; W. T. Block, "Port Arthur Resident Saw Longest Day," *Beaumont Enterprise*, June 6, 2001; Max Hastings, *Overlord: D-Day and the Battle for Normandy* (New York: Simon & Schuster, 1984), 86-88; Ambrose, *D-Day*, 274-293. Although casualties on Utah were comparatively light, Felix Soliz, a radio operator from Port Arthur, who came ashore several days later reported that "the stench of death in the area was just terrible." Vanessa Everett, "Port Arthur's Brothers in Arms," *Beaumont Enterprise*, September 16, 2002. Felix's younger brother, Don, was serving in New Guinea.

40. Quote, Ambrose, *D-Day*, 321.

41. First quote, Arlie Horn, *Beaumont Enterprise*, June 5, 1994; second quote, Jesse Cantu, in Adams, *Valley Vets*, 65. For the role of the 29th Division at Omaha and beyond see Joseph Balkoski, *Beyond the Beach: The 29th Infantry Division in Normandy* (Mechanicsburg, PA: Stackpole Books, 1989). Another member of the 29th Division, Staff Sergeant Marvin Taylor of Beaumont, actually landed on Omaha twice. Through some confusion his anti-tank gun crew came ashore on an amphibious truck an hour before the scheduled attack. An officer in a PT boat ordered them to withdraw. They went back out, circled about an hour, and then returned to the beach with the rest of the division. Marvin Taylor, *Beaumont Enterprise*, June 5,1994.

42. Joe Dawson, quoted in Stephen E. Ambrose, *The Victors, Eisenhower and His Boys: The Men of World War II* (New York: Simon & Schuster, 1998), 135.

43. Citation, G. O. 79, October 4, 1944, in *Texas Medal of Honor Recipients*, 14. Cole's exploit is described in Marshall, *Night Drop*, 367-370; Stephen E. Ambrose, *Citizen Soldiers: The U.S. Army from Normandy Beaches to the Bulge to the Surrender of Germany, June 7, 1944–May 7, 1945* (New York: Simon & Schuster, 1997), 44-45; Rapport and Norwood, *Rendezvous with Destiny*, 185-190; Bando, *101st Airborne*, 116. Perret, *There's A War To Be Won*, 326, says this was the American army's only bayonet charge of the war.

44. *Texas Almanac, 1945-1946*, 76; Peter R. Mansoor, *The GI Offensive in Europe: The Triumph of American Infantry Divisions, 1941-1945* (Lawrence, KS: University Press of Kansas,

1999), 74-78. Catarino Cueller of Lockhart, a sergeant in the 2nd Infantry, was badly wounded on Omaha. Pedro Rubio of Austin, also in the 2nd Infantry, was awarded the Silver Star for crawling under heavy machine gun fire to rescue two wounded comrades. Morin, *Among the Valiant*, 94-98.

45. John Colby, ed. and comp., *War From the Ground Up: The 90th Division in World War II* (Austin: Nortex Press, 1991), 149. Colby, a company commander in the 90th Division, describes Landrum as "short, fat, uninspiring" and unable to motivate his troops. Landrum and his assistant division commander, Brigadier General Samuel T. Williams from Denton, did not get along. Landrum relieved Williams as assistant division commander. Williams reverted back to the rank of colonel but remained in the army. He regained his rank of brigadier in 1951, became major general during the Korean War, and was chief of the first U.S. Military Assistance Group in Vietnam. He retired from the army with the rank of lieutenant general in August 1960. Harold J. "Jack" Meyer, *Hanging Sam: A Military Biography of General Samuel T. Williams, From Pancho Villa to Vietnam* (Denton: University of North Texas Press, 1990), 62-98.

46. Colby, *War From the Ground Up*, 149-163; Mansoor, *The GI Offensive*, 147-148, 265; Omar N. Bradley, *A Soldier's Story* (New York: Popular Library, 1964), 297, 331-332; Perret, *There's A War To Be Won*, 328-329.

47. Quote, Bill Lewis, in Astor, *Voices of D-Day*, 91.

48. Rob Paschall, "Walton Harris Walker," in John A. Garraty and Mark C. Carnes, eds., *American National Biography*, 28 vols. (New York: Oxford University Press, 1999), 22: 521; Richard F. Haynes, "Walton Harris Walker," in *Dictionary of American Military Biography*, 3: 1153-1154; William A. Haefner, *Patton's Bulldog: The Life and Services of General Walton H. Walker* (Shippensburg, PA: White Mane Books, 2001), 1-32; Nathan N. Prefer, *Patton's Ghost Corps: Cracking the Siegfried Line* (New York: ibooks, 1998), 13-15. For the Patton-Walker relationship see Carlo D'Este, *Patton: A Genius for War* (New York: Harper Collins, 1995), 579, 682, 711, 803.

49. Russell F. Weigley, *Eisenhower's Lieutenants: The Campaigns of France and Germany, 1944-1945* (Bloomington, IN: Indiana University Press, 1981), 218-226. Lieutenant Commander Harry Brinkley Bass of Beaumont, a graduate of Annapolis and highly decorated veteran of early Pacific naval engagements, was one of many naval airman flying support missions for the landings in south France. Bass was killed by enemy antiaircraft which shot down his Grumann Hellcat. W. T. Block, "Naval Hero from Region Overlooked," *Beaumont Enterprise*, March 21, 2001; J. Glenn Cummings, "The Legendary Brinkley Bass," paper delivered at Beaumont History Conference, January 11, 2003.

50. Gerald Astor, *Battling Buzzards: The Odyssey of the 517th Parachute Regimental Combat Team, 1943-1945* (New York: Dell Publishing, 1993), 70, 73, 91-92, 100-101, 156-206, 249; *History of the Second World War, A Memorial*, 1: 94.

51. Brager, *Texas 36th Division*, 196-207; Weigley, *Eisenhower's Lieutenants*, 226-227; Truscott, *Command Decisions*, 380-383. There is an excellent description of Major General Dahlquist in Franz Steidl, *Lost Battalions: Going for Broke in the Vosages, Autumn 1944* (Novato, CA: Presidio Press, 2000), 23-24.

52. First quote, Omar Bradley, *A General's Life: An Autobiography of General of the Army Omar Bradley* (New York: Simon & Schuster, 1983), 340; second quote, Dwight D. Eisenhower, *Crusade in Europe* (New York: Doubleday & Co., 1948), 376; *Time*, February 19, 1945, pp. 26-27; Carol Reardon, "William Hood Simpson," in Garraty and Carnes, eds., *American National Biography*. 20: 24-25; Forrest C. Pogue, *The Supreme Command: The European Theater of Operations* (Washington: Center of Military History, U.S. Army, 1996), 19-20, 265.

53. Quote, Citation, G. O. No. 20, March 29, 1945, in *Texas Medal of Honor Recipients*, 42; Art Leatherwood, "George D. Keathley," in Tyler, ed., *New Handbook of Texas*, 3: 1044.

54. Citation, G. O. No. 13, February 27, 1945, in *Texas Medal of Honor Recipients*, 22; Art Leatherwood, "James H. Fields," in Tyler, ed., *New Handbook of Texas*, 2: 992.

55. Citation, G. O. No. 32, April 23, 1945, in *Texas Medal of Honor Recipients*, 31.

56. Quote, Citation, G. O. No. 20, March 29, 1945, *Ibid.*, 1; Donald G. Taggart, *History of the*

Third Infantry Division in World War II (Washington: Infantry Journal Press, 1947), 379; Melissa Renteria, "He Says He's No Hero," *Beaumont Enterprise*, February 10, 2002.

57. Citation, G. O. No. 74, September 1, 1945, in *Texas Medal of Honor Recipients*, 50. Leonard was second in command of the company led by Captain Marion Pugh, former football star and graduate of Texas A&M in 1941. Dethloff, *Centennial History of Texas A&M University*, 467.

58. Citation, G. O. No. 77, September 10, 1945, in *Texas Medal of Honor Recipients*, 20; Colby, *90th Division*, 296, 325-326. Art Leatherwood, "Forrest E. Everhart," in Tyler, ed., *New Handbook of Texas*, 2: 910, points out that although Everhart was born in Ohio his award was credited to Texas, his state of residence when he enlisted.

59. Citation, G. O. No. 77, September 1, 1945, in *Texas Medal of Honor Recipients*, 24; Bradley, ed., *4th Infantry "Ivy" Division*, 39; Robert S. Rush, *Hell in Huertgen Forest: The Ordeal and Triumph of an American Infantry Regiment* (Lawrence, KS: University Press of Kansas, 2001), 148. Rush, 215, 215n, 216n, notes that two other Texans, Staff Sergeant Berla Childress from Waskom and Staff Sergeant Charles Monroe from Eustace, were involved in the action near Grosshau. The fighting in the Huertgen Forest was some of the most brutal in the war. For three months, mid-September to mid-December 1944, six American infantry divisions (1st, 4th, 8th, 9th, 28th, and 83rd) and part of the 5th Armored Division fought in the forest. Twenty-eight thousand casualties were incurred. For an overall account see Edward G. Miller, *A Dark and Bloody Ground: The Huertgen Forest and the Roer River Dams, 1944-1945* (College Station: Texas A&M University Press, 1995).

60. Simpson, *Audie Murphy*, 120-121; Roger J. Spiller, "Man Against Fire: Audie Murphy and His War," in Dawson, ed., *Texas Military Experience*, 148-149.

61. Simpson, *Audie Murphy*, 131-137.

62. Paul Boesch, *Road to Huertgen: Forest in Hell* (Houston: Gulf Publishing Co., 1962), 226-227.

63. Joe W. Wilson, Jr., *The 761st "Black Panther" Tank Battalion in World War II* (Jefferson, NC: McFarland & Company, 1999), 52-84, 118-119; David J. Williams, *Hit Hard* (New York: Bantam Books, 1983), 137-224; author interview with Philip Latimer, January 23, 2002, Beaumont, Texas.

64. Quote, Herman Heard, in David Colley, *The Road to Victory: The Untold Story of World War II's Red Ball Express* (Washington: Brassey's, 1999), 112; John D. Silvera, *The Negro in World War II* (New York: Arno Press, 1969), pages unnumbered. For more on the role of African American troops see Ulysses Lee, *The Employment of Negro Troops* (Washington: Office of Chief of Military History, Department of the Army, 1966) and Maggi M. Morehouse, *Fighting in the Jim Crow Army: Black Men and Women Remember World War II* (Lanham, MD: Rowman & Littlefield Publishers, 2000).

65. Steidl, *Lost Battalions*, 76-97; Brager, *Texas 36th Division*, 238-240; Lyn Crost, *Honor by Fire: Japanese Americans at War in Europe and the Pacific* (Novato, CA: Presidio Press, 1994), 185-194.

66. *Biographical Directory, U.S. Air Forces*, Vol. I., unnumbered pages; Freeman, *Mighty Eighth*, 257, 301.

67. Freeman, *Mighty Eighth*, 122.

68. *Ibid.*, 170, 250, 277; Sullivan, *Overlord's Eagles*, 85-86.

69. Astor, *Mighty Eighth*, 222, 229-230, 255-256; Freeman, *Mighty Eighth*, 242. For more on the 56th Fighter Group see *The 56th Fighter Group in World War II* (Washington: Infantry Journal Press, 1948).

70. Astor, *Mighty Eighth*, 419-420.

71. Author interview with Joe Stewart, January 18, 2002, Beaumont, Texas; Freeman, *Mighty Eighth*, 178-179, 257.

72. Author interview with Dan Dennis, January 9, 2002, Beaumont, Texas; Dennis quote, in Richard A. Wood and Robert S. Bee, eds., *War Stories of the O & W: A History of the 486th Bomb Group (Heavy)* (n.p., 1996), 148.

73. Perret, *Winged Victory*, 282, 307, 350-359. Journalist Ernie Pyle visited one of the Ninth's airbases in summer 1944. There he met Wood, at age 25 a full colonel, and Lieutenant Jim Gray from Wichita Falls, a B-26 pilot who "looked like a Texan–wind-burned and unsmooth." Pyle also met an old friend, Major Royal Roussel, former managing editor of the *Houston Press*, who was in the planning section of the Ninth Air Force. Pyle, *Brave Men*, 340-341, 356-357. Pyle noted that the Air Force "seemed to be half Texan."

74. Perret, *Winged Victory*, 232-234; Parton, *Air Force Spoken Here*, 357-435. Ernie Pyle also visited Ira Eaker, whom he had known for fifteen years. He noted that Eaker now had a command that stretched over thousands of miles and included fliers of three nations. *Brave Men*, 334.

75. Perret, *Winged Victory*, 320. Colonel Archie Old, the Texan who commanded the 45th Combat Bombardment Wing, flew a shuttle mission in late 1944. His force of 114 B-17s bombed the synthetic oil refinery at Ruhland, fifty miles south of Berlin, then flew on to Poltava and Mirgovod in the Soviet Union. That night German aircraft attacked and destroyed 44 of 72 B-17s at Poltava. Old had wanted to order up 75 P-51 fighters located nearby but the local Soviet commander had to call Moscow first and the damage was done before a response was received. There was not much enthusiasm for shuttle bombing after this disaster. Astor, *Mighty Eighth*, 278-282.

76. Stephen E. Ambrose, *The Wild Blue: The Men and Boys Who Flew the B-24s over Germany* (New York: Simon & Schuster, 2001), 35-39, 54-55, 86, 125-126, 216-219. McGovern and his crew were part of the 741st Squadron of the 455th Bomb Group. A number of Texans (in addition to those in McGovern's crew) were in the 741st. Among these were Major George B. Goetz and Staff Sergeant Henry Hutchings III of Beaumont, Lieutenant James Ross of Longview, Captain James Scott, Jr., of New Braunfels, Major James D. Mehegan of Fulton, Staff Sergeant Troy E. Myrick of McKinney, Lieutenant Colonel James A. Head of Lewisville, and Captain James H. Smith of San Antonio. Horace W. Lanford, *Partial History of the 741st Bombardment Squadron . . .* 3 vols. (Fort Lauderdale, FL; priv. printed, 1988), 3: 400-404.

77. Perret, *Winged Victory*, 352-383. For more on the 332nd Fighter Group see Charles E. Francis, *The Tuskegee Airmen: The Men Who Changed the Nation* (4th ed. rev., Boston: Brandon Publishing Co., 1997) and John B. Holway, *Red Tails, Black Wings: The Men of America's Black Air Force* (Las Cruces, NM: Yucca Tree Press, 1994).

78. Francis, *Tuskegee Airmen*, 103, 152-153, 302, 309, 394, 400. Francis, 405-413, names approximately 200 Tuskegee airmen lost in training, combat, and routine missions; among these were Lieutenant Samuel Jefferson of Galveston, Lieutenant George McCrumby of Fort Worth, and Lieutenant Neal Nelson of Amarillo.

79. Edward J. Reneham, Jr., *The Kennedys at War, 1937-1945* (New York: Doubleday, 2002), 302-304.

80. Ben Parnell, *Carpetbaggers: America's Secret War in Europe* (Rev. ed., Austin: Eakin Press, 1993), 98-100. Other Texans among the "Carpetbaggers" listed in Parnell's book are Lieutenant William L. Bales, a B-24 pilot; Captain George Bledsoe, Jr., commander of the 858th Squadron; Captain Robert W. Bronar, fight leader in the 856th Squadron; Lieutenant James A. Darby, pilot in the 850th Squadron; Sergeant Keith Gutt, B-24 gunner; and Lieutenant William A. Paul, radio-radar operator. In the index the author indicates Robert W. Fish, who eventually became group leader, was a Texan, but on p. 176, he states Fish was from Michigan.

81. Much has been written about the Ardennes offensive. One of the most thorough studies is Hugh M. Cole, *The Ardennes: Battle of the Bulge* (Reprint, Washington: Center of Military History, U.S. Army, 1994).

82. Fuller is described by military historian Charles B. MacDonald (himself a company commander in the Battle of the Bulge) as "a capable but irascible commander, a man with a cantankerous disposition." *A Time For Trumpets: The Untold Story of the Battle of the Bulge* (New York: William Morrow and Co., 1985), 134. For more on Fuller see Cole, *The Ardennes*, 179, 182, 184-185, 188, 190-191, and John Toland, *Battle: The Story of the Bulge* (New York: Random House, 1959), 74-85, 132-138, 246-247.

83. MacDonald, *Time for Trumpets*, 152, 305, 353-354, 539-540, 554-555; Trevor N. Dupuy, David L. Bongard, Richard C. Anderson, Jr., *Hitler's Last Gamble: The Battle of the Bulge, December 1944–January 1945* (New York: Harper Collins, 1994), 55, 104; John S. D. Eisenhower, *The Bitter Woods* (New York: G. P. Putnam's Sons, 1969), 193, 204-207, 253-254, 305.

84. Cole, *The Ardennes*, 307, 445-448, 449-451; Rapport and Norwood, *Rendezvous With Destiny*, 441-444, 538; MacDonald, *Sound of Trumpets*, 497-494, 524; *Texas Veterans of Czech Ancestry*, 265; Robert M. Bowen, *Fighting With the Screaming Eagles: With the 101st Airborne from Normandy to Bastogne* (Mechanicsburg, PA: Stackpole Books, 2001), 126, 127, 152, 189.

85. Dupuy, *Hitler's Last Gamble*, 194, 227-230.

86. Citation, G. O. No. 47, June 18, 1945, in *Texas Medal of Honor Recipients*, 52; Morin, *Among the Valiant*, 166-171.

87. Citation, G. O. No. 42, May 24, 1945, in *Texas Medal of Honor Recipients*, 45.

88. MacDonald, *Time for Trumpets*, 618. Among the Texans killed in the battle was Lieutenant Colonel James L. LaPrade of San Antonio. A graduate of West Point and a battalion commander in the 506th Parachute Infantry, James LaPrade was the brother of First Lieutenant Robert M. LaPrade, killed on Guadalcanal. Lieutenant Colonel LaPrade was awarded the Silver Star with Oak Leaf Cluster posthumously. *History of the Second World War, A Memorial*, 2: 751; Rapport and Norwood, *Rendezvous with Destiny*, 461-466, 810, 814. Colonel Julian Ewell, commander of the 501st Parachute Infantry, was severely wounded and never returned to combat. Donald R. Burgett, *Seven Roads to Hell: A Screaming Eagle at Bastogne* (New York: Dell Books, 1999), 242.

89. David A. Foy, *For You the War Is Over: American Prisoners of War in Nazi Germany* (New York: Stein and Day, 1984), 12-13, 61-70.

90. *Ibid.*, 13, 71-80. Lynn Harris of Nederland, a rifleman in the 29th Infantry Division, who spent seven months in a German POW camp believed "those Red Cross parcels saved a lot of lives." *Beaumont Enterprise*, June 5, 1994.

91. Interview, Joseph F. Fertitta with Angela Busceme, June 18, 1999, Special Collections, Gray Library, Lamar University, Beaumont, Texas; Matias Rodriquez, in Manning, *Courage of Common Men*, 36; R. H. Peek, Jr., in Stroud, *For Love of Country*, 216-218.

92. David Westheimer, *Sitting It Out: A World War II POW Memoir* (Houston: Rice University Press, 1992), 1-15, 170.

93. Manning, ed., *Courage of Common Men*, 89-105, 167-176; Tommy Lamore and Dan A. Baker, *One Man's War: The WWII Saga of Tommy Lamore* (Lanham, MD: Taylor Trade Publishing, 2002), 151-152. For contrasts in food rations for prisoners of war see Kenneth W. Simmons, *Kriegie* (New York: Thomas Nelson & Sons, 1960), 104-106, 144-150.

94. German-American POW figures are given by Albert E. Cowdrey, "A Question of Numbers" in Gunter Bischof and Stephen E. Ambrose, *Eisenhower and the German POWs: Facts Against Falsehood* (Baton Rouge: Louisiana State University Press, 1992), 78-92. Gavan Daws, *Prisoners of the Japanese: POWs of World War II in the Pacific* (New York: William Morrow, 1994), says 34 percent of American prisoners died in Japanese prisons. E. Bartlett Kerr, *Surrender and Survival: The Experiences of American POWs in the Pacific, 1941-1945* (New York: William Morrow, 1985), 339-340, gives 41 as the percentage.

95. Quote, Van Waterford, *Prisoners of the Japanese in World War II* (Jefferson, NC: McFarland and Company, 1994), 38. See also John W. Dower, *War Without Mercy: Race & Power in the Pacific War* (New York: Pantheon Books, 1986), 48-52.

96. First quote, Article 2, "Japanese Army Regulations for Handling Prisoners of War," in Waterford, *Prisoners of the Japanese*, 353; second quote, Refugio Medina, in Adams, *Valley Vets*, 25.

97. First quote, Thompson, *A Thousand Cups of Rice: Surviving the Death Railway* (Austin: Eakin Press, 1994), 75; second quote, William J. Weissinger, Jr., *Attention Fool!* (Austin: Eakin Press, 1998), 77; third quote, Frank Fujita, Jr., *FOO, Japanese-American Prisoner of the Rising Sun*, 153; Manning, *Courage of Common Men*, 239-240; Robert R. Martindale, *The 13th Mission: The Saga of a POW at Camp Omori, Tokyo* (Austin: Eakin Press, 1998), 181; Fiske Hanley II, *Accused American War Criminal* (Austin: Eakin Press, 1997), 122.

98. Quote, Waterford, *Prisoners of the Japanese*, 39.

99. First quote, Clyde Fillmore, *Prisoner of War* (Wichita Falls: Nortex Press, 1973), 105; second quote, Crayton R. Gordon, in Robert S. La Fonte and Ronald E. Marcello, eds., *Building the Death Railway: The Ordeal of American POWs in Burma, 1942-1945* (Wilmington, DL: SR

Books, 1993), 145; Hanley, *Accused American War Criminal*, 122; W. T. Block, "Late Physician Flew Missions Over Japan," *Beaumont Enterprise*, November 13, 2002.

100. Quotes, Robert S. La Fonte, Ronald E. Marcello, and Richard L. Himmel, eds., *With Only the Will to Live: Accounts of Americans in Japanese Prison Camps, 1941-1945* (Wilmington, DL: SR Books, 1994), 113, 160, 165; Fujita, *FOO, Japanese-American Prisoner of the Rising Sun*, 121-122.

101. First quote, Martindale, *13th Mission*, 132; second quote, Permenter, in La Fonte, ed., *With Only the Will to Live*, 163. Fiske Hanley declared that he "never received a Red Cross package during my entire imprisonment." *Accused American War Criminal*, 172. A standard American Red Cross parcel contained one 14½-ounce can, evaporated milk; one 8-ounce package of lunch biscuit (hard tack); one 8-ounce package of cheese; one 8-ounce tin of instant cocoa; one 15-ounce tin of sardines; one l-pound tin oleomargarine; one 12-ounce tin of corned beef; two 5½-ounce bars of sweet chocolate; one 2-ounce package of sugar; two 3½-ounce packages of dehydrated soup; one 16-ounce package of prunes; one 4-ounce tin instant coffee; one pack of 10 cigarettes; and one 2½-ounce package of smoking tobacco. Multinational, Canadian, and British parcels were slightly different in content. Kerr, *Surrender and Survival*, 125-127.

102. Marcello, "Lone Star POWs," 298-320.

103. Calvert died from malnutrition. *History of the Second World War, A Memorial*, 4: 679. Historians are not in agreement on the number of POWs who traveled on these ships or the number who died. Gavan Daws, *Prisoners of the Japanese*, 297, believes 10,800 of 50,000 Allied prisoners who traveled on such ships, or 21 percent, died. Van Waterford, *Prisoners of the Japanese*, 151, claims that 22,000 of more than 62,000 POWs transported on the ships, or 35 percent, died. Gregory F. Michno, *Death on the Hellships: Prisoners at Sea in the Pacific War* (Annapolis: Naval Institute Press, 2001), 282-283, believes that Daws' 50,000 is closer to the number of individuals transported, but that 21,000 men died. He notes that the 21,000 figure is greater than the 20,000 Marines killed during the entire Pacific war, the 16,000 U.S. Army troops killed in the Normandy campaign, or the 19,000 killed in the Battle of the Bulge.

104. Martindale, *13th Mission*, 131, 136-138; Weissinger, *Attention Fool!*, 77-79.

105. The Navy later named a destroyer escort in Dealey's honor. Dealey Plaza in Dallas, the site where President John F. Kennedy was assassinated, is named for Commander Dealey. At least four other Texans were on the *Harder* at the time of sinking: Seamen First Class Sylvester Lilly (Camp Ruby), Radioman Second Class Benjamin R. Medley (Marfa), Fireman Second Class John T. Swagerty (Bowie) and Ship's Cook Second Class Buford J. Young (Dozier). Lockwood and Adamson, *Through Hell and Deep Water*, 183-302, 304-306, 313-317; Art Leatherwood "Samuel David Dealey," in Tyler, ed., *New Handbook of Texas* 2: 549-550; Citation, undated, in *Texas Medal of Honor Recipients*, 17. *Texas Veterans of Czech Ancestry*, 72, states that E. Krenek Gully of Fayetteville was on *Harder* at the time of her sinking. He is not listed in the roster in Lockwood and Adamson, *Through Hell and Deep Water*. They do list Yeoman First Class Daniel John Gully on the *Harder*'s first patrol.

106. Morison, *Two-Ocean War*, 505.

107. The figures here are taken from Mendenhall's *Submarine Diary*, 190, 215, 250. They are slightly higher than those given in Blair, *Silent Victory*, 698-699. Commander Mendenhall's brother, Captain Lee G. Mendenhall, was a fighter pilot in the 355th Fighter Squadron in England. He flew more than 100 combat missions and shot down four enemy planes. Harold Scarlett, "Rice Farmer Recalls Air Combat," *Houston Post*, January 16, 1966.

108. Perret, *Winged Victory*, 448-450; Keith Wheeler, *Bombers Over Japan* (New York: Time-Life Books, 1982), 37-43.

109. Wilbur F. Morrison, *Point of No Return: The Story of the Twentieth Air Force* (New York: Times Books, 1979), 77, 84-85; Astor, *The Greatest War*, 592-593. Carmichael and his crew were systemically beaten and starved by their captors for months and kept in cages too small for lying down or sitting. When he was liberated after the war, Carmichael, who weighed 200 pounds before he was shot down, weighed only 140 pounds.

110. Manning, *Courage of Common Men*, 1-27; Johnston, *Houston*, 378. Young Roussel's father was the highly respected and well known music critic of the *Houston Post*.

111. Art Leatherwood, "Horace S. Carswell, Jr.," in Tyler, ed., *New Handbook of Texas*, 1: 997.

112. *Ibid.*; Citation, G. O. No. 14, February 4, 1946, in *Texas Medal of Honor Recipients*, 13.

113. Perret, *Winged Victory*, 400-402; Wheeler, *Bombers Over Japan*, 53-54.

114. Otha C. Spencer, *Flying the Hump: Memoirs of an Air War* (College Station: Texas A&M University Press, 1992); *Texas Veterans of Czech Ancestry*, 68, 195.

115. Buford B. Majors, interviewed by Valerie Majors Domingue, Beaumont, October 6, 1997, printed copy in author's possession; Adams, *Valley Vets*, 31-39; Spector, *Eagle Against the Sun*, 333-334, 370. For more on the subject see Leslie Anders, *The Ledo Road: General Joseph Stilwell's Highway to China* (Norman: University of Oklahoma Press, 1965).

116. Spector, *Eagle Against the Sun*, 420-421.

117. The classic account of fighting at Peleliu is E. B. Sledge's *With the Old Breed at Peleliu and Okinawa* (originally publ. 1981; New York: Oxford University Press, 1990). Sledge, later a professor at Montevallo University in Alabama, was a rifleman in the 3rd Battalion, 5th Marines, 1st Marine Division. See also Frank O. Hough, *The Island War: The United States Marine Corps in the Pacific* (Philadelphia: J. B. Lippincott Co., 1947), 291-313.

118. For Oliver Prince Smith see *Webster's Military Biographies*, 399-400; *Dictionary of American Military Biography*, 3: 1020-1024; and Clifton La Bree, *The Gentle Warrior: General Oliver Prince Smith, USMC* (Kent, OH: Kent State University Press, 2001). For Tom Lea see his own *Battle Station: A Grizzly from the Coral Sea and Peleliu Landing*, with introduction by Al Lowman (Dallas: Still Point Press, 1988) and Rebecca Craver and Adair Margo, eds., *Tom Lea: An Oral History* (El Paso: Texas Western Press, 1995). For Charles Victor Porras see Paul Morin, *Among the Valiant*, 238-243; for Marion Adam Beall see W. T. Block, "Marine Received Purple Heart for Action in WW2," *Beaumont Enterprise*, May 29, 2002. Information on Dr. Edward Crain is taken from Johnston, *Houston*, 373-374.

119. Citation, undated, *Texas Medal of Honor Recipients*, 65; Francis Collins Christian, "Charles Howard Roan," in Tyler, ed., *New Handbook of Texas*, 5: 602. Corporal Herbert N. Gibson of Rockdale and Pharmacist Mate Third Class Rex U. Daniel of Brownwood were among other Texans killed at Peleliu. Daniel was awarded the Silver Star posthumously for his action in rescuing two wounded hospital corpsmen in the fighting. *History of the Second World War, A Memorial*, 2: 837, 1005.

120. Spector, *Eagle Against the Sun*, 426-428; Robert W. Desmond, *Tides of War: World News Reporting, 1931-1945*, 429. Desmond, 438, notes that five days after the original landings one of the correspondents was killed and two others (including Stanley Gunn of Fort Worth) were seriously wounded and died later. Many of the troops who took part in the Leyte landings disapproved of MacArthur's dramatic gestures. In his memoirs John Gaitha Browning of Brownwood, a company clerk in the 692nd Engineers Amphibian Regiment, criticized MacArthur's "stupid ego." Oletha Stewart Tolliver, ed., *An Artist at War: The Journal of John Gaitha Browning* (Denton: University of North Texas Press, 1994), 259.

121. Astor, *The Greatest War*, 709-713.

122. William A. Owens, *Eye-Deep in Hell: A Memoir of the Liberation of the Philippines, 1944-45* (Dallas: Southern Methodist University Press, 1989), 1-11. The first night ashore Owens, a highly trained specialist, was ordered by a colonel to dig drainage ditches near a general's tent.

123. Historians are much divided concerning San Antonio's Walter Krueger. Ronald Spector, *Eagle Against the Sun*, Geoffrey Perret, *There's A War To Be Won*, and John Francis Shortal, *Forged by Fire: Robert L. Eichelberger and the Pacific War* (Columbia: South Carolina Press, 1987) criticize Krueger for being too cautious and devoted to minor details. Arthur S. Collins, "Walter Krueger," *Infantry Journal* 73 (January-February 1983), 15-19, defends Krueger as a highly professional officer who was concerned primarily with the welfare of his troops. William M. Leary, ed., *We Shall Return! MacArthur's Commanders in the Defeat of Japan* (Lexington: University of Kentucky Press, 1988), views Krueger as meticulous in his preparation for battle and refusing to be rushed, much as the Civil War's George H. Thomas. Kevin C. Holzimmer, "Walter Krueger, Douglas MacArthur and the Pacific War: The Wakde-Surmi Campaign as a Case Study," *Journal of Military History* 59 (October 1995): 661-685, argues that factors beyond Krueger's control contributed to his difficulties. William A. Owens, *Eye-Deep in Hell*, 31, notes that Krueger was a soldier's general, highly respected as a fighting man who had worked his way up through the ranks.

124. Samuel Eliot Morison, *Leyte, June 1944–January 1945* (originally publ. 1958; Boston: Little, Brown, and Co., 1961), 198-360, provides complete coverage of the battle of Leyte Gulf.

125. Astor, *Crisis in the Pacific*, 281-282.

126. *Ibid.*, 304-308; Morison, *Leyte*, 305.

127. Quote, Morison, *Two-Ocean War*, 455. The author expresses his appreciation to Kevin Ladd, director of Wallisville Heritage Park, for calling his attention to articles on Waldrop in the *Liberty Vindicator*, December 21, 1944, and *Liberty Sending-News and Chatter*, January 12, 1945. The *Vindictor* indicates Waldrop hit and destroyed both torpedoes, but naval historian Samuel Eliot Morison, *Leyte*, 273, says Waldrop "performed the extraordinary feat of exploding one of the torpedoes by strafing as it was porpoising toward the end of its run, and a second was deflected from its collision course by an accurate shot from the *So. Lo*'s 5-inch 38."

CHAPTER EIGHT

1. Coke R. Stevenson, Second Inaugural Address, January 16, 1945, in Martin De Boer, ed., *Destiny by Choice: The Inaugural Addresses of the Governors of Texas* (Fayetteville, AR: University of Arkansas Press, 1992), 356.

2. MacDonald, *Mighty Endeavor*, 394-398, 407-408, 417.

3. Citation, G. O. No. 79, September 14, 1945, in *Texas Medal of Honor Recipients*, 76; Art Leatherwood, "Eli L. Whiteley," in Tyler, ed., *New Handbook of Texas*, 6: 937-938; Taggart, ed., *Third Infantry*, 388.

4. Citation, G. O. No. 65, August 9, 1945, in *Texas Medal of Honor Recipients*, 62; Simpson, *Audie Murphy*, 155-160.

5. Simpson, *Audie Murphy*, 175. In the appendix, 442, Colonel Simpson lists all these awards.

6. Citation, G. O. No. 79, September 14, 1945, in *Texas Medal of Honor Recipients*, 72; Art Leatherwood, "George Benton Turner," in Tyler, ed., *New Handbook of Texas*, 6: 593-594.

7. Clark succeeded Sir Harold Alexander as group commander. Alexander had been promoted to theater commander. MacDonald, *Mighty Endeavor*, 499-501.

8. Author interview with Gene Priest, Beaumont, Texas, February 6, 2002. In February 1945 Priest's group was transferred to France to support Patton's army. Priest was hit by flak while flying over the Rhine on his twenty-sixth mission. He managed to get his plane back by gliding, but his head was crushed and his chin and both jaws were broken in the landing. After a lengthy hospital stay in England he was returned to the United States for additional surgery.

9. Quote, Citation, G. O. No. 81, September 24, 1945, in *Texas Medal of Honor Recipients*, 47; Art Leatherwood, "Raymond Lee Knight, " in Tyler, ed., *New Handbook of Texas*, 3: 1144.

10. Ambrose, *The Victors*, 254-256.

11. Citation, G. O. No. 92, October 25, 1945, in *Texas Medal of Honor Recipients*, 73; Art Leatherwood, "Herman C. Wallace," in Tyler, ed., *New Handbook of Texas*, 6: 806. Wallace, a member of Company B, 301st Engineer Combat Battalion, 76th Infantry, was buried in the Lubbock City Cemetery.

12. Citation, G. O. No. 75, September 5, 1945, in *Texas Medal of Honor Recipients*, 35. Although he was born in Texas, Herrera entered service in Phoenix, Arizona.

13. Max S. Lale, *Max's Memoirs* (Austin: Eakin Press, 2001), 141-142.

14. Author interview, Thomas A. Floyd, Beaumont, Texas, November 16, 2001. Floyd entered service July 27, 1944 at the age of eighteen. He did his basic training at Fort Hood, was sent overseas, and joined the 30th Division ("Old Hickory") as a replacement in Company G, 2nd Battalion, 119th Infantry Regiment. Floyd has recently written about his experiences in the war in a manuscript entitled "A Walk in Time: 1944-1946."

15. Quote, Russell Weigley, *Eisenhower's Lieutenants*, 423. Floyd says that he leaned later that the shelling had been "friendly fire" from U.S. artillery whose shots fell short. Interview with author, Nov. 16, 2001, and Floyd, "A Walk in Time," 21. Lale, *Max's Memoirs*, 145-147, discusses the problems associated with providing fire support for advancing infantry.

16. W. T. Block, "The World War II Years, 1941-1945," manuscript furnished the author by W. T. Block. See also *Beaumont Enterprise*, December 26, 2001. For a discussion of the fighting at Remagen by an army historian see Ken Heckler, *The Bridge at Remagen* (New York: Ballantine Books, 1957).

17. MacDonald, *Mighty Endeavor*, 441-449.

18. Harry Haines, in Manning, ed., *Courage of Common Men*, 69-88. Johnny Mitchell of Galveston, captain of an artillery battery in the 5th Infantry, was another Texan who participated in Patton's Rhine River crossing. See his account *The Secret War of Captain Johnny Mitchell* (Houston: Gulf Publishing Co., 1976), 71-74.

19. MacDonald, *Mighty Endeavor*, 450-453.

20. Weigley, *Eisenhower's Lieutenants*, 710, 714, 724. Several young Texans, including Bob L. Mikel of Ennis and Jerry J. Rotreki of Galveston, in the Third Army were disappointed that they were unable to visit relatives in Czechoslovakia because they lived in areas under Russian occupation. *Texas Veterans of Czech Ancestry*, 83, 237.

21. Harwood Hinton, "Roderick Rodman Allen," in Tyler, ed., *New Handbook of Texas*, 1: 113-114; Weigley, *Eisenhower's Lieutenants*, 707, 709; Dethloff, *Centennial History of Texas A&M University*, 471; Stanton, *Order of Battle*, 65.

22. Citation, G. O. No. 117, December 11,1945, in *Texas Medal of Honor Recipients*, 66.

23. Quote, Harrison Frank Ude, in Adams, *Valley Vets*, 98; MacDonald, *Mighty Endeavor*, 477, 479; Robert Abzug, *Inside the Vicious Heart: Americans and the Liberation of Nazi Concentration Camps* (New York: Oxford University Press, 1985), 21-27.

24. B. C. Henderson, quoted in Manning, *Texans Touched by World War II*, 110; Alfredo Garcia, in Adams, *Valley Vets*, 85. For a description of the Buchenwald concentration camp by a Texan (from Gainesville) see Joe M. Leonard, Jr., *Rockabilly, Radio, and World War II* (Austin: Nortex Press, 2002), 58-62.

25. Quoted in Nancy Caldwell Sorel, *The Women Who Wrote the War* (New York: Harper Collins, 1999), 359.

26. Richard M. Hardison, *Caissons Across Europe: An Artillery Captain's Personal War* (Austin: Eakin Press, 1990), 177.

27. Cornelius Ryan, *The Last Battle* (New York: Simon & Schuster, 1965), 317; Doris Kearns Goodwin, *No Ordinary Time: Franklin and Eleanor Roosevelt: The Home Front in World War II* (New York: Simon & Schuster, 1994), 602-603.

28. Quote, Doris Kearns Goodwin, *No Ordinary Time*, 605; Simmons, *Kriegie*, 252-253.

29. Ryan, *The Last Battle*, 319-320.

30. The Allied leaders had agreed at Yalta that Germany would be divided into zones occupied by the victorious nations. The United States, Britain, and France would occupy parts of Berlin but the other part and the surrounding territory would be occupied by the Russians. For a defense of Eisenhower's actions see Stephen E. Ambrose, *Eisenhower and Berlin, 1945: The Decision to Stop at the Elbe* (New York: Simon & Schuster, 1967).

31. In the closing days of the war the 36th Division captured hundreds of prisoners. Most prominent of these were Reich Marshal Hermann Goering and Field Marshal Gerd von Rundstedt. Casualty figures for the 36th Division are taken from Vincent M. Lockhart, *T-Patch to Victory* (Canyon, TX: Stake Plains Press, 1981), 307, and Brager, *The Texas 36th Division*, 263-264. Casualties for other divisions are taken from "Order of Battle, European Theater of Operations," published in Ambrose, *Citizen Soldiers*, 280-283, and Stanton, *Order of Battle*, 79, 119, 133, 164.

Bruce A. Olson "Texas National Guard," in Tyler, ed., *New Handbook of Texas*, 6: 369, says "its [the 36th Division's] units spent 386 days actively engaged with the enemy." Olson points out that "about one in twelve men who fought in the line companies [of the 36th Division] during World War II were native Texans, and one in five were southerners."

32. Michael Hobbs, "'Coming Home'," in Lee, ed., *1941: Texas Goes to War*, 218; MacDonald, *Mighty Endeavor*, 512.

33. Murray and Millett, *A War To Be Won*, 497.

34. Spector, *Eagle Against the Sun*, 518-528. Robert Leckie, *Delivered From Evil: The Saga of*

World War II (New York: Harper and Row, Publishers, 1987), 850, points out that Yamashita divided his troops into three groups and withdrew them to mountain strongholds.

35. Hall, *Brothers of the Fox*, 98-101. Hall, who neither drank nor smoked, carried a New Testament on his person during combat. He later wrote that "during a particularly hectic day, if possible, he would take out the holy book and read until his fears were allayed and he was at peace." *Ibid.*, 105.

36. Gerald Astor, *Crisis in the Pacific: The Battles for the Philippine Islands by the Men Who Fought Them* (New York: Donald I. Fine Books, 1996), 373-374.

37. Hampton Sides, *Ghost Soldiers: The Forgotten Epic Story of World War II's Most Dramatic Mission* (New York: Doubleday, 2001), 196-214. Forrest Bryant Johnson, *Hour of Redemption: The Heroic WWII Saga of America's Most Daring POW Rescue* (Org. publ. 1970; reprint, New York: Warner Books, 2002), 282-297, provides a list of all POWs rescued with rank and home address. Chaplain Taylor had won the Silver Star on Bataan for taking risks in moving troops from the front lines. Shortly before the surrender he had been separated from his command. He was later captured in the jungle by the Japanese who suspected him of guerrilla activity. They placed him in a "heat box" the entire summer. The ship carrying Taylor and other POWs to Japan in 1944 was sunk by an American plane but Taylor made it to shore. The second transport was also hit by an American plane but again Taylor survived. He and others were sent to a camp in Manchuria which was later liberated by the Russians. He returned home but found his wife, who believed him dead, had remarried. Taylor himself later remarried. He remained in the Army, rising to the rank of major general, the highest ranking chaplain in the Army. For more on Taylor see Billy Keith, *Days of Anguish, Days of Hope* (Garden City, NY: Doubleday & Co., 1972).

38. Sides, *Ghost Soldiers*, 272-273; Johnson, *Hour of Redemption*, 213-215. A similar rescue, primarily of interned civilians, was carried out by the 8th Cavalry Regiment, 11th Airborne Division. See Edward M. Flanagan, Jr., *The Los Banos Raid: The 11th Airborne Jumps at Dawn* (Novato, CA: Presidio, Press, 1986).

39. Quote, Paul Austin, in Astor, *The Greatest War*, 821.

40. Astor, *The Greatest War*, 824. Arlton H. Brower from Avery, Texas, a sergeant in Company D of the 34th Regiment, was also in the Zig Zag fighting. He remembers it as a "tough battle." Stroud, *For Love of Country*, 488.

41. Spector, *Eagle Against the Sun*, 522-523; Robert Ross Smith, *Triumph in the Philippines* (Washington: Office of Chief of Military History, 1963), 217-219.

42. Murray and Millett, *A War To Be Won*, 498-499.

43. Citation, G. O. No. 97, November 1, 1945, in *Texas Medal of Honor Recipients*, 67.

44. Spector, *Eagle Against the Sun*, 524-529; Smith, *Triumph in the Philippines*, 468-480; Stanton, *Order of Battle*, 113-115.

45. Manning, *Courage of Common Men*, 257-270. Walter Freeman of Beaumont was another Texan flying support missions. Flying a P-38 Lighting fighter, Freeman completed 106 missions while a member of the 432nd Squadron of the 475th Fighter Group. *Beaumont Enterprise*, February 1, 2003.

46. R. E. "Peppy" Blount, *We Band of Brothers* (Austin: Eakin Press, 1984), xi, 19, 48, 77-86, 179-184.

47. Perret, *Winged Victory*, 405-407; Dethloff, *Centennial History of Texas A&M University*, 471-472.

48. Robert E. Hayes, Jr., "'Big John' Dunning–A Texan in the Air Force," *Texas Military History* 4 (Winter 1964): 265-280. Hayes points out that on one occasion Dunning shot a sergeant who was trapped in a burning wreck and being burned to death. Dunning faced a court martial for the action, which spared the sergeant the agony of a painful slow death, but was acquitted.

49. Olson, "Texas National Guard," in Tyler, ed., *New Handbook of Texas*, 6: 369; Stanton, *Order of Battle*, 317-318.

50. John Randolph of Houston, a member of the 124th Cavalry, has described the role of the regiment in *Marsmen in Burma* (Houston: Gulf Publishing Co., 1946). See also Murray and Millett, *A War To Be Won*, 489-491; Charles F. Romanus and Riley Sunderland, *Time Runs Out in CBI* (Washington: Office of Chief of Military History, 1959), 90-91, 126-130, 183-205, 340-342.

51. Citation, G. O. No. 44, June 6, 1945, in *Texas Medal of Honor Recipients*, 46; Randolph, *Marsmen in Burma*, 191-193; Art Leatherwood, "Jack L. Knight," in Tyler, ed., *New Handbook of Texas*, 3: 1143-1144. Allen E. Stafford from West Texas, a member of L Company, 124th Cavalry, was also wounded in the 1945 fighting in Burma. Koontz and Marcello, *Heroes: Oral History Interviews*, 134.
52. Randolph, *Marsmen in Burma*, 193-194.
53. Spector, *Eagle Against the Sun*, 492-494.
54. *Ibid.*, 498-500; Bill R. Ross, *Iwo Jima: Legacy of Valor* (New York: Random House, 1986), 59-85.
55. Quote, Alfred R. Stone, *A Marine Remembers Iwo Jima: Dog Company, 2nd Battalion, 27th Marines, Fifth Marine Division* (Austin: Eakin Press, 2000), 23.
56. Ross, *Iwo Jima*, xiii.
57. Quote, Richard Wheeler, *The Bloody Battle for Suribachi* (New York: Thomas Y. Crowell Co., 1965), 8. Wheeler, later a well known historical writer, was one of 46 men of the 3rd Platoon, Co. E., 2nd Battalion, 28th Marines, 5th Marine Division. Wheeler says that Wells carried a paperback that described the sweep of the Mongols across Asia. "We converted his initials to Jenghiz Khan," said Wheeler, *Ibid.*, 9.
58. Ross, *Iwo Jima*, 91-93, 99; James Bradley (with Ron Powers), *Flags of Our Fathers* (New York: Bantam Books, 2000), 188; John Keith Wells, *"Give Me Fifty Marines Not Affair to Die"* (Abilene, TX: Ka-Well Enterprises, 1995), 207-236. Wells received the Navy Cross at an awards ceremony at the Navy hospital in Norman, Oklahoma in May 1945. Captain Phil Roach, a former football player at Texas Christian and also a veteran of Iwo Jima, received a Silver Star at the same ceremony. Wells, *Ibid.*, 284-285.
59. Full details of the flag raising and the men involved may be found in Bradley, *Flags of Our Fathers*. In Lee, ed., *1941: Texas Goes to War*, 111, Texas writer and historian A. C. Greene has an interesting story on the flag raising in which Texans Keith Wells and Bernard Holly took part.
60. Bradley, *Flags of Our Fathers*, 11, 29, 36, 80-93, 102-115.
61. *Ibid.*, 11, 229, 232-233; Ross, *Iwo Jima*, 251. For nearly two years the country did not know that it was Block in the photo. Although his back was to the camera, his mother was convinced it was her son. On January 15, 1947, the Marine Corps confirmed that Block was in the photo as his mother had always insisted. Block's remains were brought back to Weslaco for burial in autumn 1947. Bradley points out that Block's letter to his mother, saying he came through without a scratch, had not yet left the island when Block was killed.
62. Stone, *A Marine Remembers*, 84-101.
63. Citation, undated, in *Texas Medal of Honor Recipients*, 30; Derrick Wright, *The Battle for Iwo Jima, 1945* (Phoenix Mill, Great Britain: Sutton Publishers, 1999), 167; Art Leatherwood, "William George Harrell," in Tyler, ed., *New Handbook of Texas*, 3: 470. On that day, March 3, the 5th Marine Division lost eight officers and 127 enlisted men killed and had a total of 518 casualties. Five men of the division won Medals of Honor that day. Richard F. Newcomb, *Iwo Jima* (New York: Holt, Rinehart, and Winston, 1965), 222-223.
64. Citation, undated, in *Texas Medal of Honor Recipients*, 53; Art Leatherwood, "Jack Lummus," in Tyler, ed., *New Handbook of Texas*, 4: 337-338; Wright, *Battle for Iwo Jima*, 169-170. Lummus' death is described by Ross, *Iwo Jima*, 308, who points out that the mine explosion blew off Lummus' legs and the surgeons were unable to stop the bleeding. Lieutenant Howard Stackpole, a physician and fellow Texan, was with Lummus when he died. Lummus, a football star at Baylor, apparently had a contract with the New York Giants because he told his doctors the Giants had lost a good end.
65. Herman J. Dupont, "Uncommon Valor: 'I" Company, 3rd Battalion, 27th Regiment, 5th Marine Division," 15. Typed manuscript copy furnished the author by Bernard Perricone, Lamar University, Beaumont, Texas, October 31, 2002. Pearman Hardy, also from Port Arthur, was an operator of a flame thrower in Sergeant Dupont's Item Company.
66. Quote, Alfred R. Stone, *A Marine Remembers*, 151.
67. An excellent description of the people, culture, and geography of Okinawa is found in

George Feifer, *The Battle for Okinawa: The Blood and the Bomb* (Guilford, CT: The Lyons Press, 2001), 43-57.

68. Roy E. Appleman, James M. Burns, Russell A. Gugeler, and John Stevens, *Okinawa: The Last Battle* (Orig. publ. 1948; Washington: Center of Military History, U.S. Army, 1984), 69-74; James and William Belote, *Typhoon of Steel: The Battle for Okinawa* (New York: Harper & Row, 1970), 52-60; Spector, *Eagle Against the Sun*, 533-534.

69. Quote, Billy Havens, in Richard Havens, comp., *Remembering Billy . . . The Story of a West Texas Marine, His Friends, His Family, and His Sacrifices—Told by Those Who Knew Him* (Lubbock: Flatland Publishing, 1994), 158.

70. Gerald Astor, *Operation Iceberg: The Invasion and Conquest of Okinawa in World War II* (New York: Dell Publishing, 1995), 119-120, 494-495. Robert Leckie, *Okinawa: The Last Battle of World War II* (New York: Penguin Books, 1995), 198, describes Easley as a "brave little gamecock." Tenth army commander Lieutenant General Simon B. Buckner was killed by a sniper that same day.

71. Astor, *Operation Iceberg*, 24, 31, 259-260; Astor, *The Greatest War*, 894-895. John Lee Smith, Jr., an artillery officer in the 27th Infantry and the son of Texas Lieutenant Governor John Lee Smith, Sr., was another Aggie at Okinawa. *History of Second World War, A Memorial*, 5: 2133.

72. Astor, *Operation Iceberg*, 270-272. Joe S. Benavides from Dallas was one of the 77th Infantry troops who retrieved the body of Pyle. David Zimmermann, "Texas Minorities Wage War," in Lee, ed., *1941: Texas Goes to War*, 129. Pyle's body was buried in the division cemetery on Ie Shima, but later was moved to the Punch Bowl cemetery in Hawaii.

73. Quote, Joe Leech, in Manning, *Courage of Common Man*, 224.

74. Koontz and Marcello, eds., *Heroes: Oral History Interviews*, 63; Feifer, *Battle of Okinawa*, xi-xii, 387-388; Spector, *Eagle Against the Sun*, 340. Robert Delman Hejl from Austin, on the U.S.S. *Hickox*, was another Texan who survived the *kamakize* attacks at Okinawa. *Texas Veterans of Czech Ancestry*, 79-80. Over 70,000 Japanese and 80,000 Okinawans, mainly civilians, died in the three-month campaign.

75. First quote, Francis E. Abernethy, in Francis E. and Hazel Shelton Abernethy, "The Best Years of Our Lives," *East Texas Historical Journal* 34 (Spring 1996): 7; second quote, Martin E. Rutledge, in Adams, *Valley Vets*, 60.

76. Paul W. Tibbets, *Flight of the "Enola Gay,"* (Reynoldsburg, OH: Buckeye Aviation Book Company, 1989), 151-160, 206.

77. *Ibid.*, 209-228; Boyne, *Clash of Wings*, 377-378. Eatherly, the pilot of the Hiroshima weather plane, had a drinking problem and a reputation as a "loose cannon." He was discharged from the Air Force in 1947, had some difficulties with the law, and died from a throat malignancy in 1978. There were stories circulated in the tabloids that he had been the Hiroshima bomb pilot and that his conscience bothered him so badly that he turned to drink and crime after the war. Tibbets has a chapter entitled "Sad Case of Major Eatherly" in his *Flight of the "Enola Gay,"* 282-296. For more on Eatherly see William Bradford Huie, *The Hiroshima Pilot: The Case of Major Claude Eatherly Who Has Been Called "The American Dreyfus"* (New York: G. P. Putnam's Sons, 1964).

78. Beahan, a native of Jolpin, Missouri, attended Rice Institute on a football scholarship. "Ex-Baytonian Who Was On Nagaski Mission," *Baytown Sun*, August 5, 1990.

79. Potter, *Nimitz*, 386-396. In one of the last actions of the naval war the cruiser U.S.S. *Indianapolis*, which carried the final components of the atomic bomb to Tinian, was sunk by torpedoes from a Japanese submarine. Only 316 of the 1,196 crew members were rescued after several days in the water. Twenty-four of the survivors were Texans. The only Texas officer in the rescued group was Lieutenant (junior grade) Charles B. McKissick of McKinney. Names of all survivors are listed in Richard F. Newcomb, *Abandon Ship! The Saga of the U.S.S. Indianapolis* (Orig. publ.1958; New York: Perennial, 2002), 299-319.

80. Michael Hobbs, "Coming Home," in Lee, ed., *1941: Texas Goes to War*, 217-225; *Houston Post*, August 15, 1945; *Galveston Daily News*, August 15, 16, 1945.

81. Quotes, Francis Abernethy, in Roach, ed., *Collective Hearts*, 78.

82. Quote, Bruce Aiken, in Adams, *Valley Vets*, 56.
83. Quote, Fred O. Garza, Sr., in Adams, *Valley Vets*, 38-39.
84. Quote, James W. Lowry, in Stroud, *For Love of Country*, 454.
85. Quote, Max Lale, *Max's Memoirs*, 199-200.
86. Kennett, *G. I.*, 222-223.
87. Perret, *There's A War To Be Won*, 533-534.

88. Numbers of Texans in service is taken from Table 157, Armed Forces Strength, By Branch of Service and By State, June 30, 1945, in *Selective Service and Victory, The 4th Report of the Director of Selective Service* (Washington: Government Printing Office, 1948), 671-620. The same report, page 601, shows that 715,335 Texas men served in the military; the report does not give total number of women. The *Texas Almanac, 1947-1948*, 117, says 12,000 Texas women served in the armed forces during the war. Although nearly 60 percent of Texas men in service were inducted through Selective Service, Texas had a higher percentage of male volunteers (40.8 percent) than the national average (33.9 percent). Only five states (Oregon, 47.4 percent; California, 43.2 percent; Colorado, 42.4 percent; Oklahoma, 41.2 percent; and Idaho, 40.9 percent) had a higher percentage of volunteers in service. Many Texas families contributed several sons and daughters to the armed forces during World War II. The record may belong to the Stash Ripkowaski family of Liberty County. Seven brothers were in the Army and one in the Navy. A ninth brother, 18-year old Franklin, joined the maritime service in February 1945. Three other brothers later served in the armed forces. *Liberty Vindicator*, March 1, 1945; December 4, 1991.

89. Army casualties taken from U.S. Department of the Army, Center of Military History, "World War II, Korea, and Vietnam Casualties," http:/www.army.mil/cmh-pg/documents/misc/ stcas.htm; cas.htm; Navy casualties from Bureau of Naval Personnel, "Annual Report, Navy and Marine Corps Military Personnel Statistics, 30 June, 1959," 225; "Naval Personnel, U.S. Marine Corps" (U.S. Marine Corps, Historical Center), January 17, 2002; Coast Guard Casualties, from Chris Haven, Historian, to Theresa Storey, Documents Librarian, Lamar University, August 6, 2002, based on handwritten register in U.S. Coast Guard Historian's Office. This total figure is slightly less than the 23,022 reported in *Texas Almanac, 1947-1948*, 117, which was based upon 15,764 fatalities reported by the War Department and 7,258 fatalities reported by the U.S. Navy (including Navy, Marines, and Coast Guard). The *Almanac* figures for army casualties were apparently based upon a 1946 booklet *World War II List of Dead and Missing, State of Texas*, prepared by the War Department. This listed 8,403 Texans killed in action, 1,166 died of wounds, 48 died of injuries, 4,935 died from non-battle causes, 1,134 "finding of death," and 78 missing, for a total of 15,764 army deaths. Bexar County with 1,075 deaths had the highest number of army fatalities, followed by Harris (1,059), Dallas (1,038), and Tarrant (584).

90. *Texas Almanac, 2000-2001*, 444; Hobbs, "Coming Home," in Lee, ed., *1941: Texas Goes to War*, 234. For an excellent account of how the end of the war affected two Texans see Francis E. and Hazel Shelton Abernethy, "The Best Years of Our Lives," 3-13. For more on the GI Bill see Michael J. Bennett, *When Dreams Came True: The GI Bill and the Making of Modern America* (Washington: Brassey's, 1996).

91. Quote, LuQuincy Bowers, in Manning, *Courage of Common Men*, 254-255; Maria-Christina Garcia, "Marcario Garcia," in Tyler, ed., *New Handbook of Texas*, 3: 86; V. Carl Allsup, "American G. I. Forum of Texas," *Ibid.*, 1: 147-148; Julie Leininger Pycior, "Mexican-American Organizations," *Ibid.*, 4: 660-662; Patrick J. Carroll, *Felix Longoria's Wake: Bereavement, Racism, and the Rise of Mexican American Activism* (Austin: University of Texas Press, 2003), 54-85. For more on Garcia and the GI Forum see Carl Allsup, *The American G. I. Forum: Origins and Evolution* (Austin: University of Texas Center for Mexican American Studies, 1982); Henry A. J. Raymond, *The American GI Forum: In Pursuit of the Dream, 1948-1983* (Houston: Arte Publico Press, 1998); and Ignacio M. Garcia, *Hector P. Garcia: In Relentless Pursuit of Justice* (Houston: Arte Publico Press, 2002).

92. Quote, James L. Stokesbury, *A Short History of World War II* (New York: William Morrow and Company, 1989), 389.

Bibliography

In writing *Texas and Texans in World War II*, the author relied heavily upon primary materials consisting of letters, diaries, memoirs, and published interviews of participants both on the battle front and home front. In addition, numerous secondary sources providing general background information and specific descriptions of Texans involved in military campaigns were utilized. A full listing of all such material is found in the footnotes accompanying the text. A discussion of those most useful in preparing the book is presented here.

General works used include the large volume by Gerald Astor, *The Greatest War: Americans in Combat, 1941-1945* (Novato, CA: Presidio Press, 1999), a compilation of oral interviews of men at war; Martha Ann Stroud, *For Love of Country: The Price of Freedom* (Austin: Nortex Press, 2000), a collection of hundreds of interviews and personal accounts of East Texans; Ava E. Mills, *West Texans Remember the Home Front* (San Angelo: Doss Books, 1997), consisting of short sketches by West Texans; William L. Adams, *Valley Vets: An Oral History of World War II Veterans* (Austin: Eakin Press, 1999), interviews with veterans from the lower Rio Grande valley; Stephen Neal Manning, *The Courage of Common Men: Texans Remember World War II* (Plano: Republic of Texas Press, 2001), interviews with 18 veterans, and Manning, *Texans Touched by World War II* (Plano: Republic of Texas Press, 2003), a companion volume containing interviews with Texans in both military and civilian life; and Joyce Gibson Roach, *Collective Hearts: Texans in World War II* (Austin: Eakin Press, 1996), recollections by Texas men and women both in the military and on the home front. Typed transcripts of interviews with Southeast Texans are located in the Special Collections, Gray Library, Lamar University, Beaumont, Texas.

Government sponsored reports and histories prepared during and immediately after the war provide an overall view of campaigns in which Texans participated. Valuable, especially for the early part of the war, is the first of a six volume series entitled *Battle Report*, prepared by U.S. Naval officers. Volume One, *Battle Report: Pearl Harbor to Coral Sea*, compiled by Walter Karig and Welbourne Kelley (New York: Rinehart and Co., 1944), contains official reports of early naval activity with individuals identified by state of enlistment. The Office of the Chief of Military History (and later the Center of Military History) of the United States Army published a multi-volume series *The United States Army in World War II*. This massive project, more than ninety volumes and still going, known as the "Green Books" (because of their green binding), provides a valuable guide to army operations around the world. The United States Air Force employed two distinguished historians, Wesley Frank Craven and James Lea Cate, to prepare a seven volume account entitled *The Army Air Forces in World War II* (Chicago: University of Chicago Press,

1948-1958) describing air operations during the war. Also useful for this study was Samuel Eliot Morison's fifteen volume *History of United States Naval Operations in World War II* (Boston: Little, Brown, and Co., 1947-1962).

The New Handbook of Texas, six volumes, ed. Ron Tyler, et al. (Austin: Texas State Historical Association, 1996) is an essential work for any study of Texas and Texans. Particularly significant are the articles on Texas Medal of Honor recipients and military bases and airfields, many written by Art Leatherwood. Additional information on Texas airfield and bases is included in *The Stars Were Big and Bright*, 2 vols. (Austin: Eakin Press, 2000-2001) and *Wings of Change: The Army Air Force Experience in Texas* (Abilene, TX: McWhiney Foundation Press, 2003), by Thomas Alexander, a retired air force officer and businessman.

The role of Texans in the early days of the Pacific War and the subsequent imprisonment of many of them may be found in a series of oral history interviews by Robert S. La Fonte, Ronald E. Marcello, and Richard Himmel, published by SR Books of Wilmington, Delaware: *Remembering Pearl Harbor: Eyewitness Accounts of U.S. Military Men and Women* (1991); *Building the Death Railway: The Ordeal of American Prisoners of War in Burma* (1993); and *With Only the Will to Live: Accounts of Americans in Japanese Prison Camps, 1941-1945* (1994). Other oral history interviews relating to the early war in the Pacific are Paul Joseph Travers, ed., *Eyewitness to Infamy: An Oral History of Pearl Harbor* (New York: Madison Books, 1991) and Gerald Astor, ed., *Crisis in the Pacific: The Battles for the Philippine Islands by the Men Who Fought Them* (New York: Donald I. Fine Books, 1996).

A small volume, *Doris Miller: A Silent Medal of Honor Winner* (Austin: Eakin Press, 1997), written by a relative, Vickie Gail Miller, provides personal information about one of the first Texas heroes of the war. Neil Sapper's article "Aboard the Wrong Ship in the Right Books: Doris Miller and Historical Accuracy," *East Texas Historical Review* 18 (Spring 1980):3-11, corrects some of the early published misinformation concerning Miller.

Several Texans published their memoirs describing early experiences in the Pacific War and imprisonment by the Japanese. The first of these, published during the war, was written by an army air force squadron commander, William E. Dyess, *The Dyess Story: The Eye-Witness Account of the Death March from Bataan and the Narrative of Experiences in Japanese Prison Camps and of Eventual Escape* (New York: G. P. Putnam's Sons, 1944). This work has recently been edited and reissued by the University of Nebraska Press, 2002, under the title *Bataan Death March: A Survivor's Account*. Other Texas memoirs included Clyde Fillmore, *Prisoner of War: History of the Lost Battalion* (Wichita Falls: Nortex Press, 1973); John S. Coleman, *Bataan and Beyond: Memoirs of an American POW* (College Station: Texas A&M University Press, 1978); H. Robert Charles, *Last Man Out* (Austin: Eakin Press, 1988); Frank "Foo" Fujita, *A Japanese-American Prisoner of the Rising Sun: The Secret Diary of Frank "Foo" Fujita* (Denton: University of North Texas Press, 1993); Fiske Hanley, *Accused American War Criminal* (Austin: Eakin Press, 1997); Robert R. Martindale, *The 13th Mission: The Saga of a POW at Camp Omori, Tokyo* (Austin: Eakin Press, 1998); Kyle Thompson, *A Thousand Cups of Rice: Surviving the Death Railway* (Austin: Eakin Press, 1994); and William J. Weissinger, Jr., *Attention Fool!* (Austin: Eakin Press, 1998).

William H. Bartsch, *Doomed at the Start: American Pursuit Pilots in the Philippines, 1941-1942* (College Station: Texas A&M University Press, 1992), is an excellent account of the futile efforts by American pilots, several of whom were Texans, against overwhelming odds early in the war. Gregory J. W. Urwin, *Facing Fearful Odds: The Siege of Wake Island* (Lincoln: University of Nebraska Press, 1997), and Chet Cunningham, *Hell Wouldn't Stop: An Oral History of the Battle of Wake Island* (New York: Carroll & Graf, 2002) recount another futile American effort involving several Texans. Ronald E. Marcello, "Lone Star POWs: Texas National Guardsmen and the Building of the Burma-Thailand Railroad, 1942-1944," *Southwestern Historical Quarterly* 95 (January 1992): 293-321, is a description of the suffering of men of the 2nd Battalion, 131st Field Artillery of the Texas National Guard. Henry C. Dethloff, *A Centennial History of Texas A&M University, 1876-1976*, 2 vols. (College Station: Texas A&M University Press, 1976) reminds readers that twenty thousand former students of Texas A&M served in the armed forces during World War II; twenty-five of them on Corregidor in 1941-1942.

Elizabeth N. Norman, *We Band of Angels: The Untold Story of American Nurses Trapped in Bataan by the Japanese* (New York: Random House, 1999) points out that eleven of the seventy-seven army and navy nurses captured in the Philippines were Texans. More on the army nurses in the Philippines is found in Evelyn M. Monahan and Rosemary Neidel-Greenlee, *All This Hell: U.S. Nurses Imprisoned by the Japanese* (Lexington: University Press of Kentucky, 2000); Barbara Brooks Tomblin, *G. I. Nightingales: The Army Nurses Corps in World War II* (Lexington: University Press of Kentucky, 1996); Abbie C. Ratledge, *Angels in Khaki* (San Antonio: Naylor, 1975); "Hattie Brantley," in Doris Weldon Casad, *Texans of Valor: Military Heroes in the 20th Century* (Austin: Eakin Press, 1998); and articles in the *American Journal of Nursing*, March 1942, March 1945, and October 1945.

Carroll V. Glines, *The Doolittle Raid: America's First Strike Against Japan* (New York: Orion Books, 1988) and Craig Nelson, *The First Heroes: The Extraordinary Story of the Doolittle Raid—America's First World War II Victory* (New York: Viking, 2002), note that a Texan was pilot or co-pilot of eleven of the sixteen army planes that made the Tokyo raid. Otis Hays, Jr., *Home From Siberia: The Secret Odysseys of Interned American Airmen in World War II* (College Station: Texas A&M University Press, 1990), 28-54, describes the internment and escape of one of Doolittle's crews (which included a Texan) from the Soviet Union.

Ronald H. Spector, *Eagle Against the Sun: The American War with Japan* (New York: Free Press, 1985); John Toland, *But Not In Shame: The Six Months After Pearl Harbor* (New York: Random House, 1961); Walter J. Boyne, *Clash of Titans: World War II at Sea* (New York: Simon & Schuster, 1995); Gordon W. Prange, *At Dawn We Slept: The Untold Story of Pearl Harbor* New York: McGraw-Hill Book Co., 1981); Prange, et al., *Miracle at Midway* (New York: McGraw-Hill Book Co., 1982); Clay V. Blair, *Silent Victory: The U.S. Submarine War Against Japan* (Philadelphia: J. B. Lippincott Co., 1975); John B. Lundstrom, *The First South Pacific Campaign: Pacific Fleet Strategy, December 1941–June 1942* (Annapolis, MD: Naval Institute Press, 1976), and volumes three and four in *History of United States Naval Operations in World War II* by Samuel Eliot Morison are all important secondary accounts of the early phases of the war in the Pacific.

Biographies of Texan Admiral Chester W. Nimitz provide considerable information on the war in the Pacific. E. B. Potter's *Nimitz* (Annapolis, MD: Naval Institute Press, 1976) is the most complete of these biographies. *On the Treadmill to Pearl Harbor* (Washington: Naval History Department, 1973), the memoirs of Admiral James O. Richardson, the East Texan who commanded the Pacific fleet the year before the attack on Pearl Harbor, is helpful in understanding the conditions that made the disaster possible.

Biographies and memoirs of Texans in the European War include James Parton, *"Air Force Spoken Here": General Ira Eaker and Command of the Air* (Bethesada, MD: Allen & Allen, 1986); Harold B. Simpson, *Audie Murphy, American Soldier* (Hillsboro, TX: Hill Junior College Press, 1975); Don Graham, *No Name on the Bullet: The Biography of Audie Murphy* (New York: Viking, 1989); Audie Murphy, *To Hell and Back* (New York: Henry Holt & Co., 1949); Johnny Mitchell, *The Secret War of Johnny Mitchell* (Houston: Gulf Publishing Co., 1976); Ernest E. Kowalik, *Alone and Unarmed* (New York: Carleton Press, 1968); L. K. Truscott, Jr., *Command Missions: A Personal Story* (New York: E. P. Dutton & Co., 1954); Wilson A. Heffner, *Patton's Bulldog: The Life and Services of General Walton H. Walker* (Shippensburg, PA: White Mane Books, 2001); David Westheimer, *Sitting It Out: A World War II POW Memoir* (Houston: Rice University Press, 1992); Paul Boesch, *Road to Huertgen: Forest in Hell* (Houston: Gulf Publishing Co., 1962); Max S. Lale, *Max's Memoirs* (Austin: Eakin Press, 2001); Richard M. Hardison, *Cassions Across Europe: An Artillery Captain's Personal War* (Austin: Eakin Press, 1990); Kenneth W. Simmons, *Kriegie* (New York: Thomas Nelson & Sons, 1960).

Texas-born Dwight D. Eisenhower is the subject of several biographies. Particularly useful are Stephen Ambrose's *The Supreme Commander: The War Years of General Dwight D. Eisenhower* (Garden City, NY: Doubleday & Co., 1969) and *Eisenhower: Soldier, General of the Army, President-Elect, 1890-1952* (New York: Simon & Schuster, 1983), and Carlo D'Este, *Eisenhower: A Soldier's Life* (New York: Henry Holt and Co., 2002). Eisenhower's own *Crusade in Europe* (Garden City, NY: Doubleday & Co., 1948) provides valuable insights into the European war.

Carlo D'Este, *Patton: A Genius for War* (New York: Harper Collins, 1995), Omar Bradley, *A Soldier's Story* (New York: Henry Holt and Co., 1951) and Bradley (with Clay Blair), *A General's Life* (New York: Simon & Schuster, 1983) furnish material on leadership of United States forces in Europe Texan William H. Simpson, who commanded the Ninth Army in Europe, has not been the subject of a major biography but information on him may be found in the previously mentioned works and Russell F. Weigley's masterful *Eisenhower's Lieutenants: The Campaigns of France and Germany, 1944-1945* (Bloomington, IN: Indiana University Press, 1981). This volume also contains much information about one of Patton's most capable corps commanders, Major General Walton H. Walker of Belton.

The story of the 36th Infantry Division, formerly the Texas National Guard, is told in Bruce L. Brager, *The Texas 36th Division: A History* (Austin: Eakin Press, 2002); Robert L. Wagner, *The Texas Army: A History of the 36th Division in the Italian Campaign* (Austin: State House Press, 1991); Fred A. Walker, *From Texas to Rome: A General's Story* (Dallas: Taylor Publishing Co., 1969); and Lee Carraway Smith, *A River Swift and Deadly: The 36th "Texas" Infantry at the Rapido River* (Austin: Eakin Press, 1997). Several articles add insights into the role of the 36th Infantry; particularly helpful are Bruce L. Brager, "Rapido and Velletri: Problem Solving in World War II," *Military History of the West* 31 (Fall 2001): 93-116; Martin Blumenson, "The 36th Infantry Division in World War II," in Joseph G. Dawson III, ed., *The Texas Military Experience: From the Texas Revolution through World War II* (College Station: Texas A&M University Press, 1995), 128-136; and James D. Padgift, "That Long Day at Salerno," *Texas Military History* 5 (Summer 1965): 45-63.

The controversy over the attempted crossing of the Rapido River is covered in the above works and also Martin Blumenson, *Salerno to Cassino* (Washington: Office of the Chief of Military History, U.S. Army, 1969); Blumenson, *Bloody River: The Real Tragedy of Rapido* (reprint; College Station, Texas A&M University Press, 1998); Mark Clark, *Calculated Risk* (London: Harrop & Co., 1951); and Robert L. Wagner, "The Rapido River Controversy: A Review," *East Texas Historical Journal* 38 (Fall 1990): 49-51.

Ernest F. Fisher, Jr., *Cassino to the Alps* (Washington: Center of Military History, U.S. Army, 1977) provides significant information on the role of the 36th Division during the summer of 1944. Robert H. Adleman and George Walton, *Rome Fell Today* (Boston: Little, Brown, and Co., 1968) praise the work of the 36th Division in the capture of Rome. Ernie Pyle's *Brave Men* (Org. publ. 1944; Reprint, Lincoln: University of Nebraska Press, 2001), contains descriptions of 36th Division personnel. The account of the death of Captain Henry T. Waskow of Belton is especially moving and regarded as one of Pyle's most poignant writings.

The role of Texans on D-Day and in Normandy is covered in various works including Leonard Rapport and Arthur Norwood, Jr., *Rendezvous With Destiny: A History of the 101st Airborne Division* (Old Saybrook, CT: Konecky & Konecky, 1948); Ronald J. Drez, *Voices of D-Day: The Story of the Allied Invasion Told by Those Who Were There* (Baton Rouge: Louisiana State University Press, 1994); Ronald L. Lane, *Rudder's Rangers* (Manassas, VA: Ranger Associates, 1979); Gerald Astor, *Battling Buzzards: The Odyssey of the 517th Parachute Regimental Combat Team, 1943-1945* (New York: Dell Publishing, 1993); Stephen E. Ambrose, *D-Day June 6 1944: The Climatic Battle of World War II* (New York: Simon & Schuster, 1994); Ambrose, *Citizen Soldiers: The U.S. Army from the Normandy Beaches to the Bulge to the Surrender of Germany, June 7 1944–May 7, 1945* (New York: Simon & Schuster, 1997); Ambrose, *The Victors: Eisenhower and His Boys: The Men of World War II* (New York: Simon & Schuster, 1998); Cornelius Ryan, *The Longest Day: June 6, 1944* (New York: Simon & Schuster, 1959); Max Hastings, *Overlord: D-Day and the Battle for Normandy* (New York: Simon & Schuster, 1984); Adrian R. Lewis, *Omaha Beach: A Flawed Victory* (Chapel Hill: University of North Carolina Press, 2001); John Colby, *War From the Ground Up: The 90th Division in World War II* (Austin: Nortex Press, 1991); and Francis X. Bradley, ed., *4th Infantry "Ivy" Division* (Paducah, KY: Turner Publishing Co., 1987).

Joe W. Wilson, Jr., *The 761st "Black Panther" Tank Battalion in World War II* (Jefferson, NC: Macfarland & Co., 1999), David J. Williams, *Hit Hard* (New York: Bantam Books, 1983), and Philip W. Latimer, "When the Black Panthers Prowled," *Army* (January 1992), 44-46, provide excellent descriptions of an African American tank battalion that included several Texans, trained in Texas, and fought with Patton's Third Army in France and Germany.

Robert S. Rush, *Hell in Huertgen Forest: The Ordeal and Triumph of an American Infantry Regiment* (Lawrence, KS: University Press of Kansas, 2001); Edward G. Miller, *A Dark and Bloody Ground: The Huertgen Forest and the Roer River Dams, 1944-1945* (College Station: Texas A&M University Press, 1995); and Max S. Lale, *Max's Memoirs* and Paul Boesch, *Road to Huertgen*, both mentioned earlier, describe some of the most bitter European combat in which Texans were involved.

The Battle of the Bulge fought in December–January 1944-1945 involved many Texans. Several books describe the fighting: Hugh M. Cole, *The Ardennes: Battle of the Bulge* (reprint, Washington: Center of Military History, U.S. Army, 1994); Charles B. MacDonald, *A Time for Trumpets: The Untold Story of the Battle of the Bulge* (New York: William Morrow and Co., 1985); Trevor N. Dupuy, David L. Bongard, Richard C. Anderson, Jr., *Hitler's Last Gamble: The Battle of the Bulge, December 1944–January 1945* (New York: Harper Collins, 1994); and John S. D. Eisenhower, *The Bitter Woods* (New York: G. P. Putnam's Sons, 1969).

The air war in Europe has received considerable attention from historians and participants. In addition to the biography of Ira Eaker mentioned earlier, Richard G. Davis, *Carl A. Spaatz and the Air War in Europe* (Washington: Smithsonian Institute Press, 1993) provides an overview as seen by Army Air Force commanders. The works of Roger A. Freeman, especially his *Mighty Eighth: A History of the Units, Men, and Machines of the U.S. 8th Air Force* (London: Cassell & Co., 1970), are indispensable for an understanding of the largest American air force. Other works include Brian D. O'Neill, *Half A Wing, Three Engines and A Prayer: B-17s Over Germany* (New York: McGraw Hill Book Co., 1999); Geoffrey Perret, *Winged Victory: The Army Air Forces in World War II* (New York: Random House, 1993); James Dugan and Carroll Stewart, *Ploesti: The Great Ground Air Battle of 1 August 1943* (London: Jonathan Cape, 1963); Thomas M. Coffey, *Decision Over Schweinfurt: The U.S. 8th Air Force Battle for Daylight Bombing* (New York: David McKay Co., 1977); Richard A. Wood and Robert S. Bee, eds., *War Stories of the O & W: A History of th 486th Bomb Group (Heavy)* (priv. printed, 1996); Stephen E. Ambrose, *The Wild Blue: The Men and Boys Who Flew the B-24s Over Germany* (New York: Simon & Schuster, 2001); Charles E. Francis, *The Tuskegee Airmen: The Men Who Changed the Nation* (4th rev.ed., Boston: Brandon Publishing Co., 1997); John B. Holway, *Red Tails, Black Wings: The Men of America's Black Air Force* (Las Cruces, NM: Yucca Tree Press, 1997); Philip Ardery, *Bomber Pilot: A Memoir of World War II* (Lexington, KY: University Press of Kentucky, 1978); Fred Koger, *Countdown!* (Chapel Hill: Algonquin Books, 1990); Robert Morgan, *The Men Who Flew the Memphis Belle: Memoir of a WWII Bomber Pilot* (New York: Dutton, 2001); and Tommy Lamore and Don Baker, *One Man's War: The WWII Saga of Tommy Lamore* (Lanham, MD: Taylor Trade Publishing, 2002).

Later phases of the war in the Far East are covered in several firsthand accounts by Texans. See Walter Krueger, *From Down Under to Nippon: The Story of the Sixth Army in World War II* (Washington: Combat Forces Press, 1953); Corwin Mendenhall, *Submarine Diary: The Silent Stalking of Japan* (Annapolis, MD: Naval Institute Press, 1991); Otha C. Spencer, *Flying the Hump: Memoirs of an Air War* (College Station: Texas A&M University Press, 1992); Tom Lea, *Battle Station: A Grizzly from the Coral Sea and Peleliu Landing* (Dallas: Still Point Press, 1988); William A. Owens, *Eye-Deep in Hell: A Memoir of the Liberation of the Philippines, 1944-45* (Dallas: Southern Methodist University Press, 1989); Leonard G. Hall, *Brothers of the Fox: Company F, 172nd Infantry, 43rd Division* (Orange, TX: priv. printed, 1985); R. E. "Peppy" Blount, *We Band of Brothers* (Austin: Eakin Press, 1984); Oletha Stewart Tolliver, ed., *An Artist at War: The Journal of John Gaitha Browning* (Denton: University of North Texas Press, 1994); John Randolph, *Marsmen In Burma* (Houston: Gulf Publishing Co., 1946); Alfred R. Stone, *A Marine Remembers Iwo Jima: Dog Company, 2nd Battalion, 27th Marines, Fifth Marine Division* (Austin: Eakin Press, 2000); John Keith Wells, *"Give Me Fifty Marines Not Affair to Die": Iwo Jima* (Abilene, TX: Ka-Well Enterprises, 1995); and Richard Havens, comp., *Remembering Billy ... The Story of a West Texas Marine, His Friends, His Family and His Sacrifices—Told by Those Who Knew Him* (Lubbock: Flatland Press, 1994).

Other works providing material on Texans in the war in the Far East, 1942-1945 are Robert L. Sherrod, *Tarawa: The Story of A Battle* (Duell, Sloan, and Pearce, 1944); Robert L. Robertson, "A Texan At War: Sergeant Travis Moore, U.S. Marine Corps, 1942-1944," *Military History of the West* 30 (Fall 2000): 123-154; Richard B. Frank, *Guadalcanal: The Definitive Account of the Landmark Battle* (New York: Penguin Books, 1999); Lance Q. Zedrik, *Silent Warriors of World War II: The Alamo Scouts Behind Japanese Lines* (Ventura, CA: Pathfinder Publishing of California,1995); Robert B. Stinnett, *George Bush: His World War II Years* (Washington: Brassey's Inc., 1992); Charles A. Lockwood and Hans Christian Adamson, *Through Hell and Deep Water: The Stirring Story of the Navy's Deadly Submarine, the U.S. S. Harder, under the command of Sam Dealey, Destroyer Killer* (Philadelphia: Chilton Co., 1956); Clifton La Bree, *The Gentle Warrior: General Oliver Prince Smith USMA* (Kent, OH: Kent State University Press, 2001); Bill R. Ross, *Iwo Jima: Legacy of Valor* (New York: Random House, 1986); Richard Wheeler, *The Bloody Battle for Suribachi* (New York: Thomas Y. Crowell Co., 1965); James Bradley (with Ron Powers), *Flags of Our Fathers* (New York: Bantam Books, 2000); Gerald Astor, *Operation Iceberg: The Invasion and Conquest of Okinawa in World War II* (New York: Dell Publishing, 1995); and Paul W. Tibbets, *Flight of the "Enola Gay"* (Reynoldsburg, OH: Buckeye Aviation Book Company, 1989).

Several reference works furnish information on Texans in the war. The booklet *Texas Medal of Honor Recipients*, compiled by the Texas Veterans Commission (Austin, 1993), provides pertinent material and the citation for each of the Texans awarded the nation's highest military honor. *U.S. Submarine Veterans of World War II* (Dallas: Taylor Publishing Co., 1990) gives names, addresses, and brief biographical information on American submariners. A work prepared by the Czech Heritage Society, *Texas Veterans of Czech Ancestry* (Austin: Eakin Press, 1999), contains similar information for Texas Czech veterans. Paul Morin, *Among the Valiant: Mexican–Americans in World War II and Korea* (Alhambra, CA: Borden Publishing Co., 1966) provides information on Mexican Texas servicemen. The five volume *A History of the Second World War: A Memorial, A Remembrance, An Appreciation* (Dallas: Historical Publishing Co., 1948) contains hundreds of short sketches of Texans who served in the war. Shelby L. Stanton, *Ordeal of Battle, U.S. Army in World War II* (Novato, CA: Presidio Press, 1984) has information for every army, corps, division, and regiment of American ground forces in the war.

The various issues of the *Texas Almanac and State Industrial Guide* (Dallas: A. H. Belo Corp., 1941-1947) furnish valuable material on Texas' role in the war, both on the home and military fronts. The volume *1941: Texas Goes to War*, edited by James Ward Lee, et al. (Denton: University of North Texas Press,1991) is one of the finest works to appear on Texas participation in the war. The title is misleading as the book contains essays on all aspects of the war, from pre-Pearl Harbor to "Coming Home." The work is profusely illustrated with a gold mine of material relating to the role of Texas and Texans in the war.

Shipbuilding is discussed in Frederic C. Lane, *Ships for Victory: A History of Shipbuilding Under the U.S. Maritime Commission in World War II* (Baltimore: Johns Hopkins Press, 1951); Frank Karrpi, "Shipbuilding in Orange," in Howard C. Williams, ed., *Gateway to Texas: The History of Orange and Orange County* (Orange, TX: Heritage House Museum of Orange, 1988); William T. Faucett, *The Shipyard at Beaumont* (Beaumont, priv. printed, 1991); Rita Green, Joe Walker, and Marcus C. Robbins, *Beaumont at War: The Home Front, 1941-1945* (Beaumont, Tyrrell Historical Library, 1992); Marguerite Johnston, *Houston: The Unknown City, 1836-1946* (College Station: Texas A&M University Press, 1991); Robert H. Peebles, "Shipbuilding," in Ron Tyler, ed., *New Handbook of Texas*, 5: 1030; and Joseph A. Pratt and Christopher J. Castaneda, *Builders: George and Herman Brown* (College Station: Texas A&M University Press, 1999).

Diana Davids Olien and Roger M. Olien, *Oil in Texas: The Gusher Age, 1895-1945* (Austin: University of Texas Press, 2002), describe the importance of oil and oil products in the war effort. See also Roger Olien's article "Oil and Gas Industry," in the *New Handbook of Texas*, 4:1119-1128.

Louis B. Fairchild, ed., *They Called It The War Effort: Oral Histories From World War II, Orange, Texas* (Austin: Eakin Press, 1993) is an outstanding collection of interviews describing the transformation of a small Southeast Texas town from 7,500 to 60,000 residents in three years. Melanie Wiggins, *Torpedoes in the Gulf: Galveston and the U-Boats, 1942-1943* (College Station: Texas A&M University Press, 1995) discusses the impact of submarine threats upon the people of Galveston and the upper Texas coast. The role of the Civil Air Patrol, with units in Beaumont, Corpus Christi, and Brownsville, in patrolling the Texas coastline is described by Robert E. Neprud, *Flying Men: The Story of the Civil Air Patrol* (New York: Duell, Sloan, and Pearce, 1948) and Louis E. Keefer, *From Maine to Mexico: With America's Private Pilots in the Fight Against Nazi U-Boats* (Reston, VA: COTU Publishing, 1997). In an article "Memories of World War II," *East Texas Historical Journal* 30 (Spring 1992): 11-15, Buck Young recalls his experiences as a young schoolboy in Pelly (now Baytown), Texas, during the war.

The role of Texas women in the war has received considerable attention in recent years. Among these works are Charlotte A. Holliman, "Beaumont Women During World War II," *Texas Gulf Historical and Biographical Record* 31 (November 1995): 50-65; Donna Bonin, "Baytown's 'Rosie the Riveter'," in *From Humble Beginnings* (Exxon Baytown, 75th Anniversary, 1995), 50-58; Cynthia Guidici, "Women at War," in Lee, ed., *1941: Texas Goes to War* (mentioned above); Clarice F. Pollard, "WAACs in Texas During the Second World War," *Southwestern Historical Quarterly* 93 (July 1989): 61-74; Al Shire, comp. and ed., *Oveta Culp Hobby* (Houston: William P. Hobby and Jessica Hobby Cato, 1997); Julia Kirk Blackwelder, *Now Hiring: The Feminization of Work in the United States, 1900-1995* (College Station: Texas A&M University Press, 1997); William H. Chafe, *The American Woman: Her Changing Social, Economic, and Political Roles, 1920-1970* (New York: Oxford University Press, 1972); Judy Barrett Litoff and David C. Smith, eds., *We're In This War, Too: World War II Letters from American Women in Uniform* (New York: Oxford University Press, 1994); Jeanne Holm, *Women in the Military: An Unfinished Revolution* (Novato, CA: Presidio Press, 1982); and Mattie E. Treadwill, *The Women's Army Corps* (Washington: Office of the Chief of Military History, 1954).

The Women's Airforce Service Pilots (WASP) were trained in Texas and included a number of Texas women. Their experiences are described in Anne Noggle, *For God, Country, and the Thrill of It: Women Airforce Service Pilots in World War II* (College Station: Texas A&M University Press, 1990); Amy Nathan, *Yankee Doodle Gals: Women Pilots of World War II* (Washington: National Geographic Society, 2001); Cindy Weigand, "Yankee Doodle Gals of World War II," *Texas Co-Op Power* (June 2002): 12-15; Sally Van Wagenen Kiel, *Those Wonderful Women in Their Flying Machines* (New York: Four Directions Press, 1990); Doris Brinker Tanner, comp., *Who Were the WASP?* (Sweetwater, TX: *Sweetwater Daily Reporter*, 1989); Melinda Rice, "The Sky Was No Limit," *Texas Highways* (November 2002), 43-49; Molly Merryman, *Clipped Wings: The Rise and Fall of the Women Airforce Service Pilots* (New York: New York University, 1998); Ann B. Carl, *A WASP Among Eagles: A Woman Military Test Pilot in World War II* (Washington: Smithsonian Institution Press, 1999); Henry F. Snapp, "Pioneer Women in West Texas Skies," *West Texas Historical Association Year Book* 70 (1994): 19-39; and Alberta Fitzpatrick Head, "General Arnold Comes to Avenger Field," *Ibid.* 50 (1974): 92-103.

Robert W. Kirk, *Earning Their Stripes: The Mobilization of American Children in the Second World War* (New York: Peter Lang, 1994); William M. Tuttle, Jr., *"Daddy's Gone to War": The Second World War in the Lives of America's Children* (New York: Oxford University Press, 1993); and Sally Strange, "Love, Marriage & The Family," in Lee, ed., *1941: Texas Goes to War*, provide insights into the effects of the war upon children and families.

Organized sports continued to be important even in wartime. Among works describing Texas athletic events are Kern Tips, *Football–Texas Style, An Illustrated History of the Southwest Conference* (Garden City, NY: Doubleday & Co., 1964); Bill McMurray, *Texas High School Football* (South Bend, IN: Icarus Press, 1985); Howard V. Ratliff, *Autumn's Mightiest Legions: History of Texas Schoolboy Football* (Waco: Texian Press, 1963); Ty Cashion, *Pigskin Pulpit: A Social History of Texas High School Football Coaches* (Austin: Texas State Historical Association, 1998); and Bill O'Neal, *The Texas League, 1888-1987: A Century of Baseball* (Austin: Eakin Press, 1987).

Several general works provide additional information on the Texas, and national, home front during the war. Particularly useful for this study were Richard R. Lingeman, *Don't You Know*

There's A War On: The American Home Front, 1941-1945 (New York: G. P. Putnam's Sons, 1970); Geoffrey Perret, *Days of Sadness, Years of Triumph* (Baltimore, MD: Penguin Books, 1974); and Lee Kennett, *For the Duration . . . The United States Goes to War: Pearl Harbor–1942* (New York: Charles Scribner's Sons, 1985).

Texas labor problems during the war are described in Johnny M. McCain, "Texas and the Mexican Labor Question, 1942-1947," *Southwestern Historical Association* 85 (July 1981): 45-64; Charles D. Chamberlain, *Victory at Home: Manpower and Race in the American South during World War II* (Athens, GA: University of Georgia Press, 2003); Charles D. Chamberlain, III, "'On The Train and Gone': Worker Mobility in the Rural Southwest During World War II, 1939-1945," *Southwestern Historical Quarterly* 103 (April 2000): 427-451; Richard B. Craig, *The Bracero Program: Interest Groups and Foreign Policy* (Austin: University of Texas Press, 1971); Otey Scruggs, "Texas and the Bracero Program, 1942-1947," *Pacific Historical Review* 32 (August 1963): 251-264; Marcus Robbins, "'Our Inalienable Right': A Brief History of Locals 229 and 245, Oil Workers International Union, Magnolia Refinery, 1937-1945," *Texas Gulf Historical and Biographical Record* 39 (1993): 55-68; and Ernest Obadele-Starks, *Black Unionism in the Industrial South* (College Station: Texas A&M University Press, 2000).

Emilio Zamora, "The Failed Promise of Wartime Opportunity for Mexicans in the Texas Oil Industry," *Southwestern Historical Quarterly* 95 (January 1992), 323-350, notes that Mexican workers made little job advancement in the oil industry during the war. Alwyn Barr, *Black Texans: A History of African Americans in Texas, 1528-1995* (Orig.publ.1973; Norman: University of Oklahoma Press, 1996) points out that the number of black industrial workers almost doubled during the war, but Obadele-Starks, *Black Unionism in the Industrial South* (above) and Merl Reed, "The FEPC, the Black Worker, and the Southern Shipyards," *South Atlantic Quarterly* 74 (Autumn 1975): 445-467, show there was much discrimination in hiring, job assignment, and wages paid to minority workers.

Racial problems in Texas are described in James A. Burran, "Violence in an 'Arsenal of Democracy': The Beaumont Race Riot, 1943," *East Texas Historical Journal* 14 (Spring 1976): 39-52; James S. Olson and Sharon Phair, "Anatomy of a Race Riot: Beaumont, Texas, 1943," *Texana*, 2 (No. 1, 1973): 66-71; Patrick J. Carroll, *Felix Longoria's Wake: Bereavement, Racism, and the Rise of Mexican American Activism* (Austin: University of Texas Press, 2003); David J. Montejano, *Anglos and Mexicans in the Making of Texas, 1836-1936* (Austin: University of Texas Press, 1987); and Ignacio M. Garcia, *Hector P. Garcia: In Relentless Pursuit of Justice* (Houston: Arte Publico Press, 2002). The racial incident at Fort Hood involving Lieutenant Jackie Robinson is covered in his own *I Never Had It Made: A Biography* (New York: G. P. Putnam's Sons, 1972), Arnold Rampersad, *Jackie Robinson: A Biography* (New York: Alfred A. Knopf, 1997), and in *The 761st "Black Panther Tank Battalion* (mentioned earlier). Darlene Clark Hine in "The Elusive Ballot: The Black Struggle Against the Texas Democratic White Primary, 1932-1945," *Southwestern Historical Quarterly* 81 (April 1978): 371-392; "Blacks and the Destruction of the Democratic White Primary, 1935-1944," *Journal of Negro History* 62 (1977): 43-59, and *Black Victory: The Rise and Fall of the White Primary in Texas* (Millwood, NY: KTO Press, 1979) describes the successful struggle of Texas African Americans to vote in Texas primary elections.

George Norris Green, *The Establishment in Texas Politics: The Primitive Years, 1938-1957* (Westport, CT: Greenwood Press, 1979) provides a thorough account of Texas politics during the war years. In addition, see Seth S. McKay, *W. Lee O'Daniel and Texas Politics, 1938-1942* (Lubbock: Texas Technological Press, 1944); McKay, *Texas Politics, 1906-1944* (Lubbock: Texas Technological Press, 1952); Roger M. Olien, "The Republican Party of Texas, 1920-1961" (Ph.D. dissertation, Brown University, 1973); Olien, *From Token to Triumph: The Texas Republicans Since 1920* (Dallas: Southern Methodist University Press, 1982); Paul Casdorph, *The Republican Party in Texas, 1865-1965* (Austin: Pemberton Press, 1965); Kenneth E. Hendrickson, Jr., and Michael L. Collins, eds., *Profiles in Power: Twentieth Century Texans in Washington* (Arlington Heights, IL: Harlan Davidson, 1993); Hendrickson, *The Chief Executive of Texas, from Stephen F. Austin to John B. Connally, Jr.* (College Station: Texas A&M University Press, 1995); and Fred Gantt, Jr., *The Chief Executive in Texas: A Study in Gubernatorial Leadership* (Austin:

University of Texas Press, 1964). Valuable election data and other insights into Texas politics is found in Mike Kingston, Sam Attlesey, and Mary G. Crawford, *The Texas Almanac's Political History of Texas* (Austin: Eakin Press, 1992).

Numerous biographies of Texas political leaders in Washington are available. Most helpful in this study were C. Dwight Dorough, *Mr. Sam* (New York: Random House, 1962); D. B. Hardeman and Donald C. Bacon, *Rayburn: A Political Biography* (Austin: Texas Monthly Press, 1981); Tom Connally and Alfred Steinberg, *My Name Is Tom Connally* (New York: Thomas Y. Crowell, 1954); Nancy Beck Young, *Wright Patman: Populism, Liberalism & the American Dream* (Dallas: Southern Methodist University Press, 2000); Richard Henderson, *Maury Maverick: A Political Biography* (Austin: University of Texas Press, 1970); Robert Dallek, *Lone Star Rising: Lyndon Johnson and His Times, 1908-1960* (New York: Oxford University Press, 1991). Robert A. Caro's *The Years of Lyndon Johnson: Means of Ascent* (New York: Alfred A. Knopf, 1990) has considerable information but must be used with care due to the author's dislike of his subject and his failure to understand the complexities of Texas politics.

Don E. Carleton, *A Breed So Rare: The Life of J. R. Parten, Liberal Texas Oil Man, 1896-1992* (Austin: Texas State Historical Association, 1998), provides a thorough account of the hiring and firing of University of Texas president Homer P. Rainey as well as considerable information on energy matters both in Texas and Washington, D. C.. The Rainey story is also described in Alice Cox, "The Rainey Affair: A History of the Academic Freedom Controversy at the University of Texas, 1938-1946" (Ph. D. dissertation, University of Denver, 1970); and Rainey's own *The Tower and the Dome: A Free University Versus Political Control* (Boulder, CO: Pruett Publishing, 1971).

Texas housed more prisoners of war than any other state. A thorough account of this subject nationally is Arnold P. Krammer, *Nazi Prisoners of War in America* (Reprint, Lanham, MD: Scarborough House, 1996). For Texas, Richard P. Walker, *The Lone Star and the Swastika: Prisoners of War in Texas* (Austin: Eakin Press, 2001) is the most complete study but should be supplemented by Arnold P. Krammer, "When the Afrika Korps Came to Texas," *Southwestern Historical Quarterly* 80 (January 1977): 247-283; Robert Tissig, "Stalag Texas, 1943-1945," *Military History of Texas and the Southwest* 13 (Fall 1976): 23-34; Mark Choate, *Nazis In The Piney Woods* (Lufkin: Best of East Texas Publishers, 1989); Donald Mace Williams, *Interlude in Umbarger: Italian POWs and a Texas Church* (Lubbock: Texas Tech University Press, 1992); Joe D. Robbins, "Camp Hereford: Italian Prisoners on the Texas Plains, 1942-1945," *Panhandle Plains Historical Review* 62 (1989): 57-110; James Richard Keen, "The Captive Enemy? Italian Prisoners of War in Texas during World War II" (M. A. thesis, University of Texas of the Permian Basis, 1988); James S. Myers, "Prisoners of War at Camp Barkeley," *West Texas Historical Association Year Book* 61 (1985): 134-140; and Michael R. Waters, *Lone Star Stalag: German Prisoners of War at Camp Hearn* (College Station, Texas, A&M University Press, 2004).

Thomas K. Walls, *The Japanese Texans* (San Antonio: Institute of Texan Cultures, 1987) provides information on the treatment of the state's Japanese residents during the war. This should be supplemented by articles in the *New Handbook of Texas* by Emily Brosveen, "World War II Internment Camps," 6: 1082, and Robert H. Thonhoff, "Kenedy Alien Detention Camp," 3: 1066-1067, Thonhoff, *Camp Kenedy, Texas* (Austin: Eakin Press, 2003), and interviews with Japanese Americans of Southeast Texas in Fairchild, ed., *They Called It The War Effort*, cited above. Karen Lea Riley, *Schools Behind Barbed Wire: The Untold Story of Wartime Internment and the Children of Arrested Enemy Aliens* (Lanham MD: Rowan & Littlefield Publishers, 2002), describes in detail the schools at the Crystal City Internment facility.

In addition to oral interviews published in various works listed above, interviews by the author with veterans Dan Dennis, Bert Norris, Gene Priest, Lonnie Hood, Philip Latimer, Joe Stewart, Thomas Floyd (cited in footnotes) were helpful in providing first-hand views of the war. Floyd and W. T. Block also gave the author copies of manuscripts describing their wartime experiences. The transcript of an interview by Valerie Domingue with her grandfather, B. B. Majors, added information on the building of the Ledo-Burma road. Interviews with local veterans by W. T. Block published in the *Beaumont Enterprise* and clippings from the *Liberty Vindicator* furnished by Wallisville Heritage Director Kevin Ladd were most helpful.

The various annual reports of the Director of Selective Service for the war years list the number of Texans conscripted as well as the number who volunteered. Casualty figures were provided by the Center of Military History, U.S. Army, the Bureau of Naval Personnel, the Historical Center of the U.S. Marine Corps, and the U.S. Coast Guard Historical Office. The Operational Archives Branch, Naval Historical Center, provided biographical information on naval personnel.

Index

—A—
Abernethy, Francis, 170,171, 174
Abernethy, Hazel Shelton, 14, 174
Abilene Air Field, 33
Adams, Lucian, 140, 174 187
Adams, Lytle S., 33
Advanced Navigator Training School, 29
agriculture, 39
Aiken, Bruce, 171
Aikin, A.M., 116, 174
Akagi, Fukutaro, 118
Alamo Scouts, 128
Albacore, 129
Alford, Parker, 134
Allen, Fred, 99
Allen, Ray C., 146
Allen, Roderick R., 160, 174
Allen, Terry de la Mesa, 63
Allred, James, 106, 107
Aloe Army Air Field, 33
Amarillo Army Air Field, 33
Ambrose, Stephen, 137
American Women's Volunteer Services, 95
Anderson, Adrian, vii
Anderson, D., 86
Anderson, Margaret, 94
Andrews, Dana, 5
Antonesu, Ion, 68
Ardery, Philip 14, 69
Arizmendi, Ubaldo, 14
Arizona, 16, 18, 20, 21
Arkansas, 135
Arledge Field, 29
Army Aerial Gunnery School, 30
Army Corps of Engineers, 28

Arnold, H. H. "Hap," 55, 60, 71
Arnspiger, Herman, 4
Asburn General Hospital, 34
Ashlock, William "Tex," 145
Atkins, William Tom, 44
Austin, Paul, 14, 153, 163, 174
Autry, Gene, 98, 99
Avai, Saburo, 119
Avenger Field, 31

—B—
Bacom, Julia Wingate, 82
Balfanz, W. W. "Dub," 44
Barre, Agnes, 53
Barre, Lester J., 50
Bat Out of Hell, 56
Bataan Death March, 53
bat-bomb experiment, 33
Bates, Paul L., 117
Battle of the Bulge, 146
Baugh, Sammy, 6
Beaham, Kermit, 171, 175
Beall, Marion, 153
Beckworth, Lindley, 8
Beech, Joe, 170
Beeville Naval Air Station, 34
Belfabio, Guiseppe, 125
Bennett Aircraft Corp, 37
Bennett, Joseph W., 143
Bennett, Leon, 19
Bennett, Wayland, 79
Benny, Jack, 99
Bergstrom Army Air Field, 33
Bergstrom, John, 33
Berlin, Irving, 99

Berry, Noah, Jr., 98
B. F. Goodrich, 36
Bickett, John, 101
Bickford, Clara Mae, 53
Biddle, Francis, 115
Big Inch, 36
Biggs Army Air Field 1, 29
Biggs, James B., 29
Black, Evelyn, 53
Blackland Army Air Field, 31
Blanton, Thadd, 55
Blaylock, Tom, 53
Bliss, William W., 24
Block, Harlan, 167, 175
Block, W. T., vi, 159
Blondell, Joan, 5
Blount, R. E. "Peppy," 165, 175
Blumenson, Martin, 131
Boeing, 41
Boesch, Paul, 142, 175
Bologna, Sirico, 125
Bordelon, William, 78, 187
Borrega, Trinidad, 66
Bowers, LuQuincy, 173
Bowie, 170
Box, Ves, 5
Boyd, Sylvia, 90
Boynington, Gregory "Pappy," 79
Bradley, Omar ,138, 139, 162
Brantley, Hattie, 53
Brayton Flying Service, 29
Brereton, Lewis, 43, 144
Brewery Wagon, 68
Briggs, Cullen W., 41
Brin, Leonard M., 114
Britt, Richard, 69
Brooke General and Convalescence Hospital, 34
Brooks Field, 28
Brooks, Sidney Johnson, Jr., 28
Brown and Root, 39
Brown Shipbuilding Co., 38
Brown, Cecil, 98
Brown, Ellis C., 116
Brown, Herman, 110
Brown, Johnny Mack, 98
Brown, Milton, 4
Browning, John, 175
Brownshadel, Elton J., 134
Bruce Field, 29
Bruce, Andrew D., 26, 129, 154, 169, 175
Bryan Army Air Field, 34
Bryant, Frankie M., 44
Buchanan, Al, 107
Buck, Walter, 73
Buckner, Simon Bolivar, 169

Bullington, Orville, 175
Burris, Myra V., 53
Burrus Mills, 4
Bush, George H.W., 34, 128

—C—

Cabanis Field, 34
Cabell, Charles P., 143
California, 18, 21
Calvert, Bob, 96
Calvert, Wilbert A., 150
Cameron Iron Works, 39
Camp Barkeley, 72
Camp Bullis, 24
Camp Fannin, 26
Camp Hood, 25, 117
Camp Howze, 25, 26
Camp Hulen, 23, 25
Camp Maxey, 25, 26
Camp Meade (Maryland), 72
Camp Swift, 25, 26
Camp Wallace, 25
Camp Wolters, 24, 25, 72
Campbell, Robert L., 68
Campbell, Suzanne, vii
Canfield, Ivan, 68
Cantu, Jesse, 137
Caradja, Catherina, 69
Carmichael, Richard, 21, 151
Caro, Robert, 110, 113
Carrico, Carl, 73
Carswell, Horace, 151, 187
Cassin, 19
Castaneda, Carlos E., 114
Catey, Drate H., 137, 175
Cavalla, 129
Chappell, Lucius, 79
Chennault, Claire, 12, 66, 175
Chiang Kai-shek, 10, 151
Childress Army Air Field, 34
Chunn, Banker D., 117
Churchill, Winston, 61, 67
Cities Service Toledo, 86
Civil Air Patrol, 86, 95
Clarey, Bernard A., 150
Clark, Mark, 73, 129, 131, 132, 157
Clark, Tom, 112, 175
Clarkson, Percy W., 164
Clymer, J. R., 39
Cochran, Jacqueline, 31, 94
Coffey, Ruth, 95, 176
Colburn, Monroe, 84
Cole, Robert G., 135, 137, 187
Coleman Field, 29
Coleman, John S., 51, 53

Collins, Rip, 165
Combs, Cecil E., 47
Combs, Jesse M., 109
Connally, James T., 47
Connally, Tom, 7, 8, 9, 10, 12, 22, 25, 47, 105, 176
Consolidated Aircraft Corp., 37, 38
Consolidated Western Steel, 38
Cooper, Carroll, 145
Cooper, Gary, 5, 14
Corpus Christi Naval Air Station, 34
Corsicana Field, 29
Cory, James, 16, 176
Cox, Catherine, VII
Crain, Edward L., 153
Crain, Jack, 6
Crecy, Warren G. H., 142, 176
Cronkite, John, 63, 134
Crosby, Bing, 97, 98
Crosland, Don "Shorty," 44
Crossing of the Rhine, 159
Crow, Valeta, 13
Cuddihy Field, 34
Cullen, Hugh Roy, 107
Culp, Willis, 44
Cummings, 19
Cunningham, Minnie Fisher, 113
Curtis Field, 30
Curtis, Henry, 30
Curtiss, 19, 21

—D—
Dahlquist, John, 139
Dakota Queen, 145
Dale, Wayne, 165
Dallas, 62
Dallas Negro Chamber of Commerce, 115
Dallas, Bill, 14, 148
Daniel, Chal, 6
Darnell, Linda, 5
David McKelvy, 86
Davidson, Howard, 165
Davidson, Millie, 94
Davis, Chester, 104
Davis, Elmer, 4
Davis, George A., 78, 176
Davis, Richard G., 72
Dawson, Joe, 137
D-Day, 134
Dealey, Samuel, 80, 129, 150, 187
Dean, John H., 87
Del Valle Army Air Base, 33
DeLeon, Guillermo, 132
Demaret, Jimmie, 97
DeMille, Cecil B., 4

Dennis, Dan, vi, 13, 144, 176
detention camps, 120
Dethloff, Henry C., 98
Devereux, James P. S., 46
Dewey, Thomas E., 109
Dicky, Ross, 116
Dies, Martin, 9, 108, 109, 111, 176
DiMaggio, Joe, 6
Dimiceli, Vito, 13
Dobie, J. Frank, 113
Domingue, Valerie Majors, vi
Donaho, Glynn Robert, 79
Donnell, Earl, 54, 55
Dooley, Tom, 51
Doolittle, James H. "Jimmy," 28, 55, 72, 143
Dos Passos, John, 101
Dowdy, Avery, 73
Downes, 19
Drake, James T., 43, 44
Dreskin, Clarice Ann, 94
Du Pont, 41
Dugas, Louis, 82
Duke, Lee Herwin, 19
Duncan, Glenn, 143
Duncan, Robert F., 44
Dunning, John A., 165, 176
Dupont, Herman, 168, 176, 176
Dutchess, 67
Dworsky, Bertha, 53
Dyess Field, 33
Dyess, William Edwin, 33, 44, 53, 54

—E—
Eagle Pass Army Field, 31
Eaker, Ira, 60, 61, 69, 72, 143, 144, 145
Easley, Claudius, 169
Easley, Mary Carlson, 90
East Texas Electric Steel Co., 37
Easterling, Dorcas E., 53
Eastwood, Mary Walker, 90
Eatherly, Claude, 171
Eddy, Manton S., 142
Edwards, Heywood "Tex," 13
Eichelberger, Robert, 163
Eighth Air Force, vi, 59, 60, 61, 67, 71, 72, 143, 143, 144, 145
8th Infantry Division, 142
8th Marine Regiment, 64
18th Battalion of the Texas State Guard, 116
81st Infantry Division, 152
82nd Airborne Division, 72
83rd Infantry Division, 162
84th Infantry Division, 26
86th Infantry Division, 26
86th Observation Squadron, 21

88th Infantry Division, 25
89th Reconnaissance Squadron, 55
893rd Tank Destroyer Battalion, 140
Eisenhower, Dwight D., 13, 59, 72, 162
11th Armored Division, 25
Elgin Field, 55
Elkins, Ronald, 63
Ellender, Allen, 9
Ellington Field, 28
Ellington, Eric, 28
Ellison, Emit "Tex," 66
Enola Gay, 170
Enterprise, 54, 55, 58
European theater, 59
Everhardt, Forrest E., 140, 176, 187
Ewart, Arley, 80
Ewell, Julian, 134, 146

—F—
Fails, Eula R., 53
Fairchild, Marguerite, 101, 176
Fan, Leslie, 20
Farah, James, 39
Farah, William, 39
Farrow, William, 56
Faulkner, Melvin, 20
Fenoglio, Melvin, 170
Ferguson, John T., 118
Ferguson, Miriam, 101
Fertile Myrtle II, 71
Fertitta, Joseph F., 147
Fields, James H., 140, 177, 187
Fields, Wallace, 78
5th Armored Division, 162
5th Fighter Group, 165
Fifth Fleet, 128
5th Marine Division, 166, 167, 168
Fifteenth Air Force, 144, 145
15th Infantry Regiment, 73
51st Fighter Group, 67
55th Fighter Group, 143
56th Fighter Group, 143
501st Parachute Infantry, 146
502nd Parachute Infantry Regiment, 135
517th Parachute Regimental Combat Team, 139
596th Airborne Engineer Company, 139
1st Airborne Task Force, 139
1st Armored Division, 62, 133
1st Battalion, 6th Marines, 78
1st Bomb Wing, 69, 70
1st Cavalry Division, 24, 153, 164, 170
1st Infantry Division, 62, 63, 72, 77, 137
1st Marine Division, 152, 153, 169, 169
First Special Service Force, 77

Fisher, Clark, 109
Fitzhugh, William, 55
Fitzpatrick, Charles C., 49
Fletcher, Jack, 54
Floyd, Tom, vi, 159, 177
Flying Fish, 79
Flying Tigers, 66
Fomby, William W., 16, 177
Fontaine, Joan, 5
Forrest, John, 139
Forsythe, John D., 74
Forsythe, Paul, 57
Fort Bliss, 24
Fort Brown, 24
Fort Clark, 24
Fort D. A. Russell, 24
Fort McIntosh, 24
Fort Ringgold, 24
Fort Sam Houston, 24
Fort Travis, 28
Fort Worth Army Air Field, 33
Foster Army Air Field, 30
Foulois, Benjamin, 28
4th Armored Division, 140, 146, 161
4th Bomb Wing, 69
4th Infantry Division, 135, 137, 140, 143
4th Marine Division, 128, 134, 166, 168
Fourteenth Air Force, 151
14th Armored Division, 157
43rd Infantry Division, 65, 66, 163
45th Bombardment Wing, 143
45th Infantry Division, 25, 72, 76, 127, 132, 138, 139, 143, 160, 162
401st Field Artillery Group, 159, 171
435th Bomber Squadron, 78
442nd Regimental Combat Team, 119, 143
444th Bomb Group, 151
445th Bomb Group, vi, 144
447th Bombardment Group, 143
455th Bomb Group, 145
486th Bomb Group, vi, 144
492nd Bombardment Group, 145
499th Armored First Artillery, 157
Fowler, Thomas, 133, 187
Frazier, Everett, 78
Fredendall, Lloyd, 61
Frederick, Robert E., 77
Fujita, Frank, 119, 177
Fuller, Hurley E., 146

—G—
Gable, Clark, 5
Galveston Army Air Field, 33
Gambier Bay, 154
Gantt, Fred, Jr., 114

Garcia, Alfredo, 161
Garcia, Hector, 173
Garcia, Marcario, 140, 173, 177, 187
Garner Field, 29
Garner, John Nance, 10, 107, 111, 177
Garner, Roy "Tex," 154
Garson, Greer, 98
Garza, Fred, 152, 172, 177
Gaskell, Charles A., 44
Gay, George, 14, 58, 177
Gee, James W., 50
General Tire and Rubber Co., 36
George, Walter, 105
Germany, E. B., 107
Gibbs Field, 31
Giles, Barney M., 71, 177
Giles, Benjamin, 71
Gilmore, Howard, 80
Girad, Henry J., 152
Goodfellow Field, 30
Goodwin, Doris, 161
Goodyear, 36
Gray, Robert M. "Bob," 55
Grayling, 47
Great Depression, 1, 41
Green Hornet, 56
Green, Charles Clinton, 63
Greer, 13
Groce, Jim, 152
Grouper, 80
Grover, Orrin, 44
Groves, Stella, 90
Gulf Trade, 86
Gulfamerica, 86
Gulfpenn, 86
Gunn, Stanley, 153

—H—
Haddo, 150
Haggar, J. M., 39
Haines, Harry, 160, 177
Hall Aluminum Aircraft Corp., 37
Hall, Leonard, 65, 163, 177
Hallmark, Dean, 55, 56
Halsey, William, 54, 55, 154
Hamby, Thornton, 54, 148
Hampton, Charles, 66
Hanley, Fiske, 178
Hardegree, Howard, 44
Harder, 81, 129, 150
Hardison, Richard, 161
Hargrove, Marion, 100
Harker, C. E., 86
Harkness, 170, 171
Harlingen Field, 30

Harmon, 64
Harmon General Hospital, 34
Harmon, Leonard R., 64
Harper, Charles, 151
Harrell, William, 168, 178, 187
Harrington, Harold, 84
Harris, Hunter, Jr., 143
Harris, James L., 140, 187
Harris, Lynn, 178
Hart, Tommy, 49
Hascke, Marvin, 55
Hatchitt, Eunice C., 53
Hatfield, Richard, 166
Havens, Billy, 170
Havens, Weldon William, 169
Hawkins, William Dean, 77, 187
Hawthorne, Cooper, 134
Headquarters Squadron, 44
Heard, Herman, 143
Hearn, Jack, 46
Heatter, Gabriel, 98
Henderson, Bertis, 161
Henderson, Leon, 104, 112
Henningsen Co., 39
Henry, James D., 44
Hensley Field, 35, 37
Henson, Verna V., 53
Herndon, Nolan, 55
Herrera, Silvestre, 158, 187
Hicks Field, 29
Hicks, George, 98
Higgins, Ken, 145
Hilger, John A., 55
Hill, David L. "Tex," 65
Hindman, E. James, vi
Hinson, Robert, 44
Hiroshima, 170
Hitchcock Naval Air Station, 35
Hite, Robert, 55, 56, 178
Hitler, Adolf, 146, 155
Hobby, Oveta Culp, 25, 92, 93, 178
Hobby, William P., 25, 92
Hobrecht, Forrest, 44, 45
Hock, Herman, 50
Hodge, Harry, 134
Hodges, Courtney, 138
Hogan, Ben, 97
Hogan, Sam, 146
Holcombe, Oscar, 39
Holly, Bernard, 167
Holmes, Charles, 46
Homma, Masaharu, 51
Hondo Army Air Field, 31
Hood, John B., 26
Hood, Lonnie, vi, 78, 178

Hoover, Herbert, 111
Hope, Bob, 97, 98
Horn, Arlie, 137, 178
Hornet, 55, 57, 58
Horton, Gerd, 99
Hottelet, Richard, 98
Houston, 50, 51, 54, 148
Houston Shipbuilding Corp., 38
Hughes Field, 31
Hughes Tool. Corp., 37
Hughes, Hazel, 69
Hughes, Howard R., Jr., 37, 178
Hughes, Lloyd H., 69, 187
Hughett, Maurice, 44
Hulsey, Earl A., 44
Humble Oil Co., 35, 90
Hutchins, Johnnie, 77, 187

—I—
Ickes, Harold, 35, 104
Ilfrey, Jack, 63
income tax, 105
Iwo Jima, 165

—J—
Jackson, Leonard, 145
James, D. Clayton, 54
Jamison, Joseph D., 129
Jenkins, Jack, 143
Jingu, Alice, 119
Jingu, Kim, 119
Johnson, Hiram, 9
Johnson, John, 116
Johnson, Luther, 8, 10, 178
Johnson, Lyndon, 8, 10, 109, 109, 110, 111, 173, 178
Jones, Charles H., 76
Jones, Jesse, 111, 113, 178
Jones, Marvin, 104, 113, 179
Jose Carioca, 68
Joyner, Durwood, 53

—K—
Kaiser, 41
Kallus, Edward, 163
Kaltenborn, H.V., 4, 98
kamikaze, 154
Kane, John R., 69, 187
Kawamura, Mutsuo, 119
Kearby, Neel E., 77, 187
Kearny, 13
Keathley, George D., 139, 187
Kelly Field, 1, 9, 24, 28, 60, 91, 114
Kelly, George, 28
Kelly, Jack, 18, 179

Kennedy, Joe, 145
Kennedy, John F., 145
Kennett, Lee, 39
Kenney, Nat, 165
Kepner, Brigadier General William, 71
Kesner, Sam, 63
Keyes, Geoffrey, 131, 132
Kilcher, Oscar C., 64
Kimball, Warren F., 10
Kimbro, Truman, 187
Kimmel, Husband, 12, 46
King Michael of Rumania, 68
King, Ernest J., 55, 61
Kingsville Naval Air Station, 34
Kishi, Kitimatsu, 118
Kishi, Taro, 118
Kleberg, Richard M., 108, 109, 111, 179
Knight, Curtis, 165
Knight, Jack L., 165, 187
Knight, Raymond, 157, 187
Knowles, Samuel "Tex," 67
Knox, Frank, 22, 34, 46
Koger, Fred, 179
Kosan, Ernie, 139
Koym, Alfred, 87
Krammer, Arnold, 124, 126
Krueger, Walter, 13, 59, 65, 78, 127, 153, 163
Kutner, Mal, 6
Kuykendall, Matthew, 67

—L—
La Guardia, Fiorello H., 85
Lale, Max, 159, 179
Lamesa Field, 31
Lamore, Tommy, 148
Landrum, Eugene, 137
Lanham, Fritz, 110, 179
LaPrade, Robert, 64
LaSueur, Larry, 98
Latimer, Philip, vi, 14, 117, 179
Layden, Pete, 6
Le Fan, Leslie, 179
Lea, Tom, 152, 179
League of United Latin American Citizens (LULAC), 115
Lear, Ben, 13
Leigh, Vivian, 5
LeMay, Curtis, 67, 69, 70
Lend Lease Bill, 10
Leonard, Turney, 114, 187
Levingston shipbuilder, 38
Lewey, Frankie T., 53
Lewis, Bill, 138
Lewis, Spencer, 54, 55
Lexington, 57, 129

Light Crust Doughboys, 4
Little, 170
Lockridge, Patricia, 161
Logan, James M., 76, 187
Lone Star Ammunition plant, 37
Lone Star Steel Co., 37
Longhorn Army Ammunition plant, 37
Longoria, Felix, 173
Lopez, Jose M., 147, 187
Lost Battalion, v, 50, 54, 143
Louis, Joe, 5
Lovett, Robert, 71, 112, 179
Lowry, James W., 171
Lubbock Army Air Field, 30
Lucas, John, 132
Lufkin Foundry Machine Co., 38
Lukas, Paul, 98
Lummus, Jack, 168, 187
Lyle, John E., Jr., 108

—M—
MacArthur, Douglas, 43, 51, 59, 64, 65, 110, 127, 128, 150, 153, 171
MacKelvie, Jay W., 138
Madaras Steel Corp., 27
Magnolia Refinery, 90
Majors Field, 31, 45
Majors, B. B., vi, 109
Majors, Buford B. 152, 179
Majors, Truett, 44, 45
Mangrum, Lloyd, 97
Mann, Gerald, 113
Manning, Stephen Neal, 63
Mansfield, Joseph, 10, 110
Marble, Hugh H., 44
Marblehead, 50
Marcus, Sally Craighead, 95
Marfa Air Field, 33
Marfa Army Air Field, 33
Marine Squadron, 214 79
Marrett, Sam H., 44, 45
Marshall, George C., 61, 92
Marshall, Mary, 84
Martin, Freddy, 6
Martin, Ila, 90
Martin, Mary, 5
Martin, William H., 74, 131
Martindale, Robert R., 148, 180
Maryland, 16
Mathews, Forest, vii
Mathis, Jack W., 67, 187
Matula, Emil, 20, 163
Maverick, Maury, 9, 112, 180
Mayborn, Frank W., 26
Maynard, Ken, 5

McAuliffe, Anthony, 146
McCarthy, Joseph, 111
McCloskey General Hospital, 34
McCown, John L., 44
McDowell, C. K., 113
McElroy, Edward E., 55
McGovern, George, 145
McGowen, John R. C., 128
McKee, Heleln K., 94
McLain, Raymond, 138
McMurtry, Paul James, 21
McNamara, James, Jr., 139
Medina, Refugio, 148
Melody Maids, 95
Memphis Belle, 67, 70
Mendenhall, Corwin, 79, 150, 180
Midland Army Air Field, 30
Midland Army Flying School, 30
Midway, 56
Milam, Eloise, 95
Miles, Robert, 58
Miller, Ann, 5
Miller, Doris, 15, 20
Mississippi, 79
Missouri, 171
Mitchell, Johnny, 180
Mitchell, Willard, 65
Mitscher, Marc, 129
Mock, Paul O., 44
Molina, Shawn, vii
Monsanto Chemical Co., 36
Montague, Charlie, 78
Montgomery, Bernard L., 73
Moody, Dan, 106, 107
Moore Field, 30
Moore, Donald J., 79
Moore, Fred Kenneth, 21
Moore, George, 50
Moore, Harry, 132
Moore, Travis, 64, 128
Morgan, John Clay, 68, 180, 187
Morgan, Robert, 67
Morison, Samuel Eliot, 154
Moseley, Stanley P., 49
Mott, Darlene, vii
Mountbatten, Lord Louis, 62
Mueller, Alvin, Jr., 49
Munger T. Ball, 86
Murphy, Audie, 72, 127, 142, 156, 160, 180, 187
Murray, Raymond, 78
Murrow, Edward R., 98
Musick, Clay 18, 180
Musil, Joseph S., 152
Muta, Hideo, 119

—N—
Nagai, Ken, 119
National Housing Authority, 85
Naugle, Dave, 13
Nelson, Byron, 97
Nelson, Constance E., 118
Nelson, Donald, 90, 104
Neosho, 19
Nevada, 18, 21, 135
New Deal, 104
New Mexico, 170
New Orleans, 19
Nicol, James C., 44
Nies, Emma Jane, 84
Nimitz, Chester W., 15, 46, 47, 48, 54, 55, 65, 150, 171, 180,
9th Cavalry Regiment, 24
9th Infantry Division, 62, 72
19th Bombardment Group, 34
19th Bomber Squadron, 78
90th Infantry Division, 25, 127, 138, 140, 143
91st Coast Artillery, 45
95th Infantry Division, 25, 26
96th Army Division, 169
96th Bomb Group, 70
96th Infantry Division, 153
97th Bombardment Group, 61
97th Infantry Division, 26
98th Bombardment Group, 69
99th Fighter Squadron, 145
99th Infantry Division, 146
Ninth Air Force, 68, 144
Norris, Bert, vi
Norris, Edwin, 137
North American Aviation and Corp., 37
Nowlin, Jesse E., 46

—O—
O'Brien, Davey, 6
O'Daniel, W. Lee, 4, 10, 12, 23, 34, 88, 101, 106, 109, 113, 114, 180
Obadele-Starks, Ernest, 115
Office of Civilian Defense, 85, 104
Office of Petroleum Administration, 112
Office of Price Administration and Civilian Supply, 87, 104
Office of Transportation, 104
Office of War Information, 104
Ogata, Benjamin Franklin, 120
oil industry, 35
Oklahoma, 16, 18, 21
Old, Archie J., 70
Olson, Karl, 86
100th Fighter Squadron, 145
101st Airborne Division, 134, 135, 137, 146

102nd Infantry Division, 26, 27
103rd Infantry Division, 26
106th Infantry Division, 146
109th Infantry, 146
110th Infantry Regiment, 145
112th Cavalry Regiment, 24, 165
115th Cavalry of the Iowa National Guard, 25
116th Tank Destroyer Battalion, 26
120th Tank Destroyer Battalion, 26
124th Cavalry Regiment, 24, 165
131st Field Artillery, 50, 149
141st Regimental Combat Team, 74, 76, 131, 132, 133
142nd Infantry, 76
142nd Regimental Combat Team, 74, 131, 132
143rd Regiment, 132, 133
143rd Infantry Division, 74, 76, 77
147th Infantry Division, 168
Owens, William A., 153, 180

—P—
Pack, John A., 55
Page, Chuck, 45
Palm, John, 68
Pampa Army Air Field, 33
Parker, James, 55
Parnell, Garrett C., 145
Parry, Harold, 143
Parten, J. R., 101, 112, 180
Patch, Alexander "Sandy," 139, 162
Pate, James H., 44
Patman, Wright, 108, 110, 113, 181
Patterson, Robert P., 132
Patton, George S., 61, 73, 138, 139, 160,161
Paulger, Claude, 44, 119
Peacock, Howard, vii
Pearl Harbor, v, 1, 13, 23, 79
Peasley, B. J., 114
Pecos Field, 31
Peek, R. H., 147
Pennsylvania, 18, 21
Pennsylvania Shipyard, 38
Permenter, C., 149
Perrin Army Air Field, 30
Perry, George Sessions, 73
Peters, Christian R., 47
Petroleum Administration, 104
Phillips, O. A., 181
Phillips, Royal, 116
Pikley, Rita, 95
Pintado, 150, 151
Pistole, Erwin, 46
Piwetz, Florian W. "Pete," 134
Pollack, 49
Pollett, Howie, 6

Porras, Victor, 153
Prange, Gordon, 22
Priest, Gene, 157, 181
prisoner of war camps, German, 147
prisoner of war camps, Japanese, 54
prisoner of war camps, Texas, 121
Pryor, Charles C., 50
Puffer, 129
Putnam, Paul, 46
Pye, William S., 18, 46
Pyle, Ernie, 63, 73, 77, 100, 169
Pyote Army Air Field, 33

—Q—
Quincy, 134
Quine, Richard, 98

—R—
Radney, Douglas, v, 56
Rainey, Harold P., 100-102, 181
Randolph Field, 24, 29
Rankin, Jeanette, 22
Rathbone, Milton, 97
Rawleigh Warner, 86
Rayburn, Sam, 8, 9, 10, 11, 12, 22, 104, 108, 110, 181
Read, Louis, 53
Reconstruction Finance Corporation, 111
Red Ball Express, 142
Reddy, Kenneth, 55, 181
Reese, Seldon, 50
Reuben James, 80
Richardson, James, 12, 66, 181
Richardson, W. W., 116
Rigel (seaplane), 19
Rigel, 182
Ritter, Tex, 98, 99
Roan, Charles H., 153, 188
Robertson, Michael J., 181
Robertson, Milton, 73
Robertson, Robert, vii
Robinson, Jackie, 117, 181
Robinson, James, 160, 188
Robinson, Marvin E., 50
Rodd Field, 34
Rodriquez, Cleto, 164, 182, 188
Rodriquez, Matias, 147
Rogers, Ginger, 5
Rogers, Roy, 98
Rommel, Erwin, 61, 121
Rooks, Albert H., 50
Roos Aircraft Corp., 37
Roosevelt, Franklin D., 1, 6, 12, 21, 46, 50, 51, 85, 89, 104, 109, 111, 113, 137, 161
Rosenthal, Joe, 167

Roussel, Hubert J., 151
Rowan, Arch, 107
Rowe, Corliss, 73
Rowland, James W., 44, 45
Rucci, Henry, 163
Rudder, Earl, 146
Rudder, James Earl, 135, 182
Ruthie II, 68
Rutledge, Martin, 170

—S—
Sabne Transportation Co., 86
San Angelo Army Air Field, 33
San Francisco, 64
San Jacinto, 128, 129
San Marcos Army Air Field, 34
savings stamps, 95
Sawtelle, Donald, 163
Scales, Norman W., 145
Schaadt, Robert, vii
Schickele, Rainer, 39
Schmeling, Max, 5
Schroeder, Bruno, 137
Scoggins, Paul W., 70
Scott, Jean, 146
Scott, Zachary, 5
Sculpin, 79
2nd Armored Division, 162
2nd Battalion, 131st Field Artillery, Texas National Guard, 119
2nd Engineer Combat Battalion, 147
2nd Infantry Division, 24, 25, 127, 138, 147
2nd Marine Division, 128
2nd Ranger Battalion, 135
Seiser, Ed, 19, 182
Selective Service bill, 9
Seng, Gene G., 78
Sevareid, Eric, 98, 133
7th Army Division, 169
7th Infantry Division, 138, 153
7th Marine Regiment, 153
17th Pursuit Squadron, 44, 45
17th Squadron, 44
75th Squadron, 66
77th Field Artillery, 24
77th Infantry Division, 26, 129, 154, 169
78th Fighter Group, 69
78th Infantry Division, vi, 159
737th Tank Battalion, 160
756th Tank Battalion, 140
761st Tank Battalion, vi, 117, 142
Shadock, Mary, 109
Sheffield Steel, 36
Shell Oil Co., 36
Shelton, Hazel, 95

Sheppard Field, 30
Sheppard, Morris, 8, 9, 10, 13, 30, 105
Sheridan, Ann, 5
Sherman, Frederick C., 57
Sherrod, Robert L., 77
Simmons, Kenneth W., 162, 182
Simpson, Bernard, 139
Simpson, Ira, 148
Simpson, William Hood, 139
6th Marine Division, 169
6th Ranger Battalion, 163
63rd Infantry Division, 160
Skelton, Red, 99
Sloman, Wiley, 46
Smith, Carlo C., 74
Smith, Herbert Weldon, 49
Smith, John Lee, 115, 116
Smith, Kate, 99
Smith, Oliver Prince, 152, 182
Sneed, Charles, 44, 45
Snowden, William, 145
Solace, 19
Soliz, Felix, 182
Sothern, Ann, 5
South, Charles L., 109
Southern Aircraft Corp., 37
Spaatz, Carl "Tooey," 60, 72
SPARS, 92
Spatz, Harold S., 56
Spector, Ronald H., 43
Spencer, Otha C., 152
Spock, Benjamin, 96
Spruce Goose, 38
St. Lo, 154
Stach, Stanfield A., 146
Stambaugh, Jack R., 78
Stampolis, Nicholas, 68
Starett, Charles, 98
Stark, Luther, 182
Stevenson, Coke, 23, 41, 74, 101, 102, 108, 113, 114, 116, 155, 182
Stewart, James, 5
Stewart, Joe, 144, 182
Stewart, Manton, 163
Stewart, Thomas, 63
Stiborik, Joe, 171
Stockton, Clyde, 165
Stokesbury, James L., 161
Stone, Alfred, 166, 168, 182
Stone, Fred C., 116
Storey, Theresa, vi
Stovall, Oran, 133
Straight Flush, 171
Strange, Adrian, 78
Strickland, D. Frank, 101

Strother, Dora Dougherty, 94
Stroud, Martha Sue, 14
Stueber, Joe, 85
Sumners, Hatton, 8, 9, 80, 110, 182
Suwannee, 154
Sweeney, Charles, 171
Swing, Raymond Graham, 4, 98
Swint, Barney, 73

—T—
Tanamachi, Saburo, 120
Taylor, John D., 63
Taylor, Maxwell, 134
Taylor, Robert, 98, 163, 183
Taylor, Zachary, 24
Tennessee, 18, 21
Tenth Air Force, 165
Terrell, Henry, 137
Texarkana Ordnance Center, 37
Texas, 62, 135, 139, 169
Texas Guardettes, 95
Texas National Guard, 13
Texas Oklahoma, 86
Tharp, Blucher, 51
3rd Armored Division, 146
3rd Fleet, 154
3rd Infantry Division, 72, 127, 139, 140, 142, 143, 156, 160, 162
3rd Marine Division, 129, 166, 168
3rd Pursuit Squadron, 44
13th Combat Bombardment Wing, 143
27th Infantry Division, 128
30th Infantry Division, vi, 138, 143, 159, 162
31st Infantry Division, 53
34th Division, 62, 77
34th Pursuit Squadron, 44, 45, 53
35th Fighter Group, 165
36th Infantry Division, v, 9, 13, 14, 25, 63, 73, 74, 76, 77, 127, 129, 131, 132, 133, 134, 139, 143, 158, 160, 162
37th Infantry Division, 164
Thomason, Ewing, 111
Thompson, Kyle, 148
Thorne, Hank, 44
301st Fighter Squadron, 145
302nd Figher Squadron, 145
308th Bombardment Group, 151
326th Squadron, 92nd Bomb Group, 68
327th Glider Infantry Regiment, 146
332nd Fighter Group, 145
342nd Fighter Squadron, 78
353rd Fighter Group, 69, 143
389th Bomb Group, 69
Tibbets, Paul W., 170

Tips, Kern, 5
Toland, John, 53
Torpedo Squadron, 8 58
Torrez, Patricio, 66
Townsend, Frank, 18, 183
Triton, 49
Truman, Harry S., 109, 162
Truscott, Lucian, 62, 72, 133, 139, 157
Turkel, Studs, v
Turner, George B., 156, 183, 188
Tweedy, Ann, 14, 69
Twelfth Air Force, 63, 144, 157
12th Armored Division, 25, 160
12th Cavalry Regiment, 24
Twentieth Air Force, 151
20th Bombardment Command, 29
21st Pursuit Squadron, 44
23rd Fighter Group, 66
24th Infantry Division, 134, 153, 164
24th Pursuit Group, 43, 44, 45
25th Infantry Division, 163
26th Infantry Division, 142
27th Infantry Division, 128, 169
27th Marines, 168
28th Infantry Division, 146
29th Infantry Division, 135, 137, 138, 143
Tye Field, 33

—U—
U.S. Eighth Army, 163, 164
U.S. Fifth Army, 73, 76, 129, 157
U.S. First Army, 157, 159, 162
U.S. Maritime Commission, 38
U.S. Ninth Army, 139, 159, 162
U.S. Second Army, 13
U.S. Seventh Army, 138, 157, 160, 162
U.S. Sixth Army, 65, 153, 163, 164
U.S. Third Army, 13, 25, 65, 138, 157, 160, 161, 162
United Service Organization (USO), 95

—V—
Valenta, Marcus, 183
Vandagriff, Tony G., 47
Vandenberg, Hoyt, 144
Vaughn, Herbert E., 47
Venable, James C., 46
Venta, Marcus A., 20
Vestal, 18
VI Corps, 139
Victory Field, 29
VIII Bomber Command, 61, 70
Vinson, Willie, 115
Vrana, Lee Raymond, 18, 183

—W—
W. E. Hutton, 86
W. W. Anderson, 86
Waco Army Air Field, 31
Wade, George, 80
Wadsworth, 64
Waggoner, C. W., 84
Wagner, Boyd, 44
Wainwright, Jonathan, 51
Wake Island, 23, 46, 47, 148
Waldron Field, 34
Waldrop, Leonard E., 115
Walker, Edwin A., 77, 183
Walker, Fred, 13, 63, 73, 131, 132, 133, 134, 183
Walker, Richard P., 121
Walker, Walton H., 138, 160, 183
Wallace, Henry A., 111, 112
Wallace, Herman, 158, 188
War Food Administration, 104
War Manpower Committee, 90
War Production Board, 87, 104
War Relocation Authority, 120
Ward, Billy, 137, 183
Ward, Orlando C., 26
Ward, Robert, 87
Warnick, Harold, 165
Wash, Carlyle, 65
Washington, George, 9
Waskow, Henry T., 77
Waterford, Van, 148
Waters, Jerome J., 95
Weaver Shipyards, 38
Weigley, Russell, 159
Weissinger, William, 148
Welles, Orson, 5
Wells, John Keith, 166, 183
Wentrek, Dan, 18, 184
Werner, Richard J., 74
West Virginia, 15, 18, 21
Westheimer, David, 147, 184
Wheeler, Burton, 9
Whiskey Pete, 55
Whitaker, Francis H., 47
White, Eugene, 66
White, Jack J., 19, 184
White, William L., 100
Whiteley, Eli, 156, 184, 188
Whitman, Leona, 88
Wiggins, Melanie, 86
Wilder, Ross, 55
Wiley, Catherine H., 94
Wiley, Estus F., 94
Wilke, Wendell L., 10
Wilks, Ted, 6

Index ★ 255

William Beaumont General Hospital, 34
Williams, Jim, 117
Williams, Robert B., 69, 70
Williams, Ted, 6
Williamson-Dickie, 39
Willis, Phillip, 20, 184
Willke, Wendell, 100
Wills, Bob, 4, 99
Willy, Wildford "Bud," 145
Wilson, Lucy, 53
Wilson, Woodrow, 7
Winning Run, 70
Winsor, Kathleen, 100
Wirtz, Alvin, 112, 184
Wissinger, William J., 50
Woman's Ambulance Corps, 95
Women Accepted for Voluntary Emergency Services, 92
Women's Airforce Service Pilot (WASP), 31, 94
Women's Army Auxiliary Corps, 92
Women's Army Corps (WACs), 93, 118
Women's Auxiliary Ferrying Squadron (WAFS), 94
Women's Flying Training Detachment, 94
Women's Motor Corps, 95
Women's Reserve of the Marine Corps, 92
Wood, William, 144
Woodson, J. D., 58
Wooster, Edna, vii
Wooster, Jessie, 85
Wooster, Robert, vii
Worley, Francis, 109
Worth Garment Co., 37
Wyatt, Aaron, A., 45, 131

—**XYZ**—

XX Corps, 138, 160
Yamamoto, Isoroku, 57
Yorktown, 54, 57, 58
Young, Buck, 88, 184
Youngblood, Lucian, 55
Zaharias, Mildred "Babe" Didrikson, 97, 184
Zalman, Rudolph, 19, 184
Zamora, Emilio, 114
Zeilin, 171

www.ingramcontent.com/pod-product-compliance
Lightning Source LLC
Chambersburg PA
CBHW080535170426
43195CB00016B/2566